GEOPOLITICS IN THE DANUBE REGION

Hungarian Reconciliation Efforts, 1848–1998

edited by
IGNÁC ROMSICS and BÉLA K. KIRÁLY

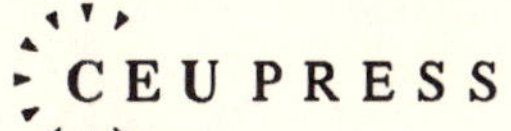

CENTRAL EUROPEAN UNIVERSITY PRESS
BUDAPEST

Volume No. 97 of the Series "Atlantic Studies on Society in Change"
of Atlantic Research and Publications, Inc.
Series Editor in Chief *Béla K. Király*
Series Associate Editor in Chief *Kenneth Murphy*
Series Editor *László Veszprémy*

Published by
Central European University Press
Október 6. utca 12.
H-1051 Budapest
Hungary
400 West 59th Street
New York, NY 10019
USA

Translated by Nóra Arató

Maps by Béla Nagy

Distributed by
Plymbridge Distributors Ltd., Estover Road, Plymouth PL6 7PZ,
United Kingdom

ISBN 963-9116-29-7 Cloth
ISBN 963-9116-28-9 Paperback

Library of Congress Cataloging in Publication Data
A CIP catalog record for this book is available upon request.

Printed in Hungary by Akadémiai Nyomda Kft.

GEOPOLITICS IN THE DANUBE REGION

HUNGARIAN RECONCILIATION EFFORTS,
1848–1998

To the memory of
PAUL JONAS
one of the founders of this series

CONTENTS

ERA OF UPHEAVALS (1918–98)

PRESENT AND THE FUTURE

CONTRIBUTORS

Piroska Balogh, Eötvös Loránd University, Budapest, Hungary
Gáspár Bíró, Institute on Central Europe, Teleki Foundation, Budapest, Hungary
Judit Boda Pálok, Attorney, Budapest
István Csucsuja, Babes-Bólyai University, Cluj-Napoca, Románia
Ágnes Deák, József Attila University, Szeged, Hungary
András Gergely, Eötvös Loránd University, Budapest, Hungary
György Gyarmati, Eötvös Loránd University, Budapest, Hungary
Péter Hanák, Member of the Hungarian Academy of Sciences; Central European University, Budapest, Hungary
László Katus, Pázmány Péter Catholic University, Piliscsaba, Hungary
Béla K. Király, Brooklyn College of the City University of New York, USA
György Litván, Institute of History and Documentation of the Hungarian Revolution of 1956, Budapest, Hungary
Tibor Zs. Lukács, Eötvös Loránd University, Budapest, Hungary
Ambrus Miskolczy, Eötvös Loránd University, Budapest, Hungary
János M. Rainer, Institute of History and Documentation of the Hungarian Revolution of 1956, Budapest, Hungary
Imre Ress, Institute of History of the Hungarian Academy of Sciences, Budapest, Hungary
Ignác Romsics, Eötvös Loránd University, Budapest, Hungary
György Szabad, Member of the Hungarian Academy of Sciences; Eötvös Loránd University, Budapest, Hungary

PREFACE TO THE SERIES "ATLANTIC STUDIES ON SOCIETY IN CHANGE"

The present volume is a component of a series that, when completed, will constitute a comprehensive survey of the many aspects of East Central European society.

The books in the series deal with peoples whose homelands lie between the Germans to the west, the Russians, Ukranians, and Belorussians to the east and north, and the Mediterranean and Adriatic seas to the south. They constitute a particular civilization, one that is at once an integral part of Europe, yet substantially different from the West. The area is characterized by a rich diversity of language, religion, and government. The study of this complex area demands a multidisciplinary approach, and, accordingly, our contributors to the series represent several academic disciplines. They have been drawn from the universities and other scholarly institutions in the United States and Western Europe, as well as East and Central Europe. The contributors of the present volume are prominent Hungarian experts of the field.

The editors, of course, take full responsibility for ensuring the comprehensiveness, cohesion, internal balance, and scholarly quality of the series we have launched. We cheerfully accept this responsibility and intend this work to be neither justification nor condemnation of the policies, attitudes, and activities of any persons involved. At the same time, because the contributors represent so many different disciplines, interpretations, and schools of thought, our policy in this, as in the past and future volumes, is to present their contributions without major modifications.

Budapest, March 15, 1998

BÉLA K. KIRÁLY
Editor in Chief

PLANS AND PROJECTS FOR INTEGRATION IN EAST CENTRAL EUROPE IN THE 19TH AND 20TH CENTURIES: TOWARD A TYPOLOGY

IGNÁC ROMSICS

The history of East Central Europe during the 19th and 20th centuries teems with plans to integrate whole or specific regions in order to overcome linguistic, ethnic, and political heterogeneity. Despite their general similarities, the objectives underlying these integrating ideas differ vastly. Among the factors that may have a role in these objectives include the economic advantages of expanded markets, territorial expansion motivated by strategic and security considerations, national and linguistic unification, solidarity among kindred peoples, and common protection against an external threat. These plans and related political movements, fall into four well-defined trends, which continue to the present:

—an ideology of a federative Habsburg Empire;
—the evolution of German *Mitteleuropa* concepts;
—the unification of Slavic peoples (Pan-Slavism), including the later expansionist policy of the Soviet Union; and
—various confederative aspirations of those nation states formed as successors to the multi-ethnic Ottoman, Habsburg and Russian-Soviet Empires.

In Hungary those integrating plans stemmed from its cultural heritage with a focus upon pacification of the peoples in the Danube Basin either by federalizing the Austro-Hungarian Monarchy or by creating a confederation of nation states which would replace the Monarchy. No Hungarian plan has ever advocated incorporation into Pan-Slavism, while acceptance of German *Mitteleuropa* plans have never gained substantive support.

*

Plans to modernize the Habsburg Empire evolved into three major groups, apart from centralism resulting from Western-European absolutism, a doctrine that had been discredited by the end of the 18th century.

One group includes plans that make allowance for local features by creating a federation of the Empire. There are three further subgroups within this group. The first group is built on local historical-political traditions and sought a state formation based on either early or later Medieval organic traditions, yet in the form of a federative state. One example is that branch of the Illyrians who wanted to restore the Croat Trionite Kingdom within the Monarchy. Another example is the Czech trialism that alluded to the pre-1525 Czech-Moravian statehood. A third is Baron Miklós Wesselényi's 1843 plan ("pamphlet"), one of the 19th century Hungarian reform ideas. As Ágnes Deák writes in her essay, Wesselényi outlined five political-legal units: (1) permanent Austro-Hungarian provinces, (2) united Czech and Moravian provinces, (3) Galicia, (4) Hungary, and (5) Lombardy in Northern-Italy. The Transylvanian baron, Wesselényi's only linguistic-ethnic concession was to divide Istria along ethnic lines between the Italian speaking Lombardy with the Croatian side included within Hungary. Furthermore, Slovenia would have received autonomy within German-Austria.[1] In general, a historical-legal approach characterized the main stream of Hungarian concepts about the future of the Monarchy. This approach is also an essential element in the 1867 Austro-Hungarian Compromise since it necessitated the restoration of the unity of the Hungarian State dissolved in 1526.

A different subtype of federative ideas, built on nationalities as opposed to historical or political traditions, wished to restructure the Empire according to territorially distinguishable linguistic-ethnic groups. The first plans of this sort were devised by the Croat Ognjeslav Ostrozinski (1817–1890) and the Czech František Palacky (1798–1876) who proposed the creation of seven or eight such units in 1848–1849.[2] The most comprehensive ethnically structured federative plan of the Monarchy was outlined by Aurel Popovici, a Romanian politician, at the beginning of the 20th century. He conceived of fifteen territorial units. It is most remarkable that besides the central Hungarian area and the Romanian Transylvania, Székely (Szekler) land would have formed a separate Hungarian entity.[3] There had not been a Hungarian thinker or politician who would have accepted such an idea of total disintegration of historical Hungary.

Yet another subtype of federative plans combines both historical-political and linguistic-ethnic principles. The Hungarian Oszkár Jászi's plan is best known. He devised it in the spring of 1918 and it was published in the fall. As György Litván describes in his essay, similar to Wesselényi, Jászi also counted on five equal federative units. However, unlike his predecessor, he attached great importance to nationality status. For him it was obvious that Croat–Slavonia ought to be part of Illyria and not that of Hungary since Illyria united the South-Slav areas. He also insisted on the unity of Hungary and did not advocate organizing Eastern-Galicia as a Ruthenian political unit. Based on his plan the five states creating a federation would have been Austria, Bohemia, Poland, Hungary, and Illyria.[4]

A newly revived concept of the past few years, which has advocated cultural and personal autonomy, differs from all the three preceding subtypes. It first surfaced during the 1848–49 Austrian constitutional work (Kremsier) and later it became a central motif in the projected constitution of the Hungarian revolutionary, Lajos Kossuth. According to György Szabad's essay, Kossuth envisioned the "personal" or "cultural-national autonomy" with linguistically diverse citizens founding territorially independent national associations to nurture and develop social, cultural, and educational national interests. They would have the right to hold national assemblies, elect national leaders, and frame laws.[5] Although elaborating his plans Kossuth had the future of Hungary, rather than the Monarchy, in mind. His influence is visible in the late 19th and early 20th century propositions to modernize and save the Monarchy. Karl Renner and Otto Bauer, Austrian Social Democrats, had synthesized earlier plans into a coherent system. The essence of their ideas, similar to that of Kossuth's, radically separated the state, state government, and citizens on one side and the national community, national-cultural self-government, and personalities on the other. Stratified administrative units were to correspond to geographic and economic rationalities, not to ethnic borders, and there was no significance attached to the ethnic-linguistic status. While in religious, linguistic, and ethnic matters, every community and individual would have possessed complete autonomy. In this way a dual structure was posited that would assure both the centralization needs of a modern governing system and the needs of ethnic regionalism.[6]

Both of the preceding ideas were intraterritorial; that is, they elaborated on solutions within the borders of the Monarchy.

However, there was also a third, expansive or imperial concept that envisioned integration of the whole imperial area by devouring the neighboring small states. In the early 19th century Metternich projected an expansion of the Empire into German principalities and into Switzerland, while later in the century Archduke Rudolf discussed a possible annexation of Romania, Serbia, Montenegro, and Russian-Poland to the Empire after getting even with the "Barbaric czarism". It is worth noting that the intention to reinforce the imperial status of the Monarchy was an integral part of plans drawn up by both conservative, reactionary and progressive, opposition politicians. In Miklós Wesselényi's concept both Wallachia and Moldova, as well as the Bulgarian, Serbian and Bosnian territories, would have been tightly connected with the Monarchy.

In Oszkár Jászi's concept even Greece, Albania, and Russian-Poland would have been involved. Contrary to Metternich and Rudolf, Wesselényi and Jászi were motivated by the common self-defense of the area against external, imperial, primarily Russian, threats, rather than by Habsburg expansion.

Debates about the future of the Monarchy terminated at the end of World War I with the creation of small and medium sized states that defined themselves as nations. The Paris Treaty sealed the fate of a state that had assured a political framework for the co-existence of a handful of ethnic groups for over 400 years. The assumption was that a more modern and democratic alliance of the Danube peoples would replace the hierarchical, "obsolete" and "repressive" form of integration. Yet, the close cooperation of the peoples of the defunct Habsburg Monarchy did not materialize then and it is doubtful whether it ever will. Owing to this unrealized promise, and other bitter experiences of the 20th century, nostalgia for a Habsburg Monarchy still endures. It also endures because it has been the region's most successful form of integration for the peoples of the Danube Basin despite its problems and drawbacks.

*

The Habsburg Empire historically has faced two alternatives for integration: (1) integration into one or both of the two bordering empires of Germany and Russia, resulting in an even larger economic and political unit, or (2) close cooperation with the liberated smaller nations, while accepting them as more or less equal partners. In the first option, German and Russian political thinkers had been preparing for expansion and aggressive integration of the area since the 18th century. Gottfried Wilhelm von Leibniz (1646–1716) was the first German intellectual who connected the federation of all or some of the European nations under the geographical, geopolitical, intellectual, and cultural aegis of the Germans. In the following decades, especially at the end of the 18th and the beginning of the 19th century, a whole series of German intellectuals (Kant, Herder, Fichte, and Schlegel) engaged in discussing the questions of integration beyond German linguistic borders and of the civilizing mission of the Germans in Europe with primary emphasis upon East Central Europe.

It was a South-German, Friedrich List (1789–1846), who developed a specific and detailed political program and thus became the father of the German *Mitteleuropa* concept. In 1841, his major work departed from two prior suppositions. One predicted that the future belonged to large economic units that would compete with one another. While according to the second, neither Prussia nor the future Germany would be able to exert influence on British or French colonies, or on overseas territories belonging to the sphere of the United States, even if they had a fleet and thus could set foot on the tropics. In his view "...the future of a German state lay on the continent; it would have to seek its colonies there." To assure economic competition and efficient defense against a Franco–Russian coalition, List envisioned an East Central European cohesion which extended as far as Persia on its south-eastern borders. He proposed the development of a railroad from the German seashore across Central-Europe and the Balkans to the Persian Gulf, and the regulation of the Danube and its tributaries. "We have our backwoods like the Americans: the lands of the Lower Danube and the Black Sea, all of Turkey, the entire Southeast beyond Hungary is our hinterland." Besides *Drang nach Osten,* List also advocated westward expansion. In that direction he counted on states bordering German language areas: Belgium, the Netherlands, Denmark, and Switzerland in the south.[7]

The *Mitteleuropa* concept has been present in German political thinking ever since. It evolved into a political program during the economic boom following German unity in 1871 by relying on the political power of the new state from the 1890's on. The numerous plans and ideas released between 1890 and 1918 reflect two major groupings. First, liberal-imperialistic concepts, supported by manufacturing, banking and industrial interests, aspired to develop a multi-national economic bloc with a united customs policy. This would have included the German–Austrian–Hungarian core, the Balkans, the Benelux states, France, and Scandinavia. Note that advocates did not strive to destroy world-trade connections so important for Germany, nor did they want to subjugate member countries belonging to a Germany-led customs union, nor deprive the member nations of their statehood. The most well-known of these concepts is that of the Lutheran theologian, Friedrich Naumann (1860–1919), whose book, *Mitteleuropa* was published in 1915 in German and in the following year translated into Hungarian.[8]

The second group of Mitteleuropa concepts, imbued with various different *völkisch* and racial-biological elements propagated by big estate owners, military circles, and especially by the Federation of All Germans (*Alldeutscher Verband*), included plans for politically subjugating the Central-European area through military intervention, such as fusing and integrating areas of Poland, the Baltic states, and Russia in the east and Northern-France and Belgium on the west. During World War I this program was managed by the German Chief of Staff Field Marshal Eric Ludendorff and his clique.[9]

Despite these significant differences there was one feature common to both trends: the economic and political expansion of the German Empire created in 1871 to the Atlantic Ocean in the west and to the Black Sea in the south. The German neo-mercantile economy would function as a fourth world empire to ensure the security and prosperity of the area, even in crisis situations, in competition with the three prevalent world powers, England, Russia, and the United States.

These German-inspired concepts were debated by various circles of the Hungarian intelligentsia during World War I. Generally the 1848 Independence Party and István Bethlen (later prime minister) dismissed all extra-mural infringements on the sovereignty of his country. The influential circles of the 1867 or Compromise Party, led by the historian Gyula Szekfű, favored those plans integrating Hungary into the "Christian-German cultural circle." And finally, the liberal-imperialist variants of the German plans, as conceived by Friedrich Neumann's *Mitteleuropa*, impressed a minority of Hungarian progressives, such as Oszkár Jászi. According to György Litván, Jászi reasoned that his position offered protection against Russian expansionism.

After the Russian revolutions, in the spring and summer of 1918, the eastern half of a German-led economic and political grouping was established. An agreement signed in Spa, May 12, 1918, between the Austro-Hungarian Monarchy and Germany stipulated tight economic, political, and military cooperation between the two parties—essentially leading to a customs union. The Baltic countries, Poland, Serbia, and Romania were occupied by German and Austro-Hungarian forces, while Bulgaria, Turkey, Finland, and the newly established Ukraine were conceived as belonging to the German Alliance.

Following the final defeat of the Central Powers, the possibility of a German continental hegemony temporarily dissipated. However, that soon changed with the dissolution of the Monarchy, the atomization of the entire area, and the permanent weakening of the rival super-power, Russia. Between the two world wars, for many in the conservative, traditional German leading circles, the *Mitteleuropa* concept became an economic objective, nevertheless, still respected the independence of the nations involved. In this respect it was a continuation of pre-war liberal-imperialist plans that still enjoyed some support in Hungary as described in György Gyarmati's essay. The ideas of the National Socialists, on the other hand, were imbued with a racially motivated and aggressively hegemonic *Lebensraum* concept that harked back to aggressive Pan-German ideologies from the turn of the century, i.e., territorial expansion, subjugation of "inferior nations," and leadership by a "superior" German race.

The victory and the reign of Nazism between 1939 and 1944 discredited the German *Mitteleuropa* concept for a long time to come in the eyes of other nations in the area. Beginning in the latter half of the 1960's the West German policy of *Ostpolitik* seemed to parallel German activities concerning East Central Europe during the second half of the 1920's. However, it was only in 1985–86 that an open scientific debate about *Mitteleuropa* commenced, with the first conference with this title on German territory organized only in 1987. Until the 1980's only a few dared to allude to a deeper and more permanent force within the Nazi *neue Ordnung* than Hitlerism, or to suggest that this force surviving the post-war chaos might have served as the pillar of the Western-European integration by the 1960's. Arnold Toynbee, who was among this few, concluded in 1955: "Hitler's forcible military, political, and economic unification of Europe had been a practical answer to Europe's most pressing need; and though Hitler's brutal way of solving Europe's problem had been made odious to the reluctant beneficiaries by the acts of aggression through which it had been achieved, the methods of barbarism by which it had been enforced, and the selfish German national purposes for which it had been exploited, it was, nevertheless, a grave misfortune for Europe that part of the price for her release from German tyranny should have been the loss of the one great benefit that this tyranny had brought with it."[10] Although Toynbee spoke primarily about Western Europe, his statement was even more appropriate for East Central Europe.

*

Similar to German *Mitteleuropa* plans, the antecedents of Pan-Slav and Pan-Russian ideas reached farther back than the 18th century, when the first Russian emperors referred to the Slavs to buttress their North-Western and South-Western expansions. Peter the Great (1672–1725) annexed the Eastern shore of the Baltic Sea to the Empire, while Catherine the Great (1729–1796) occupied Lithuania, Courland, White Russia, Eastern Poland, and the Northern shore of the Black Sea. However, Pan-Slavism played a subsidiary role in both Emperors' ideologies when compared with the liberation of orthodox nations and Constantinople from the Turks. Between 1801 and 1825 emphasis shifted towards liberating and unifying Slav nations. During the reign of Alexander I (1777–1825), Finland (1809), Bessarabia (1812), and the remnants of Poland (1815) were annexed. The first serious Pan-Slav, Pan-Russian plans for unification of East Central Europe and the Baltic states were formulated against Napoleon's imperial intentions.

After its expulsion of Napoleon, Russia reached a peak in its influence upon Europe. Although no Great Balkan vassal state was ever established, the 1815 Vienna Congress recognized the 1809 annexation of Finland and the 1812 annexation of Bessarabia, and also placed the remnants of Poland under Russian protectorate. Henceforth Alexander I changed his policy. Instead of absorbing further European territories both he and his successor Nicholas I (1796–1855) resolved to integrate the occupied territories and to consolidate the Empire. It is well-established that while linguistic-cultural Russianization failed, economic integration succeeded, especially after the termination of customs borders within the Empire in 1850. The vast Polish textile industry around Lodz thrived under the new economic policies of the Russian Empire.

Despite the relative passivity in foreign trade and the hardly fraternal attitude towards the Poles, numerous representatives of young Slav intellectuals of East Central and South-Eastern Europe looked upon Russia as liberator and natural leader of Slav nations. Pan-Slavism, as extolled by the Czech Antonin Marek (1785–1877), the Slovak Jan Kollár (1793–1852), and the Croat Ljudevit Gaj (1809–1872) all professed Slav relatedness and dreamed about a Great Slav Empire led by Russia. Some of them, like the Polish Kazimierz Krzywicki (1820–1883) or the Slovak Ĺudovit Štúr (1815–1856), advocated complete assimilation by surrendering language, religion, and national identity, adopting Orthodox religion and the Russian language.

It was in the second half of the 1860's and the first half of the 1870's that Pan-Slav views propagating Slav unity under the aegis of Russia were cast in detailed political molds by Mikhail Petrovich Pogodin (1800–1875), history professor at the University of Moscow, by General Rostislav Fadeiev (1826–1884), and by natural scientist Nikolai Danilevski (1822–1855). To extend Russian influence in East Central and South-Eastern Europe was the essence of the program, as voiced by Fadeiev, "Russia either expands its leadership as far as the Adriatic Sea or will be driven back behind the Dnieper River."[11]

Russian objectives during World War I adhered to the canons of Pan-Slavism. The minimal goal was the Bosporus and Istanbul in the south and in the north the Ruthenian territories (Bukovina, Sub-Carpathia, Eastern Galicia), and the strategically important Eastern Prussian seashore. Yet west of the Russian–Ukrainian–Lithuanian language areas Russian foreign policy planned to establish only a nominal alliance with a belt of vassal states managed from Belgrade and Poland. By 1916 the outcome of the St. Petersburg debates about the future of the Austro-Hungarian Monarchy resulted in a consensus about the division of the Empire and the organization of new nation states. Russia wished to establish particularly strong ties with Czechoslovakia. While formal integration due to cultural and religious differences was not feasible, still a Russian king was planned to head the new Slavic state, as in Poland. There were no established plans about the future status of Hungary, Romania, and Bulgaria. Nevertheless, it is quite obvious that in the event of a Russian victory their only choice would have been to join the alliance of the vassal states of Poland, Czechoslovakia, and Serbia.[12]

Iosif Vissarionovich Stalin materialized Nicholas II's (1868–1918) plan a quarter of a century later. However, it had nothing to do with Pan-Slavism, which had been discredited among the Slav nations in World War I. After the German attack in 1941 the Soviet leadership tried to revive solidarity among the Slav nations. However, along with the Hungarians, Romanians, Finns, and Baltic nations, the Croats, Slovaks, and many of the Ukrainians fought for the Germans and not for their "Slav brother." Moreover, Soviet relations with Poland and Serbia were laden with controversies. The 1946 Belgrade Pan-Slav Congress had no sequel. After 1947 the sole ideology of the Soviet-Russian hegemony reflected unity through "peoples' socialism," the so called proletarian internationalism, and not Pan-Slavism.

Hosts of experts both West and East have analyzed different aspects of Soviet integration of East Central Europe up to 1990. Some have denied its existence. Yet it resembled *Mitteleuropa* before and during World War II in many respects. In both scenarios a superpower tied down vassal states along its borders and imposed upon them its own policies. Both superpowers had advocated exclusive ideologies and the popularization of their cultures and languages, German or Russian respectively. The significant difference was that the earlier system at least reflected an advanced level of Western ideas and technical development, whereas the latter demanded adherence to a semi-Asian culture which seemed retrogressive. It never became a model for emulation by the vassal states. A saga of the failure of the Soviet experiment is to be found in this discrepancy.

*

In addition to the plans for a federative transformation of the Austro–Hungarian Monarchy; to the expansive and hegemony-oriented regionalism of imperial Germany and the czarist Russia; and to the plans of the Third Reich and the Soviet Union, there exists a fourth trend in the integrating efforts of 19th and 20th century East Central Europe. This fourth trend also includes those movements that aimed to defeat one or another of the three empires dominating the area and also aimed to create more or less ethnically homogeneous nation states which could later become a tight confederation of states. This anti-dynasty, revolutionary attitude did not preclude the possibility of resorting to the support of one or the other Great Powers, sometimes Russia or Turkey, and most frequently France. This usually happened due to tactical considerations. Another great paradox of these anti-dynasty, revolutionary movements was that most of the oppressed nations waiting to be liberated expected to be "first among the equal" as a minimal requirement, but more often expected a leading-dominating role. This odd "small nation" nationalism was almost as expansive and repressive as the "big nation" variety. Still, the former created more sympathy than antipathy in the West, which was not due to a quality difference, rather due to the fact that small nations lacked resources.

The underlying thesis of nationalism is that the ideal political form for people of identical origin and language is the nation state. In the first half of the 19th century Greece and Poland, both with the greatest imperial traditions in the Balkan and East Central Europe, connected this form of nationalism with the idea of an alliance of nations. Serbian and Romanian statesmen and political thinkers also came forward with similar propositions. Such plans usually emerged when the *status quo* broke down as in 1848–1849, at the end of World War I, in the first half of the 1930's, during World War II, and in our own time, at the beginning of the 1990's.

From among the 1848–49 East Central European revolutions Hungary went farthest in the dethronement of the Habsburgs and in a declaration of independence. Unlike other anti-dynastic, revolutionary movements, Hungary did not strive to gain or reclaim territories, only to protect what it had. Some Hungarian revolutionaries, in the grip of national ambitions and Habsburg absolutism, leaned towards accepting a comprehensive territorial autonomy of the non-Hungarian peoples and even counted on the disintegration of historical Hungary. By 1849 László Teleki announced: "not only Austria died but also St. Stephen's Hungary." Even if a historical Hungary still existed, it should be reconstructed on "confederative basis."[13] Later, as is well documented in Ambrus Miskolczy's essay, surrendering the idea of a historical Hungary and the acceptance of national autonomy or at least comprehensive national self-governments, characterized the activities and visions of György Klapka, Bertalan Szemere and Ferenc Pulszky. The majority, however, was unable to come to terms with this perspective. It was only in 1862 that Kossuth accepted the separation of Transylvania and Croatia and the autonomy of the Serbian Voivodina, and announced the plan about the Southern Slav, Romanian, and Hungarian United States of the Danube Region.[14]

The establishment of Italian unity (1859–61), the Austro-Hungarian compromise (1867), and the birth of the German Empire (1871) stabilized the political situation in East Central Europe for several decades. Anti-dynasty revolutionary ambitions lost ground for a long time and regained strength only during the second half of World War I. Tomaš G. Masaryk's 1917 concept, *The New Europe,* was the most extensive plan among the integrating concepts presented during and after World War I. In his *New Europe,* Masaryk also included the Lithuanians, Latvians, Estonians, Romanians, and Italians in addition to the close cooperation between the Poles, Czechoslovaks, and Southern Slavs. The Hungarians also could have joined provided "they are content with governing their own people and understand that the Slavs and the Latins are not their adversaries."[15] Masaryk's goal of creating an anti-German protective belt which would cooperate with France and England would have strengthened the prospects for peace and the balance of power in Europe.

However, none of Masaryk's integrating concepts during and after World War I materialized. Ethnic divisiveness and territorial haggling among the new or reformed states of the area proved to be stronger than economic rationality or security requirements. As Péter Hanák stresses in his paper, by defining their national goals in terms of "small irredentism/ small nationalism," the majority of Poles, Serbs, Romanians, and Greeks ended up defending the post-1918, post-break up of the Monarchy, status quo. This posture helped transform an originally defensive Hungarian nationalism into a nationalism charged with revisionism and irredentism. The "small nationalism" antagonism manifested itself in the anti-Hungarian military cooperation among Czechoslovakia, Romania, and Yugoslavia called the Little Entente by 1920–21.

Due to the world depression and Hitler's rise to power in 1933, Great Britain and France made several attempts in the 1930's to initiate a mutually advantageous cooperation among East Central European small nations. Customs union and other plans hallmarked by Briand, Tardieu, Hodža and others never attracted the minimally needed East Central European support. This was especially true in Hungary where revision was claimed to be the requirement for any regional cooperation, as György Gyarmati indicates in his essay. A peculiar exception was "Transylvanism." Its several representatives set out to reconcile the Romanian and Hungarian population of Transylvania without demanding any territorial revision, as Piroska Balogh indicates in her essay. "Transylvanism" assumed that the common past and a certain territorial isolation produced a regional consciousness that both Romanians, Hungarians, and Saxons would possess irrespective of language or origin. But the plan was hopeless. Added to political antagonism was economic incompatibility. In the preceding one and a half decades, with the dissipation of traditional bonds offered by the Monarchy, each state had pursued economic independence. While in the early 1920's more than half of Czechoslovakia's exported goods were sold in the Danube states, by the end of the decade the amount fell to only one third. For example, the flour needs of the country were met through greater overseas purchases rather than from neighboring agricultural exporters. In spite of the proximity and shared historical traditions, trade among the East Central and Southern-Eastern European countries decreased by 10–15% during the mid and late 1930's, while between 70% and 80% of trade occurred with the western half of the continent.[16] Due to structural changes, however, the British and French share was becoming insignificant and the German more prominent. In 1932 the German foreign trade had accounted for only 10–25% of the export–import business of the South-Eastern European countries. But by 1938–39 it had increased to 40–55%, and in the case of Bulgaria it was 65–70%. The Romanian, Yugoslav, Hungarian, and Bulgarian economies had become dependent on Germany.[17]

During World War II even more detailed and serious plans were considered about the transformation of the states between Russia and Germany into a confederation. American and British geopoliticians conceived of three units: Baltic-Polish, the Danube Basin, and the Balkan area. The Greek–Yugoslav Treaty of January 15, 1942, and the Polish–Czechoslovak declaration of intention of January 25, 1942, were designated the first steps taken in that direction. The principle of ethnically unified borders was one of the requirements outlined by these confederative plans. In Hungary's case both the Czechoslovak, Romanian, and Southern-Slav frontiers were to be corrected with linguistic-ethnic distribution as the dividing lines.[18] Without being aware of these plans, István Bibó, the outstanding Hungarian political theorist of this century, offered conciliatory solutions in his 1945/46 essays. According to Tibor Zs. Lukács, Bibó broke with the historical, geographical, and economic aspects of Hungarian revisionism between the two world wars and came to the conviction that in East Central Europe borders following linguistic-ethnic demarcation lines could stabilize. As Bibó put it, "in East Central Europe...if we wish to see borders that can be viewed democratically legitimate, then we must use lines of demarcation that in fact separate peoples in this region: linguistic and ethnic lines."[19] If the Red Army could have been contained at the historical borders of the Russian Empire, true reconciliation, compromise, and the evolution of a mutually beneficial security and economic cooperation might have evolved.

Instead of free states in free association, all the post-1945 East Central European nations found themselves in the Warsaw Pact and Comecon. During the nearly half century when Hungary was part of the Soviet bloc there was no opportunity to pursue an independent foreign policy. Hungarian communist leaders were obliged to represent Soviet interests, not Hungarian, and the reconciliation of the Danubian nations remained an empty slogan. There were a few exceptions. As János M. Rainer attests, Imre Nagy, the leader of the 1956 Hungarian Revolution and War of Independence, earnestly considered the cooperation of the "small nations along the Danube" against common threats to be especially important. In his view the goal of Hungarian politics was to realize the Kossuthian ideals. But after the USSR smashed the 1956 Revolt, the idea of collaboration among the Danubian nations again faded. Regional integration, when it existed, was the instrument of Soviet policy. Its historical prototypes were the federative plans of the Austro-Hungarian Monarchy, the utopias of the 19th century anti-dynastic, revolutionary movements, the customs union plans between the two world wars, and the Anglo-Saxon-American peace plans during World War II. Yet all of this was empty theory.

None of the most recent proposals such as Brzezinski's call for a Polish-Czechoslovak confederation in 1990, or the idea of a loose cooperation of states between the Baltic Sea and the Black Sea, or Ukraine's 1993 initiative to develop a Central-European safety belt, ever entered even an initial phase of implementation. Either the participants were indifferent or the proposals were perceived to be antagonistic to their best interests. Even those initiatives, such as the policy of rapprochement starting in the 1970's among the Baltic states, the Central European Initiatives stemming from the Alps-Adriatic cooperation (called *Pentagonale* and later *Hexagonale*), the cooperation of the Visegrád group, the Polish,

Slovak, Hungarian, Ukrainian, and Romania sub-regional cooperation in the Eastern Carpathian area, which had promising starts, quickly failed. The reasons were similar to those of the inter-war period, either political fears prevailed or the countries involved were not complementary economically. An example of the former is the failure of the Carpathian subregional collaborative plan. Both Romania and Slovakia considered it to be a Trojan horse from the Hungarians, while Polish nationalists attacked it for endangering the territorial integrity of Poland. The withering Visegrád cooperation is an example of the latter and is usually blamed on Vaclav Klaus and Czech selfishness. But the truth is that in spite of the enthusiastic propaganda, the Visegrád association was not and could not be as attractive from either an economic or a military point of view as joining the European Union or NATO. After the demise of communism only the economic cooperation of the Baltic states with Scandinavia and of Turkey with the Black Sea states seem deep-rooted and promising from among the several East Central European initiatives. In both cases a highly developed regional center with solid capital attracted a backward, poor, but culturally related periphery. Political analysts[20] rightly say that the missing economic complements have become more crucial during the past forty years. Linguistic and cultural heterogeneity, on-going virulent ethnic hostilities, and continued territorial disputes, as well as the absence of a great power, spelled failure for East Central European and South-Eastern European confederative plans.

Even without the prospect of a tight regional cooperation, the search for different forms of reconciliation remains vital. Mutual recognition of common borders through separate treaties and respect for nationalities as state-creating factors, rather than only ethnic minorities, are essential. The last two essays of this book discuss relevant Hungarian efforts.

NOTES

1. Baron Miklós Wesselényi, *Szózat a magyar és szláv nemzetiség ügyében* [Manifesto Concerning Hungarian and Slav Nationalities]. Prepared for the press by István Gál (Kolozsvár), vols I–II.

2. The proposals are outlined in Stephan Pejakovic, *Aktenstücke zur Geschichte des kroatisch–slavonischen Landtages und der nationalen Bewegung vom Jahre 1848* (Wien, 1861), Appendix; and in Rudolf Wierer, *Der Födera-*

lismus im Donauraum [Federalism in the Danube Basin] (Graz, Köln, 1860), 33-40.

3. Aurel C. Popovici, *Die Vereinigten Staaten von Gross-Österreich. Politische Studien zur Lözung der nationalen Fragen und staatsrechtlichen Krisen in Österreich-Ungarn* (Leipzig, 1906).

4. Oszkár Jászi, *A Monarchia jövője. A dualizmus bukása és a Dunai Egyesült Államok* [The Future of the Monarchy. The Fall of Dualism and the United States of the Danube Region] (Budapest, 1918). See also, Péter Hanák *Jászi Oszkár dunai patriotizmusa* [Oszkár Jászi's Danube Patriotism] (Budapest,1985), 67-80.

5. Lajos Kossuth, *Summary of the Principles of the Future Political Organizations of Hungary, I-II.* (*The Daily News,* November 25, 1851), 5, and (November 26, 1851), 6. Also published by Daniel Irányi and Charles-Louis Chassin, *Histoire politique de la révolution de Hongrie 1847-1849 I.* (Paris, 1859), 365-398.

6. Springer [Karl Renner], *Grundlagen aund Entwicklungsziele der österreichisch-ungarischen Monarchie* (Wien, Leipzig, 1906) and Karl Renner, *Das Selbtbestimmungsrecht* [Self-determination Rights] (Wien, 1918).

7. Henry Cord Meyer, *Mitteleuropa in German Thought and Action 1815-1945* (The Hague, 1955), 13-15. See also, William Henderson, *Friedrich List* (Reutlingen, 1989).

8. Friedrich Naumann, *Mitteleuropa* (Berlin, 1915) and Frigyes Naumann, *Középeurópa* [Central Europe] (Budapest, 1916).

9. For more details see Gyula Tokody, *Össznémet Szövetség (Alldeutscher Verband) és középeurópai tervei (1890-1918)* [Federation of All Germans and its Central-European plans] (Budapest, 1959).

10. Quoted by Anthony McElligott, Reforging Mitteleuropa in the Crucible of War, in *Mitteleuropa: History and Prospect,* ed. Peter Stirk (Edinburgh, 1994), 130.

11. Rostislav Fadeiev, *Mnenie o vostochnom voprose po provodu poslednih recenzi na Vooruzonnie sili Rossii* (St Petersburg, 1870), 90.

12. *Russian Diplomacy and Eastern Europe 1914-1917*, Introduction by Henry L. Roberts (New York, 1965).

13. László Teleki, *Válogatott munkái II.* [Selected works] (Budapest, 1961), 27-28.

14. *Kossuth Lajos iratai* [Lajos Kossuth's Papers], ed. Ferencz Kossuth (Budapest, 1898), 9-12. See also István Hajnal, *A Kossuth-emigráció Törökországban* [The Kossuth Emigration in Turkey] (Budapest, 1927) and László Katus, A magyar politikai vezetőréteg a délszláv kérdésről 1849 és 1867 között [Hungarian Political Leadership on the Southern-Slav Question] in *Szerbek és magyarok a Duna mentén II.* [Serbs and Hungarians along the Danube], ed. István Fried (Budapest, 1987), 147-184.

15. Thomas G. Masaryk, *The New Europe. The Slav Standpoint* (Washington D.C., 1918), 60.

16. Iván T. Berend, A közép- és kelet-európai gazdasági integráció kérdéséhez [To the Question of Central-Eastern European Economic Integration] in Iván T. Berend and György Ránki, *Gazdaság és társadalom* [Economy and Society] (Budapest, 1974), 123-126.

17. David E. Kaiser, *Economic Diplomacy and the Origins of the Second World War* (Princeton, 1980), 130-169.

18. *Wartime American Plans for a New Hungary. Documents from the U.S. Department of State, 1942-1944,* ed. Ignác Romsics (Highland Lakes, NJ., 1992)

and *Pax Britannica. Wartime Foreign Office Documents Regarding Plans for a Postbellum East Central Europe,* ed. András D. Bán (Highland Lakes, NJ., 1991), 78.

19. István Bibó, *Democracy, Revolution, Self-Determination. Selected Writings,* ed. Károly Nagy (Highland Lakes, NJ., 1991), 78.

20. See, e.g., Péter Kende, Volt-e valaha is esélye egy dunai államszövetségnek? [Has There Ever Been a Chance of a Danube Association of States?] in Péter Kende, *Miért nincs rend Kelet-Közép Európában?* [Why Isn't There Order in Central-Eastern Europe?] (Budapest, 1994), 105–128.

THE BEGINNINGS

MIKLÓS WESSELÉNYI ON THE FUTURE OF THE HABSBURG EMPIRE AND HUNGARY

ÁGNES DEÁK

The pamphlet, "Manifesto Concerning Hungarian and Slav Nationalities" was a climactic point of Baron Miklós Wesselényi's oeuvre. Exiled to Gräfenberg the "civil dead" presented "a cry of warning"..."from the depth of his grave" to his nation "about the danger threatening land and nation": "Disaster is hanging over us, my land! A disaster we have never had."[1] The end of the 1830's and the 1840's brought both a dynamic reform movement and also increasing antagonisms between Hungarian and non-Hungarian nationality movements in the Austro-Hungarian Empire. The Hungarian liberal movement advocated a combined program of a bourgeois society, consisting of citizens of equal rights and obligations, with a program for a modern political state modeled on Western European examples, thereby aspiring to assure for their country as many criteria as possible of a nation state within the Habsburg Empire. Until 1844 when Hungarian became a fully integrated official language, the movement had mostly campaigned for the cultivation and political and public emancipation of the language. However, in addition to Hungarian liberals, who wished to assure the public dominance of Hungarian, non-Hungarian nationalists also became active in protecting their own national language and culture. They demanded the subsequent use of Latin and the integration of their own language in local administration, education, and church. In the early 1840's the relationship between Hungarian and Croatian national movements became strained when the issue of Slovak language use created a stir both domestically and internationally following Lutheran Inspector-General Count Károly Zay's unification plans regarding Lutheran and Calvinist churches of Upper Hungary.

Pronounced differences produced a flood of pamphlets and articles discussing nationality issues. According to his diary Wesselényi had already been working on the *Manifesto* in June 1842 and had completed it by January 10, 1843. It was published by Otto Wigand in Leipzig the same year. In the meantime Wesselényi also tried to publicize his views through the press. He planned to publish an article on Russian Pan-Slav propaganda in the *Pesti Hírlap*, but was rejected by the censor. In the fall of 1842 in his Address, delivered at the Hungarian Academy of Sciences, Count István Széchenyi criticized the linguistic aspirations of the Hungarian national movement and considered the non-Hungarian national movements as reactions to the former. Consequently, he contested the liberal argument that nationality movements were mostly incited by subversive Russian propaganda. Wesselényi raised objections to Széchenyi's conduct in a proclamation sent to Kossuth which he subsequently published in the *Pesti Hírlap*.[2]

Wesselényi's *Manifesto* exposed one of the most important theses of Hungarian liberal nationalism; that the greatest threat to Europe actually came from the centuries long expansionism of a backward Russian Empire. Known as the Open Eastern Issue, the thesis held that a diminishing Ottoman Empire left a power vacuum in South Eastern Europe which provided ample opportunity for Russia to build new bridge-heads to Europe, this in addition to the already occupied territories of Poland. To do this Russia utilized national and denominational sympathy of Slavs to weaken and undermine European states, first of all Austria. To cope with this threat, co-operation among the non-Slav peoples of the area (Germans, Hungarians, Italians, and anti-Russian Polish) would be necessary, in the name of freedom and constitutionalism. It would realize a "real holy alliance."[3]

While similar writings discussed the topic from the point of view of Hungary and Hungarian national interests, Wesselényi's writings examined the Hungarian phenomena from a wider imperial and European perspective. Beyond indicating specific things to be done, he offered a roughly outlined program to transform the political institutions of the Habsburg Empire in a way which would recognize national sentiments and yet still reinforce existing federative elements. These were very distinctive features of Wesselényi's political writings.

Prognoses about the future of Europe and the impacts of Pan-Slavism greatly concerned Hungarian politicians of the Reform Era. As if Herder's prophecy had taken shape, Hungarian politicians were haunted by the image of Hungary disintegrating or dismembered, perhaps during an unfavorable international situation—a scenario attested to in Ferenc Deák's letter to his brother-in-law József Tarányi-Oszterhueber in November 1842. Although Deák privately reflected on the possible disintegration of the Empire and of historical Hungary,[4] these fears were hardly ever discussed publicly. Count Leo von Thun was duly surprised when, during a debate he initiated with Ferenc Pulszky on the Slovak-Hungarian language controversy, Pulszky commented on the threats Pan-Slavism carried for the future of Hungary "during a turmoil which would be unavoidable at the collapse of one of the neighboring Empires, Hungary would cease to exist as a political entity. Certain parts would be incorporated by German and Slavic provinces of Austria and other parts would be annexed by Serbia and Croatia, thus directly or indirectly by Russia."[5]

Despite open analyses of European power relations, there were political reasons why there was no analytical writing done concerning the structure of the whole Empire.[6] In Széchenyi's description the Empire was like a mixed marriage—feudal constitutionalism in Hungary married to absolutism in the rest of the Empire. This situation induced both liberal and conservative Hungarian politicians to protect Hungary's constitution and to abstain from expressing views on the prevailing governing system in the rest of the Empire. Conservative Count Aurél Dessewffy said in 1941, "Remain silent about the heterogeneity in the different parts of the Monarchy. If our constitution is respected by the government, we have nothing to do with the system of other provinces."[7] The Hungarian liberal movement embraced the program of the personal union which constituted the political law between the Empire and Hungary. It originated with the Pragmatica Sanctio and was enforced by Article 10:1790 of the constitution. The actual political system only remotely resembled a real personal union since political separation really existed only in the legislature, the Diet, and in municipal executive power. In most other respects a direct dependence upon the imperial government prevailed. In addition, the personal union referred only to Hungary proper; any political plans or criticism of the political system in the rest of the Empire would have caused controversy between the liberal opposition and the government. As Zsigmond Kemény stated, "whether Austrian provinces should become constitutional is not asked by Hungarians whose country is "regnum unum et independens," unless for general cosmopolitan or freedom interests. After all, we have so much to do that we have to use both hands to accomplish our own affairs and we never reach the last item on the agenda. Kossuth has named so many vital issues, which are of crucial importance for the survival of Hungarians, that it is impossible to take on the issue of the provinces as has been suggested. Széchenyi often indicated that our "mixed marriage with Austria" should be included in our everyday considerations, but his suggestion went just as much unnoticed as Wesselényi's writing. There was nobody among the constitutional reformers who would have included the following important question in his plans, not even as an afterthought–"What practical position should Hungary occupy in case other provinces, effected by the state of events, also follow the path of constitutionalism? Can we prepare for such an event and can we make an impact?"[8]

The 1847 *Proclamation of the Opposition* was the first official document to consider that constitutional institutions in the rest of the Monarchy could actually safeguard Hungarian constitutionality. Lajos Kossuth raised it as a political demand in his address to the Lower House on March 13, 1848 amidst the excitement caused by the Paris Revolution. However, the opposition in the rest of the Monarchy apparently felt no great need for political dialogue and/or cooperation with the Hungarian liberal opposition, and so there were only a few scattered initiatives after 1847.[9]

Wesselényi's writings were a unique exception in the void of comprehensive reform propositions. Mihály Horváth listed the following motivations for Wesselényi's *Manifesto:* nationality conflicts in Hungary, Széchenyi's Address at the Academy (although Wesselényi had started writing well before Széchenyi delivered it), and ensuing polemics in the press.[10] All the above affected Wesselényi who remained connected to Hungarian intellectual and political life through his readings and correspondence even in Gräfenberg. In a letter to the Governor of Croatia, Ferenc Haller, he emphasized the importance of the international context in evaluating the Hungarian situation "which is the product of our century and age, the product of world events, created within all European states, and which is only one symptom of an illness you attributed to us and, consequently, regard the Hungarian nation and whoever has advocated our cause as assaulting and aggressive while the Slavs are suffering and defensive. This mistake has misled you and it is bound to happen this way. Because of your conviction and opinion you limited yourself to a small-scale local viewpoint which prevented you from a wider Monarchical and European awareness."[11]

In 1844 Wesselényi's pamphlet was also published in German in an effort to influence the German and Austrian public.[12] Different intellectual-political circumstances during his Moravia solitude must have also motivated his writing and helped to form a wider scope because "...during his extended visits abroad he noticed things and heard of issues neither belligerent politicians at home nor doctrinaires abroad were aware of." [13] As his contemporary Zsigmond Kemény wrote, "in the sanatorium he became closely acquainted with aristocratic Slavs and Wallachian Boyars because attentive and sympathetic foreigners gathered around this proclaimed hero and a martyr of liberal ideas. Interactions with authorities of neighboring Slav and Romanian provinces made him increasingly gloomy. He started dreading Eastern intellectual movements."[14] He often conversed with Austrians and Germans as well.[15] Hardly anything is known about Wesselényi's readings of the time. He himself only referred to the *Augsburger Allgemeine Zeitung* in his work. But since his eyesight deteriorated and he resorted to his future wife's assistance, contemporary German literature must have constituted the bulk of his reading.[16] Contemporary German publications and brochures also discussed nationality conflicts in Hungary. In 1843–44 the Hungarian version of the *Vierteljahrsschrift aus und für Ungarn* and shortly thereafter the *Jahrbücher für slawische Literatur, Kunst, und Wissenschaft* were published in order that "the intellectual battle would be fought within the sight of neutral Germany."[17] The *Augsburger Allgemeine Zeitung* regularly published writings of this kind and pamphlets, for and against, were also available. Consequently, a review of pamphlet battles might reveal aspects of Wesselényi's work which would be lost in a purely Hungarian context.

By 1848 nation states had become the generally accepted political form. Yet the Habsburg Empire remained a conglomerate of nations with dynastic legitimacy as its cohesive force. In the midst of unfolding modern political ideas and controversial challenges of constitutionality and nationality, the leading conservative elite viewed the Empire as a besieged fortress which, jointly with the conservative forces of the Holy Alliance, was the bulwark against revolutionary ideas. The reign of Emperor Franz I was a period of immobility and inertia when any suspicious intellectual initiative was hindered or even banned. After his death, the 1840's brought a period of intellectual and political revival in all the provinces. Different groups of political opposition gradually formed, Bohemian and Lower Austrian nobility became active and liberals both at home and in exile embarked on intensive propaganda campaigns. The most seriously debated question was how to transform the Monarchy from a "big colorful chaos of peoples" into a modern state.[18] As the writer of the most effective pamphlet, Viktor Franz von Andrian-Werburg, elaborated, "Austria is an imagined name which does not mean a people, a country or a nation. It is a conventional name of a composite of totally separate peoples. There are Italians, Germans, Slavs, and Hungarians who constitute the Austrian Empire but there is no Austria, Austrian, or Austrian nationality and they have never existed, except in a small area around Vienna."[19] Heterogeneous parts had been held together by overpowering absolutism. However, the lack of public spirit, a conscious divisive policy by the government, and "divergent nationalities" made the future of the Empire uncertain. A well-known playwright of the era, Eduard Bauernfeld contemplated about Austria's mission in his memoir when Franz I died, "Concerning its origin Austria is German. Its earlier task was to fight the Barbarians and its later task was to cultivate them. Unfortunately it failed to do the latter. It does not help if somebody calls himself Emperor. He has to be one. During Franz I's rule a united Austria existed in name only....The improvised perpetual Empire relied on implied external and internal compromises, on patriarchal sentiments, and on the benevolence of other great powers who could not allow the Empire, 'this recognized necessity,' to fail; or it did not rely on its peoples. A state should not exist for external needs or by the grace of others; it has to invent its own necessity in itself."[20] Each pamphlet contemplated two issues: (1) how to define the Empire's mission under modern circumstances, and (2) how to establish a "public spirit" in order to hold the Empire together under constitutionality (as well as what changes that might entail).

Three main ideological trends emerged from the Austrian–German opposition: Bourgeois-liberal, Josephian, and feudal liberal-conservative.[21]

I. *The Bourgeois-Liberal Trend.* Like German bourgeois-liberal ideology, the image of Russia was an important factor in Hungarian liberalism. With a centuries long expansionist policy, absolutism, and oppressive governing system Russia was an immediate threat to European culture, civilization, and freedom. German nationalism further deepened anti-French sentiments. It was a generally accepted theory that an alliance between France and Russia would be the result of a united Germany or Austro-Germany since France had been angling for the Rhine Valley and Russia for Galicia, while the latter also aspired to be the protector of South Eastern Europe after the decline of the Ottoman Empire. In the face of these dangers co-operation between Austria and Germany was necessary.[22]

Exiled Franz Schuselka was the best known publicist of Austrian–German liberals of the 1840's. Schuselka considered the German guiding role the most essential factor in European development and their cultural and political contributions main integrating forces of the Austrian Empire. It was imperative for the elite of small peoples to absorb German culture, even if ethnic masses retained their national languages and traditions along with their uncivilized existence. "The Slavs do not become Germanized to increase Germany's population but simply because the Slavs cannot resist German culture. The overpowering German spirit will Germanize them against their will as it is happening to every civilized human being. With pleasure and eagerness they themselves want to be Germanized as they are aware of the advantages of German culture. It is also their civic and moral duty to Germanize because armed with German culture they can serve the state on a higher level and it is the moral duty of every human being to improve and perfect himself."[23] Schuselka's pamphlets did not contain direct proposals for changing the political system of the Empire. Yet the prevailing German cultural and political monopoly indicated a tendency towards constitutional centralization and he expressed some understanding only towards Lombardy's autonomy. Each pamphlet, which dealt with the Hungarian question was a little different. The *German Words of an Austrian* envisioned the annihilation of Hungarians–either a slow death of the nation or a glorious downfall.[24] *Austria and Hungary* echoed old stereotypes in a modernized style in order to mock the Hungarian language reform movement. Hungarians applied the same "barbaric force" in the present time as they did when they first appeared in Europe. "Whatever Hungary presently possesses of higher culture ought to be attributed to the diligence and talent of its non-Hungarian population. Ardent self-respect and a certain chivalry distinguish Hungarians from the rest but these are characteristics of the nobility. Hungarian peasantry fall short of the German and even the Slav as is demonstrated by the sight of Hungarian villages."[25] Hungarians were to blame for this backwardness because even though they were full of fear they obstinately insisted on a "literal interpretation of the constitution and in this way they evoke the barbaric spirit that once dictated those words."[26] In his view Hungary owed a lot to the Empire since it did not share in the common expenses (consequently it remained a foreign land for the others). Schuselka was more insightful in *Is Austria German?* where he mused that Hungary's "national pride in freedom" could be the Germans' alliance in the fight against the East.[27] Since Hungarians were such an isolated ethnic group, their access to civilization was through the Germans. Hence, German intellectual dominance should prevail in Hungary as well. It was to no purpose to try to dominate the Slav population since Hungarians lacked the intellectual superiority which would induce the Slavs to assimilate voluntarily. Further, aggressive assimilation was not acceptable. Implementing German as the official language would solve the Hungarian language reform issue.

In foreign policy Schuselka supported a close alliance with Germany and advocated Austria's further presence in Italy to counterbalance France and to assure Austria's intermediary mission between Italy and Germany. He promulgated an alliance with England and France against Russia to restore Poland, a Hellenic-Christian Empire with Constantinople as center, and a drive to push Russia back to Asia where it would be an "Apostle of lights," a messenger of civilization.[28] Following that, Prussia would gain influence around the North Sea in Sweden and Finland, while Austria would be granted the Danubian Romanian principalities. The liberal followers of the German mission combined the program of a nation state with the project of a new Central European state which would extend its sphere of influence to the Balkan. Friedrich List enthusiastically advertised the creation of a big Central European economic unit and the necessity of a large scale German settlement along the lower Danube. The plans were eagerly received by certain circles of Austrian–German liberals.

II. *The Josephian Trend.* Franz Grillparzer, a celebrated playwright of the period held enlightened Josephian imperial ideas. He opposed modern nationalism whether Slav, Hungarian, or Austrian–German. Yet there was a German element prevalent in this trend as well, even though it never planned to expand the Empire beyond a cultural rapprochement towards Germany. Josephian imperialists also advocated centralization and considered provincial separatism an impediment to advancement. In his notes Grillparzer stated that German provinces supported by a civilized Germany had to retain leadership, and that "when Vienna is the intellectual center of the Monarchy, it will become the political as well and it will stay that way." He expected that Slav and Hungarian ambitions would spring asunder like soap-bubbles. Otherwise, Hungarians should be motivated enough to eagerly renounce their constitution. "...I am not an advocate of constitutions" but it would be necessary to give a common constitution to the rest of the Empire beyond Hungary, which could trigger the need for a union with the Hungarians. Based on Schuselka's principle that the Hungarian language and culture were undeveloped and isolated, Grillparzer rejected the idea of making Hungarian the official language and proposed German as an alternative. "...the Hungarian language has no future...whatever they did against Latin will be an advantage for German. Hungary is already Germanized and will become even more so with every passing year. If one expects to be educated, he must know German."[29]

III. *The Feudal, Liberal-Conservative Trend.* The liberal and predominantly feudal-conservative policy, hall-marked by Andrian-Werburg, also promulgated a twofold orientation concerning the foreign policy of the Empire. On one hand, Andrian advocated tight connections with the German federation entailing a customs union (although he did lack the missionary zeal of Schuselka). On the other hand, referring to trade interests, he stated that "Serbia, Moldova, and Wallachia will secure their status, development, and membership in the European family of peoples in a permanent alliance with us. We, however, can feel safe and independent from every side through such a tight alliance."[30] Within Austria, Andrian did not profess a German hegemony. On the contrary, he tried to harmonize nationality sentiments and ambitions by means of a homogeneous public spirit. Even his first pamphlets criticized the bureaucratic centralized administration. Instead, it was desirable to revive a feudal institutional system, to extend the jurisdiction of the nobility over taxation and the budget and to grant them the right to partake in the discussion of Bills brought in by the government. This program maintained the feudal constitution with its execution remaining with the Emperor; there was no demand for a responsible executive authority yet. The need for a local self-governing system had already arisen, focussing on the provincial level and provincial constitutions. The program argued that the national awakening of the peoples of the Empire did not threaten the Empire itself since their demands could be satisfied through provincial separatism. There were only obscure allusions to traditions and institutions which might bring further political demands to the surface. However, pamphlets of this kind outlined an imperial assembly of the Estates indicating a need for a common imperial constitution as a depository of the desired "public spirit." Andrian-Werburg sounded pro-Hungarian in his pamphlets when he considered Hungary as a model that could revive the Estates of the Land. According to his pamphlets, both in 1841 and in 1847, he held Hungary up as an example to the Austrian nobility as a liberal constitutional state with a relatively efficient administrative system. However, it was also evident from his diary that he had been politically motivated to say that and did not have such a high opinion of Hungarians and their wisdom at all.[31] Yet his program included references to the development of constitutional institutions which would entail a higher degree of integration of Hungary within the Empire, an idea contrary to the strategic objectives of the Hungarian opposition.

From the early 1840's on the number of writings on Slav nationalistic demands increased and their views on the present and future of the Empire became more succinct. The first example of this trend was a pamphlet by the Czech–German aristocrat, Count Leo von Thun in 1842.[32] His writing was the first proclamation of an emerging Austro–Slavism which drew a favorable response among the Slav peoples of the Empire. The unknown author of *Slawen, Russen, Germanen* (1843) followed Thun's footsteps, although he was more outspoken and assertive.[33] Like Thun he also considered the linguistic-cultural alliance of Pan-Slavism the only viable option. He was also aware of the danger Pan-Slavism might pose to the Empire, but distinguished between the Western and Eastern Slavs since the impending Russian threat might affect the former just as much as other European nations. The last part was a solemn message from the Western Slavs to the Germans inviting reconciliation and alliance. "...We are turning to You great, virile, sparkling German nation....Oblivion and forgiveness! we exclaim to you, German men, who really care for the greatness and fame of your country and we extend our hands in reconciliation....We are the protecting wall of German culture towards the advancing East. We are your allies, so the enemy may enter German soil only through our body. However, if you turn away from us, you force us to become their allies. Thus you thrust enemy weapon into the heart of your country and they will enter your land unfearingly with no enemy at their back."[34] In concert with Thun, the author agreed that unhindered development of the peoples within Austria should be made possible, adding that in the Western Slavic view the Empire had a special mission. "Our civilization, language, nationality, and faith are in danger and only Austria can save the greatest and the holiest for us. Austria is obliged to help us in the threatening danger. We fought with her against the Turks and the Mongols; we helped to build Austria and elevate it to its present level; we strived for culture and humanity with the Austrians; we suffered and thrived, cried and rejoiced with them; we shared her days of misery and humiliation and days of victory and elation as well. Our trust and hope are in Austria."[35] To fulfill its mission the Empire "will have to give up the idea of a pure German state since it has not been one ever since it became the Austrian Empire and cannot now be one. It is not more or less than Austria and it should stay that way. It has to make do with the fact that it has a hegemonious impact on the Parliament and understand that its influence over the German states should be generated by its own internal resources. To achieve that it is necessary that the four main nations would be in a co-ordinate, not in a subordinate relationship."[36] Since Slavs made up half of the population of the Empire they should receive attention from the imperial government accordingly. The author demanded the renewal of the bonds between Bohemia and Moravia, as defined by political law. This way the two provinces of the crown would be united by their feudal constitution and would be elevated to the level of Hungary and Northern Italy within the Empire. He also spoke about the linguistic-cultural unification of the Southern Slavs who would form a strong, new nationality, yet without mentioning its possible political consequences. Still the idea of a Southern Slav union to be created by destroying existing boundaries lurked not far behind the lines. Although Hungarians were only mentioned in passing, they were "exposed" as sworn enemies of the Slavs. Finally, his elaboration of a program of Czech–Moravian–Slovak unity would have directly affected the future of Hungary.[37]

Count Thun disapproved of an extensive use of Hungarian as an official language and demanded language rights for the Slovaks in education and religious services. He considered Czech and Slovak one language, thus emphasizing the indivisible unity of Czech national recovery and Slovak needs. He also blamed Hungarians for separatism within the Empire and mentioned that Hungarian government agencies sent Hungarian official documents to agencies of other provinces. "This is a way to confer with foreign countries. But does Hungary have to remain foreign forever for the rest of the provinces within the Austrian Monarchy? Unification in a vast Empire deserves special attention and the use of a common language when not only one party is affected is certainly one of the crucial issues. The way you, Hungarians, do not want to adjust seems to be an impractical demonstration. If there is an ulterior motive, I find it even more foolish."[38]

*

Wesselényi's *Manifesto* was one among many pamphlets of this time. It proposed different viewpoints and presented a radical Hungarian perspective in the heated debate over the future and role of Austria. On the international scene, Wesselényi fully shared the German liberal views of Russia's role, of a probable French alliance, and of lurking dangers for Austria and Germany. He offered a Hungarian view on an alliance with Germany. "...Both its constitutional existence and the possibility of national survival make Russian or any Slav revolutionary ambition alien and distant for Hungarians. Hungary's existence depends on keeping its distance from this. For Germany and the whole civilized Europe, this fact makes Hungary a trusted relative and a reliable and faithful ally....Hungary will be a bulwark of Germany and Europe against Russia. However, this possibility postulates intellectual, constitutional, and national development in order to bear the brunt of the attack."[39] The Hungarian view deviated from that of the German liberals for whom political advancement was equivalent with Germanization. Wesselényi offered a "real holy alliance" of German, Austrian-German, Hungarian, Italian, and Polish peoples in which the principle of a free national development would be sustained. The Austro-Slav idea contrasted the same principle with the German romantic missionary zeal.

Wesselényi emphasized Austria's Western orientation above all. Austria was expected to play a leading role in Germany (in alliance with Prussia and considering Prussia's claims) and to become the leading power in Europe. This echoed the secret dream of Austrian-German liberals. "If Austria adopts constitutionality as its slogan and becomes the leader of civilization and the leader of lawful and peaceful advancement, it will become the leading power of Europe."[40] He is less embracing towards an eastern orientation which appeared in the Reform Era but advocacy of an increased cultural and political influence towards Romanian Danubian principalities emerged mostly after 1848/49.[41] Wesselényi shared the German liberal views that this area should not be under Russian predominance after the dissolution of the Ottoman Empire. He envisioned a Southern Slav Kingdom made up of a revived Byzantium, Greece, Bosnia, Serbia, and Bulgaria and a united Romanian Principality. They would seat members of Austrian, Prussian, and French dynasties on the throne; hence they would be included in the international spheres of interest.[42] Wesselényi did not view the Balkans as an exclusively German sphere of interest and neither did he consider it of direct Hungarian interest. However, he shared the German liberal views about Poland's restoration under the auspieces of the Prussian dynasty.

To sum up, in foreign policy Wesselényi shared basic elements of German liberal views on the situation in Europe. His program, however, stipulated a certain balance and cooperation among European great powers instead of supporting German claims for preeminence.

He stated two important principles of Austrian internal affairs: (1) the mixed governing system of the Empire should be terminated and every part of the Empire should be granted constitutionality. Since he did not expatiate upon constitution types, his program was not contrary to restoring feudal constitutions in the provinces. Yet presumably his ideas, which corresponded to the objectives of the Hungarian liberal movement, would have called for a bourgeois constitution. (2) He only expounded on provincial and national constitutions so that "every country and province of the Empire would enjoy the benefit and security of its own bourgeois and representational constitution."[43] He did not mention a common imperial constitution which made his program distinctively different from Schuselka's aspirations for centralization and from Andrian-Werburg's plans as well. From this respect Wesselényi followed the ideas of the Hungarian liberal movement. However, he advocated a federative reconstruction of the Empire which was not in tune with an emerging Hungarian dualist conception of a "dual political federation of states."[44]

Historical law formed the basis of Wesselényi's plan. He outlined five political units: Austrian-German provinces (proposing Slovenian autonomy similar to that of the Croats and Transylvanian Saxons), united Bohemia-Moravia, Galicia, Hungary, and Lombardy. Quoting historical references Dalmatia, which "came to us through Hungary anyway," would be annexed by Croatia; Slovakia would be annexed indirectly by Hungary. Apart from the Slovenian case, ethnic-nationality principle would be observed only in the case of Istria–by joining its sections inhabited by Italians to Lombardy and its sections inhabited by Slavs to Dalmatia.[45] His plan was dissimilar from the confederative plans prepared by Hungarian and other nationalities' exiles during the 1840's and 1850's. Wesselényi himself disapproved of them as "revolutionary propaganda." His work was also different from the 1848–49 Austro-Slavic federative plans that proposed ethnic-nationality divisions and different from programs that proposed extending intra-imperial dualism to trialism in order to include a third, unified Southern Slav political entity.[46]

Since Wesselényi's plan focussed on the provincial level, it did not fully describe characteristics of imperial supervision over those provinces. At the imperial level he emphasized features intended to sway the public of the rest of the Empire. One of the reproaches to Hungary had been that it did not proportionately share the common expenses of the Empire owing to the nobility's fiscal immunity. Wesselényi stressed that under certain conditions Hungary was ready to assume its share in expenses and in debts, an idea which proved to be the most factual offer to the Austrian-German public in his plan. The impact of this element would be demonstrated in 1848 when Hungarians refused to share the national debts of the Empire and it received an unfavorable and heated response from the imperial authorities.

The 1840's in Austria was a period when the liberal opposition became an organized body and explored the possibilities of alliances. Wesselényi's intention was to include Hungarian reform movements in this process, to define Hungarian interests, and to seek opportunities for concessions. However, his "offer for alliance" rejected the idea of German cultural and political hegemony.

That of his objectives–to change the unfavorable response towards the Hungarian language reform movement and to justify Hungarian ambitions–followed the main direction of the Hungarian liberal movement. He shared and advocated the common doctrine of European liberals that establishing a modern civil society and a liberal constitutional political administration would cure nationality conflicts and "could transform hostile and menacing Slav peoples into harmless but reliable allies."[47] Wesselényi fully embraced the demand for Hungarian as an official language. In his view nationality rights were attached to people while communities were historically empowered with rights. "The state has the right to oblige its citizens, to require severe and unappealing responsibilities from them, to limit them in their individual rights, in some measure, for the sake of the rest, and to involve them for their own sake."[48] Thus, for the beneficial sake of the Whole, there should be a unilingual political administration. Non-Hungarian languages were not to be used in any level of administration; Hungarian would be used in education, although teaching in Hungarian was not to be enforced in lower elementary schools; and Hungarian proficiency would be required of priests of any denomination. Beyond the ability to read and write, Hungarian proficiency would be necessary for acquiring political and even certain private ownership rights, with the restriction that it was not applied at fee absolute transactions.[49] "...It is our Slavs' civic duty to confine the use of their mother tongue within limits set by the common good. In other words, it is their duty to exercise and cultivate their tongue to an extent which will not impede on the use and proficiency of Hungarian since this is an indispensable requirement for national unity."[50] In private life the use of one's mother tongue should not be limited, nor should nationality sentiments be ridiculed or insulted. In this respect he professed tolerance, denounced force, and "rowdy Hungarianism...rudeness, coarseness, and stupidity."[51] Yet this part of his program followed the paradigm of Hungarian liberal nationalism of the Reform Era, unlike his plans concerning a political transformation of the Habsburg Empire.

Bloody nationality encounters of 1848–49 greatly affected Hungarian liberal views and different groups of the Hungarian political elite were compelled to re-evaluate their views on nationality policy and national language use. Wesselényi's work was an inspiring contribution to exploring ways of peaceful coexistence among different nationalities within the Habsburg Empire and historical Hungary.

NOTES

1. Miklós Wesselényi, *Szózat a magyar és a szláv nemzetiség ügyében* [Manifesto Concerning Hungarian and Slav Nationalities] (Budapest, 1992), 15–17.

2. Zsolt Trócsányi, *Wesselényi Miklós* (Budapest, 1965), 453; Wesselényi's Manifesto published in, *Gróf Széchenyi István írói és hírlapi vitája Kossuth La-*

jossal, I. [Count István Széchenyi's Literary and Newspaper Debate with Lajos Kossuth], ed. Gyula Viszota (Budapest, 1927), 205–206.

3. Wesselényi, *Manifesto*, 186.

4. Ferenc Deák's letter to József Tarányi-Oszterhueber, Pest, November 10, 1842. published in, Pál Sándor, Deák politikai koncepciójához. (Ismeretlen levele 1842-ből) [On Deák's Political Theory. His Unknown Letter from 1842] (*Történelmi Szemle*, 1979), 262–282.

5. Graf Leo von Thun, *Die Stellung der Slowaken in Ungarn* [The Slovaks' Situation in Hungary] (Prague, 1843), 262–282. The correspondence was also published in *Vierteljahrsschrift aus und für Ungarn,* 1.1843, 61–91. Thun reacted to László Pulszky's observation: "That is new! Do we have to say more about it? Do we have to seriously contemplate whether Slovakia's political integration with Bohemia and Moravia and that of Hungary with the Principality of Austria and Styria are possible? Would it be the next step towards the Slovaks' national development? As far as we know this is the first time these concerns are voiced and are Mr. Pulszky's personal views. We have nothing to do with him any more, only with the Party he is a representative of. We'll see what reception his opinion will get."

6. See, János Varga, *Helyét kereső Magyarország. Politikai eszmék és koncepciók az 1840-es évek elején* [Hungary Seeking Its Place: Political Ideas and Theories in the Early 1840's] (Budapest, 1982), 115–141; András Gergely, Liberalizmus és nemzet. Eötvös József és a Habsburgok az 1840-es években [Liberalism and Nation: József Eötvös and the Habsburgs in the 1840's] (*Világosság*, 31. 1990), 4–5.

7. Aurél Dessewffy, *Pesti Hírlap és Kelet Népe közti vitály* [Dispute between Pesti Hírlap and Kelet Népe], in, *Gróf Dessewffy Aurél összes művei* [Count Aurél Dessewffy's Complete Writings], ed. József Ferenczy (Budapest, 1887), 47.

8. Zsigmond Kemény, A két Wesselényi Miklós [Two Miklós Wesselényis], in, *Magyar szónokok és statusférfiak (Politikai jellemrajzok)* [Hungarian Orators and Statesmen: Political Portraits] (Pest, 1851), 173–174.

9. See V.F. von Andrian-Werburg, *Oesterreich und dessen Zukunft. Zweiter Theil. Bei Ludwig Giese* (Hamburg, 1847), 188–197; Karl Moering, *Guter Rath fuer Oesterreich. Mit Bezugnahme auf das Programm der Liberalen Partei in Ungarn* (Leipzig, 1847).

10. Mihály Horváth, *Huszonöt év Magyarország történetéből, 1823–1848* [Twenty-five Years of the History of Hungary, 1823–1848]. 3rd ed, vol. 2. (Budapest, 1886), 324; Michael Horváth, *Fünfundzwanzig Jahre aus der Geschichte Ungarns von 1823–1848.* trans. from Hungarian by Joseph Novelli. 2nd ed. (Leipzig, 1867), 114–118.

11. In Ferenc Szilágyi, *Ifjabb B. Wesselényi Miklós. Élet és korrajz.* [Miklós B. Wesselényi, Jr. Biography and Description of a Period] (Budapest, 1876), 76.

12. *Eine Stimme über die ungarische slawische Nationalität* (Leipzig, 1844).

13. István Gál's preface to the following edition: Miklós Wesselényi, *Manifesto*, ed. István Gál (Kolozsvár: Minerva, I.), 25.

14. Kemény, 163.

15. Trócsányi, 451.

16. *Wesselényi Miklós naplója* [The Diary of Miklós Wesselényi] (Film Library of the Hungarian National Archive, Box 5496.)

17. "den geistigen Kampf vor dem neutralen Deutschland auszufechen," in, *Jahrbücher für Slawische Literatur, Kunst und Wissenschaft* (J. P. Jordan, Jr., 1843. 3.), 181.

18. "...dieses grosse bunte Völkerchaos" in, Oesterreich und das constitutionelle Princip. (Leipzig, 1844.), 88.

19. Viktor Franz von Andrian-Werburg, *Oesterreich und dessen Zukunft*, 3rd.ed. (Hamburg, 1843), 6-7; Andrian-Werburg quoted in Friederike Glanner, Viktor Franz von Andrian-Werburg. Ein Lebensbild (Dissertation. Wien, 1961); Fritz Fellner, Die Tagebücher des Viktor Franz von Andrian-Werburg (*Mitteilungen des Österreichischen Staatsarchivs*, Bd. 26. 1973), 328-341.

20. Eduard Bauernfeld, *Erinnerungen aus Alt-Wien* (Wien, 1923), 216-217.

21. Georg Franz, *Liberalismus. Die deutsch-liberale Bewegung in der Habsburgischen Monarchie* (München), 37-38; Ignaz Beidtel, *Geschichte der österreichischen Staatsverwaltung 1740-1842*, vol. 2. (Innsbruck, 1898); Viktor Bibl, *Die niederösterreichischen Stände im Vormärz. Ein Beitrag zur Vorgeschichte der Revolution des Jahres 1848.* (Wien, 1911); Viktor Bibl, *Der Zerfall Österreichs. Kaiser Franz und sein Erbe*, vol. 2. (Wien-Berlin-Leipzig-München, 1924), 39-101; Karl Eder, *Der Liberalismus in Altösterreich. Geisteshaltung, Politik und Kultur* (Wien-München, 1955), 78-104; Eduard Winter, *Frühliberalismus in der Donau-monarchie. Religiöse, nationale und wissenschaftliche Strömungen von 1790-1868* (Berlin, 1868); Péter Hanák, Österreichischer Staatspatriotismus im Zeitalter des aufsteigenden Nationalismus. In *Wien und Europa zwischen den Revolutionen (1789-1848). Wiener Europa-Gespräch 1977* (Wiener Schriften Heft 39). (Wien-München, 1978), 315-330; Hanák, Osztrák állampatriotizmus a hódító nacionalizmus korában (*Világosság*, 19. 1978), 151-157.

22. About Russia's image in Europe see also, Alfred Fischel, *Der Panslavismus bis zum Weltkrieg. Ein geschichtlicher Überblick.* (Stuttgart-Berlin, 1919), 225-227; Hans Kohn, *Pan-Slavism: Its History and Ideology.* (Notre Dame, Indiana, 1953), 11-28, 50-60; Dieter Groh, *Russland und das Selbstverständniss Europas. Ein Beitrag zur europäischen Geistesgeschichte* (Neuwied, 1961), 180-195; Olga V. Pavlenko, Russland und die Donauslaven (1848 bis 1871). In *Der Austroslavismus. Ein verfrühtes Konzept zur politischen Neugestaltung Mitteleuropas*, ed. A. Moritsch (Wien-Köln-Weimar, 1996), 156-177.

23. Franz Schuselka, *Ist Oesterreich deutsch? Eine statistische und glossirte Beantwortung dieser Frage.* (Leipzig, 1843), 24; Fritz Fellner, *Franz Schuselka. Ein Lebensbild.* (Dissertation, Wien, 1948); Márta S. Lengyel, Egy osztrák röpiratíró útja a negyvennyolcas forradalom felé [An Austrian Pamphlet Writer's Road to the Revolution of 1848] (*Századok*, 1960.5,6), 750-793, (1961.1), 47-82.

24. Schuselka, *Deutsche Worte eines Oesterreichers* (Hamburg, 1843), 210.

25. Schuselka, *Oesterreich und Ungarn* (Leipzig, 1843), 6; The *Jahrbücher für slawische Literatur, Kunst und Wissenschaft* enthusiastically reviewed "the best pamphlet ever written by a German about Hungary. Germany seems to have finally discovered the real situation of nationalities in Hungary." (Jg.1, Heft 4.), 284. In later issues of the periodical, Schuselka's views of the Slavs are fiercely criticized; See also, Schuselka, *Ungarn als Quelle der Befürchtungen und Hoffnungen für Oesterreichs Zukunft* (Leipzig, 1845).

26. Ibid., 25.

27. Schuselka, *Ist Oesterreich deutsch*, 48.

28. Franz Schuselka, *Die Orientalische das ist Russische Frage.* (Hamburg, 1843), 81-85.

29. Grillparzer's notes from early 1843, see: Franz Grillparzer, *Tagebücher und literarische Skizzenhefte*, ed. August Sauer (Wien, 1924), 11-12; Grillparzer, Von den Sprachen. in, *Prosaschriften I.F.G. Sämtliche Werke I. 13. Band*, ed., August Sauer and Reinhold Backmann (Wien, 1930), 179-180; about Grillparzer see, Peter Kuranda, Grillparzer und die Politik des Vormärzes, in, *Jahrbuch der Grillparzer-Gesellschaft* (28, 1926), 5-21; Friedrich Kainz, Grillparzers Stellung im österreichischen Sprachen- und Nationalitätenkampf (*Historische Zeitschrift*, 161. 1939), 498-531; Eduard Winter, *Revolution, Neoabsolutismus und Liberalismus in der Donaumonarchie* (Wien, 1969); Waltraud Heindl, Die österreichische Bürokratie. Zwischen deutscher Vorherrschaft und österreichischer Staatsidee (Vormärz und Neoabsolutismus), in *Österreich und die deutsche Frage im 19. und 20. Jahrhundert.* ed. Heinrich Lutz and Helmut Rumpler (Wien, 1982), 73-91; Péter Hanák's quoted article.

30. Andrian-Werburg, 1847, 198.

31. *Tagebücher von Viktor Franz von Andrian-Werburg.* (Archiv mesta Brna, Grossgrundbesitz Lisen), H 2, Karton 116, Inv. Nr. 671.

32. Leo Graf von Thun, *Über den gegenwärtigen Zustand der böhmischen Literatur und ihre Bedeutung* (Prag, 1842).

33. *Slawen, Russen, Germanen. Ihre gegenseitigen Verhältnisse in der Gegenwart und Zukunft.* (Leipzig, 1843). It was reviewed by Heinrich Ritter von Srbik, *Aus Österreichs Vergangenheit. Von Prinz Eugen zu Franz Joseph.* (Salzburg), 254. The author was unknown even to his contemporaries. According to an Austrian government agent the pamphlet was written by Dr. Kuhninge who also contributed to *Jahrbücher für slawische Literatur, Kunst und Wissenschaft.* The publisher of the report, Karl Glossy, claimed in his notes that Kuhnige had arrived in Leipzig on a Russian commission and his contact was Minister Uvarov. Glossy, however, did not take a stand on the issue of authorship. See *Literarische Geheimberichte aus dem Vormärz* (Wien, 1913), 1. Teil 360, 2. Teil 89; Géza Petrik, *Magyarország bibliographiája 1712–1860* [Bibliography of Hungary, 1712-1860] (Budapest, 1890), 861. named a certain "Németh" as author, although the author identified himself as a Slav. Dieter Groh mistakenly mentioned the work as a product of Polish revolutionary Pan-Slav propaganda, see Groh, 189. The content rather indicated somebody from Bohemia. Josef Koci quoted Thun's words from the *Augsburg Allgemeiene Zeitung* from the early 1840's. They were also included word for word in the pamphlet on page 199. See Josef Koci, Der Austroslawismus und seine Rolle in der tschechischen Politik. in, *Ludovít Stúr und die slawische Wechselseitigkeit*, ed. Ludovit Holotik (Bratislava-Wien-Köln-Graz, 1969), 103. The author of the pamphlet frequently alluded to Thun's pamphlet from 1842, but sounded more assertive politically (even though his ideas were similar to those of Thun's). There were two reviews of the pamphlet published in *Jahrbücher für slawische Literatur, Kunst und Wissenschaft* (Jg. 1. Heft 3.), 178-197.

34. *Slawen, Russen, Germanen*, 234-236.

35. Ibid., 2 28-229.
36. Ibid., 171-172.
37. Ibid., 191-193.
38. *Die Stellung der Slowaken in Ungarn,* 21.
39. *Manifesto*, 159.
40. Ibid., 184.
41. Domokos Kosáry, *Széchenyi Döblingben* [Széchenyi in Döbling] (Budapest, 1981), 46-48.
42. *Manifesto,* 191.
43. Ibid., 188.
44. Varga, 131-132.
45. *Manifesto,* 186-190.
46. Foreign language reviews place Wesselényi's plan among the ones of revolutionaries in exile. This misunderstanding must have been based on the article published in the April 12, 1849 issue of *Deutsche Reform* which attributed a plan for a Federative Danubian Republic with its center at Budapest to Wesselényi. "I want a Federative Danubian Republic with the flexibility that a republic of different countries and of a tolerant nationality policy are capable. It would form an alliance with the Dako-Romans in the east, with the Southern Slavs in the South, and with the united provinces of Germany in the west. Hungary would be the central state and Budapest would be the capital of Central Europe," in István Gál, I. 139; Ernst Görlich, Südosteuropa in der deutschen Publizistik um die Mitte des 19. Jahrhunderts. (*Donaueuropa,* Jg. 2. 1942), 210-215. See also Joachim Kühl, *Föderationspläne im Donauraum und in Ostmitteleuropa* (München, 1958), 21-22; Rudolf Wierer, *Der Föderalismus im Donaruraum* (Graz-Köln: Böhlaus Nachf., 1960), 59; Fobert A. Kann, *The Multinational Empire. Nationalism and National Reform in the Habsburg Monarchy, 1848-1918* (New York, 1950.) vol. 1, 119-120, 310; *Das Nationalitätenproblem der Habsburgermonarchie.* 2. Band. *Ideen und Pläne zur Reichsreform.* 2. Auflage. (Graz-Köln, 1964), 114-117. Wesselényi's plan is discussed by Horst Haselsteiner. Ungarische Nationalkonzepte, die Slaven und der "Austroslavismus", in *Der Austroslavismus,* 89 and András Gergely, Ungarische Föderationsprojekte während der Reformära und der Revolution, in *Friedenssicherung in Südosteuropa. Föderationsprojekte und Allianzen seit dem Begin der nationalen Eigenstaatlichkeit,* ed. M. Bernáth und Karl Nehring (München, 1985), 35-41. For Wesselényi's and Frantisek Palacky's ideas based on ethnic-nationality division and disintegration of existing historical-imperial borders, see Gyula Szekfű, *Három nemzedék és ami utána következik* [Three Generations and What Comes After], 2nd ed. (Budapest, 1935), 117; Gábor Benedek, Történelem és politika Palacky életművében [History and Politics in Palacky's Ouvre], in Frantisek Palacky, *A huszitizmus története. Fejezetek a cseh nemzet történetéből* [The History of the Hussites: Chapters from the History of the Czech Nation] (Budapest, 1984), 684. For Wesselényi's plan compared with the Trialist plans inspired by the Southern Slavs see Zsolt Trócsányi, 460, 466. Gyula Mérei stresses the prevalence of ethnographic principles as well in Gyula Mérei, *Föderációs tervek Dél-Kelet-Európában és a Habsburg-monarchia, 1840-1918* [Federative Plans in South-Eastern Europe and the Habsburg Monarchy, 1840-1918] (Budapest, 1965), 16-21.

47. *Manifesto, 181.*
48. Ibid., 216.
49. Ibid., 222–228.
50. Ibid., 218.
51. Ibid., 221.

THE HUNGARIAN NATIONALITIES ACT OF 1849

ANDRÁS GERGELY

Hungarian historiography records that "In Europe of the mid-19th century period, there were countries where laws and monarchial decrees regulated one or several aspects bearing upon the nationality issue. However, for the first time in history, Hungarian legislation devised a system which spanned the whole problem area while demonstrating extensive self-restraint."[1]

For technical as well as for constitutional reasons the nationality statutory provision of July 1849, promulgated by the Hungarian Parliament, was a parliamentary resolution not a legislative act. The Legislature had prepared for an overall settlement of the nationality question and raised the issue of a new constitution after passing the Declaration of Independence in April, 1849. However, due to compelling circumstances the nationality issue had to be dealt with quickly and a resolution was passed.

THE NATIONALITY-MINORITY ISSUE IN PRE-1848 EUROPE

In general, prior to 1848 legislation existed only in Western Europe. Absolute governments in Central and Eastern Europe ruled through decrees. The majority of Western European countries were ethnically homogeneous and there was no apparent reason for a legal settlement of the nationality-ethnic issue.

British legislation considered its ethnic groups integral parts of the British nation unified by the English language and the Church of England. The Catholic Church gained equal rights only in 1828. Granting additional rights for the Catholic Irish or for non-represented weaker ethnic groups was out of the question.

In 1789 France declared the incontestable principle of "a unified and indivisible nation" and also declared and endorsed equal rights and participation in state life for all citizens. At the end of the 18th century most of the population still spoke local dialects, but these were also Latin languages. Acquiring French, the official language of the state, was a natural process, although centralized administration, the military, and schools accelerated linguistic assimilation. Equal rights for everyone were granted irrespective of linguistic-ethnic background, whether through immigration or new territorial acquisition. In return, however, individuals or ethnic groups could not demand linguistic or ethnic rights. The concept of the French "national state" served as an example for Central and Eastern European states when popular representation in state life was considered. Holland, which revised its old constitution, Spain, which drew up a liberal constitution in the 1830's, and the Scandinavian states all followed the French example. Their nationalities, Frisians, Basques, Norwegians, etc., lived on the peripheries, constituted minorities, and could not enforce their rights. However, they were linguistically related to the national majorities who had developed from smaller ethnic groups themselves and who considered assimilation of existing minorities to be a straightforward matter of course.

Essentially, the French national state model consisted of one political community–the nation–without intermediaries between the individual and the state and without linguistic, religious, or social distinctions. This national political community established, operated, and controlled power, i.e., the state. After Switzerland, Belgium was established in 1830 as the first state in Western Europe to include two relatively similar ethnic groups, the Flemish and the Walloons, with two quite different languages. Yet the 1831 Belgian constitution did not settle the language/ethnic issue. Instead it declared the free use of state languages: Flemish, (almost identical with Dutch), Walloon, (a variant of French), and French proper–and authorized the legislature to settle the language issue. Although French became the language of Parliament, public administration and higher education, the majority of the population, which spoke Flemish, did not protest for historical reasons. The Walloons, who had torn Belgium away from Dutch supremacy and established the Belgian state, did not consider Flemish to be an endangered ethnic language. Advocacy of Flemish, its use in church and school, was initiated in the 1840's. The use of Flemish in state life and administration was only initiated in the 1870's, without any spectacular successes or failures. The 1831 Belgian constitution, later used as a model for quite a few Central European constitutions, e.g., the Hungarian constitution of 1848, implied that functional states could be established even in multi-national countries as long as they were based on the French "political nation" model.

THE 1848 CENTRAL EUROPEAN LEGISLATURES AND CONSTITUTIONAL DRAFTS

Strong central power had not existed in Switzerland before its constitution was passed in 1848. The new constitution declared a trilingual state and Switzerland became the first multi-lingual state in history. But it had little direct effect in 1848 on other countries since the new constitution was the result of the internal 1847 Civil War (*Sonderbund-Krieg*), not of a contemporary revolution–the constitution had become law only later in the fall of 1848. Besides, European contemporaries did not regard Switzerland as a model country since it was both sparsely populated and mostly inhabited by poor mountain people.

The 1848 revolutions aspired to restructure the state and to implement popular participation in state life. The Frankfurt German National Assembly in Germany, the Imperial Assembly (*Reichstag*) in Vienna and later in Kremsier acting for the western part of the Habsburg Empire, the Representative Parliamentary Session in Pest acting for the Hungarian Kingdom were all expected to legalize and stabilize those ambitious goals.

The task of establishing Germany started with outlining its borders. The Preliminary Parliamentary Session (*Vorparlament*) decided in April 1848 that the "Deutscher Bund," founded in 1815, would form the basis of the area involved. Consequently, the state would be organized according to historical rights, not according to territories inhabited by Germans. The Austrian delegates to the Preliminary Parliament immediately suggested that nationality rights ought to be guaranteed separately as well. However, they only declared that non-Germans were granted their language and culture and otherwise were free to share the "good and bad" lot of "free Germans."[2] The new German state, to be founded on the territory of the German Federation, would be complemented by annexation of East and West Prussia (*Ost- und Westpreussen*) and a part of the Posen Principality (*Grossherzogtum Posen*), itself also part of the Prussian Kingdom. Thus, only the central part of Germany would be ethnically homogeneous. There were Danish living in the north in Schleswig but they did not belong to Germany. Limburg, in the west, was a Dutch province and so was left out of the German unity. In the east, at the Frankfurt National Assembly, a huge debate flared up about the Polish population of Posen (*Polendebatte*). Since the province was divided ethnically, areas inhabited by Germans were annexed.

Provinces belonging to the German Federation, first of all Bohemia, were of real concern for the Habsburgs. Many of the politically inclined in German territories would not know that Bohemia had Czech majority and not German. The leader of the Czech national movement, František Palacky, refused to participate in the Frankfurt session, causing general consternation. He has been frequently quoted for the famous statement—"If Austria did not exist, it should be invented for the benefit of humanity"—included in his letter of resignation April 11, 1848. However, his real reasons were more significant: He had historical arguments which pointed out that Bohemia had not been part of the German-Roman Empire, in contrast to other German provinces. The Frankfurt goals would change the course of history since imperial-historical rights would be exchanged for popular ones, a different organizational standpoint based on ethnic principles. Consequently, the Czechs should not be forced "to sacrifice themselves for the sake of their neighbors."[3]

Palacky's argumentation was built on a new range of thoughts originating in German territories. From this viewpoint, the people existed and could be identified, with or without a state. A people may live in a state either as a minority or majority or may live in several states without having anything to do with the state life. They are united by language, culture, historical customs, and traditions. Through historical development a people might constitute a nation even without a state. The new definition of nation as a cultural nation originated with the 18th century poet Herder and became very popular in the 19th century. It argued that, at a certain point of development, the cultural state aspires to establish a legal/political state and becomes a nation state. This perfect opportunity seemed to have arrived, and stateless nationalities and ethnic groups saw a perfect opportunity to implement this theory in the year 1848.[4]

The Frankfurt German Assembly, however, endorsed the historical approach and chose the French type of nation building.

Palacky was mistaken to believe that they had acted upon the theory of the supremacy of the people. After heated debates at the end of 1848 the first paragraph of Basic Rights *(Grundrechte)* stated that "*das deutsche Volk besteht aus Angehörigen der Staaten, welche das deutsche Reich bilden.*" Consequently, only the citizens of the state were considered German, and the Basic Rights was not applied to German speakers beyond the borders of the Empire.[5] Following the French pattern, the Assembly simply ignored the existence of non-German peoples in the Empire.

A left-wing democratic representative of Gratz, Titus Mareck, warned them about the importance of the nationality issue just when the delegates of the Hungarian Parliament arrived at the Frankfurt Assembly. The Hungarians received a festive welcome and were seated at places of honor. Mareck purposely annoyed the Hungarian delegation by proposing that nationality rights in Germany should be assured by a separate law and that Germany should seek alliance with countries that abided by the same approach in their own land.[6]

Mareck's anti-Hungarian motion had a strange journey. The Frankfurt Committee for Basic Rights accepted his motion and entered "free development of nationalities" and free language use (in church, education, administration, and jurisdiction) within their compromise list of basic rights and, in this way, granted cultural-national autonomy.[7] Then in July of 1849 seeking ways of reconciliation, Hungarian liberals and nationalities in Hungary chose cultural-national autonomy as the model for the Nationality Act.[8]

Laying down the foundations of constitutionality in a multinational Empire was almost impossible, since ethnic groups had cohabited for different lengths of time. They had not been subjected to the same dynasty since ancient times, and they belonged to different families of languages and denominations. Germans, Slovenes, and Czechs had lived in the Habsburg Empire since the 16th century; the Italians joined in the 17th century and later, the Poles, Ukrainians, and Romanians in the second half of the 18th century. The Czechs and the Poles had had independent states of their own in the past, while the cultural role of the Italians in Europe is well-known and did not need support.

The Austrian Empire, which did not include the Italian provinces and Hungary unlike the Habsburg Empire, received its constitution from Emperor Ferdinand on April 25, 1848. The constitution declared under Section 4 that "*allen Volkstämmen ist die Unverletzbarkeit ihrer Nazionalität und Sprache gewährleistet.*"[9] (*Vokstamm* means tribe and it is a term which had a long career from then on.) However, within a few days the constitution was swept away by the turn of events and the legislative assembly (*Reichstag*) was convened in Vienna. The assembly was convened under the principle of universal suffrage and, as a result, quite a few peasant representatives, mostly from Galicia, showed up who did not know or hardly spoke German. There were scandalous scenes until a new system was implemented to interrupt discussions and to inform non-German speakers before a vote was taken ...The Basic Rights Committee of the Imperial Diet, which was adjourned in Vienna after the repression of the Vienna October Revolution and was reconvened in Kremsier, endorsed the principle at the end of 1848 that "*alle Volksstämme des Reiches sind gleichberechtigt.*"[10]

Section 5 of the tentative constitution stated that "*alle Volksstämmen sind gleichberechtigt und jedes Volksstamm hat ein unverletzliches Recht auf Wahrung und Pflege seiner Nationalität und Sprache.*"[11] Hence, in theory the Germans of the Empire also belonged to one of the several "tribes," a phrase of great publicity value in appeasing nationalities. If national equality were a true objective, endorsing unambiguous basic principles would be the greatest hardship, although the use of "*Volkstamm*" implied nationality and not comprehensive national rights.

The Constitutional Committee of the Kremsier *Reichstag* discussed nationality rights in February 1849. Committee Chair Palacky tried to substantiate nationality rights with a new system of provinces and by expansion of rights. He aspired to implement a new, ethnically oriented system of provinces. (From this respect, he assumed a revolutionary point of view, one with a the basis in common law). Where it was impossible, as for example in the Czech Basin, he advised the subdivision of larger provinces into regions with possibly pure ethnic districts. The Committee eventually endorsed the historical approach, which would have subdivided the six largest of the 14 provinces into 31 districts.[12]

The solution would have assured a long-lasting peaceful coexistence within the Habsburg Empire. However, it was never passed nor enacted. On March 4, 1849, the Kremsier meeting was dissolved with the excuse that the whole Empire needed a constitution, but that Hungary and the Italian provinces had not been represented. At the same time a constitution was announced from Olmütz which adopted the wording about "tribal" equality and cultural nation. The Olmütz Constitution was not enacted either and, since it was formally retracted in 1851, its nationality promises were never realized.[13]

HUNGARY'S DEVELOPMENT INTO A "CIVIL" NATIONAL STATE IN 1848

For centuries several nationalities had lived together in the Hungarian Kingdom, that is, in the Countries of the Hungarian Holy Crown (as its name of the day was). Forty percent of the population was Hungarian with the majority living in the center of the country and smaller groups occupying the easternmost areas. Croats lived in autonomy in the south-west. Slovaks lived in the north, Serbs in the south, Romanians in the east, and Ruthenians (Transcarpathian Ukrainians) in the north-east. All the Slovaks lived within Hungary, while the majority of Romanians and Serbs lived outside of Hungary in principalities subordinated to the Turks. The Germans were dispersed in smaller blocks within Hungary. Hungarians, Germans, and Slovaks were either Roman Catholics or Protestants, hence belonged to western Christianity. Romanians were divided between the Greek Catholic and Greek Orthodox Churches, while the Serbs were all Greek Orthodox. Therefore, in Hungary, with a population of fourteen million, ethnic dividing lines represented cultural and civilization boundaries as well between Western and Eastern Europe.

Before 1848 Hungary was a unified state only in principle. In practice the country was divided into the Hungarian Kingdom, the Southern Military Border areas governed by Vienna, and the Transylvanian Principality in the east (with Romanian majority). The Kingdom of Croatia, within Hungary proper and with an exclusively Southern Slav population, had a certain degree of provincial autonomy. The River Drava between Hungary and Croatia formed the only distinct ethnic dividing line and all the other nationalities were mixed.

The French type of a "civil" national state, which did not differentiate among nationalities when rights were granted or expanded, appealed to pre-1848 Hungarian liberals. The theory became especially popular in the 1830's and its prevalence was facilitated by the Hungarian nobility's centuries old "*hungarus*" concept that had distinguished between "*the natio,*" that is, the nobility, and the privilege-deprived "*plebs.*" Hence, the basis of distinction was law and privilege, not language. Therefore, religious or language differences were ignored; everybody was considered Hungarian, that is, "from Hungary." The "*hungarus*" concept was expanded and developed into the idea of a modern nation of equal citizens as the national objective.

Two elements of this future objective were implemented in 1848: the unification of the country under one state and individual civic equality under the law (abolition of serfdom and enforcement of equal rights). In April 1848 the last Diet enacted the unification of Hungary, declared a union with Transylvania, subjected the Southern Military Border areas to the Pest-Buda government, and retained the old subordination of Croatia, joining it to the new Hungarian administration.

Everybody, irrespective of nationality, had political rights conferred on them in April 1848. This fact should be emphasized because both the *Reichstag* and the press wrongfully accused Hungary on several counts: that only Hungarian speakers were enfranchised, that nationality education and church services were terminated, that municipal and communal administrations were ordered to be in Hungarian, and that only Hungarian language newspapers were published.[14]

There were no language and nationality distinctions in the laws of April 1848 that eliminated feudal privileges. Hungarian as an official language, instead of Latin, had already been enacted in 1844. From among the laws only two temporary ones included language resolutions. One of them designated Hungarian as a temporary official language of the counties until detailed regulations were completed. Theorctically this statement might have violated equality before the law. However, all the 49 counties of Hungary, each within its own sphere of authority, had already decided in favor of using Hungarian: therefore the law did not cause grievance. Rather, it temporarily endorsed a status quo which might have been considered detrimental, but only in the long run. The second resolution concerned the Hungarian language proficiency of parliamentary representatives. Even though the *Reichstag* called it "the grievance of 11 million people," it concerned only four hundred. Moreover, almost all the politicians and intellectuals spoke Hungarian. With hindsight knowledge of the linguistic Babel later created in the *Reichstag*, we might understand the 1848 legislators' concerns about running a seven-language Parliament.[15] It is certainly a deficiency of the April Laws of 1848 that they did not include any statements about language use in municipalities, cities, the newly established National Guard, churches, schools, or private and social circles–places where the traditionally used mother tongue still remained in use.[16] A liberal politician of the pre-1848 era, Miklós Wesselényi, with the right political instinct, tabled a proposition in the Upper House of the Diet relating to a separate law about the Romanians' religious and language rights. However, Romanian nationality politicians, in Pest at that point of time, found his Bill unsatisfactory and rejected it.[17] Romanian representatives of the Chamber of Deputies also prepared similar Bills but they were never discussed.[18]

Hungarian politicians were taken by surprise when nationalities, shortly after hailing the revolution, came forward with claims for territorial autonomy. They could not fathom why "expansion of liberties" and the "blessings of public freedom" had not satisfied nationalities who had hardly expressed demands earlier. They had not considered internal developments and ensuing demands; therefore, in their view, "Pan-Slav agitators" and the machination of "Viennese reactionary forces" underlay such claims.[19]

Disparate use of terms affected the discourse, increasing misinterpretations. Nationalities interpreted "nation" as cultural nation and a community in the mother tongue that had the same rights to independent existence as did the Hungarian nation. Nationalities considered the new constitutional state as belonging to the Hungarians and not as a common country. Thus, they did not demonstrate any civic loyalty towards the new 1848 national state, driving Hungary into a political crisis and a civil war. Hungarians frequently inquired what kinds of "freedom" the nationalities still lacked and what their actual demands were–apart from the rejected territorial claims.

In 1844 the introduction of Hungarian as a national language replacing Latin was a concrete grievance, but no discourse followed up on this issue. There seemed to have been a consensus about replacing Latin with a living language, although Croatia still insisted on continuing the use of Latin. Hungarians claimed that administration ought to be unilingual and a five/six language administration, parliament, etc., was inconceivable, while the nationalities felt threatened by the forced acquisition of Hungarian and the use of Hungarian language in higher education, something which might lead to full assimilation. Although the assimilation could not have been rejected, unless the alternative of the division of the country was considered, it remained psychologically and emotionally unacceptable for the minority nationalities.

Claims for territorial autonomy were flatly refused, with objections based on political considerations, not ideological concerns. One of the arguments was that territorial autonomy would soon lead to independence, separation, and then unification with neighboring kindred peoples. Thus would begin the eventual disintegration of the country with both the nationalities and the Hungarians falling prey to the czar. The nationalities acknowledged that the creation of several small provinces would disintegrate Hungary, but they were reassured that the Habsburg Empire as a protective community would survive. Therefore, they accepted subordination to Vienna, resulting in an alliance with the Counter-Revolution.

Another liberal counter-argument proved to be indisputable. In Hungary, owing to the mixture of peoples and nationalities, homogeneous nationality territories or provinces could not be established nor could accurate borders dividing ethnic groups be set up because even partial satisfaction of nationality requirements would result in the subordination of one people by another people. (E.g., only one third of the population of Southern Slav Voivodina, demanded by the Serbs, would have been Serbian.) The response to this irrefutable argument was a resort to arms, first by the Southern Slav Serbs, then by the Transylvanian Romanians who ventured out to implement a policy of ethnic cleansing. A devastating civil war began with the aim of creating a nationally homogeneous area.

The intellectual leadership of all the nationalities mobilized and rallied the masses by abolishing serfdom and by manipulating unsolved social problems of Military Border Area peasants, by preying on their ignorance and fanning religious fanaticism. The Austrian counter-revolutionary army launched an attack, with the resulting bloody war being fought in the hinterland. This all made nationality reconciliation even more difficult, but not impossible. On the one hand, the intensity of nationality fights awakened the Hungarian political leaders to the extent of grievances underlying the conflicts. On the other hand, military fiascoes made nationality politicians recognize that their military was too weak for a complete victory. As a result both parties initiated peace talks.

THE NATIONALITY ACT OF 1849

The acceptance of Croatia's demands came quickly since these were based on an earlier Croatian autonomy along with a Southern Slav homogeneity. In August of 1848 the Hungarian government presented a Bill to assure autonomy for Croatia with the recommendation that even secession could be considered.[20]

Nationality demands within "smaller Hungary" focussed on many church-related issues. The Serbs already had the privilege of holding "national congresses" for the self-government of the church. Beyond this privilege, Hungarian Serbs wanted to achieve independence from the existing Serbian patriarchate, thus elevating their newly independent metropolitan to the rank of patriarch. This demand was endorsed by the Hungarian government. Now since the Romanian Orthodox Church belonged to the same organization, they intended to separate. Since schools were church related, ethnic church self-governments (separate Serbian and Romanian bodies) assured independent and national school administration. One result of strengthening the Orthodox Church was a plan to establish a university department of orthodox theology. On the issue of language use in in municipal administration, including the language of instruction of the National Guard, the Hungarian Government leaned towards the language of the majority, Hungarian. However, applications and petitions could be submitted in one's ethnic tongue as well. The judiciary would officiate in the nationality language of the accused or litigious parties.

In this way, nationality jurisdictions were outlined, an undertaking later called cultural autonomy. In return the Hungarian government asked for a cease-fire, loyalty sealed with an oath of allegiance, and the renouncement of territorial demands. It then offered an amnesty. There were negotiations but there was no final settlement ever made.[21]

Following the imposed constitution of Olmütz and the successful 1849 spring campaigns of the War of Independence, the independence of Hungary was declared on April 14, 1849, and "The Declaration of Independence" was passed on April 19, 1849.

In the changed political circumstances the elected head of state, Lajos Kossuth, considered a new constitution that would include nationality rights. The War and unexpected events hindered its completion, but preparatory work was still carried out in the appropriate ministries.

To assure its new independence, Hungary needed foreign political allies. Only the Southern Balkan principalities responded. This is probably because the prerequisite of such an alliance was reconciliation of the Hungarian government with their related nationalities, Serbs and Romanians, groups that could urge the parties to seek ways to compromise.

Nationalities did not raise objections to the official use of Hungarian in state life. However, there were two areas which lacked consensus: the language of county administration and the nature of communal-territorial rights. Counties were both centers of administration and of political life; therefore the question of language use was an important issue.

The Czartoryski group in exile played a major role in settling the differences. The leader of Polish politics in exile, ex-foreign minister of the czar Prince Czartoryski, directed an independent organization pertaining to foreign affairs and an influential network of agents in Paris. His ultimate goal was to restore independent Poland. Czartoryski recognized early that Hungarian independence, disintegration of the Habsburg Empire, and establishment of a new system of alliance could not take place without a Hungarian-nationality reconciliation. Using his organizational and personal influence, he strove to foster reconciliation through the Hungarian ambassador to Paris, László Teleki, and through General Dembinski who was sent to Hungary to impress politicians. Through his agents in Paris, Constantinople, and Hungary, Czartoryski tried to influence nationalities and to encourage their willingness to compromise.

Through these efforts the Wallachian revolutionary, Nicolae Bălcescu, came to Hungary and engaged in successful discussions with Hungarian government officials. As a result Kossuth and Bălcescu signed the "*Project de pacification*" on July 14, 1849. In the agreement the Hungarian party made further concessions beyond granting the rights mentioned above. The Romanians renounced their demand for territorial autonomy and the Hungarian party agreed to multi-lingual communication and administration in multi-ethnic counties, and they also agreed to recognize nationalities as communities, which opened the door to validating collective rights.[22]

Governing President Lajos Kossuth and Prime Minister Bertalan Szemere recognized the significance of the Hungarian–Romanian agreement and considered it a model for reconciliation with other nationalities. On July 21, Prime Minister Szemere presented the draft of a general nationality guideline to the Chamber of Deputies in Szeged. Trying not to be prejudicial to the constitution, he submitted it as a parliamentary resolution–not as a Bill. Hungarian historiography discusses it as a "nationality law" and lists this resolution among the laws which is conceptually incorrect, but right in essence.[23]

The proposal was first discussed in a closed session of the Chamber of Deputies. There are no reliable documents of closed sessions in general and memoirs must serve as sources of information. It is, however, quite certain that some of the deputies objected to adding this item to the agenda saying "this is not what we have fought for." Foreign Minister Count Kázmér Batthyány pointed out at the first session that either they should destroy the nationalities by fire and swords,[24] which was absurd, or they should appease them with concessions.[25] At a closed session on July 26, reputed liberal politician, Pál Nyáry, expressed objections to the draft indicating that "if the nationalities are the shareholders of the Hungarian state, we can bury the state." He argued that there were not separate nationality rights in the United States either. Moreover, the Anglo-Americans were town-dwellers and merchants, whereas in Hungary the Hungarian element was absent from cities, trade, and industry. Therefore it was fatal to recognize the nationalities and give them concessions.[26] At the last closed session, on July 26, the objection was not raised although several suggested that it should not be on the agenda of the open session the day after. The government, however, stood by its proposition.[27]

The plenary debate of the Bill began July 28, 1849. Prime Minister Szemere stated that the first two considerations of the revolutionary government–changing the form of the government to a responsible governing system and granting individual rights–had already been implemented. The third consideration–"the free development of nationalities and ethnicities"–was the remaining major task of the revolution, and the time had arrived for its realization. "Let the world see...while it was only freedom that old revolutions wished for and gained, we understand the new revolution of of a new history. We do not grant only freedom, but also national rights."[28] Szemere recognized and emphasized the significance and uniqueness of the Bill. Justice Minister Sebő Vukovics said that if the Counter-Revolutionary enemy won, they would not speak about the Hungarian language use at all because German would then become the language of the government. The proposal, however, was a significant contribution to "saving the country" in his view. According to leftist deputy József Irinyi they should have passed the act a long time before. "Reconciliation of nations" within the country and an "alliance of nations" between countries were the major tasks, and the two were mutual prerequisites. Otherwise, Hungary would not survive, he argued. While according to Transportation Minister László Csányi, political considerations influenced the government and they did not act under the pressure of circumstances.[29]

All the members of the government present intervened on behalf of the proposal. In fact, nobody expressed opposition at the open session, while only a few voted for postponement. Yet the debate demonstrated that the governmental-political elite recognized the necessity of concessions much earlier than did those deputies sitting in the back row. In fact, the European tendency for radicals to be more impatient than liberals manifested itself in the parliamentary debate.

The Bill finally passed with a great majority.[30]

The first section of the Nationality Resolution stated that "a free nationality development of all the nationalities of the Hungarian Empire is hereby granted," identical to the resolution of the 1848 German Assembly in Frankfurt. A detailed enumeration of nationality rights followed the first item. Nationalities were entitled to use their own tongues at municipalities (counties and cities) in addition to use in their own communities. Minutes could be kept in their own languages, making state administration multi-lingual. Nationality languages could be used at verbal court procedures. The commanding language of the Civil Guard would be identical with that of the corresponding community. The language of the school would be that of the community or church and registers were also to be kept in the language of the community. Applications could be submitted in the mother tongue. Synods of the Orthodox Church were entitled to settle their church and school related issues, and were also eligible for public support. A Greek-Orthodox Department would be established at the University. An ethnic ratio would be observed at tenure of office. Nationalities could present their additional grievances to the government, which would seek redress by submitting Bills. Insurgents, after laying down their arms, received amnesty.[31]

Varga states that the Hungarian Nationality Resolution "does not explicitly state it but Hungary has given up on the idea of a homogeneous Hungarian political nation, thus on the manifestation of Hungarian supremacy. Although the Resolution did not declare the recognition of nationalities as nations, it laid down the conditions for them to live as nations."[32]

The evolution of the Nationalities Resolution refutes the criticism that it was improvised or that it was established because of the approaching defeat of the War of Independence. The Hungarian Government was aware of the extraordinary significance of the Resolution. Therefore, it announced it immediately and tried to utilize it both in its European propaganda and in the appeasement process. Nationality politicians favorably reacted to the measures which, however, were not implemented owing to the course of the War of Independence.

On August 13, 1849, the independent Hungarian state ceased to exist with the capitulation of the rebel army at Világos. Hungary, divided and deprived of its self-determination, was re-attached to the Habsburg Empire. There was no time left for the great experiment to test the political co-existence and cooperation of nationalities within a multi-national Hungary.

NOTES

1. János Varga, *Románok és magyarok 1848–1849-ben* [Romanians and Hungarians in 1848/49], Inaugural address at the Hungarian Academy of Sciences, October 3, 1991, (Budapest, 1995), 69; János Beér–Andor Csizmadia, Az 1848–49. évi népképviseleti országgyűlés [The 1848/49 Representative Parliamentary Session], in *Az 1848–49. évi népképviseleti országgyűlés* [1848/49 Representative Parliamentary Session], ed., János Beér (Budapest, 1954), 96; Endre Arató, Az 1849. évi júliusi nemzetiségi törvény és helye Európában [The July of 1849 Nationality Act and Its Place in Europe] (*Kortárs,* 1975) 19, 1330; György Szabad, *Kossuth Lajos politikai pályája ismert és ismeretlen megnyilatkozásai tükrében* [Lajos Kossuth's Political Career as Reflected in His Known and Unknown Statements] (Budapest, 1977), 163.; Endre Kovács, *Szemben a történelemmel. A nemzetiségi kérdés a régi Magyarországon* [Facing History. The Nationality Question in Old Hungary] (Budapest, 1977), 365.

2. *Verhandlungen des deutschen Parlaments.* ed., Friedrich Siegmund Jucho (Frankfurt a. M., 1848, II.), 55–62.

3. Franz Palacky, *Gedenkblätter. Auswahl aus Denkschrifte, Aufsätzen und Briefen aus den letzten fünfzig Jahren* (Prague, 1874), 150. Palacky happened to write his letter of resignation when the Hungarian "April laws" were sanctioned.

Palacky mistakenly assumed that "den Grundsatz aufsellt, dass man vor allem Magyare and dan erst Mensch sein müsse." (Palacky), 150.

4. To distinguish between state and cultural nation, see Fiedrich Meinecke, *Weltbürgertum und Nationalstaat* (Berlin, 1909).

5. (Reichs-Gesetz-Blatt, December 28, 1848.) with its publication, the law went into effect. The statement does not define who is German. It defines who the German people constitute, which shows the influence of the "cultural nation" since the "people" constitute the state and not the "citizens."

6. *Stenographischer Bericht über die Verhandlungen der konstituierenden Nationalversammlung zu Frankfurt am Main*, ed. Franz Wigard (Frankfurt, 1848–1849, I.), 118. Hungarian delegates resented the initiative, (Frankfurter Ober-Post-Amt-Zeitung, May 29, 1848), see the report by Ambassador Dénes Pázmándy: Karl Nehring, Die Beziehungen Ungarns zur deutschen Nationalversammlung im Jahre 1848. (*Südostvorschungen,* 1977), 37. For the German–Hungarian relationship of the day see András Gergely, *Das Bündnis zwischen Frankfurt und Pest-Buda und die österreichische Frage in 1848/49. Revolutionen in Ostmitteleuropa* (Bad Wiesseer Tagungen des Collegium Carolinum Bd. 18., München, 1996), ed. Rudolf Jaworski and Robert Luft. It is noteworthy that even in Frankfurt the nationality question emerges at the concurrence of foreign and domestic political connections.

7. See Par. 13. of the Basic Rights (Grundrechte) in *Die Grundrechtsdiskussion in der Paulskirche. Eine Dokumentation,* ed. Heinrich Scholler (Darmstadt, 1973). It was praised as a step towards cultural-national autonomy by Hansrothfels, Das erste Scheitern des Nationalstaates in Ost-Mitteleuropa 1848/49 (1955), in, *Die deutsche Revolution von 1848/49* (Wege der Forschung, CLXIV), ed. Dieter Langewiesche (Darmstadt, 1983), 231.

8. Historiography did not recognize the probable connections. All the above does not contradict the statement that the Hungarian Nationality Resolution was the first to cover the whole problem area because the Basic Rights had only one paragraph on the issue and it was not an independent law.

9. *Die österreichischen Verfassungsgesetze mit Erläuterungen,* ed. Edmund Bernatzik (Wien, 1906), 103.

10. *Protokolle des Verfassungs-Ausschusses über die Grundrechte,* ed. Alfred Fischel (Wien, 1912), 86.

11. Bernatzik, 150.

12. *Die Protokolle des Verfassungs-Ausschusses im Österreichischen Reichstage 1848–1849* (Leipzig, 1885), 10–15, 52, 73–86, 298–304.

13. According to unidentified Hungarian sources of the day: "what the nationalities received as reward was punishment for the Hungarians," that is, a state of lawlessness. For more on the topic see Gerald Stourzh, Frankfurt–Wien–Kremsier 1848/49. Det Schutz der nationalen und sprachlichen Minderheit als Grundrecht, in *Grund- und Freiheitsrechte von der ständischen zur spätbürgerlichen Gesellschaft.* (Göttingen, 1987), 437–456.

14. From the debates in the Reichstag: *Verhandlungen des österreichischen Reichstages nach stenographischer Aufnahme,* Wien 1849; 1971/2. Bd. IV. 213. (December 21, 1848) – The Hungarian nobility does not pay taxes; Bd. V. 196. (February 22, 1849) – Hungarian is the exclusive language of education and the

language of discussion in cities and municipalities; Bd. V. 279/ (March 2, 1849) - It is time to establish popular representation instead of the rule of the nobility. Similar completely ignorant quotations from the Austrian and German press and erroneous statements from modern historical works could be endlessly listed.

15. On the official language of the counties: Article 1848:XVI Par.2; on the Hungarian language proficiency of the deputies: Article 1848:V Par. 3. The 1848 Hungarian laws on cities, municipalities, and the national guard do not include language resolutions. The April Laws reflected the new situation in Hungary, see András Gergely, Ungarns staatsrechtliche Stellung in der Habsburgermonarchie in den Aprilgesetzen von 1848, in *Gesellschaft, Politik und Verwaltung in der Habsburgermonarchie 1830-1848*, ed. Ferenc Glatz (Stuttgart, 1987), 41-54.

16. Failing to create a language law which would have acknowledged the existing status quo was considered to be a mistake even by the contemporary historian Mihály Horváth in Mihály Horváth, *Magyarország függetlenségi harczának története 1848 és 1849-ben* [The History of the Fight for Independence in Hungary in 1848 and 1849 (Pest, 1871/2, I), 131. It was not so much the result of the legislators' extreme nationalism, rather of their liberalism since they did not consider the language-nationality question to be a political and legislative issue.

17. According to Wesselényi's suggestion the self-government of Romanian (Greek Catholic and Greek Orthodox) Churches would be established, the minutes of church meetings would be kept both in Hungarian and Romanian, elementary schools could have instruction in Romanian, municipal minutes would be bilingual, and existing Romanian private documents, contracts, etc. would remain valid. Characteristically the way the Upper House reacted to the suggestion assumed that everything mentioned had already been incorporated into the equality law, hence enforcing equality laws would be sufficient and they called onto the ministry to take a stand. In Beér, 861-862. On the unsympathetic attitude of Romanian politicians see Zsolt Trócsányi, *Wesselényi Miklós* (Budapest, 1965), 546.

18. Beér, 862-867.

19. For a bibliography of Hungarian 1848/49 nationality question see György Spira, *A nemzetiségi kérdés a negyvenyolcas forradalom Magyarországán* [Nationality Question in Hungary of the 1848 Revolution] (Budapest, 1980), 123-138. and *1848/49. Revolutionen in Ostmitteleuropa, in* Bad Wiesseer Tagungen des Collegium Carolinum, 18. (Rudolf Jaworski and Robert Luft, München, 1996), 414-415. For important foreign papers see György Spira, Die Nationalitätenfrage in Ungarn 1849 (*Österreichische Osthefte,* 1983, 25), 197-222; Zoltán I. Tóth, The Nationality Problem in Hungary in 1848-1849, (*Acta Historica Academiae Scientiarum Hungariae,* 1955, 4), 235-277; Gyula Mérei, Über de Möglichkeiten eines Zusammenschlusses der in Ungarn lebenden Völker in den Jahren 1848-1849, (*Acta Historica Academiae Scientiarum Hungariae,* 1969, 15), 253-298; Ambrus Miskolczy, Roumanian-Hungarian Attempts at Reconciliation in the Spring of 1849 in Transylvania, (*Acta Universitatis Budapestiensis Section Historica,* 1981, 21), 61-81; István Deák, István Széchenyi, Miklós Wesselényi, Lajos Kossuth and the Problem of Roumanian Nationalism, (*Austrian History Yearbook,* 1976/77, 12-13), 69-77; R. Florescu, Debunking a Myth: The Magyar-Romanian National Struggle of 1848-1849, (*Austrian History Yearbook,*

1976/77, 12–13), 82–89; Keith Hitchins, *The Rumanian National Movement in Transylvania* (Cambridge, Mass., 1969). Other important sources are: *A tót nemzetiségi kérdés 1848–49-ben, I–II* [The Slovak Nationality Question in 1848–49, I–II] ed. Lajos Steier (Budapest, 1937); *A magyarországi szerb felkelés története I–II* [Serbian Uprising in Hungary, I–II] ed. József Thim (Budapest, 1930–1935); and *1848–1849. évi iratok a nemzetiségi megbékélésről* [Nationality Question Documents from 1848/49] (Budapest, 1848).

20. György Szabad, Hungary's Recognition of Croatia's Self-determination in 1848 and Its Immediate Antecedents, in *East Central European Society and War in the Era of Revolutions, 1775–1856,* ed. Béla Király (New York, 1984), 591–609.

21. Cessions gradually changed in the first half of 1849. See above, I. Tóth and note 19.

22. The full text of *Megbékélési nyilatkozat* [Declaration of Reconciliation] in, *Kossuth Lajos Összes Munkái XV. Kossuth Lajos kormányzóelnöki iratai* [Complete Works of Lajos Kossuth, XV. Lajos Kossuth's Presidential Documents] ed. István Barta (Budapest, 1955), 725–727. In the French text the Romanians used the expression "une nationalité a part" meaning "forming a separate nationality."

23. Beér, 454–456. It also mentions the nationality resolution (Article 1849:VIII) among the laws.

24. In 1848 in an article on the Posen issue Bismarck raises the extirpation of the Poles, thus this kind of a solution had already been conceptualized.

25. Beér, 553.

26. Ibid., 553–554.

27. Ibid., 555. According to the rules only open sessions could pass resolutions.

28. Ibid., 472.

29. Ibid., 476.

30. Ibid., 476. "Most of the deputies stood up." There is no record of the number of deputies participating in the Chamber of Deputies' session in Szeged. Historiography mentions the Bill as the "Szeged Nationality Act."

31. Ibid., 868–869.

32. Varga, 70.–The Resolution was further developed by Kossuth's constitutional draft of 1851 in exile. See György Szabad's essay. The Nationalities Act of 1868 was a retrogression since it stated that "In Hungary... there is one political nation, the united, indivisible Hungarian nation and every citizen of the country is an equal member of it irrespective of his nationality." (Article 1868: XLIV).

CROSSROADS BETWEEN REVOLUTION AND THE COMPROMISE (1849–1867)

LAJOS KOSSUTH'S ROLE IN THE CONCEPTUALIZATION OF A DANUBIAN FEDERATION

GYÖRGY SZABAD

How familiar Kossuth was with the confederative ideas that surfaced among the opponents of the 1815 European reorganization is unknown. Following his appearance at the 1832 Diet in Pozsony (Bratislava) he might have heard that Giuseppe Mazzini contemplated, first in a pamphlet and later in his persecuted periodical, a Hungarian-led Center-European confederation that could replace the disintegrating "botchwork" of the Habsburg Empire. Mazzini had sought contact with Deputy István Borcsiczky of whom the young Kossuth had become an admirer of. Whether the Italian revolutionary's effort was successful is debatable owing to Borcsiczky's circumspection, but Mazzini's personality and bold ideas might have been familiar to Kossuth.[1]

Kossuth, who rose to become leader of the Reform Opposition between 1833 and 1848, and his colleagues aspired to modernize the obsolete feudal structure via constitutional means or, at the very least, to force the Habsburgs to recognize Hungary's parliamentary autonomy. Because of the growing influence of absolutist doctrines and of Pan-Slav aspirations over East Central Europe—owing to the alliance between the Austrian Empire and czarist Russia—Kossuth had been interested in the relationship between Hungarians and cohabiting nationalities from early on in his career. He wanted to assure Hungary's national integrity and character on the one hand, and yet use civic reforms to counterbalance Austrian and Russian "divide et impera" absolutism on the other hand.[2]

The Reform Opposition's policy did not directly serve federative or confederative goals, although looking back Kossuth ranked them as his most important ambitions. In 1850 he claimed that "Real freedom emerges only in its federative form. Ever since my intellectual coming of age it has been my conviction. Several years ago when I was asked what I thought about the future of Hungary, I responded that either it did not have a future or its future is a federation with neighboring smaller nations which would assure political freedom and independence both against the domination of any great power and against assimilation of nationalities."[3]

Kossuth's overstatement stemmed from the fact that by the middle of the century the elements of his federative aspirations had evolved into a succinct concept, influenced by the experiences of 1848–1849 and his discussions projected back to earlier days as if the concept had rooted in him before. In spite of the exaggeration about a developed ideology, his references to certain elements were not ungrounded.

"If you ask me why I am for the county system, I will answer that by placing it on a popular basis the concept of federation will be integrated in my country's internal organism." He considered having popular representation in counties, and in local governments generally, to be indispensable, furthermore disregarding it would be "national suicide." It was a condition of national reconciliation, he claimed—both as a member of the opposition and as a minister in the spring of 1848. His insistency almost caused a government crisis.[4]

In retrospect, Kossuth also claimed that well before 1848 he considered that "artificially roused or naturally awakened conflicts are reconciliable...through the idea of federation." He mentioned an example from 1842 when he proposed to eliminate the Metternich government incited Croat–Hungarian antagonisms by offering autonomy to Croatia. Even though the majority of the Reform Opposition did not support the idea, Kossuth's proposition became the theoretical antecedent to the Batthyány Government's reconciliation proposal, which preceded the Jelačić attack in the fateful summer of 1848.[5]

The fate of his proposal for an autonomous Croatia and the cold reception given to his mentor Miklós Wesselényi's book *Manifesto for the Hungarian and Slav Nationalities* (Szózat a magyar és szláv nemzetiség ügyében) published in 1843, indicated what reform proposals for national and nationality co-existence could look forward to. In a private letter Kossuth enthusiastically welcomed Wesselényi's significant work,[6] which proposed a federative Habsburg Empire to avert the Pan-Slav threat. But in his newspaper, he praised it in a more subdued tone, and not necessarily because of the censorship. The spiritless public reaction must have cautioned him that even if the Hungarian public was now only mildly alarmed, it would become even more alarmed by indications of structural changes including federalization.[7]

In addition, beginning with the publication of his paper in 1841, Kossuth repeatedly cautioned that Hungarians, "thrown into the middle between two formidable nationalities," would have to take charge of their future, including re-unification with Transylvania, self-determination, and Western orientation. Otherwise, the country would become either a "Russian province" or a "German colony." However, he did not come forward with ideas about federation.[8] What is more, he denied that counties–thoroughly reformed but maintained–"would directly sail towards North American federalism."[9]

The turn of events in the spring of 1848 both justified worries[10] of the Reform Opposition Party and yet also gave rise to new hopes for Hungarian autonomy or even self-determination. Both were connected with the contemporary assumption, all over Europe, that in the wake of revolutionary changes German unity would be implemented, thus precipitating the disintegration of the Habsburg Empire.[11] First of all "the Pan-Slav threat," frequently noted by Wesselényi, Kossuth, Deák, and followers, caused alarm. Reformers proposed the antidote of the Kossuthian "task of the tasks"–the abolition of serfdom thus reassuring or at least neutralizing the ethnic peasantry. The hope was that Hungary would be able to assert its independent statehood, to reconstruct its national integrity, non-existent since the 16th century, and to integrate its smaller neighbors such as the Southern Slavs and Romanians, who were dependent territories on the Turks or the czarist empire.

This general approach persisted in the Batthyány Government and became a calling during the feverish days of the Revolution. It was attested to by Joseph Andrew Blackwell, emissary to Hungary from the Vienna British Embassy, in his account to Lord Posonby, the British ambassador in Vienna. On March 19, 1848, he wrote of the development of the "lawful revolution"[12] and quoted the moderate government deputy, József Eötvös,[13] saying during a private conversation that "the independence of the country is the ultimate goal so that Hungary would become powerful enough to be accepted by countries who want to stop the Russians."[14] Blackwell also reported his private opinion that the heterogenous Habsburg Empire, which he had considered unsustainable and which was traditionally also considered to be an important element of the English balance of power, could only be replaced by a confederation that Hungary would create with the Romanians and the Southern Slavs.[15]

Blackwell might have been inspired by the ardent hopes of some of his Hungarian companions. The main concern and aspiration of the Batthyány government and personally that of Kossuth was to acquire the power that would assure Hungary's surviving the disintegration of the Empire, and not to extort as much as they could from the shaken Habsburgs. In 1848–49 Batthyány's government tried to avoid the sort of situation that Hungary finally faced in 1918–20.

The fact was that they tried to avoid any statement which would have hinted at underlying imperial ambitions. In 1847 Kossuth stated that "in our time the greatness of nations is to be found in subsistence and the demonstration of internal strength, not in conquest and expansion." He opposed to maintaining even a formal claim to the provinces of divided Poland, which had been attached to the Habsburg Empire, instead considering them inherently Polish.[16] Their aspiration was to restore the integral Hungarian state which had been disintegrated by the 16th century Ottoman conquest. Although the separated Transylvanian Principality came into Habsburg hands in 1690, it had not been reunited with Hungary. A few counties on the edge of Transylvania, generally known as the "Partium," were also governed separately, although their integration was enacted in 1836. In addition to that, the 17th and 18th century Hungarian opposition ineffectively demanded the reintegration of the Military Border,[17] which was directly subordinated to the Imperial Military Authority in the name of defense against the Turks. The majority Southern Slav border guards (who were similar to the Cossacks in Russia) did not have to obey Hungarian Authorities.

Under these circumstances the Batthyány Government, formed in the spring of 1848 with Kossuth among its members, set out to reconstruct Hungary's national integrity and took great care not to burden this process with the politically charged idea of a confederation. They focused all their efforts on modernizing the country. Beginning with a country with four-fifths of its population in serfdom, with a government of feudal and semi-absolutist structures, and with economical and political dependence on Austria, the Batthyány reformers worked to form it into a country with equal rights, with a parliamentary and constitutional structure, and with local autonomy. The laws of the spring of 1848 were not illusory, but rather reflected hopes based on a sense of security. On April 16, 1848, Kossuth and his co-envoy said of their plans that "They do not contain the complete future of the nation, but are the foundations of our future development." Voicing their worries they spoke about the danger that "despotism," by which they meant czarism, might come to "European civilization," and especially to Hungary since "we are next-door neighbors to the giant of the North." Kossuth claimed that "We will not fall victim unless we are isolated in the struggle." On one hand, "it is the common interest of the European free community to make the future brighter." On the other hand, "within the borders of our country" 'the constitutional freedom' might become a foundation where "the interests of peoples of different languages may be unified."[18]

Among alternating hopes and worries, on July 11, 1848, Kossuth gave his famous speech reminding Hungarians of "the endangered homeland." In his foreign policy overview he realistically noted that "the English will support us as long as it is in their own interest." He forewarned against overrating French sympathy since "Poland used to rely on sympathy and Poland does not exist any more." He cautioned that near the frontiers of the country "a vast Russian army is stationed which may turn left or right, may be amicable or inimical, but since it might behave any way, the nation needs to be prepared." He spoke about nationality movements as well. He did not stop at pointing out deliberate trouble-making and provocation. Instead, Kossuth, who was an adamant abolitionist and against privileges, openly declared that "the nation and the authorities have been late at extending justice....The moment when justice could have been served to the people is gone and, therefore, social relations have been disintegrating." Thus, in areas where the actual power was in the hands of the Imperial Army, as in the military border zone and Transylvania, fratricidal wars have developed.[19]

Kossuth knew and professed that "hatred among nations and generally among people empowers tyrants." Alternately, "the mutual love of peoples, ethnicities, and nations is the source of national well-being and is a deterrent for tyrants."[20] However, it was in vain for him to warn that "the issue of Hungarian-Dacian confederation is stipulated by the philosophy of the situation."[21] It was a wasted effort to try to avert Jelačić's attack by offering the "secession" of Croatia.[22] It was equally wasted when on September 12, 1848, Kossuth, in the Chamber of Deputies, declared that "from among all the nationalities of Europe, the Hungarian and the Dacian have the mission to develop a mutual sympathy and harmony, if they want to survive." For this reason, he offered amnesty to rioters, an amnesty that would be one of several "'tools' to destroy dirty plots to oppress Hungary and the freedom of the Romanian nationality within Hungary."[23]

All proved to be too little. Risking his own political support in the Chamber of Deputies, Kossuth admitted that "in Transylvania, if anybody is entitled to complain about the past, they are the Romanians" and tried to offer new guarantees to reassure them.[24] Yet the Romanians broke off the negotiations leading to bloody anti-Hungarian activities in Transylvania. The situation was developing towards a civil war. Peasants retaliating against the miseries of serfdom broke into country houses, sometimes even into estates of abolitionist reformers like Wesselényi (whose thresher was destroyed). The violence did not spare innocent women or children. Priests, embittered by religious grievances or presumed dangers, incited the rioters; young intellectuals saw them as national heroes; and imperial commanders utilized them as tools to implement the concept of "divide et impera." Transylvania was swept over by a tragic fratricidal war. Kossuth, the President of the Defense Committee elected by the Hungarian Parliament, considered it his major and only possible task–temporarily–to organize the Hungarian self-defense.[25]

For long months fights went on in Transylvania, in "Voivodina," and in the contiguous areas of Croatia. The Imperial Habsburg army had a major impact on the fighting, openly attacking the Hungarian government, which relied on support from the Parliament and the majority of the population. The defense and successful counter-attack in the spring of 1849 led the Habsburgs to request czarist intervention to help in dissolving the Parliament of the Empire and in governing by absolutistic measures while still making frequent references to the imposed constitution. How hard the participants in the fratricidal war strove for reconciliation has been debated for a long time. On June 6, 1849, a special council meeting of the Hungarian Government discussed an offer of reconciliation and to switch sides attributed to a Serbian military leader of the uprising. The Hungarian government, as if anticipating the judgment of history, stated that "Since early on, the Hungarian government has tried to end the bloodshed and destruction of this wild war incited by our enemies in the Bács-Bánság (Bac-Banat) area.[26] The government was always eager to seek and utilize opportunities for reconciliation. In conjunction with the legislature, it has tried to reconcile with the Serbs and Croats on multiple occasions. Therefore, the Governor[27] of the country and the Council of Ministers, just as in the past, consider it their utmost concern in the present as well...again to try to achieve reconciliation with Serbian, Wallachian, and all other ethnicities in order to secure the independence of the country."[28]

It is not in the focus of this essay to summarize all the reconciliatory endeavors or analyze political figures for missed or overdue measures.[29]

Even after the armed confrontations in the fall of 1848, Kossuth frequently gave proof of his willingness to negotiate and promote reconciliation on such issues as language, church policy, and administration, but rejected what he considered were attempts against the unity of the state. Kossuth's basic instructions given on April 26, 1849, to Ioan Dragoş Romanian Deputy to the Parliament, for negotiations with Romanian insurrection leader Avram Jancu, exemplified his willingness to negotiate. Kossuth had unconditional trust in Dragoş, who was appointed Secretary in the Ministry of Finance after he wrote an important proposition in the summer of 1848. Kossuth supported Dragoş' parliamentary initiatives for Hungarian-Romanian rapprochement and appointed him government commissioner to the successful Romanian synod in the spring of 1849.[30] The instruction Kossuth gave to Dragoş was a peace offer so that "we become equally free citizens of a free country to heal the wounds of the past in brotherly love and harmony." He emphasized that Romanians, returning to peace "would be extended common rights and freedom in equal measures with every inhabitant of Hungary irrespective of language and religion." Even though Parliament and the government were uni-lingual, the Romanians should be reassured that "the free use of their language in their schools, churches, at religious services, and communities are granted." Furthermore, laws and decrees were to be declared "in the language of the people" and individuals had the right to apply to the government and defend themselves in court in their own language. He also added that "not only do we want to allow for a free use of every language and for free ethnic development, we also want to promote it for the sake of civilization." He gave two tangible examples. In case Romanian foundations did not have the necessary resources for the improvement and "scientific development" of its schools, "the state will provide it just as it will in case of educational expenses of any other language and citizen." He also stated that the state would be "glad" to offer help to develop "the Vlach language for higher scientific standards with appropriate methods." In accordance with the principle of equality before the law, Kossuth committed the state to offering employment to Romanians in any "civic and military" job "according to merit and ability, without fear or favor." He assured Romanians that they would receive all "a state is able to offer to its citizens." Less than this would "lower Romanians to servitude." And the government's goal was the opposite–"to stop their centuries long suffering and servitude." After reiterating his intention to assure individual and community rights, Kossuth said, "this is what I offer to the Romanian people as an act of peace and appeasement." Kossuth then drew the line: "Whoever wants more, he wishes to dismember the country and wants to tyrannize others," adding that to prevent it was "the determined will of the nation" and "his obligation."[31]

The terms, or rather concessions, were essentially identical with the ones included in the–finally abandoned–Bill about the establishment of the Transylvanian Union. The delegated committee of the Hungarian Parliament on September 27, 1848, tabled the Bill in order "to assure the equal political rights of the Romanian state."[32] However, the Bill differed in two points from the one Kossuth was ready to support, according to his statement in the late fall of 1848. The Bill 1) would establish the possibility of disbanding the para-military organization of the border guards, and 2) would establish the office of governor, just as the Croatian governor had been established "by recognizing the request of the Serbian people."[33]

Gheorghe Magheru, the exiled military leader of the 1848 Wallachian Romanian revolution, indicated in his letter to Kossuth from Baden early March 1849 that they had found the offer insufficient, but were willing to consider it as a basis for future confederative reorganization. On behalf of the "Romanian nation" living in three countries, and also personally "convinced" about the agreement of the "Southern Slav population" he offered "an alliance of defense and resistance" against czarist Russia.[34]

It could not have been a mere coincidence, and probably was connected with the active intermediary role of the Polish government in exile[35] that in the early spring of 1849 Kossuth kept receiving encouragement to establish a confederation with the neighbors. This all followed the first Transylvanian intervention of the czarist army and the Battle of Kápolna announced as a major triumph of the Imperial Military, simultaneously with the release of the Imperial Constitution, which dissolved the Imperial Diet and broke Hungary into provinces in order to merge the country into the Empire.

László Teleki, the Paris ambassador of warring Hungary, in his letter of March 7, 1849, to Kossuth recommended several ideas about a "secure future" including "an authority extending to the Black Sea" for consideration by the peace-mongers. He believed that these ideas "will reconstruct Hungary as a confederation."[36] Concurrently with Teleki's letter, Kossuth must have read the call, anonymously written by Albert Pálffy editor-in-chief of the opposition paper the *Marczius Tizenötödike* (March the Fifteenth), that "Hungary, Transylvania, Croatia, or even Slavs of the upper counties" should form "the foundation of future federative republics, united by the Pest government."[37]

The above, and similar advice, did not divert Kossuth from the road he had taken. Not because he knew that taking the advice would cause disturbances in his own party, in neighboring princely courts, within Turkish and czarist empires anxious for their Serbian and Romanian interests, but because he did not approve of their form or content. Rather, Kossuth proceeded along with the plan of extending rights and equality before the law in order to help to form an alliance of peoples living together and super-ordination and subordination of nations in order to protect the common freedom. On the one hand the basic instruction given to Dragoş contained Kossuth's statement that the disintegration of the country could not be the price of reconciliation, as had been hinted at by Magheru's proposal. And on the other hand, the instructions included a federative offer to recognize the independent statehood and integrity.

At Kossuth's initiative, the response to the imperial imposition of rule on Hungary, which would have meant the break up and assimilation of Hungary, was to advocate the Habsburgs from the throne, reconstruction of an independent Hungary, and a federative proposal. Kossuth's original proposal stated "When the Hungarian nation, by virtue of its inalienable natural right, joins the European community as an independent, free state, we declare that if our own rights are not violated, we are determined to initiate and maintain peace and friendship and to form friendly alliances on the basis of mutual interest with peoples who have been subjected to the same emperor with us, and also with the neighboring Turkish Empire and the Italian provinces."[38]

At that point Kossuth did not commit himself to confederative ideas. However, still in 1849, and on his initiative the Hungarian Parliament was the first in the area to declare independence. It then offered a tight union with its neighbors and initiated a "proposal" to become the potential organizer of the union of nations which would survive the disintegration of the Habsburg Empire.[39]

The Declaration of Independence did not meet the expectations of those who had hoped for an immediate reassurance to the nationalities and envisioned a secure future in an instant confederation. In his letter of May 14, 1849, László Teleki expected a "reassuring manifesto...to the peoples" which would have acknowledged that "the peoples also want their nationality existence acknowledged." He stressed that after implementing its practical consequences "Hungary will be gladly accepted as a center and a queen of the future Danubian Confederation, whose power will forever break the monster of absolutism and will extend from the Baltic states to the Black Sea."[40]

Teleki's letter reflected the atmosphere of the negotiations between the Paris ambassador and certain Polish and Czech leaders in exile. They came to an agreement concerning the situation of the region following the disintegration of the Habsburg Empire. There was to be an alliance of the countries to be liberated, located between Western Europe and the Russian and Turkish Empires, with the participation of Hungary which had gained respect following the successful spring campaign of the Hungarian army. There is no proof of Kossuth's familiarity with the negotiations. In fact, it is certain that he had not authorized an agreement.[41] It was a slightly different situation with the diplomatic circular released by Foreign Minister Kázmér Batthyány following the June 6, 1849, resolution of the Council of Ministers. The resolution called upon Batthyány to inform "all the governments that Hungary has shared, and will readily share, civic rights with all the nationalities without any exception...consequently, oppression of nationalities on Hungarian territory is not at all true....In case, at the intervention of neighboring Wallachian and Serbian governments and nations, the appeasement of Serbs and Wallachians were necessary, Hungary would want to achieve that."[42] In his circular dispatched to Hungarian diplomats and frontier military commanders, Foreign Minister Batthyány followed Kossuth's approach of presenting the nationality question as a domestic issue. With respect to concessions and assurances, he was also in accord with Kossuth except for one unfortunate issue. Despite the principle of free language use Kossuth himself insisted on Hungarian as the diplomatic language of the country for practical reasons, that is of the Parliament and the central government. Batthyány, however, spoke about the "supremacy...of the Hungarian element" and described a more extensive use of "diplomatic" Hungarian than Kossuth. At the same time, in his view the aim of "reconciliation and negotiations" was to establish a "common alliance or confederation" against "the common enemy"—"now Austria and Russia."[43]

Kossuth continued to advocate a "reconciliation" policy which would satisfy "legitimate wishes of every citizen of any language and religion as long as they comply with the unity of the state." He insisted on the idea of the "unity of the state" and declined any direct or indirect demand which threatened the dismemberment of the country. His argument was that Hungary was not only a multi-national but also a mixed-national country. His principle stated that a country "where different ethnic groups do not live separately...divided from one another, but rather mixed and mingled...cannot be divided or governed according to languages, unless we want to carve up the country." He drew the conclusion that "the government can never comply with the suicidal move of creating separate Hungarian, Slovak, German, Saxon, Romanian, Serbian, and Russian provinces." On July 5, 1849, Lieutenant-Colonel József Simonffy, engaged in renewed negotiations with Avram Jancu, was instructed on these points. At the same time Kossuth also clarified another important concept. "Hungary may form a federation with Wallachia, Serbia, etc. But Hungary cannot form a federation with itself, that is, with its own citizens. This is absurd."[44]

Kossuth made the above statement one week before signing the noteworthy agreement with Nicolae Bălcescu, the Wallachian political leader of the Romanian revolution, on July 14, 1849, coincidentally the 60th anniversary of the fall of the Bastille. The agreement, or officially "a reconciliatory draft" since the Romanian politician served only as an intermediary between the fighting parties, validated several points of the judicial process which had broken down in the fall of 1848. It realized concessions with regard to language use, education, and church policy that Kossuth had made earlier. Changing the term "Wallachian" to "Romanian" was of fundamental importance, while eliminating the residue of serfdom and redressing the grievances of the peasantry were of practical significance. The sides agreed upon a cease-fire (which was a bit late since the Russians had already intervened), on amnesty for the insurgents, and on the establishment of a Romanian legion which would be committed both to Hungary and "Romania."[45]

On July 28, 1849, the Hungarian Parliament passed a nationality policy resolution. In the Preamble it stated that it was drawn up "to reassure...the non-Hungarian speaking citizens of the fatherland" and that it served as "a provisional instruction for the government" until the Parliament could act upon "a constitution to be propounded." The resolution recognized the use of the Romanian language at county meetings and as a language of command of the local militia, and reinforced the religious and educational rights of the Orthodox Church.[46] As had been anticipated, the principle stating that "free national development of every nationality ...is hereby granted," was of fundamental importance.[47]

The Hungarian Parliament persevered until the final days of the 1848–49 freedom fights and created a nationality policy resolution[48] which became both a requiem to the reconciliatory ambitions of the "lawful revolution" and an obligatory norm for all future national coexistence.

*

After the defeat, Kossuth was forced into exile where he took upon himself the tasks of unraveling the reasons why the reconciliation policy had failed and of continuing to develop new norms of coexistence for the Danube Basin peoples.

Within a few weeks Kossuth emerged from the shock of the defeat and ruthless retributions. He set out to do his work, first as a refugee, then later as an internee in the Turkish Empire, where he was permitted to re-establish his western contacts. There he reiterated his earlier nationality policy concept: "The nationalities are entitled to everything within the state...but no concession ought to be given to the extreme demands which threaten the existence of the state."[49]

Kossuth did not alter his basic principles regarding Hungary, its nationalities, and its relationship with neighboring countries. Nevertheless, after the events of 1849 and in the aftermath of the defeat, confederative ideas played an increasing role in various political solutions. What Kossuth considered the ultimate threat in April of 1848 was fulfilled when Hungary became isolated as the forces of despotism and constitutionalism clashed. Kossuth also recognized that the czarist intervention had traumatized the nations involved and had had a similar affect on western public opinion. All the entanglement with the English-Russian conflict, which time and again rose and then abated before exploding in the Crimean War, justified Kossuth's cautious diplomatic moves. In addition to the increasing activities of Polish and other East Central European emigrant groups, the influence of Hungarian diplomats (Former Foreign Minister Kázmér Batthyány, former Paris ambassador László Teleki, and former London ambassador Ferenc Pulszky), and Charles F. Henningsen, British envoy to Turkey and a real advocate of confederative ideas, had a great impact on Kossuth.[50]

Beyond English and Turkish exploratory talks, it is of utmost significance that Kossuth believed that the long due nationality reconciliation, as an integral pre-requisite of the liberation of Hungary, was more and more connected to the idea of alliance or confederation with neighboring countries. This is testified to in Kossuth's renowned June 15, 1850, essay written to László Teleki from Kütahya, the place of his Turkish internment.[51] In this letter Kossuth tried to untangle the "Gordian knot" of modern Hungarian history–the coexistence of diverse people of different languages and religions.

Since Kossuth had been adamant on Hungary's integrity, many considered him an opponent of federative solutions. However, Kossuth insisted that he had been committed to "federative principles" for a long time and "it is not a concession to the present sad situation of my country." He reiterated that within the given situation "only a tight federation of smaller nations would assure their political existence, national integrity, and independence." (Solving the paradox underlying the above statement became his major concern in his ensuing polemics.) Hungary's situation was aggravated by the fact that "powers of absolutist inclination surrounded the country."[52] One of them was Russia, which threatened "European civilization" itself. However, Europe was gravely mistaken if it thought it had found a protecting wall "against this threat...in the Austrian Empire...at the price of oppressing so many peoples." Since the Habsburg Empire needed the assistance of the Russian Empire to maintain its rule, it was obvious that to assure the balance of power, "Europe is in dire need of a confederation." In want of a confederation, "smaller nations would fall prey to Russia, which would increase Russia's power so much that even the Germans would not be able to withstand it. Hence, the Germans, as much as the Italians and the French, would not be able to avoid Russian dependence." Consequently, Europe "will bitterly suffer" for its failure to promote the confederation.

He maintained that, due to geographic endowments, the center of the confederation should be in Hungary, although not in the country's capital.[53] Listing the possible members of the confederation, Kossuth did not exclude the German provinces of Austria either. Rather Kossuth noted that "for them the direction of the German unity seems to be" reasonable, while the Slavs "can retain their national identity only within this confederation. Otherwise the Poles, Czechs, Croats, Slavonians, Serbians, Dalmatians...will be absorbed totally or one by one. Each of them will lose its national identity within the ideology of Pan-Slavism (which necessarily coincides with the Russian protectorate). The Hungarians and the Wallachians, as isolated breeds, are also exposed to danger."

In the process of clarifying the structure and operation of a confederation, Kossuth noted that an alliance of nations or confederation cannot be accompanied by a "domestic federalization"–that is by forming ethnic territorial units–because this would dissolve the unity of the state, giving rise to interventions into the domestic policy of these multi-national countries. This is the reason why the basic requirement that "every confederate state is completely independent of one another and the whole confederation as far as its domestic issues are concerned" was at the very top of his "principles." Allied countries would be required to be jointly responsible to defend "the independence and national integrity" of individual countries, primarily a security requirement.

Beyond a common defense against the "foreign enemy" Kossuth's proposal stipulated a common diplomatic and customs union as well. The "federal council," whose president would alternate annually and whose number would be proportional to the population, and a federal government would head the federation. A government member from each country would report on federal issues to his own legislature. The federal contract would determine the rate of financial obligations from common expenses. The contract would be revised every 25 years and on that occasion members would be allowed to withdraw from the federation.

Enclosed within his proposal was a draft proposed to renew the state structure of Hungary. It was based on the Declaration of Independence, ratified by the Hungarian Parliament on April 19, 1849, which had assumed the obligation of preparing an up-to-date constitution. The letter written to Teleki testifies that, as early as the tenth month of his exile, Kossuth was well advanced in outlining a renewed national and democratic government construction incorporating aspects of the nationality policy. In the following year he further developed his ideas and summarized them in his "Constitution Proposal".

One point in his letter to Teleki should be mentioned here. It was the specific role that he would assign to representative self-governments and, most particularly, to county self-governments. "The state, which gives complete freedom to individuals, families, communities, and counties in their own affairs, should not consider the civil society eternally minor and itself to be a committed tyrant guardian; instead...it should supervise...through its administrative organs so that the community or the county would not compromise the public interests of the state or violate its laws." Responding to Teleki's inquiry about the establishment of an "internal federation," Kossuth responded, "That is how the idea of an internal federation will be approached. I use the word approach because internal organization cannot solely be organized on federative bases. Through this approach, the nationality needs of different ethnic groups can be met." Kossuth was aware of the facts and had the intellectual courage not to reject the idea of a structural correction to the county system. "Good departmental division according to potentially equal counties, which meet the natural requirements of administrative success." He emphasized that such a division should "first of all consider the nationalities so that possibly one uni-lingual ethnic group would live in one county." Then he stressed that "this division will appease the nationalities or nothing can do it–and then the peoples are condemned to be subjugated while tearing each other to pieces."

As early as June 1850, Kossuth summarized his ideas concerning the reform of the state structure in his "Constitution Proposal," but did not leave any trace of doubt regarding the democratic character of the proposal. In his letter to Teleki, Kossuth restated what linguistic measures would be desirable within the self-governments, "It stems from the autonomy of communities and counties that the majority decides about the language of the administration within the community and the county." Even though the official language would be decided this way, he still adhered to the right of language use and the right of assembly. "So that this basic principle will receive perfect assurance, it is desired that the natural rights of minorities should be safeguarded and their associational rights should be respected."

Kossuth attached a note to his voluminous letter in which he responded to Teleki's reflection. He quoted Teleki, "So that our country would become the center of the federation, it is of utmost importance to accept the principle of federation within its own heart, etc. The Wallachians are not satisfied with the Hungarians. Still we will have to establish an alliance with them as well. We will have to understand that the Transylvanian Wallachians should also see their nationality secure." Kossuth responded immediately,

> Count Teleki, would you please tell me for once what you mean by this internal federation because beyond what I said in my letter[54] accompanied by these notes, I cannot comprehend it...The Wallachians know what they mean by it; namely, Transylvania, Krassó, three quarters of Bihar, Szathmár, and Máramaros would be detached from Hungary so that they become Wallachia, which would graciously promise to enter into alliance with us. Still they reserve the right to merge with Wallachia and Moldavia, their natural relatives.

Then Kossuth continued heatedly, "Thank you! I cannot ever, ever accept this. Its obvious consequence would involve detaching 15 counties to the Slovaks, down in the south, Bács, Baranya, half of Zala to the Serbs, the northern border territory to the Russians, the western to the Germans." (We have to point out that Kossuth envisioned and rejected the same sort of "reorganization" that was realized in the Trianon Peace Treaty in 1920, within the framework of the Versailles Peace agreements. This "reorganization" came at the expense of Hungary, considered "guilty" of maintaining the Monarchy, and of ignoring the right of self-determination of four million Hungarians.)

In his notes Kossuth dismissed the charge that he would deny anything to the Romanians he would give to the Serbs or others. The legal system could not make such a difference anyhow. And "I have always been a good friend and a supporter of the Wallachians since I feel that we owe them more for the bygone sins of the Hungarian–that is, rather Transylvanian–aristocracy." At the same time, he described certain unidentified Romanian exiles who had learnt about his ideas about the desired ways of co-existence as influenced by "numbing thoughts." When he described that "the proper territorial division would consider nationality interests ... to assure departmental and communal nationality autonomy and ethnic interests, in other words everything that common sense, equality, and fraternity might wish for, they were not pleased at all but rather detested the fact that we had not changed the name of our country since it was inhabited by several nationalities."[55]

In those days Kossuth's ideas could not expect much sympathy among the exiled leaders of co-existing and neighboring nationalities. Even Bălcescu, whom Kossuth had pursued successful talks with in 1849, voiced more and more reservations about him and promoted a federation completely different from that of Kossuth's.[56]

Already in the spring 1850 Bălcescu outlined a confederation called the Danubian United States. It would not only have included Hungarian, Bukovina, Moldova, Wallachia, and Serbia, but instead would have transformed it into a federation of Hungary, Romanian, and Serbian nationalities by eliminating former borders.[57] Kossuth became familiar with both the initial idea and the finished version, and the fact that its dying author intended to be the basis of Hungarian-Romanian reconciliation. According to Bălcescu's plan, only one of the parties would have been expected to give up national integrity according to the argument of natural law.[58] At Kossuth's request Sebő Vukovics, Minister of Justice of the 1849 Szemere Government and who was of Serbian ancestry, analyzed the plan. Vukovics' writing of March 17, 1851, emphasized the importance of focusing power as the main message of Bălcescu's confederation plan, a benefit to Hungarian political interests. He was also convinced by the examples of Switzerland and the United States of America. Both Switzerland and the United States were created as defensive alliances of smaller entities, not by dissolution existing units. It was also enticing that ethnic considerations were not determinative when they were created. However, the plan itself did not sustain Bălcescu's logic since by breaking up Hungary it would again create multi-national units. Vukovics' critical remarks reinforced Kossuth's view that Bălcescu's plan would not solve the differences of opinions, a view that was not contested by Teleki either.[59]

Teleki was deeply impressed by Kossuth's nationality theory of June 15, 1850, even if their disagreements about organizational questions concerning the exiles became strained. Teleki's letter of

August 16, 1850, stressed that their differences of opinions concerning the nationality question was that "I would allow collective rights, that is a provincial diet as well, to the Serbs and Wallachians beyond municipal rights."[60] This was a troublesome question for Kossuth. He was aware that, on the one hand, provincial diets might induce disintegration, but that, on the other hand, confining nationalities within municipal limits might be a source of constant irritation for minorities. Quite soon he had the opportunity to develop his theory and to assure "collective" rights beyond the municipal ones. At the request of Giuseppe Mazzini, who tried to create a unity of exiled groups against absolutism, Kossuth had to summarize his views concerning "the principles of future political organization" of Hungary.[61]

In the letter sent to Mazzini, Kossuth also felt obliged to satisfy the goal of having a written constitution for Hungary reflecting the transformation based on 1848–49 laws. He considered his work "a proposal" for the "constituent" Parliament of Hungary and also a starting point for negotiations or concluding an alliance with the political leaders of nationalities within or outside of the country. Kossuth translated the work from the original French himself, provided corrections and modifications, and gave the title "Proposal for the Future Political Organization of Hungary with Respect to the Solution of the Nationality Question."[62]

Kossuth's Proposal was the most concrete plan of the 19th century for a democratic restructuring of Hungary. It stated that the "people," which was the source and consignatary of law, were the "summary of citizens...without racial, linguistic, and religious differences." The Proposal required an itemized list of democratic liberties according to constitutional norms because "limits of these liberties are the invulnerability of others' rights." Drawing up the ambitious requirements of a personal autonomy it stated that "individual rights cannot depend on the mercy of family, community, county or the state."

The Proposal aspired to enforce the principle of "popular sovereignty" through universal suffrage both at autonomous county and parliamentary elections. Members of the Chamber of Deputies would be elected directly while the Senate, as a second chamber, would be elected indirectly through County Assemblies. Since ethnic nationalities were in the majority in several counties, they could gain substantial influence in the Senate, in the self-governments, and in the Chamber of Deputies. Kossuth expressed views on the questions of free language use and religion similar to those of 1850. His major step forward was to promote national minority "collective life," something Teleki had found wanting earlier.

Returning back to the issue of individual liberties, Kossuth claimed that to unite with others either for moral reasons or for supporting and assuring financial interests belonged to "inviolable human rights." He compared churches uniting "individuals of one faith and one religion" with local societies of "citizens of one nationality." He suggested that the latter unite in a common "national association." The national minority associations should then state their goals, rules, elect leaders. Hence, "with the freedom of an associative self-government they would promote moral and social interests called 'nationality.'" Kossuth contrasted this version of self-government, which did not require a separate "territorial authority" and could be adjusted to the operation of a democratic government organization, with the tragic consequences of dividing "the territory of the state according to languages" while claiming nationality interests. He was convinced that "it is either practically impossible, because ethnicities are mixed, or completely impossible without the dissolution of the state and without violating the rights and the security of other citizens."

The democratic nature of the plan–majority rule, self-government, and personal autonomy associated with the opportunity of developing national ethnic organizations–indicated how far Kossuth was willing to go to cooperate for reconciliation, against absolutism, and for the foundation of a confederation.

Kossuth felt obliged to state his views on three issues which had changed over time. In his view the Croats and cohabiting Southern Slavs were entitled to self-determination. Their separation from the Hungarian state had been observed by Hungarian constitutional law since the Middle Ages and in 1848, preceding the Jelačić attack, the Batthyány Government with Kossuth's active participation would have approved their secession in order to ensure peace. Kossuth offered a "mere treaty of alliance," maintaining Hungary's right to Fiume and the adjoining seashore for transportation rights.[63] In 1851 when there were obvious signs of Croat disillusionment with Vienna,[64] Kossuth–while emphasizing their right to secede–offered internal autonomy to motivate them towards an "associative connection" with Hungary. This was a change from 1848. Now Kossuth hoped to dissuade the Croats from opting for the Habsburg monarch in case of secession. In addition, Kossuth stated "Fiume ought to be given the free choice between Hungary and Croatia" or the option of becoming a "free port" guaranteed by both Hungary and Croatia. The 1859 published version, however, did not mention secession but proposed an "associative connection" which "would assure national self-government and would confine connections to a confederative relationship." This way confederation would merely be an "assurance against external absorption, for internal freedom, and national development."[65] Summarizing his Croat policy at the end of 1861, Kossuth again resigned himself to the possibility of a Croat secession. Besides Fiume he mentioned Muraköz (Medimurje)–the area between the Drava and Mura Rivers with majority Southern Slav population–as a contested area.[66] "...After gaining independence with common effort and submitting the issue to universal suffrage, we are willing to abide by the arbitration of a monarch who governs his country by the principle of the sovereignty of the people."[67]

Kossuth added a substantial section to his constitutional draft in order to deal with Transylvania.[68] The Saxons, who settled in Transylvania in the Middle Ages, and the Széklers (*Székely*), who constituted a branch of Hungarians, could keep their self-governments to assure "equal rights for every inhabitant" and so could Romanians who had lived within Saxon and Székler self-governments and had been excluded from the privileges before. However, since the majority of Transylvanian Romanians lived within the county system, his proposal referred to them directly. Kossuth hoped that his initiative would seem desirable to "our Transylvanian Wallachian relatives on nationality, civic, and political grounds." Nevertheless, the Transylvanian population should be able to vote, via plebiscite, for maintaining the union with Hungary or for an autonomous Transylvania with its own Parliament and independent internal affairs. Either way, the common state would still to be maintained with Hungary. Once again, the possibility of a plebiscite and ensuing developments were excluded from the 1859 version of his proposal.[69] In November of 1861 in his letter to Irányi, he compensated for it saying,

> Concerning Transylvania, as soon as we are advanced enough in the fight for independence so that a renewed discussion about the union cannot serve as a pretext for the Austrians to oppress us, we will submit the Transylvanian question to universal suffrage. It will decide whether the union should re-

main the way it was decided in 1848 or whether Transylvania should have a separate legislative and administrative autonomy. Still, it would retain its status quo with the Hungarian Crown; consequently, the unity of a common defense, foreign policy, diplomatic representation, customs and trade systems, and finances would be preserved.[70]

In 1851 Kossuth appealed to the Serbs and called their attention to the fact that his proposal was especially advantageous for them. This was so because the territories of Serbian Voivodina and Temes-Banat, separated from the Hungarian state by the Emperor by a promise of autonomy,[71] had Serbs mixed with other nationalities and in a proportion hardly exceeding one quarter of the population, according to the 1851 Census. Still, "to prove how much I wish that mutual appeasement and fraternal concord will replace nationality discord, which has caused so much misfortune and common servitude to the common fatherland," Kossuth was willing to acquiesce that areas which "are inhabited by Serbs in pure compact masses" would be transformed into a Serbian Voivodina and its population would elect its own Voivod. Again, the latter passage was not included into the 1859 version of the Constitutional Draft.[72] In the fall of 1861 Kossuth again felt obliged to make some modifications. In order "to assure Serbian municipal and county administration for the Serbian people, adjustment of county borders would be reasonable since most of them live in counties with no absolute Serbian majority."[73]

Differences in Kossuth's texts of spring 1851, early 1859, and the end of 1861 were not due to his changeable moods or to varying chances of Hungarian self-determination. Rather, they were mostly due to internal political events and relationships. Kossuth was aware of these things and claimed that in exile "we might gain importance if we are acknowledged representatives of national aspirations. For the sake of our nation it is our obligation to maintain solidarity with our nation and to make sure that the nation would maintain solidarity with us."[74] This same political fact also restrained him from going too far ahead with reconciliation and federative plans that his nation could not and would not follow him, something he bitterly suspected. However, he never wavered on three issues: reconciliation would happen only among peoples with fundamental freedoms; dividing Hungary could not be the price for reconciliation; and connecting the protection of liberties with a readiness to accept confederation was reasonable.

All the above explains why Kossuth considered collaboration an indispensable tactic to use when faced with absolutism. In his 1851 conclusion to the Constitutional Draft he expressed his wish "to overcome nationality discords and to create again a free homeland with a common will for all of us irrespective of language, ethnicity, or religion. We have suffered enough for nationality matters. We Hungarians were oppressed; you others were cheated and oppressed together with us. All of us have been victims of lost freedom. God help us that we will have learnt from our past." On November 18, 1858, Kossuth's Glasgow speech reflected the same goal. In the closing passage he stated "Each of the various races had something to forget, something to learn. I know they have. Shocked by past errors and by present servitude, I trust the next time when the moment comes...the great moment of regeneration shall find us united in heart and mind, shall find us united in will and act, for common right and common liberty."[75] Yet Kossuth did not seek reconciliation by all means. In the summer of 1861 he wrote to his companion in exile, General György Klapka, "nobody wants nationality reconciliation more than I do....However, there is a price I am not willing to pay and that is the linguistic division of the country," an event he labeled "suicidal."[76]

Kossuth aspired to get down to facts in the nationality issue which, in his view, were formed by "an unavoidable law...like the law of gravity in the material world." Thus, one should not play "hocus-pocus" with it.[77] With the confederative issue he remained on a theoretical level. His constitutional draft includes only a general warning that "an alliance with neighboring nations" might well serve Hungarians' "own security" and "solidarity" with "other peoples' fate." He claimed that "this is the only way to secure the independence of small nations against assimilation and the excess weight of larger nations." "This idea has application south of the German territories, along both banks of the Danube." He repeatedly cautioned that "countries which are part of such a confederation should not vie for each other's territory and should not violate each other's independence," but rather "confine their alliance to withstanding external dangers."[78]

However, in the course of diplomatic encounters Kossuth alluded to palpable ideas as well. His talks in the spring of 1859 with Prince Mihailo Obrenović are illuminating. Shortly before the French–Italian–Austrian war, the Serbian heir-to-the-throne, whose elderly father had been reinstalled on the throne a few months before, traveled to London to meet Kossuth at the advice of Napoleon III. Kossuth's memoir is very informative about the meeting. Jovan Ristić, the tutor and political advisor to the heir and who later became the head of his government, was also present at the talks. Yet Ristić completely relied on Kossuth's interpretation in his own historical work. Ristić notes that the Prince stated at the meeting that restoring Hungary's independence was desirable for Serbia's independence and for its unification with the Southern Slavs, still to be liberated from the Ottoman rule, since Hungary would help counter-balance Austrian and Russian hegemonic aspirations. Kossuth stated that the "freedom of the people" not the Russian czarist or Austrian imperial despotism should replace the fracturing Ottoman Empire in the Balkans. In his view the Hungarian middle power would not threaten liberated peoples since Hungary could not and would not want to increase its rate of national territory and population. A federation, on the other hand, would also act to hinder the increase of excessive power in the area. After confirming that their views matched, including on the issue of confederative plans, they hoped to reach practical results through further talks.[79]

Simultaneously, in the spring of 1859 there were promising developments between Hungarian exiles and the Romanian Principality. General Klapka, a protege of the initiating Cavour and Napoleon III, who was amidst preparation for war, appeared in Cuza's Court and concluded two agreements with Cuza. The first one aimed at military cooperation, especially in case the Italian war would entail a Hungarian military campaign launched from the east. In return for using the Romanian Principality as a base Klapka offered his support for liberating Bukovina, which had a majority Romanian population. The first agreement was concluded on March 29, 1859, and was followed by a second within two months. The Italian military operations were well under way when the second agreement declared a "complete" reconciliation among Hungarians, Romanians, and Serbs. It assured equal rights and free language use for every citizen of Hungary in the spirit of Kossuth's Constitutional Draft. Perspectively Kossuth promised that, following the war of liberation, a majority vote at the "meeting" convened in Transylvania would decide whether to maintain the 1848 Union with Hungary or to renew Transylvania's autonomy. The agreement concluded that "Fraternal principles should inspire all of us. Only these principles can lead us to our goal which is the confederation of three Danubian nations: Hungary, Serbia, and Moldova-Wallachia."[80]

There was no common military action taking place in 1859 due to Napoleon III's Villafranca maneuver and also due to the pressure of the great powers who feared a general European upheaval. However, the internal crises of the Empires, caused as they were by dynastic factors and poor judgment, were not over yet. The survival of the Austrian, Russian, and Turkish Empires mostly depended on the principle of "divide et impera" and on how successful they were in turning the centrifugal forces against each other or in appeasing these forces. Problems of national co-existence and the complications of the Transylvanian issue played significant roles in these crises.

In May of 1859, early in the Italian war, the Hungarian National Board of Directors was founded in Paris, with the participation of Kossuth, Klapka, and Teleki, in order to function as a temporary government in exile. Establishing a "fraternal" relationship with the nationalities was "of utmost importance" according to the information sent to Hungary. The 1848 laws, which dissolved a number of antiquated privileges, served as "starting points" but did not limit the issue. "...We want to expand and develop the implied theories so that every interest, both nationality and religious, would be satisfied under the auspices of the Hungarian constitution." Kossuth's Constitutional Draft was attached, (the version published in the Irányi-Chassin book), as a "guiding line" which "has our consent in its basic principles." Teleki was concerned that replacing the Upper House with a democratically elected Senate would "unnecessarily frighten the aristocracy."[81] However, Kossuth's known "rigidity" on the Transylvanian issue gave rise to much more tension.

Undoubtedly Kossuth was, and remained, a unionist as he was obliged both rationally and emotionally to the unity of historical Hungary. However, his political rationality always prevailed. During 1841–42, at the time of his first statements about the union, he considered it of vital importance that Hungary unite with Transylvania–since "it is thrown in the middle between two giant nationalities," the Germans and the Russians, and it does not wish to be either a "Russian province" or a "German colony." The nation should understand that besides the "reminiscences" about historical antecedents and "sympathy for a unified nation...it is a common interest of the two brotherly countries to unite. It is advisable to unite and they need to unite, even if they have never been united."[82]

Kossuth's rationality was substantiated by Viennese power-political considerations. Minister of Public Safety, Count J. Sedlnitzky warned in 1846 that in the event the union was realized "the central gravity of the Monarchy would necessarily shift towards Hungary."[83] In his secret memorandum to the Monarch on March 20, 1848, the first day of his prime ministership, Count F.A. Kolowrat declared that the prevention of a union between Hungary and Transylvania was one of the most important things to be done.[84] Power politics and interests hid behind the facade of protecting nationality interests during both the absolutist and semi-constitutional periods of the Vienna Court. However, during the July 19, 1861 meeting of the Council of Ministers, A. Schmerling very honestly summarized the policy the Court had put into practice "The Transylvanian Union is not of interest for the Empire because in this way a vast administrative unit would be created, stretching from the River Leitha to the border of Moldavia. With regards to its size and population it would surpass any other country of the Crown, even the largest ones. Transylvania is of military importance, which will be lost if it is united with Hungary." (This remark also alluded to the fact that such a military power could also be applied against Hungary.)[85] This attitude prevailed throughout the absolutist period. For instance, speaking to a delegation of Transylvanian Romanians Franz Joseph said that "...as far as the union between Transylvania and Hungary is concerned, I will never let it happen."[86]

The Opposition movement in Hungary having played a decisive role in forming the public mood in 1860–61 and being organically connected with the exiles, found themselves in an increasingly difficult situation on the Transylvanian question. Legally they demanded the reinstatement of the 1848 constitutional situation, which would have entailed the Union. Extra-legally, however, the Opposition also considered the possibility of a liberating war coordinated with the Italian unity movement. Its logical requirement would have been to maintain Prince Cuza's cooperation and his indirect support in order to promote Hungarian–Romanian reconciliation. The latter was especially crucial because of the news and rumors spread about provocateurs in Transylvania sowing the seeds of discord among the people. As a result, the Hungarian National Board of Directors–via Teleki's authorship–summarized its political ideas in a voluminous memorandum for Prince Cuza, dated on September 10, 1860. It focused on the fact that in the event of the inevitable dissolution of the Ottoman Empire, the Danubian principalities would either gain independence or they would have to make do with an exchange of masters, in case the Great Powers would divide up the area. Only the existence of an independent Hungary could prevent the latter from happening. Thus, it is in the interest of the Principalities to restore independent Hungary. The memorandum also summarized the basic nationality principles of the Board in accord with Kossuth's 1859 version of the Constitutional Draft; hence, it did not elaborate on the possibility of a separate Transylvania–contrary to Teleki's original intention.[87]

According to Teleki Kossuth wished to ignore the Transylvanian alternatives because "the Transylvanian gentlemen were not in the mood" for a different solution. However, Kossuth also stated that the question was important enough for two or three people to decide in Hungary. They asked the envoy "to pursue" the issue, stressing that "especially" Kossuth decided not "to say or do anything without verifying acceptance at home ahead of time." Concerning the Transylvanian alternatives Kossuth wanted to rely on the views of the home organization to avoid any devaluation of the exiles. In his letter, the last one Teleki could write to Kossuth before he was caught and imprisoned, Teleki informed Kossuth that he had received a cable indicating "that they are in agreement[88] about the Hungarian Crown retaining its rights to Transylvania, about the territorial unity of Hungary, about a legislative connection between Transylvania and Hungary, about the form of internal administration, and about the question whether Transylvania should have a provincial diet besides sending representatives to the Hungarian Diet, which should depend on the plebiscite of the Transylvanian population." Teleki added, "This sounds very reassuring to me. This way we can make a greater impact on Cuza."[89]

Kossuth appeared to be less accommodating towards the demands of co-existing and neighboring peoples than either Teleki or Klapka. However, he was more cautious with regards to concessions on nationality policies. His strong point was that his national aspirations were always accompanied by a consistent long-term view of democracy. Unlike Teleki, he did not despair over the vacillation of the "resistance fighters" during the Habsburg crisis.

Nor did he develop extreme alternatives: Garibaldi or Deák as Ferenc Pulszky and several other friends in exile. He fought against any swashbuckling-type risking of lives and against bargaining with anti-democratic and crypto-absolutist powers since this would endanger future prospects. For Kossuth, the moral of 1848-49, of the 1849-59 absolutist period, and of the 1859-61 crisis was that agreement should be sought within the community of the oppressed.

That is why he heavily criticized his fellow-citizens who failed to utilize the crisis and urged them to search for a way out based on reconciliation. He also criticized the work of the nationality committee of the 1861 Parliamentary session, led by Eötvös, since it had not achieved the desired level of linguistic emancipation. Kossuth declared that "...if they are not willing to step forward, I am sorry to say that the roads we have taken have separated and our policies do not agree."[90] His correspondence at the end of 1861 and in early 1862 indicates that he and Dániel Irányi were going to make a comprehensive political "manifesto" regarding nationality policy and coexistence with neighboring peoples. Kossuth's correspondence also reveals that several concessions which he had left out of the 1859 version of his Constitutional Draft would be revived and even exceeded–as mentioned above. The planned release of a manifesto was delayed by Kossuth's differences of views with Klapka concerning the character and rate of concessions, by the death of his beloved daughter in the spring of 1862, and by the deterioration of his wife's health. In addition, since Cavour's death in 1861, Kossuth had not received the unprecedented cooperation from the Italian government that he had enjoyed before.[91] Faith in Italian-Hungarian interdependence survived Cavour since some of the Italian statesmen still counted on Hungary as a potential ally, and a potential pressure on the Habsburgs, even after the dissolution of the Hungarian Parliament and inconsistencies in Hungarian policy. It was clear that many of these inconsistencies were related to unsolved issues of national and nationality co-existence. That is why the Italians tried to retain their intermediary role. It was also noted that György Klapka, who some considered "the man of the future" in contrast with the temporarily inactive Kossuth, was more flexible towards the demands of nationality leaders and neighboring princes than Kossuth had been.

In April 1862, M. A. Canini visited Kossuth, who had just arrived in Torino from his daughter's funeral. Canini, an Italian secret agent in Bucharest and personal envoy of Victor Emanuel, was familiar through Klapka with the exiles' views about a future alliance.[92]

According to Kossuth, after their long discussion about the confederation, Canini asked him to summarize his views by the following day. Due to his family obligations Kossuth was unable to comply and Canini himself offered to try to make a summary. The following day Canini appeared with the summary, with which Kossuth essentially agreed, although he did recognize Ferenc Pulszky's handwriting, from whom he had been alienated. The summary relied heavily on György Klapka's work which had been finalized before Canini's visit to Kossuth. (Klapka's writing to the Italian Government was dated April 15, 1862. The text was mostly a blend of Klapka's, Kossuth's, and László Teleki's plan and it must have had Pulszky's consent.[93])

In Torino on May 1, 1862, after a few handwritten modifications, Kossuth signed the text as ex-governor of Hungary based on notes of his discussion with Canini and Klapka's summary.[94] (Ferenc Kossuth translated and edited the original text which included the note "accepted as the basis for negotiations."[95])

The confederative plans of the Hungarian exiles–Kossuth's draft of June 15, 1850, Klapka's work of April 15, 1862, and Camini's summary–would require a thorough philological study. The present essay does not attempt to do that since it is limited to discussing the plan for the Danubian Federation.[96]

The plan for the Danubian Federation envisioned the alliance of "old historical states" bordered by the Carpathians, the Danube, the Adriatic Sea, and the Black Sea. Contrary to Kossuth's 1850-51 plans it did not include Polish or Czech territories. Hungary, Transylvania, Romania, Croatia, Serbia, and the Southern Slav provinces–after their liberation from the Ottoman rule–would be considered as potential participants in the alliance.

The introduction declared that "the legislature, jurisdiction, and administration of each state would be independent" except for certain issues referred to the "federal authority." The reference to free development through decentralization when "every people could occupy its own place in the large family of mankind" might well allude to a further development of the state structure.

The condition for the establishment of the Confederation was "the voluntary agreement of each people in the Danubian provinces, either in the form of a legislative meeting or through a general plebiscite." Obviously the possibility of a plebiscite was connected to Transylvania. Nearly all the alternative solutions to this problem, which had troubled Kossuth the most during his twelve years in exile, were listed. "Will the inhabitants of Transylvania decide through a plebiscite whether their homeland should be united with Hungary? Or should it be politically united with Hungary and administratively separate? Or should it be in alliance with Hungary and other allied states as an autonomous state on completely equal footing?" As a rare exception Kossuth expressed his view in the first person singular when he indicated that Hungary and Transylvania should have their head of state in common just in case the Transylvanians opted for political independence within the confederation.

The "legislative gathering" would draw up a federal contract. The contract would declare a common defense of the federal territory, common foreign policy, and a common economic alliance to divide the customs profit among the states through the Parliament. The legislative assembly would decide whether the Parliament would have one or two chambers. If it were the latter, the deputies would be elected by the population of each state, in proportion to the number of inhabitants, while each state would have the same number of senators in order to protect the rights of the smaller states. The legislative assembly would also decide about the "official" language at each level of government, yet still assuring free language use. The seat of the executive authority would alternate between Pest, Bucharest, Zagreb, and Belgrade. (This complied with Bălcescu's plan even though contrary to Kossuth's proposal of 1850, which envisioned the seat on Hungarian territory.)

Every member of the confederation should have a constitution which would correspond to their interests which, however, should not contradict the confederative agreement. Kossuth's views concerning free language use, basic freedoms, and communal rights, described in the Constitutional Draft and summarized in eight points, were considered desirable. They had been brought to Prince Cuza's attention by the Hungarian National Board of Directors in September 1860.

If everything was accepted, an agreement of the respective peoples might be realized and "the ancient, rotten states, which keep them in servitude" would be dissolved.[97] Blending logic with rhetoric the text continues,

> I invoke my Hungarian, Slav, and Romanian brothers to cast a veil over the past and to extend a hand to one another. Rise up as one people for the common freedom and fight for all as all fight for one....Accept the plan, which is not a concession. It is a mutual and voluntary alliance. Any state of the lower Danube, should it even be successful in rallying around itself all its racial brethren now belonging to other states, could be at best only a state of second rank, the independence of which would be continuously menaced and inevitably subjected to foreign influences. However, if the Hungarians, the Southern Slavs, and the Romanians would accept this plan [of confederation], they would together become a wealthy, powerful state of the first rank...which would have a heavy weight in the scales of Europe....Unity, concord, fraternity between Hungarians, Slavs, and Romanians! This is my most ardent wish, my most sincere advice![98]

Because of indiscretion born of enthusiasm the whole world soon became familiar with the text.[99] Due to Viennese initiatives Kossuth's old and new adversaries discussed and commented on the text in the heavily censored Hungarian press. Most of the opposition had to remain silent. In spite of Kossuth's information to them[100] they did not discuss the real function of the proposed Danubian Confederation nor the fact that the exiled statesman still considered the promotion of reconciliation and co-operation among nationalities as his primary task. They endured that the government press would first respond to sympathetic nationality statements. It was due to this unfavorable response in Hungary that the Draft was not properly appreciated by the various political circles in neighboring countries.[101]

Until the spring of 1867 Kossuth continued to state the view that "in the event of the obvious annihilation of Austria, a great task is awaiting both the Hungarian nation and all the nationalities whose lands are washed by the River Danube...Our calling is to work and to play leading roles in the political and social solutions of the great questions of freedom and equality. Our calling is to go ahead in the work that develops and stabilizes freedom and national co-existence along the Danube."[102]

Kossuth considered the Compromise to be the same as an alliance, established over the heads of the respective peoples, with a Power that sought refuge in a retrograde and absolutist government. Beyond moral objections he found it devastating that Hungarians, who were declared to be a ruling nation, would be isolated from their natural allies and in the event of the unavoidable dissolution of the Monarchy, they would be considered an "Austrian accomplice."[103]

During the more than 25 remaining years of his exile, Kossuth often referred back to the Danubian confederation plan. Unfortunately, the Plan was deemed useless, and became useless, by the narrow-minded. He was always saddened by this outcome and was full of fear about the consequences. In 1882, twenty years after the plan was published, he wrote at the end of the third, and what he considered final, volume of his writings,

> The Danubian Confederation would have been possible with an independent Hungary. But Hungarian independence has been given up and this way the idea of a confederation, as so many other ideas, belong to the *pium desiderium* . Although the details may be debated, the idea itself is so rational, is so much required by Hungary's security, and is so much required by the national freedom of eastern peoples that, if the Hungarian nation had not abandoned me in my aspirations towards independence, the idea would have prevailed and the Hungarian homeland would have been spared enormous ordeals.[104]

NOTES

1. Jenő Koltay-Kastner, *A Kossuth-emigráció Olaszországban* [The Kossuth Exile in Italy] (Budapest, 1950), 8–10; Magda Jászay, *Mazzini* (Budapest, 1977), 41–43, 77–79; See also, *Kossuth Lajos Összes Munkái I.* [Complete Works of Lajos Kossuth, I] ed. István Barta (Budapest, 1948) 11, 16, 26, 30; and Kossuth, *Complete VI*, ed. István Barta (Budapest, 1966), 397 and passim.

2. See *Gróf Széchenyi István írói és hírlapi vitája Kossuth Lajossal* [Count István Széchenyi's Written Debate with Lajos Kossuth], I–II. ed. Gyula Viszota (Budapest, 1927–1930); Domokos Kosáry, *Kossuth Lajos a reformkorban* [Lajos Kossuth in the Reform Era] (Budapest, 1946); *Emlékkönyv Kossuth Lajos születésének 150. évfordulójára, I–II.* [Memorial Volume on the 150th Anniversary of Kossuth's Birth] ed. Zoltán J. Tóth (Budapest, 1952); György Szabad, *Kossuth Lajos politikai pályája* [Lajos Kossuth's Political Career] (Budapest, 1977); János Varga, *Helyét kereső Magyarország* [Hungary Seeking Its Place] (Budapest, 1982).

3. Kossuth's significant letter was published in Tivadar Ács, *Kossuth demokráciája* [Kossuth's Democracy] (Budapest, 1943),33–50; The quotations are from the original letter, *Lajos Kossuth to László Teleki* (Kütahya, June 15, 1850), Hungarian National Archives, R. 90. I. 797.

4. See also, *Pesti Hírlap,* 1842. Nos. 161, 165, 1843; Nos. 233, 234, 236, 266-267; Gyula Viszota II. 1068-1076; György Szabad, 1977. 75-83, 121-122.

5. See György Szabad, Hungary's Recognition of Croatia's Self-Determination in 1848 and Its Immediate Antecedents, in *East Central European Society and War in the Era of Revolutions, 1775-1856,* ed. Béla K. Király (New York, 1984.), 591-609.

6. Ágnes Deák's essay discusses this topic in this book.

7. See *Pesti Hírlap* 1843. No. 244; Zsolt Trócsányi, *Wesselényi Miklós* [Miklós Wesselényi] (Budapest, 1965), 452-473.

8. *Pesti Hírlap,* 1841. No. 30; 1842. No. 179.

9. Ibid., No. 107.

10. See János Varga, 1982. 115-141.

11. For the whole question see István Hajnal, *A Batthyány-kormány külpolitikája* [The Foreign Policy of the Batthyány Government] (Budapest, 1957); see Gábor Erdődy, *A magyar kormányzat eruópai látóköre 1848-ban* [The Hungarian Government's European Vision in 1848] (Budapest, 1988), 10-76.

12. István Deák, *The Lawful Revolution: Louis Kossuth and the Hungarians 1848-1849* (New York-London, 1979). Blackwell's reports well justified the appropriateness of his definition.

13. See Paul Bödy, *Joseph Eötvös and the Modernization of Hungary, 1840-1870* (Philadelphia, 1972).

14. Quoted by Tamás Kabdebó, *Blackwell küldetése* [Blackwell's Mission] (Budapest, 1990), 166-168.

15. Blackwell drafted his concept on a map that indicated Hungary as the leading power between the new Germany and Russia, István Hajnal, 15. and Tamás Kabdebó, 169, 172-175.

16. Kossuth, *Complete* XI. ed., István Barta (Budapest, 1951), 187-188.

17. See Gunther E. Rothenberg, *The Military Border in Croatia, 1740-1881: A Study of an Imperial Institution* (Chicago-London, 1966).

18. Kossuth, *Complete* XI. 742-43; György Szabad, 1977, 117ff.

19. Kossuth, *Complete* XII. ed., István Sinkovics (Budapest, 1957), 424-438; Szabad, 1977, 133ff.

20. Kossuth, *Complete* XII. 385.

21. Ibid., 394.

22. *Az 1848-1849 évi minisztertanácsi jegyzőkönyvek* [The 1848-49 Minutes of the Council of Ministers] ed. Erzsébet F. Kiss (Budapest, 1989), 65.

23. Kossuth, *Complete* XII. 924-925.

24. Ibid., 939; *Az 1848/49. évi népképviseleti országgyűlés* [The 1848-49 Representative Parliamentary Session] ed. János Beér (Budapest, 1954), 228-229, 491-492, 576-591.

25. Ambrus Miskolczy, Erdély a forradalomban és a szabadságharcban, 1848-49 (Transylvania in the Revolution and War of Independence) in *Erdély története* [History of Transylvania], editor-in-chief, Béla Köpeczi (Budapest, 1986), 1384; Szabad, 1977. 150, etc.; Dániel Irányi-Charles-Louis Chassin, *A magyar forradalom politikai története, 1847-49* [The Political History of the Hungarian Revolution, 1848-49] (Budapest, 1989), II.70, etc.; György Spira, Polgári forradalom, 1848-49 [Bourgeois Revolution, 1848-49] in *Magyarország története*

[History of Hungary], VI, editor-in-chief, Endre Kovács, 2nd edition (Budapest, 1987), 287, etc.

26. The text here connects peace efforts to military events, but further on it makes reference to general events and issues.

27. Kossuth, elected by the Parliament, served in office as temporary head of state.

28. *Az 1848–1849 évi minisztertanácsi jegyzőkönyvek* [The 1848–49 Minutes of the Council of Ministers] ed. Erzsébet F. Kiss (Budapest, 1989), 77–78.

29. For the issue, also see József Thim, *A magyarországi 1848–49-iki szerb fölkelés története, I–III.* [The History of the 1848–49 Serbian Uprising, I-III] (Budapest, 1930–1940); Lajos Steier, *A tót nemzetiségi kérdés 1848–49-ben, I–II.* [The Slovak Nationality Question in 1848–49, I-II.] (Budapest, 1937); Daniel Rapant, *Slovenské pvstanie roku 1848–49, I–II.* (Sv. Martin, 1937–1950); *1848–1849. évi iratok a nemzetiségi megbékélésről* [1848–1849 Documents about Nationality Reconciliation], published by the Hungarian–Romanian and the Hungarian–Yugoslav Societies, (Budapest, 1948); Radoslav Petrovič, *Gradja za istoriju srpskog pokreta u Vojvodini 1848–1849 godine.* (Beograd, 1952); Endre Kovács, *Magyar–délszláv megbékélési törekvések 1848/49-ben* [Hungarian–Southern-Slav Reconciliatory Efforts in 1848/49] (Budapest, 1958); Zoltán I. Tóth, *Magyarok és románok* [Hungarians and Romanians] (Budapest, 1966); Zoltán Sárközi, *Az erdélyi szászok 1848–1849-ben* [The Transylvanian Saxons in 1848–1849] (Budapest, 1974); *Revolutia de la 1848–1849 din Transilvania*, ed. Ştefan Pascu–Victor Cheresteşiu, (Bucuresti, 1977); György Spira, *A nemzetiségi kérdés a negyvennyolcas forradalom Magyarországán* [The Nationality Question in the Hungary of the 1848 Revolution] (Budapest, 1980).

30. Kossuth, *Complete* XII. 650, 801, 921, 925; János Beér ed.,1954, 862-863; Ambrus Miskolczy, *A kőröskisjenői román egyházi zsinat, 1849* [The Romanian Synod of Kőröskisjenő, 1849] (Budapest,1991),14–26, etc.

31. Kossuth, *Complete* XV. ed.; István Barta (Budapest, 1955), 136–139; The tragic outcome of Dragoş' mission was not the direct result of the instructions, see in János Varga, *Románok és magyarok 1848/49-ben* [Romanians and Hungarians in 1848–49] (Budapest, 1993).

32. János Beér ed., 1954. 576–577, 583–585.

33. Kossuth, *Complete* XIII. ed. István Barta (Budapest, 1952), 439–442; György Spira, 1980. 85–86, 187–188.

34. Zoltán I. Tóth, Kossuth és a nemzetiségi kérdés 1848–1849-ben [Kossuth and the Nationality Question in 1848–1849] in *Emlékkönyv Kossuth Lajos születésének 150. évfordulójára* [Memorial Volume on the 150th Anniversary of Kossuth's Birth] ed. Zoltán I. Tóth, Budapest, 1952. II. 32; Endre Kovács, *A Kossuth-emigráció és az európai szabadságmozgalmak* [The Kossuth Exile and the European Freedom Movements] (Budapest, 1967), 284–285; György Spira, 1980.103, 201–205.

35. *Memoirs of Prince Adam Czartoryski*, ed. A. Gielgud (London, 1888); Marcel Handelsman, *Adam Czartoryski* (Warszawa, 1949); Zoltán Horváth, *László Teleki I–II* (Budapest, 1964); Endre Kovács, A magyar–délszláv megegyezés ügye 1849. tavaszán [The Case of the Hungarian–Southern-Slav Agreement in the Spring of 1849] in Endre Kovács, *Népek országútján* [On the Highway of the Peoples] (Budapest, 1972).

36. *Teleki László válogatott munkái* [László Teleki's Selected Writings], ed., Gábor G. Kemény (Budapest, 1961), II. 18-21.

37. *Márczius Tizenötödike, 1849. márc. 6, 10.* published by György Spira, 1980, 197-200.

38. Kossuth, *Complete* XIV. 882.

39. György Szabad, *Magyarország önálló államiságának kérdése a polgári átalakulás korában* [The Question of Independent Hungarian Statehood in the Period of Bourgeois Transformation] (Budapest, 1986), 48-49.

40. Teleki, *Selected,* II. 25-29.

41. Eszter Waldapfel, *A független magyar külpolitika 1848-1849* [The Independent Hungarian Foreign Policy in 1848-1849] (Budapest, 1962), 218-221.

42. *Az 1848-1849 évi minisztertanácsi jegyzőkönyvek* [The 1848-49 Minutes of the Council of Ministers] ed. Erzsébet F. Kiss (Budapest, 1989), 77-78.

43. The French text of the circular is included in József Thim, III. 783-784. Its Hungarian translation is in Ferenc Pulszky, *Életem és korom* [My Life and My Age], ed. Ambrus Oltványi (Budapest, 1958), 543-547.

44. Kossuth, *Complete* XV. ed. István Barta (Budapest, 1955), 661-664.

45. Ibid., 723-728 735-736; Zoltán I. Tóth, 1952. 327; Zoltán I. Tóth, *Bălcescu Miklós élete* [The Life of Nicolae Bălcescu], ed., Dániel Csatári (Budapest, 1958), 119-147; György Spira, 1980, 104-107, 225-226.

46. It tacitly corrected Article 1848:XVI, which was contradictory to Kossuth's aspirations in many ways.

47. See his instructions on April 26, 1849, to Dragoş and on July 5, 1849, to Simonffy in Kossuth, *Complete* XV. 137, 662.

48. Közlöny, July 29, 1849. *Az 1848/49. évi népképviseleti országgyűlés* [The 1848-49 Representative Parliamentary Session], ed. János Beér (Budapest, 1954), 469-475, 552-553, 861-869.

49. Jenő Koltay-Kastner quotes, 1960, 101; Eugenio Kastner, *Mazzini e Kossuth* (Florence, 1929), 134.

50. István Hajnal, *A Kossuth-emigráció Törökországban, I.* [The Kossuth Exile in Turkey] (Budapest, 1927); Ferenc Pulszky, I. 550-553; Teleki, *Selected* II. 39-40, 52-61; Imre Deák, *A száműzött Kossuth* [The Exiled Kossuth] (Budapest), 224-228, 371; Zoltán Horváth, II. 190-213; Gyula Mérei, *Föderációs tervek Délkelet-Európában és a Habsburg-monarchia 1840-1918* [Federative Plans in South-Eastern Europe and the Habsburg Monarchy, 1840-1918] (Budapest, 1965), 64-66; Endre Kovács, 1967. 168-178.

51. See note 3.

52. Kossuth made it clear in his later talks that multi-national empires formed by conquests and dynastic connections lacked internal cohesion and could survive only by absolutist means; György Szabad, *Kossuth and the British "Balance of Power" Policy* (Budapest, 1960).

53. His idea is strikingly similar to what was realized a century later in selecting the capital of the European Union.

54. See note 3.

55. Lajos Kossuth, *Észrevételeim* [My Observations], June 15, 1850, in the Hungarian National Archives, R.90.I. 795, Zoltán Horváth, II, 221-232.

56. Endre Kovács, 1967, 284–289; *Miklós Bălcescu válogatott írásai* [Miklós Bălcescu's Selected Writings] ed. Zoltán I. Tóth (Budapest, 1950), 212–214; Béla Borsi-Kálmán, *Nemzetfogalom és nemzetstratégiák. A Kossuth-emigráció és a román nemzeti törekvések kapcsolatának történetéhez* [Nation Theory and National Strategies. To the History of the Kossuth Exile and Romanian National Ambitions] (Budapest, 1993), 75–78.

57. Bălcescu, *Selected Writings*, 214–215; *Deák Ferenc beszédei* [Ferenc Deák's Speeches] (Fourth edition, Budapest, 1903), V. 17–18. Hungarian National Archives, R.90.I.1568.

58. Bălcescu, *Selected Writings,* 215–220; Zoltán Horváth II, 236–240; Endre Kovács, 1967, 291–298.

59. See Sebő Vukovics's text in the Hungarian National Archives, R.90.I. 1568, published in Zoltán Horváth, II. 264–280; See also Endre Kovács, 1967. 298–301.

60. Teleki, *Selected Writings,* II. 54, 58–61; Ibid.

61. Originally Kossuth, *Exposé des Principe de la future organisation politique de l'Hongrie*, Kütahya, April 25, 1851 sent to Mazzini attached to a letter, and published by Eugenio Kastner, 1929, 120–140.

62. Kossuth, *Javaslat Magyar Ország jövő politicai szervezetét illetőleg,—tekintettel a nemzetiségi kérdés megoldására* [Proposal for the Future Political Organization of Hungary—with Respect to the Solution of the Nationality Question] (Hungarian National Archives, R.90.I. 1554). Review of editions and text variations, György Spira, *Kossuth és alkotmányterve* [Kossuth and his Constitutional Proposal] (Debrecen, 1989, 7, and others); Kossuth stopped modifying the Constitutional Proposal only in 1862, see György Szabad, *Forradalom és kiegyezés választútján, 1860/61* [On the Crossroads of Revolution and Compromise, 1860/61] (Budapest, 1967), 556–559.

63. The 1848/49 Minutes of the Council of Ministers, 65; Szabad, 1984, 602-604.

64. György Szabad, *Az önkényuralom kora, 1849–1867* in *Magyarország történte 1848–1890* [The Era of Absolutism, 1849-1867 in History of Hungary, 1848–1890], ed. Endre Kovács and László Katus, 2nd ed. (Budapest, 1987), I. 478–479).

65. Irányi-Chassin, I, 309–310.

66. Miklós Kring, *A muraközi országhatár a magyar–horvát viszony történetében* [The Muraköz (Medimurje) Border in the History of Hungarian-Croat Relations] (Budapest, 1942).

67. Lajos Kossuth (San Francesco d'Albaro, November 18 and 20, 1861); *Irányi Dánielnek* [To Dániel Irányi] (Hungarian National Archives, Dániel Irányi's Documents]; György Szabad, 1967, 558.

68. I refer to historical Transylvania which became a Principality, dependent on the Turks, after Hungary was divided into three parts in the 16th century. After almost one and a half centuries, in 1690, Transylvania was transferred to Habsburg hands. The Habsburgs governed it separated from Hungary until 1848 when Parliament (still feudal) declared the Union. In *Erdély története, I–III.* [The History of Transylvania] editor-in-chief, Béla Köpeczi (Budapest, 1986). Everyday Hungarian refers to a much larger area than the Trianon Treaty area sanctioned to join to Romania in 1920.

69. Irányi-Chassin, I, 310–311, 364.

70. See note 67.

71. For the unrealized promise see György Szabad, 1987. I. 479–480.

72. Irányi-Chassin, I, 311, 364.

73. See note 67.

74. Lajos Kossuth, *Irataim az emigrációból I.* [My Documents from Exile, I.] (Budapest, 1880), XXI.

75. Hungarian National Archives, R. 90. I. 3437–3839; Irányi-Chassin, I, 312–313, 364; György Szabad, 1960, 7–8; Louis Kossuth, *La question des nationalités. L'Europe, L'Autriche et la Hongrie,* 2nd ed. (Bruxelles, 1859), 19–27; György Szabad, 1967, 401.

76. Kossuth (Cossila, June 23, 1861); *Klapkának* [To Klapka] Hungarian National Archives, R.91.I, 3764; also in Lajos Kossuth's Writings, III. (1882), 629.

77. Kossuth (London, March 4, 1859); Ludvigh Jánosnak [To János Ludvigh] in *Iratok a Kossuth-emigráció történtéhez, 1859* [Documents to the History of the Kossuth Exile, 1859] ed., Jenő Koltay-Kastner (Szeged, 1949), 27–28.

78. Irányi-Chassin, I, 308–309.

79. Kossuth, *My Documents,* 336–337, 341–344, 386–403; János Risztics (Jován Ristić), *Szerbia külügyi viszonyai az újabb időben* [Foreign Affairs of Serbia in Newer Times] (Nagybecskerek, 1893, I) 213–221; Koltay-Kastner, 1960, 108, 120–121; Szabad, 1967, 121, 410–411, 537–540.

80. Endre Kovács, 1967, 318–356; Zoltán Szász, Az abszolutizmus kora Erdélyben, 1849–1867 [The Era of Absolutism in Transylvania] in *Erdély története* [The History of Transylvania] (Budapest, 1986), 1465–1469; Kossuth, *My Documents,* I.369–382, III.69–70, 241; Luigi Chiala, *Politica segreta di Napoleone III. e di Cavour in Italia e in Ungheria, 1859–1861* (Torino–Roma, 1895); Magda Jászay, *Cavour* (Budapest, 1986), 191–192, 199–200; Béla Borsi-Kálmán, 1993, 99, 202–204.

81. Kossuth, *My Documents,* 453; Dániel Irányi (Genova, June 27, 1859); *Kossuthnak* [To Kossuth] Hungarian National Archives, R. 90. I, 2821/A.

82. *Pesti Hírlap,* 1841, No. 30–31; 1842, 179, 181.

83. Quoted by Ambrus Miskolczy, Az Erdélyi Nagyfejedelemség 'birodalompolitikai' jelentősége az 1848. májusi válságban [Imperial Political Significance of the Transylvanian Principality in the Crisis of May 1848] in *A magyar polgári átalakulás kérdései* [The Question of Hungarian Bourgeois Transformation] ed. Zoltán Iván Dénes, András Gergely and Gábor Pajkossy (Budapest, 1984), 288.

84. Árpád Károlyi, *Németújvári gróf Batthyány Lajos első magyar miniszterelnök főbenjáró pöre* [Trial of the First Hungarian Prime Minister Count Lajos Batthyány de Németújvár] (Budapest, 1932), II. 610.

85. Josef Redlich, *Das österreichische Staats- und Reichsproblem* (Leipzig, 1920–1926), II. 118–119; György Szabad, 1967, 395.

86. Quoted by Zoltán Szász, 1986, 1483.

87. Its text in Teleki, *Selected* II. 192–202, 288; Kossuth, *My Documents,* II. 498–501, II. 59–66; Gyula Tanárky's Diary (1849–1866), selected by Jenő Koltay-Kastner (Budapest, 1961), 174–175; Endre Kovács, 1967, 361–364.

88. His biographer used the past tense, which is not only a question of different tenses but also indicates a closure of the question; Zoltán Horváth, I, 447; More than twenty years later Kossuth referred back to Teleki's passage of Tran-

sylvania written on November 26, 1860, as if it had been significantly different from his view of the time, although essentially they agreed on what was later elaborated on in his correspondence with Irányi in the fall of 1861; Kossuth, *My Documents,* III. 168-169.

89. László Teleki (Geneva, November 7, 26, 1860); *Kossuthnak* [To Kossuth], Hungarian National Archives, R. 90. 3450, 3477; László Teleki, *Selected II,* 202-208.

90. Kossuth (San Francesco d'Albaro, December 28, 1861); *Jósika Miklósnak* [To Miklós Jósika], Hungarian National Archives, R. 90. I. 3910.

91. György Szabad, 1967, 556-559; Kossuth, *My Documents,* III. 735.

92. See Annibale Strambio, Italian Chief Consul (Bucharest, June 28, July 29, 1862); Giacomo Durando külügyminiszternek [To Minister of Foreign Affairs Giacomo Durando] I, in *Documenti Diplomatici Italiani. Prima Serie* (Roma, 1959), II, 475-477, 601-604; Endre Kovács, 1967, 408-409.

93. Documenti Diplomatici, II, 293-295; Kossuth, *My Documents,* III. 735-738, VI, ed., Ferencz Kossuth (Budapest, 1898), 8.

94. See original text signed by Kossuth in Archivio Centrale dello Stato, Roma. Fondo-Ricasoli. B. 1. F. 2/g.

95. Lajos Kossuth, My Documents, VI. 9.

96. We rely on the original text quoted in endnote 94, but our words follow the Hungarian text published in Lajos Kossuth, *My Documents,* 9-12.

97. According to Lajos Kossuth, *My Documents,* 12—"that is Austria and Turkey." The interjection is contextually indicated but is not part of the original text.

98. Almost three decades earlier Kossuth, who had just started his career, argued similarly for his bourgeois reform policy, in Kossuth, *Complete VI.* ed., István Barta (Budapest, 1966), 378-379.

99. The hastily translated Italian text was published on the front page of the L'Alleanza on May 18, 1862, without any commentary. Kossuth had sent it as a political guiding principle to editor Ignác Helfy with the note "quite clearly, ... as the issue is under consideration, it is not for the public." Kossuth (Torino, May 19, 1862); *Helfynek* [To Helfy], Hungarian National Archives, R. 65/6; and Kossuth, *My Documents,* VI. 1, 12-13, 23-25.

100. Kossuth, *My Documents,* VI. 1-9, 12-23.

101. The issue of the reception of the Draft has a vast bibliography. See some guidance in *Hungarian Historical Bibliography, 1825-1867,* ed. Zoltán I. Tóth (Budapest, 1950), III. 161-162, IV. ed. Gábor G. Kemény and László Katus (Budapest, 1959), 9798; Lajos Lukács, *Magyar függetlenségi és alkotmányos mozgalmak, 1949-1867* [Hungarian Movements of Independence and Constitution, 1849-1867] (Budapest, 1955), 317-323; and György Szabad, 1987, 710-713, 1630-1631.

102. *Negyvenkilencz* [Forty nine], 1866, 1/7.

103. Ibid., 1867, 5/30, 32.

104. Kossuth, *My Documents,* III. 739.

THE DIALOGUE AMONG HUNGARIAN AND ROMANIAN EXILES IN 1850–1851

AMBRUS MISKOLCZY

Even though the Hungarian–Romanian negotiations in 1850–1851 did not produce palpable results, they were more than a passing episode. These talks were important because they constituted a "clean" incident in the history of ideas. They were clean because the participants disregarded, for this time only, the compelling atmosphere and tactical maneuvers of petty politics. They engaged in both long and short term political planning at the same time. Both sides felt they were the masters of their future, and could blend the ideas of nation and freedom together into an optimal outcome. They felt their views could be better expressed without the binding concerns of current policy, which had been a liability so many times in the past. The fact that in 1848 they both had fought for their own freedom awakened the consciousness of the parties to the need for these negotiations. This was heightened by the belief of both sides that defeat was the result of outside force. As Ion Ghica wrote in 1850, the idea of unifying the two Romanian principalities had been only in the heads of a few, but "now it is on the agenda".[1] Both the Hungarians and the Romanians were convinced that a general European war was about to break out. Because they were conscious of their responsibilities and the possibilities before them, there was less ambiguity regarding any underlying intentions than a year or two before. Moreover, everything that was said in 1850–51 helped in understanding events and rhetoric from years before. How did Hungarian and Romanian exiles envision the future of their nations? Let's take a look at the chronology of events and ideas.[2]

ANTECEDENTS

The Hungarian–Romanian dialogue of 1850–1851 was a lesser-known but significant and more developed chapter of the approximately two decades of alternating Hungarian–Romanian opposition and alliances to overcome this opposition. Our story has two points of view since, depending on their respective interests, the Hungarians and the Romanians alternated in initiating negotiations. This was the world of plotting and of intrigue hidden behind the scenes of official policy and diplomacy. On the one side was the British Palmerston, who manipulated the strings of worldwide diplomacy; on the other was Mazzini, organizer of international conspiracies. The exiles of Southeastern and East Central Europe maneuvered between these two extremes, while trying to exploit any and all emerging opportunities.

It was not a coincidence that the exiles of the Polish National Liberation Movement of 1830 were the first ones to envision some sort of confederation to replace the Habsburg Empire. Its agents tried to disperse and propagate this idea. The Romanians of the Danubian Principalities tried to cooperate with the Polish exiles in Paris since already in the 1830's and 40's they viewed the Poles as examples and drew encouragement from them.[3] Mazzini also raised the issue of the Danube Confederation quite early in an article he wrote on Hungary in 1832.[4] However, the policy-makers of Western European powers would have disapproved of any alliance with him, even though national efforts to abstain from social disorder and revolutionary movements could be counted on as future potential allies. (The liberal form of government automatically had to tolerate foreigners who accepted its rules of the game.) Meanwhile, beginning in 1847, a few French political writers adopted the idea, e.g. H. Desprez, J. Ubicini and P. Bataillard. In place of the Habsburg Empire they conceived of a confederation consisting of ethnic blocs, arguing that the new order would be in the best interest of Hungarians even if it meant sacrifices for them.[5] Nicolae Bălcescu announced in 1847 to Romanian students in Paris that "our aim cannot be other than the national unity of Romanians. First, the unity of ideas and feelings; this will eventually lead to political unity."[6]

Let there be no misunderstanding: the concept of Romanian national unity was not imported. It was an inherent part of the contemporary European national unity movements. It emerged in unison with the plans for a Danubian confederation. Neither were these just simple fantasies. The concept of the confederation seemed like a guarantee of sorts that the restructuring of the region would not lead to chaos. The parties to the deal committed themselves to moderating and coordinating their national aims. The brutal law of nationalist self-centeredness could not be allowed to prevail freely.

Hungarian contemporaries were not attracted to the future described in the articles of the French and Polish journalists. They were trying to find a place for an independent Hungary within the Habsburg Empire. Their aim was a "State Alliance," as described by Miklós Wesselényi.[7] Liberal ideas were implemented with resolute pragmatism. Making use of the opportunity, they created the modern constitutional Hungary in the spring of 1848. The liberalization of the whole Empire, however, ended in failure. No program for doing this had been elaborated because it was simply impossible to do so and because there was no time left for establishing compromises. The counter-revolution striving to re-establish the centralization of the Empire skillfully exploited the transitional period.

Subsequently the policy opted for by the Hungarian government was very often judged as falling victim to its own pitfalls. It did not decide whether it wanted to compromise with Austria or not, and it did not come to terms with its relationship with its national minorities. You could say, for example, that the compromise with the Romanians would have been simple. And you could go on saying much more. The opposite could also be stated if the Romanian efforts at national unity were presented as an implacably resolute and all-defining irredentism, for which there were copious Hungarian and Romanian examples. (In a paradoxical way the spiteful Hungarian and Romanian national martyrdom did find a common denominator—the very issue of martyrdom. And both groups expressed it in the cheap publicism that quoted references from the work of historians contrary to the lessons of everyday politics; we try to show the essence of history, the way contemporaries experienced the events.)

It is to the credit of Hungarian history writing that it has provided the most thorough analysis to date of the Romanian confederative efforts of 1848.[8] It was a Hungarian historian who, in a monograph, first described Romanian national unification efforts. He did this because of the desire to mobilize against these efforts.[9] The majority of sources were by Romanian historians, but amid the atmosphere of "holy national egoism" and national-communist autarchy, these were embarrassing sources in many cases, primarily a marked anti-Russian and anti-Czar feeling. It is ironic that the most thorough analysis of the Romanian confederative efforts was hidden in the explanatory endnotes of the exemplary collection of Bălcescu's correspondence.[10]

The Wallachian revolution was prepared in Paris in the hope of a "Swiss-type" Hungarian–Romanian confederation. This was also well known in Transylvania. What this means exactly is something we ignore today and it also was not clear during 1948–49. It could not really become widely publicized because the dream was to unify the Romanians dispersed in different countries. This, however, was not something that could be disclosed because it would have led to overturning the European status quo. (It is very likely that they were following the Parisian dream of the new status quo.) The "Swiss" metaphor expressed the demand of the parties for a peaceful arrangement, for a compromise. In the midst of the ever changing transition period the Wallachian delegates did not strive to represent, at any cost, the ideas of the Spring of Nations. In April of 1848, A. T. Laurian, despite receiving a directive from Bălcescu to establish good relations with the Hungarians, tried to support a policy asserting Romanian autonomy in Transylvania, and thus acted against the Hungarian government. It is also true, though, that he wrote an article before the May crisis supporting the unification of Transylvania with Hungary, which was published only later in the summer.[11] At the time, Brătianu was conducting negotiations of sorts, although there is little of his activity in the specialized literature. Then only the innermost circle of confidants had access to the results of his trip. A. G. Golescu, his friend, provided some information on the events. He disclosed that the Hungarians rejected the confederation, alleging their own weakness as the reason. The Hungarians also cited the importance of maintaining good relations with Russia. True enough, the Hungarians also held out the prospect that "They will step in for Russia and ensure that the Turkish Porte supports the Romanians." (Russia at the time was exercising protectorate over the Romanian principalities.) The Hungarians justified their policy regarding Romanians of Hungary and Transylvania by pointing to the French policy on Alsace and Lorraine while at the same time requiring that the Transylvanian Romanians embrace anti-Croatian and anti-Serbian positions. When Brătianu explained to the Hungarian Prime Minister, Lajos Batthyány, in the presence of Lajos Mandel, the Hungarian-born envoy of the French government, that France would like to see a Polish–Hungarian–Romanian confederation,

Batthyány expressed readiness for a confederation with the Polish, but he also remarked that they would do nothing until the French army arrived.[12] The Hungarian statesmen probably did not talk about this meeting at the time since Kossuth only found out about Brătianu's visit in Pest as a delegate of the Wallachian revolution two years later.[13] In any case, the whole incident is characteristic of the primitive nature of contacts on the governmental level since, instead of achieving rapprochement, it left behind a wider gap.

Most of Hungarian public opinion and policy makers were influenced by the spiritual atmosphere of the times since they accepted the imperialist claptrap, i. e., proclaiming that the Danube Principalities should belong to the Hungarian Crown. This assertion, although not feasible, promised the possibility of breaking out of Hungary's isolation amid circumstances where everybody would, if they saw a way, present similar demands. There were several instances of declarations to this effect by loudmouthed students and even informed statesmen with realistic policy requirements as the Transylvanian Dénes Kemény and the Hungarian government delegate in Frankfurt, László Szalay. They generally claimed the rights of the Holy Crown in hopes that the Romanian Principalities would choose the historically well-trodden path in order to escape the pressure of the Czar's policy. (Consider that the feudal allegiance of Hungarian kings and Romanian voivods was always nominal, serving the interest of both parties. Furthermore, it promoted the dispersion of Western court culture.) Thus, the Hungarian endeavors of the 1840's regarding the East was an expression of the political need for a confederation of nations with some sort of historical basis rather than a greedy and naive imperialism, the hopelessness of which was quite evident to them.

Otherwise, Hungarian statesmen never made irresponsible statements. The Minister of Interior Affairs, Bertalan Szemere, wanted to secure the independence of Hungary united to Transylvania through an alliance with revolutionary Wallachia and by winning over the Romanians residing in Hungary. Lajos Kossuth, on the other hand, pointed out in August the requirements of a Hungarian–Romanian alliance and the risk of a civil war.

Hungarian imperialist propaganda was a direct result of the awareness of Hungarian weakness and of an alarming vision of the nation's death. It even wanted to mobilize the masses by overstating the threat. One tactic was to diminish the size of the Hungarian population, approximately five million at the time, to four million. The Romanians did the opposite by exaggerating their numbers, announcing that there were 8-12 million Romanians instead of the correct number of 6-7 million. A good example of overstating the threat was the case of Alecu Russo. He was arrested in Dés, on July 9, 1848, while traveling to Bukovina. He was later held in prison in Kolozsvár (Cluj) until Government Commissioner Miklós Vay set him free by a government directive.[14] Some observers emphasized his courage, while others emphasized his protest against Hungarian despotism and his wit.[15] Some noted that he condemned fake patriotism and tyranny while proclaiming freedom.[16] In any case, there was less attention paid to his letter of July 4 to Nicolae Bălcescu. Still, it was interesting because it constituted a document of Romanian imperialism—called fake patriotism by the author—awakened vis-à-vis Hungarian imperialism. A Romania stretching from the Dniester to the Tisza rivers was the vision of a generation, a dream. According to Alescu Russo the basis of Romanian imperialism was ethnicity, which was nonexistent in Hungary, itself only a name. "There are 1,500,000 and 3,000,000 renegades originating from other different nations who want to superimpose their language, laws, and customs on 4,000,000 Romanians and 8–10,000,000 Slavs and Germans." Incidentally, Russo considered that the disintegration of Hungary was inevitable. The Transylvanians disapproved the Wallachian government having sent an agent to Pest. The Hungarians must be presented with an ultimatum: "if not independence, potentially with us Romanians here, then at least recognize an independent Romanian nationality in the Bánát, Transylvania, and Hungary"—that is, territorial autonomy. Although it is true that "the Romanians here struggle with poverty and helplessness," Russo's final hope lay in the larger numbers of Romanians. And—as his phrasing suggested—he also believed in the death of the Hungarian nation.[17]

Russo's letter clearly indicated the objectives of the Romanian national policy, its reasoning, and assessment of the situation. To Russo national unity was an ideal concept, although he clearly saw that he could not yet organize a mass movement. Hopes and aspirations, planning and plotting were what characterized the political orientation. With or against the Hungarians—this was and remained the dilemma. And by what means? The Wallachian delegate A. G. Golescu directly recommended a joint armed fight with the Croatians and Serbs in his August letter. The letter was intercepted and ended up in the hands of the Hungarian government and became the basis of constant mistrust. Ioan Maiorescu, on the other hand, was against instigating rebellion by the Romanians against the Hungarians.[18] He hoped to achieve Romanian unification by diplomatic means under the protectorate of Germany—more of a nominal supervision than a real power burden on the Romanian state. In September and November of 1848 he submitted two petitions to the German Joint Ministry in Frankfurt. The latter of the two raised the issue of the exchange of population. The Hungarians should leave Transylvania and the various fractional ethnicities—Hungarian and Romanian—should trade places. The two countries, Hungary and Romania, should make full use of the advantages of the protectorate annexed to Germany.[19] At the same time, Golescu also started to campaign for the same objective. He wrote several brochures in favor of the German alliance. In the last days of September he talked in Paris to the French Minister of Foreign Affairs about a Hungaro-Czech-Croat-Romanian federation to take the place of the Habsburg Empire.[20] At the beginning of October he was already seeking opportunities for agreement with László Teleki, the Hungarian delegate to Paris.[21]

Meanwhile, Constitutional Austria also proved to be an attractive alternative to counterbalance Hungarian pressure. Due to this, military intervention commenced. The Romanian peasants of Transylvania were readily gathering to the call to arms. The pro monarchic feelings of the peasantry were not the result of political immaturity or propaganda. The service to the "good emperor" was the only legitimate formula by which, following the abolition of serfdom, the peasants could realize those aspirations they held which had fed on a "peasantry-utopia." This was a widespread model, in a specific situation, amid specific social conditions and a specific history of events, as we have shown earlier.[22] In Hungary, however, the majority of Romanian political forces tried to assert their objectives while integrated into the constitutional political scene. They found that the Hungarian government was their ally against the hegemony of the Serbs in church life.[23] Their long-term objective was Romanian national autonomy in the Banat, and perhaps Romanian national unity. This is the reason they supported the *Declaration of Independence,* in order to pressure Hungarians to fulfill Romanian requests. Meanwhile the Habsburgs wanted to unify the Romanians—including those in Bukovina—within the Empire. All of this corresponded to the usual practice of Hungarian-Romanian confrontation: the Hungarians reiterated their social preeminence, while the Romanian insisted on their numerical superiority.

A division of labor of sorts evolved among Romanian political forces in Hungary, Transylvania, and the Principalities. They all professed and tried to assert national solidarity while they often faced each other on "the barricades." The uprising and war of national liberation by Transylvanian Romanians secured the basis for the assertion of Romanian national interests. A few Wallachians represented the wider European political orientation. First, they hoped that no matter how much "advantage the imperial reactionary force achieved," Transylvania and the Banat could be disannexed from Hungary, a first step towards national unity. At the same time they also sensed the drama of the situation. For instance, Bălcescu exclaimed bitterly, "Oh! All the misfortune that ethnic feelings brought to these regions." [24] Ion Ghica shared his friend's opinion and mused whether it was "our clumsiness" or the Hungarians' "blindness or a little of both" that led to a situation where "Romanians have no other alternative but to have to choose between fighting liberal ideas or fighting their own ethnicity." Ghica also shared the view that the downfall of Hungarians was in the best interest of the Romanians' political survival.[25] The Hungarian military victories of 1849 modified this position. The proclamation of Hungarian independence on April 14 made the most decisive effect.

Romanians rightfully counted on the supporters of an independent Hungary also to embrace the idea of a confederation. Or rather, that the Hungarians would have to embrace it as the only possibility to secure their place in the European power structure. "Austrian Hungary or Romanian Hungary"–this is the choice that Hungarians have, according to Bălcescu in early July, 1849.[26]

From among the Hungarians, László Teleki was the first to enter the realm of planning a Danube Confederation. In Paris on March 7, 1849, he wrote to Kossuth that "it is not so much the Austrians that we should unite with, but with the Serbs, Croats and Wallachians." The result for him was that "our dominion would stretch all the way to the Black Sea."[27] However, he did not altogether break ties with the Habsburg Empire. Two days later László Teleki's secretary, Frigyes Szarvady, turned to the head of confederative diplomacy, Prince Adam Czartoryski, and discussed the feasibility of restructuring the "monarchy" into "an alliance of nations," into a "confederation." In the name of total equality of ethnic rights, "the Hungarian government would be ready to allow the Serbs to establish a Serbian Voivodeship." It would recognize Croatia's independence and the autonomy of Transylvania, trusting that all the people residing in Hungarian territory (which in its wider interpretation includes Croatia and Transylvania) would be joined by common interests. Thus, the entire Hungarian territory would constitute a natural unit, further strengthened by its common history.[28] Although Szarvady was quite independent, and later László Teleki parted with him, he presumably did not act totally on his own. However, it cannot be proved that the ideas he put down on paper were unequivocally those of Teleki. On the other hand, he could have written about ideas that had been discussed at least as possibilities.

On May 14, 1849, László Teleki broke with the aspirations to transform historical Hungary into an ethnically homogeneous nation. "Austria has died, but so has Saint Stephen's Hungary," he wrote to Kossuth. Actually the proposition he put forth was in the spirit of the great Hungarian King's *Admonitions*. King Stephen warned that a nation of one language and the same customs is weak and fragile. László Teleki turned away from the French nation state ideal when he dreamed about Hungary acting to realize the goals of the Great French Revolution: "The role of France in the year '89, which was the emancipation of Europe, is now our task." Because, if a new system could be established, then "the lack of ethnic unity will be supplemented by the coordination and recognition of individual and ethnic rights." That is, the Hungarian government would grant regional autonomy to the Serbs and would provide extensive county self-government to all the nationalities. The results would be that "all ethnic groups, and not only those in Hungary, but also outside our boundaries, will look at us in yearning, and will happily accept Hungary as the center and queen of a future Danubian Confederation, whose power shall forever break the monster of absolutism and which will spread from the Baltics to the Black Sea."[29] A few days later a meeting was held under the chairmanship of Czartoryski, and with the participation of László Teleki, Ferenc Pulszky, Frigyes Szarvady, and former Czech representative Rieger, on the issue of "reciprocal concessions" in Hungary and the internal transformation of the country.[30] The memorandum prepared at the meeting seemed to have made it faster into the hands of the Austrian secret police than to the desks of Hungarian statesmen.[31] The policy of the Hungarian government inevitably pointed in the direction of the plans and aspirations generated in Paris, even if László Teleki would have expected larger and faster steps to be taken.

The initiatives of the Romanian parliamentary representatives in Hungary and of the Wallachian Romanian émigrés offered a new perspective on progress on breaking the deadlock surrounding the national confrontation since their ideas were in line with the Hungarian government's efforts on social evolution and stability. Romanians could start developing the autonomy of the Orthodox Romanian Church, which signaled that Lajos Kossuth was not making empty promises when he voiced his support for respecting church self-government and freedom of language use. True enough, the mid-May pacification efforts of Ioan Dragoş ended in a tragedy resulting in the civil war escalating in the Erzgebirge. Meanwhile the Romanian exiles in Istanbul reconsidered the feasibility of All-Romanian objectives and accepted reconciliation with the Hungarians amid the civil war. Did they return to the Wallachian revolutionary policy determined in Paris? Yes, partly. Bălcescu presumed to find the following stages in the course of history: war of joint liberation by several nations; collective liberation; then the individual struggle, the fight of nations, corresponding to the class wars of the West; and finally the arrival of the "real confederation." The Romanian exiles intended to use the help of the Hungarians to liberate the Danubian Principalities and then later planned to make use of their ethnic predominance. "We have to make sacrifices in the present for the benefits of the future," he wrote to Ioan from Pest on June 6, 1849.[32]

In 1849 both parties continued where they had left off. Lajos Kossuth, in agreement with his fellow ministers, offered the Hungarian Holy Crown to the Czar's family in the beginning of August, provided that they accepted the constitutional freedom of the country.[33] However, in October in Vidin, he was already considering the prospects for a Danube Confederation. With this he entered the realm of theoretical projections. He might have been influenced by the renowned European publicist C. F. Henningsen who had been in Vidin since September, and who supposedly had earlier considered the possibility of a Danube states alliance.[34] Henningsen later became Kossuth's secretary and celebrated in him the liberating hero who united all the enemies of the Czarist Empire.[35] He also proposed that Poland, Serbia, Croatia, Hungary and Romania unite in a confederation of states called the Banda

Orientale, under the nominal protectorate of the Turkish Sultan.[36] Towards the end of October and after delivering a "long and brilliant speech" on the past and the present to the emissary of Polish exiles, the exiled Hungarian Governor described his hopes regarding the confederation.[37]

At the same time, the Romanians also made some initiatives. What is more, their plans seemed more specific. In his letter of December 25, 1849, to Bălcescu, Ion Ghica outlined the idea of some sort of a Hungarian-Romanian-Serbian "Eastern Confederation" aimed against Pan-Slavism and envisioned under the suzerainty of the Porte.[38] By the end of January, Benedek Jancsó knew the contents of Bălcescu's answer and concluded that it was Ghica who first raised the issue of the Eastern Confederation.[39] The question of who first proposed the idea was more complex than simply relating it to the inspiration or realization of a single person. As a matter of fact, Kossuth had taken some practical steps as early as January 1850. As an agent of Hungary he sent a merchant from Piemonte, by the name of G. Carosini, on a mission to Belgrade to explore the grounds for the establishment of a confederation.[40] Henningsen traveled to London where Bălcescu also soon arrived. Later he proudly announced in his letter to Ghica that he successfully organized a committee with three representatives from each of the six nations (Romania, Hungary, Poland, Russia, Czech-Moravia, and the Southern Slavs).[41] It is characteristic of the time that a contest of sorts evolved to decide who was the original author of the confederative idea since it seemed to be such an effective plan.[42] The organizational efforts, however, did not have any practical results. It is clear from the inaccurate and mutilated edition of Gyula Tanárky's memoirs that during the January 10 London meeting of the Hungarian exiles, László Teleki and György Klapka explained that "if we have to reconstitute ourselves in Hungary, why would we need to renounce our Hungarian national supremacy? Since their ethnic demands are sufficiently mature, we should provide everything that Serbs, Croatians, and Wallachians request–but not the Slovaks. Since they are not ready for it yet. We should establish a federative state with the Hungarians as *natural* and not superimposed leaders since they are the most developed of all, politically, numerically, and in terms of their character."[43]

In March Ghica prepared what he called a Memorandum, which was rather just a note, and which he sent to Kossuth. He addressed Kossuth as the person whose name was "synonymous with future success," and whose hands operated the "lever" to rejuvenate political life. The value of Ghica's letter lay in the fact that it reflected the dilemma of Romanian policy: "the Romanian people only respond to two concepts, religion and ethnicity. The first one channels us directly to the Russians since in policy, just as in physics, the law of nature prevails and the larger mass attracts the smaller. It is very probable that the nationality concept, both in its present and its extreme future form, shall surpass our objectives. This, however, is the only one capable of saving us, or you, or all of Europe. After victory reaction could follow and then it would be easy to eliminate the dangerous and maleficent character of this idea." This was the contribution that Ghica wished to make when he offered to express, on a regular basis, his opinion on the Hungarian–Romanian confrontation to Kossuth.[44]

Probably Ion Ghica was the author of the 1850 handwritten bulletin of the exiles, the one and only copy of which that has been found was part of his estate. This is an important document of the political "opening." It was with great satisfaction that he acknowledged, in the May 5 *Bulletin,* that the Hungarian General recognized the impossible oppression by Historical Hungary on the Romanian and Slavic peoples, even if the Hungarians were not on the right road yet. In their writings of Kiutahia, they talked about a confederation of five parts: 1) Croatia, Dalmatia, Illyria and the Serb Voivode of Turkey all constituting one state, 2) the united Czechland and Moravia, 3) Poland, before its partitioning, 4) the united Wallachia and Moldavia, and 5) Hungary. On the other hand, Ghica did not only ponder in the May 25 issue of the *Bulletin*, whether Romanian participation in the unification project was to the benefit (or loss) of Austria or Turkey, but he also reinterpreted the 1848 tradition in a Hungary-friendly way. In the June 5 issue he wrote, "From all Romanians, the luckiest are those originating from the so-called 'clean' Hungary because, even though they fought for a foreign cause, as did the Transylvanians or the people from the Banat, they at least fought for the liberation of a nation or fought under Bem and Dembinski on the fronts in their disciplined battalions. The 16 Romanian battalions are treasures for the Romanian Nation. Austria may draft them today, but he who once fought for liberty cannot be loyal to oppression."[45]

The Ghica-type thorough discussion never materialized. Bălcescu continued to play the key role in Hungarian–Romanian negotiations.

When Ghica was describing his ideas, Nicolae Bălcescu was still under the spell of the euphoria of unlimited possibilities. On March 4 he wrote to A. G. Golescu that the union of the two Danube Principalities was a "fact." The Austrian Romanians will also "unite into an ethnic mass of three and a half million." And the two Romanian blocs will inevitably merge. Thus, "our Romania shall live." And "You have to be blind not to see it." With the help of Austria and Turkey, or against them, he argued. "The enlightened Hungarians do not oppose it any longer and they are happy to pay this price to live in one confederation with us."[46] Unfortunately, the plan for an "Austrian Romania" soon failed and they had to find new Hungarian partners for their negotiations. On April 6, 1850, Bălcescu wrote to Ghica from Paris that he approved of Ghica's letter to Kossuth but that the negotiations with Kossuth were in vain because he obstinately stood by his ideas. On the other hand, Bălcescu thought, Teleki and Klapka would look upon the Romanian plans favorably. The "United States of the Danube" would constitute three nations, three territories, and three administrations: Hungarian, Romanian and Southern Slav. When it comes to dividing up the territory, the majority of the county population should be the norm. The minority, if significant, shall receive linguistic, religious, and municipal guarantees. The Danube Confederation should unite the Hungarian Kingdom, Bukovina, Moldavia, Wallachia, Serbia, and Bessarabia. The Federal Assembly should have 150 representatives, with each nationality delegating 50 representatives. The official working language would be German or French or other. Every year the Federal Assembly would elect a three-member government, with joint Ministers for Foreign Affairs, National Defense, Trade, and Transportation.[47]

In the meantime, Bălcescu's investigations analyzing the events of the revolution amalgamated into a vision of the apocalyptic struggle between Good and Evil, with him putting his full trust into Divine Providence and the cleansing power of suffering.[48] However, less than a year had elapsed before Bălcescu addressed the leaders of the Hungarian exiles in Paris (in February 1851) with his plans for confederation. Bălcescu could not really tell them more about the alliance of nations than he had before, but he did give a somewhat more precise definition of the scope of power of the joint Ministers indicating that the Minister of Trade would also have the Financial portfolio and that Internal affairs would be outside the scope of the federal government. Also it is of importance that the Danube state, with a population of 22 million, was to be modeled after Switzerland and the United States. It provides a better grasp to understand what his contemporaries meant by Swiss and American models. Much of the few page treatise was a historical and political exposition. Three ideas should be pointed out: legitimizing the new confederation of states, interpretation of history, and the need to normalize Hungarian–Romanian relations.

The legitimizing concept is obviously the ethnic nation. This "is the most developed and perfect form of the life of an ethnicity, often surviving independence, and is the only one capable of winning it back again. It is the ultimate legitimization of nations." Its significance was well reflected in the near past. The Hungarians had heroically fought with the Austrians for their national independence while still denying it to other nationalities in Hungary, who, on the other hand, held a promise from Austria that they would get what they want, that is the recognition of their own nationalities.

The historical approach was correspondingly nationality-centered. The Hungarians were unable to assimilate the nations they conquered and they could not be assimilated either. Thus, both sides still stood facing each other just as they had a thousand years ago. Hungarians treated the Romanians the worst since they fought with the most persistence. The three Transylvanian feudal nations, Hungarians, Saxons, and Széklers *(Székelys),* were in close alliance against the Romanians, thus dishonoring their name even in their laws. In 1784 the Romanians started a revolutionary movement. Although their luck soon abandoned them, their belief in their nation lived on. In 1848 when the Transylvanian Diet united with Hungary without the prior consent of the Romanians, it ignited a cruel war. The solution to all this is federation and the equality of nationalities.

Hungary should accept this. "It seems to me that the Hungarians would misunderstand our intentions if they interpreted the separation of the three nations as the dismemberment of Hungary. This separation is necessary because it is the only alternative satisfying the instincts of ethnic nations. Furthermore, this separation is more fictional than realistic since the three nations are destined to share the same political existence, following the model of Switzerland and the United States. And finally, under the present circumstances this can only benefit Hungary because it makes survival possible and because it contributes to the development of the federal state, with the Romanians joining from the Principalities." Yes, it was true that the Turkish Porte would not be very happy to lose its protectorate of the Principalities. However, "we represent a revolutionary position and postulate a Europe-wide revolution and in this case the Romanian people must decide their fate by themselves." It was essential for the Romanians from the Principalities to join for it would finalize Romanian unity and, lacking it, the development of the federated state would be hindered.[49]

Bălcescu's plan clarifies the puzzling answer he gave to Kossuth at the end of May 1849 when the Hungarian Governor accused the Romanians of harboring Daco-Roman aspirations. Bălcescu said "rather than tearing Transylvania away from Hungary, we wanted to unite the two. Actually, we even wanted to do more for Hungary."[50] Since time was running out, there was no opportunity for a thorough discussion. But in May 1849, even though they were getting ready for an approaching war, the proposal had to be answered. All the more so since, in the meantime an unprecedented ferocious debate broke out among the Hungarian exiles. There had been arguments before in Hungarian public life, but this time two of the most committed personalities of national liberation and democracy turned against each other, Lajos Kossuth and László Teleki (with Bertalan Szemere also expressing his opinion). This time they tried to clear the controversy with lengthy written exposés, although in the past such sensitive issues had been resolved orally. It was a case of friendly and loyal discussion, but at the same time it also constituted a real intellectual duel. [51]

The Teleki–Kossuth dispute had started in Paris in 1849 perhaps even without László Teleki, the initiator, fully recognizing what he had unleashed. Imre Deák, a researcher of the dispute, thinks that Teleki came to the conclusion that his earlier discussions were unsuccessful. He no longer believed in the salvation of the confederation and consequently forewarned Kossuth that the plan of confederation under the protectorate of the Porte was not expedient.[52] On January 26, 1850, Teleki asked Kossuth to write "of the latest events in Hungary." Since "you are the greatest man in Europe, (...) the leaders of Hungary will always gather around you. But foreign countries should be informed of the idea Hungary represents–the idea of Liberty, the idea of constitutional order–and not the idea of revolution. This should be made public to the whole world, and you are the only person capable of doing it. Only you can tell the different nationalities that Hungary has been just to all nationalities since it has planned to establish a federation and has never demanded supremacy over other nationalities and will never vindicate it in the future." Teleki believed that Kossuth should write about it and should give permission to Teleki and his circle to apply stylistic changes and even omissions.[53] Teleki then explained his ideas to Kázmér Batthyány, sending them on to Kossuth. This is how Kossuth came to have an inciting ally in his friend László Teleki.[54] In his response of June 15, 1850, Kossuth described in the greatest detail his position on the Danube Confederation or, as he called it, the confederation "of northeastern free allied states." Since he did not prohibit the publication of this piece of writing, his words received a special emphasis.

Kossuth was driven by the conviction that he couldn't make any further compromise for the benefit of "the motherland and freedom." He could only lead the liberating fight as a dictator and, if they did not want to follow his route, he would still continue on his own way. His course of action originated from the county and parliamentary life of the reform era. For him the future lay in the confederation with neighboring nations, the potential guarantee of real freedom. His solution was not the French type centralized system, but rather a system of counties. "I see the idea of federation in its popular implementation: this is how it becomes feasible for the internal organization of my country." When he explained that "theory is a building and practice provides the base," the practical side or "practical experience" he refers to was actually inspirations which he drew from the Hungarian past and American present. The leading force in Hungary, the aristocracy, both culturally and politically assimilated the non-Hungarian elements of the society and also captivated the urban world. This was all done by the integrating power of political freedom and not by force. If language is the basis of a nation, it will have a disintegrating effect. Language is not the basis in America. Hungary would also become a Babel impossible to govern if the linguistically defined nation became the state-making standard and equality of rights for the linguistic nations was introduced. "Territory and not language can and should be the basis for government." If the Serbian Voivodine were established, the Serb nation would rule over all the others. Nationality, then, is similar to religion–it can only be one of the many factors that constitute a state. A country, however, cannot be organized solely on this one basis.

The ultimate value is freedom since it guarantees everything else. Instead of erecting a wall in defense against Russian imperial aspirations, Austria became the "servant of the Russians, their vanguard." This is why "smaller nations can only secure their political existence and their national autonomy and independence by establishing a close federation with each other." Therefore "this confederative idea was sent by Heavenly Providence, so evidently present in molding events, and destined it to be the only salvation for Europe." This is what can save small Slavic nations from Pan-Slavism and will counterbalance the isolation of Hungarians and Romanians.

At the beginning of the letter the concepts of federation and confederation are blurred into one idea in Kossuth's mind. In this case he used them synonymously. He might have done this to illustrate the absurdity of federalizing the country. A year earlier he argued that the Transylvanian Romanians "may have a hazy concept of federation before their eyes. Hungary can be in a federation with Wallachia, Serbia, etc. But Hungary cannot be in federation with itself, i.e. with its own citizens. This is nonsense."[55] This time he tried to satisfy the demand for an internal federation by a comprehensive system of county autonomy or "municipalism" while trying to keep it in line with the need for a unified state. Simultaneously, state federation ties also stressed this harmony. "For it is undeniable that only the nationality that has a secure political existence can be considered safe. And this confederation would guarantee political existence on their own political territories for Czech, Polish, Wallachian, Serb, Slav, Croatian, Dalmatian, and Hungarian nationalities. Not only would it guarantee their nationality, but given the confederate ties, it would also assure that the Wallachians, Serbs, and Slovaks living in Hungary or the Hungarians living in Moldavia can find support in the civic development of their nationalities and thus will never again have to fear absorption."

Kossuth's concept was based on some shaky ground. It took for granted a considerable self-restraint on behalf of the leaders of non-Hungarian national movements, something which even Kossuth could not have honestly accepted in their place, especially if the pressure of the circumstances were less accommodating. The majority of Hungarian public opinion might have accepted it if they seriously considered all the potential consequences of realigning the country's borders. On the other hand, Kossuth's vision also promised a future of peaceful development–the harmony of bourgeois development and the surmounting of national differences via everyday compromises. It was a positive utopia in comparison to the threat of national and social wars of extermination. This is why Kossuth emphasized that if one thought that Kossuth's ideas "are not satisfactory, then he does not want freedom and rather wishes for the disappearance of Hungarians. And if this is one's goal, he shall find an enemy in me even if we were born from under the same heart."[56] This was from the work of a politician who had already been confronted with Hungarian public opinion, but who, as a representative of public views, could also be merciless with his comrades of yesterday. He even publicized the first such case. He bitterly remembered his isolation in 1841 when he proposed that if Croatia did not want to have state ties with Hungary, it should become totally independent. The second case he always kept silent about. On June 18, 1848, his good friend Miklós Wesselényi, who even stood by him against István Széchenyi, wrote him a letter in which he raised the issue of giving up the historic borders of the country and the establishment of a more homogeneous Hungarian national state through population exchange. The letter was written to Gábor Klauzál, but Kossuth must have read it since it ended up with his documents. They must have discussed the matter also since the Transylvanian press alluded to the idea.[57] As a consequence, the former "disciple" never wanted to see his idol again. And it was Kossuth who stressed to László Teleki the differences in their viewpoints, namely that Wesselényi's proposal endangered the existence of the Hungarian nation. It is not clear, however, whether their views differed all that sharply then and there.

The letter from Teleki urging a discussion and clarification of differences was lost. We can reconstruct his viewpoint and his reproaches from Kossuth's response and from an earlier comment he wrote down the same day. While Kossuth acted as a realistic politician believing only in the driving force of interest, Teleki believed in the universal nature of freedom and that differences could be surmounted. Ignorant sophistry and bad words said in Paris were insults to him, while good words brought salvation. The 1848 Minister of Foreign Affairs, Bastide, explained to him that the Hungarians, as a catholic Slav tribe (sic), should stand in the forefront of the liberation of the Slavic peoples.[58] However, Teleki might consider it to his credit that Victor Hugo abandoned his anti-Hungarian course. He would remember forever that he could call the great French writer his compatriot. Hugo told him that "the *common idea* is a common motherland!" This is why László

Teleki could truthfully write, in his letter to Victor Hugo on January 29, 1850, that he had found his lost motherland in the great writer's words.[59] At the same time he also believed in the cleansing power of self-criticism. He wanted an internal federation. "We have to agree that the Wallachian from Transylvania should also see his nationality secured. What we want to do for the Serbs, why don't we do it for the Wallachians as well?" He blamed Kossuth for his "Werbőczy-type Hungarian supremacy" and believed that "maintaining a historic counter-revolutionary platform against Slavs and Wallachians is an impossible contradiction."[60] But it was due to Kossuth's detailed response, intended as a potentially public document, which stimulated him to clarify his own ideas. (He confessed to Kossuth at the end of June and early July.)[61] Teleki opposed dictatorship. As for his ideas on the nationality issue: the problem cannot be solved "by the stroke of the pen." Otherwise, he mused that "the difference of opinion in our case is not too big in the matter of nationalities. I believe that besides the communal, county, jurisdictional, church, and schooling concessions, the Wallachians and Serbs should also have permission to form a provincial assembly so that they can decide their own internal matters, in compliance with existing regulations. For this is the collective national life that the Serbs and Wallachians covet. The ties between the government and their legislation would still be in place. And in the delimitation of Voivodina and the Wallachian regions, one should ensure where possible that other nationalities do not fall under Serbian or Wallachian rule. This would not be as difficult as it might seem since this is not the delimitation of two independent countries. Therefore, completely surrounding all the territories is not required. We all remember what Felső-Fehér (Upper-White) county was like. Still administration was not overtly difficult there."[62]

László Teleki was right: the gap between his and Kossuth's vision was not all that wide. He did not want the dissolution of Hungary either. Nevertheless, by recognizing the legitimacy of establishing regional autonomies, he also recognized ethnicity as a legitimate component of power policy. This, in Kossuth's view, endangered the interest and even the existence of the Hungarian nation. For there was one thing Kossuth did not accept—the ethnic principle, i. e., that national-ethnic affiliation would be the principle of state legitimization, as opposed to "history" and the people's sovereignty. In his August 22 response, Kossuth even mentioned "the equality of rights of the nationalities," a detested Austrian formula. He did not use it in the same sense as the Austrians did, however. They used it as a state legitimizing concept while Kossuth never took it very seriously for it proved to be inapplicable under the circumstances Hungary faced. At the same time Kossuth's argument relied on the functional capacity of the state. He considered that even the Austrian system was better than the dismemberment of the country because that system would leave Hungary with a larger territory. And the "idea of territory is decisive. It is the container, in the absence of which the life fluid of a state will not come to boil." Correspondingly, Kossuth wrote, "I want a *territory* for Hungary, and on this territory I want equality for every nationality under the protection of common justice, common freedom, and common laws."[63]

Meanwhile the Kossuth–Teleki debate was further expanded by Ioan Eliade Rădulescu joining in. Rădulescu addressed a letter to the former Governor in mid-August 1850. The letter has been lost and the little we know about it is from Kossuth's comments. Rădulescu also turned to László Teleki roughly at the same time, but no exchange of views took place and Teleki responded with "total generalities" "on behalf of Kossuth."[64]

The Romanian exile's letter did not carry any weight since he had turned against the majority of the Romanian exiles, and wherever he could, he would vilify them as selfish and irresponsible Russian agents. Incidentally, Rădulescu also proclaimed and promulgated the idea of Romanian national unity. However, in his proclamation of December 1849 to his fellow exiles, he denied having Daco-Roman unity aspirations saying that the whole idea had been invented by St. Petersburg propaganda so that they could represent the Romanians as "fools" and "dreaming children" who dissolved peace. He assumed that the big goal, a strong Romania, would be realized by time and circumstances. Language connects nations much more anyway. Notice that the Hungarians also constitute a nation, while being divided by religion.[65] At the same time he believed that he would find the way to a strong Romania more easily than his contemporaries if he separated himself from them. Supposedly he offered Sándor Karacsay, an unrelenting advocate of Hungarian nationality issues, the annexation of two Danubian Principalities and Bessarabia to Hungary. On one hand, Rădulescu was aware of the fact that some politicians had been toying with the claims of the Hungarian Crown and thus wanted "to dangle a carrot in front of the donkey." On the other hand, the medieval Hungarian suzerainty, which would have observed the internal autonomy of the principalities and would have maintained equality rather than subordination, could have served as a legal ground to fend off Russian influence, based as it was on power relations.[66] Moreover, Rădulescu wanted to persuade Kossuth to join the Ligue des Peuples. The letter did not make a big impact on Kossuth, although he extensively expounded on his views of Romanian politics in his letter to Teleki of September 18, 1850. He did not believe Rădulescu's claim that it was a fabrication of Russian foreign policy that the Romanians aspired for a national unity and for "a Daco-Roman Empire." The Russians did this, according to Rădulescu, in order to discredit the Romanian revolution and impress the western powers enough to intervene. According to Kossuth, unity was, in fact, true "because it is the natural instinct of every nation to strive for complete independence as a final goal. This condition is existential and relies on the national past. This instinct cannot be eradicated." Kossuth considered the Wallachians' Transylvanian propaganda for unity natural and realistic. He believed that Transylvanian developments were the results of mass revolt directed from the top. "The mass rose up, with no conscious goal, because that is what their leaders, who found old hatred in the flammable bosoms of the masses and the memory of past oppression, wanted and, thus, they exploited the predatory desire." The Romanian leaders wanted "to use" the Austrians. They wanted to establish a Transylvanian-Banat "province" which would be united with the principalities in the future. As for any reconciliation of differences, Kossuth believed in equal rights for every nationality in the state, but not to the detriment of the state or beyond the state–as Kossuth explained in German in order to emphasize the verbal similarity and practical differences between the Hungarian and Austrian concepts.[67] Truly, while the constitution which looked so good on paper did not have deep intellectual and practical antecedents, Kossuthian politics were rooted in the Hungarian constitutional development.

Paradoxically, it was Teleki who advocated St. Stephen's principle and the Werbőczy constitution. Teleki did not discard old legal relations as Kossuth did. Kossuth accepted the idea of boundaries being laid out by ethnic lines. Teleki, however, brought up the example of Felső-Fehér county which was already considered an economic impossibility by contemporaries. Felső-Fehér county included a dozen separate areas which looked like an archipelago on a colored map. According to evaluations based on practices of past years, Teleki's idea would be considered a feudal remnant. However, such a use of historical experiences and traditions was a rather western trait. It was obvious that the effectively working feudal system of old Hungary had a great influence on Teleki. All his life the past accompanied him, as his letter to his sister indicates: "I love Transylvania. My memory always shows it in golden colors. I spent there the brightest period of my life....Everything is so dreadfully far from me; still sometimes it feels like yesterday."[68] He also was affected by the memory of his first political experiences. In the Reform Era Romanian Boyars of the Fogaras region faithfully elected him as their deputy to the Diet.[69] This experience obviously affected Teleki's views of Hungarian–Romanian interethnic relations and his trust that even non-Hungarians would stay loyal to Hungary. By emphasizing it he wanted to put an end to his dispute with Kossuth. On September 27 he diplomatically noted, "Whether we accept what you want or what I propose, we will not achieve any result. Knowing the influential members of different nationalities in Hungary, for the present, none of the plans would satisfy them." He did not see any sense in making constitutional drafts and "we do not have the right either. If Hungary ever has a future, my wish would be that instead of any constitution we declare one principle–the principle of universal suffrage–and I would subordinate everything to that. Despite the Austrian tyranny, 10 million people declared themselves Hungarian in Hungary, so this principle is not dangerous for our nationality."[70] Consequently, the basis of his optimism was the belief that in the Census the majority (more than two thirds) of the population claimed Hungarian nationality. (It is unclear how this idea was born, but it is included even in slightly anti-Hungarian works.[71]) At the same time the Paris atmosphere, meaning the need for democracy, had a stimulating effect on him, not to speak about the fact, not mentioned in his letters, that he became an active free-mason.[72]

The language and the needs of the contemporary democratic press were mediated to Teleki by his secretary, Frigyes Szarvady. One of the sneaky Austrian informers obviously exaggerated when he found Szarvady intellectually more significant,[73] but the fact is that the secretary moved more around in the world of the press and was more affected by the democratic environment than his boss. That is why, early in 1850, he turned to Kossuth and asked his views about the nationality question. Szarvady sounded as if he had vulgarized Teleki's views when he said, "We have to promise much, as much as each nationality wants. I believe that a nation that has written so much on the sheets of history as ours, that has produced organizational talents, constitutional maturity, so much dedication for liberty, and unparalleled heroism like Árpád's people, should not fear for her natural supremacy, not even after granting the greatest concessions."[74] We do not know what views Szarvady professed after he broke with Teleki and frittered away his talent in an undignified way amid the personal grind of the exiles. We have quoted Szarvady in order to outline Teleki's views as translated into the language of daily propaganda.

László Teleki's and Lajos Kossuth's direct dialogue terminated with the letter of September 17. Their differences, which surfaced in connection with the nationality question, were still discussed and debated among the Hungarian exiles. In the question of a close alliance with Turkey, Teleki's rejection was accepted and Kossuth's flexibility was not appreciated. As Dániel Irányi, a true and devoted follower of Kossuth, wrote, the ex-governor "indicates grouping the Central European federation around Istambul."[75] However, in the question of territorial integrity, the majority agreed with Kossuth. According to sources, Bertalan Szemere and György Klapka's positions were similar to Teleki's, although it is unknown whether they ever expressed them. Further on, Bertalan Szemere's change of view will be mentioned. Sándor Karacsay justly characterized Szemere as "this man is a whole labyrinth."[76] Klapka compiled a program which was flatly refused by Gyula Andrássy in his letter of April 16. Andrássy wrote to him fair and square that he did not see any sense in pursuing theoretical debates about the constitutional form of the state since the Hungarians would fight for old Hungary and under those circumstances a constitutional assembly would only cause problems. "As far as the equality of nationalities is concerned, either the issue is irrelevant as nobody wants their inequality or it means what Szemere told me–which is the exact opposite of your views–dismemberment of Hungary."[77] (Klapka learned a lot from this letter because in his book published both in French and German, he expressed only cautious and general sympathy towards the Danubian Confederation.[78])

László Teleki, however, really proved to be a diplomat, even if it wore out his nerves. Perhaps in his correspondence with Kossuth he avoided verbal duels. However, in his letter he did not conceal the fact that he could not reconcile with Kossuth's or, as he wrote with aristocratic superiority, with Lajcsi's dictatorship, attitude, and manners. Something might have leaked out about the disharmony between them since Bălcescu, according to his letter of February 17, 1851, hastened to compile his draft requested by the Hungarian Exiles' Committee in Paris in order to foreclose Kossuth's objection. Bălcescu hoped that "Klapka and Teleki are close in theoretical issues" to him.[79] None of them discussed the Bălcescu Draft; at least there is no source relating to it. Although according to Sebő Vukovics's letter to Kossuth on March 6, 1851, Teleki supposedly had asked the Romanian politician whether he would inform them about his "federative and nationality ideas."[80] When the draft was complete, Vukovics thoroughly analyzed it.

The Greek-Orthodox Sebő Vukovics, of Serbian origin but who learned to speak Hungarian in his adolescence, was an example of spontaneous assimilation that sometimes took place especially among those incorporated into Hungarian national nobility. He was an enlightened liberal who, at the age of 20, commented that "our religion is a very dumb religion." In his view, Catholicism was obscure and Protestantism was "the simplest and most natural" religion. Consequently, he would be delighted if the Romanians converted to Protestantism as well.[81] Later, as a dedicated representative of Hungarian liberalism, Vukovics became a government commissioner and a year later a minister. Until the end of his life he remained Kossuth's follower and admirer. Vukovics was a practical politician who understood the techniques of county and state bureaucracy. He also knew how to take a person to task–even though he always tried to overcome internal conflicts. On August 14, 1850, he wrote to Kossuth straightforwardly that it was not wise for Kossuth to publish his letter to Teleki about the confederation. It would only encourage the enemy because it would verify the belief of some that "the idea of an independent Hungary was a chimera." In confederations, decisions about common matters are made in common, and so fellow-countries "would form a majority against Hungarian interests. To awaken nationalities of the country to demand separate rights, now that everybody is united in the desire to throw off the Austrian yoke and honestly wish for the unity and independence of Hungary, would be to destroy the country's unity, instead of to stabilize it." If the time comes that "we will have to find salvation in the confederation, then your plan will be a secure foundation to acquire the alliance of neighboring peoples in harmony with the interest of our country."[82]

Vukovics wanted to appease rather than reinforce antagonisms and it was an appeasing tone he used in writing to Kossuth in January 1851. Accepting universal suffrage would "exclude any preliminary discord."[83] It was a hopeful sign that at the end of Vukovics' letters to Kossuth the ailing László Teleki also added some lines. However, once again the Hungarian exiles quarreled, this time upon receiving Bălcescu's letter. In his letter to Kossuth on March 6, 1851, Vukovics claimed the draft to be a post hoc condemnation of the Hungarian War of Independence and indicated an interest in the dismemberment of the country. "A Hungarian will never feel the urge to revolt for something like that."[84]

Within ten days, on March 17, 1851, Sebő Vukovics presented a detailed analysis of the Bălcescu Draft for Kossuth. The analysis could be considered a reception of Kossuthian ideas and a starting point for their future interpretation. Vukovics stated two basic principles for the near future: (1) independence for Hungary, and (2) "complete democratic freedom with respect to politics, nationality, and religion." Vukovics insisted on the unity of historical Hungary. Therefore he did not give up Transylvania but did acknowledge the independence of Croatia, and proposed the establishment of a Serbian Voivodeship of Szerémség (Srem) within Croatia. Instead of a confederation he proposed an alliance with the neighboring Danubian states, obviously vis-à-vis Austria. Vukovics subordinated the nationality question to the issue of universal suffrage while "not keeping up any supremacy for the Hungarian nationality." Since the "central power" would decide only in national affairs, county autonomy could satisfy nationality claims. The official language in national affairs would be decided by the state, in county affairs by the county, and in municipal affairs by the community. Vukovics contested Bălcescu's view of history and the proposals he made. He objected that certain of Bălcescu's details about the federation were obscure and objected to the fact that it "does not present any views on the nationality dissonance." For Vukovics, the idea of unity of the country was a force that mobilized non-Hungarians as well, saying that the concept of homeland "is more forceful than the concept of nationality." In his experience during the War of Self-defense and Independence "the call of the homeland was able to mobilize non-Hungarian speaking people as well. However, we could not have mobilized for the idea of nationality." Hungarians did not fight for their nationality "because nobody contested that." Germans, Slovaks, Romanians also did not fight for the Hungarian nationality or for their own; "all of them fought for the homeland." He claimed that more than 80% of the population "adhered to the territorial integrity of the country." If there were any doubt, the first national assembly, convened on the basis of universal suffrage, could decide. For Vukovics, this loyalty is the reason that "the strength of our nation is greater than its proportion of the population." A further weakness of Bălcescu's draft, according to Vukovics, is that his solution would not be "national equality, but the establishment of supremacy of three nations in separate territories." These were areas with mixed population. Consequently, if they were consistent with their plans of territorial demarcation, the areas of the new countries would be mosaic-like, giving birth to "real monsters."[85] The latter argument was directed not only to Bălcescu but also to László Teleki, who had earlier informed Kossuth that he did not fully share Vukovics' opinion and hoped that "from this respect we will be able to reconcile our views."[86]

Vukovics was the most practical politician among the Paris exiles. He probably truly believed that the Transylvanian Romanians were instigated by Imperial agitators. Also, he slightly exaggerated when he described the fighting spirit of the people of the country. But his statements were based on facts as subsequent events demonstrated. The anti-Hungarian Romanian national movement did not develop among the Máramaros (Maramureş) and Bihar (Bihor) Romanians; the Slovaks were successfully recruited into the army; the majority of the Banat Romanians also complied with Hungarian policy, albeit due to Serbian pressure; the Germans enthusiastically lined up behind Hungarian policy; and when the Transylvanian Romanians were recruited into the Hungarian army, they did not desert but instead fought valiantly. When Bălcescu's plan was discussed, it was probably Vukovics whose opinion made a difference. Besides László Teleki, Vukovics also disagreed with his ex-Prime Minister, Bertalan Szemere, because Szemere "fully agrees" with Teleki whose views "mostly agree with Bălcescu's propositions," Vukovics wrote to Kossuth. Contrary to that, "with slight differences the majority, namely Klapka, Andrássy, Czecz and Gorove, agree with me with regards to the unity and the territory of the country."[87]

There was nothing else left for Teleki to do but to write a polite and evasive response to Nicolae Bălcescu on March 22.[88] This was despite the fact that he did not agree with Vukovics. How exactly these disputes took place or what questions they discussed, we do not know. Most probably they debated the principle of whether nationality legitimizes political aspirations or not and, if yes, to what degree. On April 7 Teleki was so quick at informing Kossuth that he did not have time to review the note and did not put the accent marks at all the places needed. "There are many things in Bălcescu's letter that cannot be supported," he wrote. "We, that is Szemere and I, can support him, as I already mentioned it in my previous letters, as long as we consider the confederative solution the most advantageous for Hungary. Otherwise I managed to respond to Bălcescu in the way we all agreed, in which we say that we want to apply the principles of freedom, equality, and fraternity both to individuals and nationalities. And, we cannot settle on the system we consider the most advantageous without learning about the wishes and views of the absent members of the exiles, first of all those who have acquired a lot of influence on the public and on the future of Hungary." Teleki especially emphasized that they would not let the disagreements among the Hungarian exiles be leaked out. He considered the national question the most important and reckoned so strongly that a general European war would happen that he wanted a decision by any means. "Even if we choose the path of supremacy, although I am convinced that its is harmful for our nation, it is much better than not choosing anything."[89]

It is characteristic of the way information spread in those days that on July 24 Ferenc Pulszky, whom László Teleki came quickly to oppose, informed Kossuth that the "Parisians...presented half of the country to the Wallachians and the Serbs, obviously only on paper. And finally, Andrássy took a stand against this matter."[90] Gyula Andrássy reported to Kossuth earlier, on May 7, that after they had received "Bălcescu's memoir, which dismembered our poor Hungarian homeland," they were in a definitely "unpleasant situation" because "his impossible demands still found a few supporters among us. But we soon put an end to this abnormal situation. Latzi (Teleki), seeing how unpopular he has become among us because of his ideas, which are well-known to you, agreed with some of us that we will not allow the negotiations to shift over to territorial issues. He was adamant that we should promise to the Wallachians that they will be able to speak their own language in Parliament and we did not find a big problem with that." Andrássy and his followers emphasized that their opinions were private and could not speak for Kossuth and the others.

Kossuth's response to the questions raised during the Hungarian-Romanian discussions was his constitutional draft–"The most palpable Hungarian draft of the 19th century...for a bourgeois democratic restructuring of Hungary's government structure."[91] Later negotiations developed as recounted above. When the need to live with real life possibilities occurred, then personal conflicts were pushed into the background and service and solidarity with the Hungarian nation again came to the foreground.

NOTES

1. N. Georgescu-Tistu, *Ion Ghica scriitorul* (Bucureşti, 1935), 129.

2. For the early period of the exile, Endre Kovács, *A Kossuth-emigráció és az európai szabadságmozgalmak* [The Kossuth Exile and the European Freedom Movements] (Budapest, 1967); Lajos Lukács, *Magyar politikai emigráció 1849–1867* [Hungarian Political Exile, 1849–1867] (Budapest, 1984); Béla Borsi-Kálmán, *Nemzetfogalom és nemzetstratégiák* [Nation Theory and National Strategies] (Budapest, 1993).

3. Ambrus Miskolczy, A román nemzeti egység kérdése és az 1840-i havaselvi forradalmi mozgalom [The Issue of Romanian National Unity and the 1840 Wallachian Revolutionary Movement] (*Századok,* 1973), 2.

4. Magda Jászay, *Mazzini* (Budapest, 1977), 201.

5. Olimpius Boitos, Paul Bataillard et la Révolution roumaine de 1848 (*Mélanges de l'École Roumaine en France,* 1929, II); *Raporturile romanilor cu Ledru-Rollin si radicalii francezi* (Bucureşti, 1940); Cornelia Bodea, *Lupta romanilor pentru unitatea nationala 1834–1849* (Bucureşti, 1967), 95–118; Dan Berindei, *Românii si Europa* (Bucureşti, 1991); N. Isar, *Publicisti francezi si cauza romana 1834–1859* (Bucureşti, 1991).

6. Bodea, 87.

7. Miklós Wesselényi, *Szózat a magyar és a szláv nemzetiség ügyében* [Manifesto Concerning Hungarian and Slav Nationalities] (Lipcse, 1843).

8. Zoltán I. Tóth, *Magyarok és románok* [Hungarians and Romanians] (Budapest, 1966).

9. Benedek Jancsó, *Szabadságharczunk s a dako-román törekvések* [Our War of Independence and the Daco-Roman Aspirations] (Budapest, 1895).

10. N. Bălcescu, *Opere, IV.* ed., George Zane (Bucureşti, 1964).

11. Ambrus Miskolczy, Erdély a forradalomban és szabadságharcban [Transylvania in the Revolution and the War of Independence], in *Erdély története III.* [History of Transylvania III], editor-in-chief, Béla Köpeczi (Budapest, 1987), 1363.

12. Ambrus Miskolczy, *Dumitru Brătianu pesti küldetése* [Dumitru Brătianu's Pest Mission], in manuscript.

13. Zoltán I. Tóth, *Magyarok és románok* [Hungarians and Romanians] (Budapest, 1966), 264; István Hajnal, *A Batthyány-kormány külpolitikája* [The Foreign Policy of the Batthyány Government] (Budapest, 1987), 99.

14. Mária Magyaródi, Contributii documentare la cuuoasterea vietii si activitatii revolutionare a lui Alecu Russo in Transilvania anului 1848. (*Studia Universitatis Babes-Bolyai.* Sectio philosophica, 1966), 2.

15. Cornel Regman, *Nu numai despre critici* (Bucureşti, 1990), 47.

16. Al Dima, *Alecu Russo* (Bucureşti, 1957), 106.

17. B.A.R. S36-LXIV. The original French text is published with a few misleading errors: Petre V. Hanes, *Alexandru Russo* (Bucureşti, 1930), 174-176; and in good Romanian translation: *Al Russo: Scrieri postume*, 141-143.

18. N. Banescu and V. Mihailescu, *Ioan Maiorescu* (Bucureşti, 1912). 220.

19. Ion Ghica, *Amintiri din pribegia dupa 1848, I.* (Craiova), 135-136.

20. Zoltán Horváth, *Teleki László I.* (Budapest, 1964), 248.

21. *Teleki László válogatott munkái, II.* [László Teleki's Selected Writings, II], ed., Gábor G. Kemény (Budapest, 1961), 16.

22. Miskolczy, Transylvania in the Revolution, 1389-1407; in *Erdély rövid története* [A Short History of Transylvania], editor-in-chief, Béla Köpeczi (Budapest, 1989), 442-451; Zsolt Trócsányi-Ambrus Miskolczy, *A fanariótáktól a Hohenzollernekig* [From the Fanariotas to the Hohenzollerns] (Budapest, 1992), 11-114.

23. A newer summary of these ambitions: Ambrus Miskolczy, *Egyház és forradalom. Biserica şi revolutie.* [Church and Revolution] (Budapest, 1991); *Arról, amit Erdély történetében írtunk...* [About What We Wrote in the History of Transylvania] (Aetas, 1992), 150-157.

24. Bălcescu, Opere, IV, 118-119.

25. Ion Ghica, *Opere, V.* (Bucureşti, 1988), 588.

26. Bălcescu, Opere, IV, 210.

27. Teleki, Selected Writings, II, 19.

28. Ibid., 21-24; Horváth, Teleki, 255, 172-174; Domokos Kosáry, Teleki László és a nemzetközi politika [László Teleki and International Politics] in *Teleki és kora* [Teleki and His Era], ed., Mihály Praznovszky and Ágnes Rozsnyói (Salgótarján, 1987), 33.

29. György Spira, *A nemzetiségi kérdés a negyvennyolcas forradalom Magyarországán* [The Nationality Question in Hungary of the 1848 Revolution] (Budapest, 1980), 216-217.

30. Horváth, Teleki II, 177-179.

31. Wien, Haus-, Hof- und Staatsarchiv (hereafter WHHStA), Informationsbüro (hereafter IB) 1849: 450/A.

32. Bălcescu, 185-186.

33. *Kossuth Lajos összes munkái, XV.* [Lajos Kossuth's Complete Writings, XV] ed., István Barta (Budapest, 1955), 839-843.

34. István Hajnal, *A Kossuth-emigráció Törökországban, I.* [The Kossuth Exile in Turkey, I] (Budapest, 1927), 53, 171.

35. C.F. Henningsen, *The Past and Future of Hungary* (Cincinnati, 1852).

36. Hajnal, 172.

37. Ibid., 529.

38. B.A.R.S 34-10/DCXII. and see Ion Ghica, *Opere IV.* (Bucureşti, 1985), 618.
39. Jancsó, 183.
40. Hajnal, 671.
41. Bălcescu, 266.
42. Hajnal, 377.
43. Hungarian National Archives, (hereafter MOL), R 195. 1.cs. 1.k. January, 1850; see *A Kossuth-emigráció szolgálatában. Tanárky Gyula naplója (1849-1866)* [In Service of the Kossuth Exile: Gyula Tanárky's Diary, 1849-1866] ed. Jenő Koltay-Kastner (Budapest, 1961), 26.
44. Ion Ghica, *Opere, VI.* (Bucureşti, 1988), 75-76.
45. B.A.R. Arhiva Ion Ghica, V, 300-322.
46. Bălcescu, Opere, IV, 278.
47. Ibid., 291-292.
48. Nicolae Bălcescu, *Opere, I.* (Bucureşti, 1953), 308-313.
49. Bălcescu, Opere, IV, 359-362.
50. Ibid., 177.
51. Horváth, Teleki, I, 330.
52. Imre Deák, Az első magyar-román konföderációs tervek [First Hungarian-Romanian Confederative Plans] (*Magyar Kisebbség,* 1932), 338.
53. MOL, R 90 *Kossuth Lajos iratai,I.* [Lajos Kossuth's Documents, I], 692.
54. György Szabad, *Kossuth politikai pályája* [Kossuth's Political Career] (Budapest, 1977), 170.
55. Imre Deák, *1848. A szabadságharc története levelekben* [The History of the War of Independence in Letters] (Budapest, 1944), 395.
56. MOL, R 90. I. 797; With minor literal errors published by Deák, 376-392.
57. Ambrus Miskolczy, Társadalmi és nemzeti kérdés az utolsó erdélyi rendi országgyűlésen [Social and National Question at the Last Transylvanian Feudal Diet] (*Századok,* 1979), 5.
58. György Klapka, *Emlékeimből* [From My Memories] (Budapest, 1886), 314.
59. Library of the Hungarian Academy of Sciences (hereafter MTAKK), Ms. 5086/244.
60. Deák, 456-467; Horváth, Teleki II, 221-232.
61. Teleki, II, 52.
62. Deák, 508-512.
63. MOL, R 90.I, 882; Deák, 542.
64. MOL, R 216. *Vukovics Sebő hagyatéka, 1. cs.* [Sebő Vukovics' Legacy]—László Teleki-Sebő Vukovics (Zürich, August 21, 1851).
65. BNCS, Fond Brătianu, XL/12.
66. Béla Borsi-Kálmán, *Nemzetfogalom* [Nation Theory], 109.
67. MOL, R 90 i. 991; Deák, 602-608.
68. MTAKK Ms. 4757/138.
69. Ambrus Miskolczy, *Teleki László szereplése a reformkori Erdély politikai életében* [László Teleki's Role in the Political Life of Transylvania of the Reform Era]; Nicolae Edroiu, Teleki László és a fogarasi román nemesség [László Teleki and the Fogaras Romanian Nobility] in *Teleki és kora* [Teleki and His Era] ed. Mihály Praznovszky and Ágnes Rozsnyói (Salgótarján, 1987).
70. Deák, 602.

71. Julian Chownitz, *Handbuch zur Kenntniss Ungarns* (Balnerg, 1851), 130.
72. MTAKK, Károly Óváry-Avari, *Teleki László élete, IV.* [László Teleki's Life, IV], 26.
73. HHStA, IB 1849: 660.
74. MOL, R 90 I, 693.
75. MOL, R 90 I, 822.
76. Klapka, 329.
77. MOL, R 295, György Klapka's Writings, 6.d.
78. George Klapka, *La guerre en Orient* (Geneva, 1855), 191.
79. Bălcescu, Opere, IV, 357.
80. MOL, R 90 I, 1128.
81. Archivele Statului, Timisoara, Fond Ormos, 700. *Vukovics Sebő levele Ormos Zsigmondnak* [Sebő Vukovics's Letter to Zsigmond Ormos], May 18, 1834.
82. MOL, R 90 I, 873.
83. MOL, R 90 I, 1054.
84. Deák, 634.
85. Horváth, Teleki, II, 264-280.
86. Deák, 634.
87. Ibid.
88. Alexandru Marcu, *Conspiratori si conspiratii in epoca renasterii politice a Romaniei 1848-1877* (Bucureşti, 1930), 39.
89. Deák, 722-723; MOL, R 90 I, 1174.
90. Deák, 724.
91. Szabad, 174.

ERA OF DUALISM (1867–1918)

JÓZSEF EÖTVÖS AND FERENC DEÁK: LAWS ON NATIONALITIES

LÁSZLÓ KATUS

On December 6, 1868, Franz Joseph I signed the law "concerning equality of nationalities" and the following day it was formally announced in Parliament making Act 1868: XLIV part of *Corpus Iuris*.

To put this law in historic perspective, there are two aspects to be considered. First, Act 1868:XLIV was the end point of a process, not its climax. That process, "a period of nationality law" development, began in the late summer of 1848 and ended with the parliamentary debate in November 1868. Finally, only Article 28 made its way into the *Corpus Iuris*. However, the two decade long political deliberations, debates, and impressive works of political theory (materializing in books, newspaper articles, pamphlets, parliamentary speeches, private letters, or unpublished manuscripts) magnified the importance of this Act. József Eötvös and Ferenc Deák, two classical figures of political liberalism in Hungary, played outstanding roles in this process.

The second aspect to be considered is the very nature of Hungarian nationality policy before 1848. Pre-1848 language laws sanctioned Hungarian as the language of public life on every level and all over the country; minority languages were to be limited to private life.[1] Underlying the language laws was the illusion that non-Hungarian inhabitants of the country would be gradually "Hungarianized" and that the linguistic border would coincide with the borders of the country. Bourgeois transformation was expected to promote and accelerate the process. However, because of the traumatic experience of 1848–1849, Hungarian liberal political thinking broke with the illusions of the Reform Age and shaped more realistic reactions to the nationality problem.

A PERIOD OF LINGUISTIC LAWS

Historic antecedents of the 1868 nationality law stemmed from the end of the 18th century and primarily related to regulation of language use rights. Between 1790 and 1848 the Diet ratified a whole series of language laws establishing the Hungarian language as a subject, not the language of education in secondary schools and institutes of higher education. Gradually Hungarian was made the official language of the Diet, laws, administrative authorities, and of secular and church courts. According to these language laws, Hungarian was a prerequisite for appointments in public offices, it was the language of legal board exams, and knowledge of Hungarian was even required for ecclesiastical positions in all denominations. The latter was important since religious registration was thus in Hungarian. Finally, in 1844 it was codified that "in schools within the borders of the country, Hungarian was to be the language of public education." In fact, the Transylvanian Diet codified Hungarian as the official language of Transylvania in 1847.[2]

Hungarian was given predominant consideration in the language laws. The intent was to implement its use in each area of public life. The linguistic rights of all the other nationalities in the country were ignored. At best a few years of grace was permitted for these nationalities to learn Hungarian. For these reasons, non-Hungarian representatives were justified in protesting the linguistic laws. Even some Hungarian politicians such as István Széchenyi considered the use of Hungarian as an official language too extensive. It had been common knowledge since Elek Fényes's thorough statistical surveys of the late 1830's that only 37% of the population claimed to be ethnic Hungarian. The proportion was 44% in "central" Hungary whereas in Transylvania it was only 28%.[3]

The reform politicians of the 1840's with Kossuth at the lead, wished to solve the nationality problem by establishing "the grand principle of equal freedom, equal rights, and equal responsibility for all the Christian population of the Hungarian crown regardless of racial, linguistic, or religious differences."[4] However, liberal hopes proved to be illusory. The non-Hungarian inhabitants of this multi-ethnic country welcomed the bourgeois revolution but were not ready to give up their nationality in exchange for freedom. In addition to freedom and personal equality before the law, they also demanded an assurance that their national identity and ethnic rights would be respected.

Under these circumstances it was unfortunate that the April 1848 laws, which founded a new bourgeois Hungary, did not discuss the nationality problem—with the exception of a few decrees which touched upon the linguistic rights of the non-Hungarian population. In the meantime the demands of non-Hungarian peoples, with their suggestion of eventual armed conflict, clearly showed that a solution to the nationality problem was required.

The Transylvanian Union committee, delegated by Parliament, took the first important step towards that solution with its September 1848 Bill "to assure the equal rights of the Romanian nationalities." This Bill launched a two decade long process leading, after various different propositions, bills, and ideas, to the birth of the Nationality Act. The July 1849 resolution of the National Assembly of Szeged on the "free ethnic development of every nationality in the Hungarian empire," as well as Lajos Kossuth's constitution plan outlined in exile in 1851, were vital steps in this process.

THEORETICAL CLARIFICATION AND POLICY MAKING IN THE 1860'S

Following the defeat of the war of independence, the basic principles of the March 1849 Olomutz forced imperial constitution became valid in Hungary also. The constitution almost literally quoted the proposition of the Constitutional Imperial Assembly: "every ethnic group is equal and has an inviolable right to retain and maintain its national identity and language" (Article 5). The constitution also stipulated that corresponding public and civic institutions would assure equal rights to all nationalities and languages (Article 71).[5] However, measures to institute equality could not be fully implemented because in 1851 the March Constitution was repealed and Imperial Absolutism was re-instituted. The 1851 New Year's Eve Announcement did not even mention national equality.

Years later, after the defeat of neo-absolutism, the national equality issue in the Habsburg Monarchy came back to the foreground. In the meantime, affected by the events of 1848–49, the mental outlook of the Hungarian political elite also changed, developing into a new national policy for the situation both inside and outside Hungary. The main lesson learned from the events of 1848–49 was that a simultaneous fight against the Habsburgs to free the country and at the same time to maintain Hungarian control over rising ethnic groups were incompatible. Many shared László Teleki's view that the disintegration of historical Hungary was inevitable. Thus the state should be reorganized into a federative form with the nationalities given territorial self-governing rights, including the right of self-determination. Finally, even the principle of secession ought to be acknowledged.[6] Opposing this position were those who claimed that "the price of our reconciliation with Austria and its immediate surroundings is not as high as the one the nationalities demand."[7] Between these two extreme views were those who wished to save the territorial integrity and unity of historical Hungary by placing it within a liberal or democratic state, by legally sanctioning ethnic equality, and, if necessary, by partially or fully surrendering Hungarian political supremacy.

After the October Diploma of 1860 restricted political activities, the nationality problem became the major topic of debate. Prominent representatives of the Hungarian political elite repeatedly disclosed their wish to fulfill "the legal and reasonable demands" of non-Hungarian nationals. The challenge now for liberal publications was to develop clear theories that went beyond general cliches to the realm of building practical programs. In those days the main body of the liberals was constituted by the former "centrists" (József Eötvös, László Szalay, Zsigmond Kemény, Móric Lukács) who succinctly represented the Western European bourgeois ideas of the 1840's. Similar to Kossuth's draft constitution, their solution of the nationality problem was to be carried out within a state based on communal and county autonomy with the central sphere of authority reduced to the minimum.

Liberal publications of the early 1860's reflected important changes in presenting the nationality problem compared with pre-1848 decades. It was now fully recognized that Hungary was a multi-ethnic state where different ethnicities could not be merged into a single nation. The liberal writers heavily criticized the nationality policy of the Reform Age and the revolution. They denounced the excesses of linguistic laws, forced language diffusion, and Hungarianizing efforts. Learning from the 1848–49 experiences they discarded the quixotic view that a bourgeois constitution, individual freedom, and civic equality would automatically solve the nationality problem. They stressed the legitimacy of non-Hungarian nationality demands both for individual freedom and those nationality rights which would assure free language use in public life and in education. Thus, in their view, the 1848 code ought to be completed by passing laws codifying ethnic equality and laws codifying the use of the nationalities' native tongues.

"Our exclusive rule is untenable...the complete emancipation of nationalities is inevitable in our country. A fair settlement of the nationality problem is our main task and it is our solemn obligation to fulfill the justified nationality demand of every non-Hungarian fellow-citizen."[8] Zsigmond Kemény, who criticized the language laws of the Reform Age and the nationality policy of the revolution in his political pamphlets as early as 1850–51, also wrote the following in the *Pesti Napló*: "It is quite certain that in the 19th century an unchangeable desire developed in the ethnic groups to participate in bourgeois development in their own language and according to their own national identity. We can only state this fact and cannot change it." To accept this was "to refuse the Sisyphean task of Hungarianization." He declared that the Hungarian nation "will be ready to acknowledge the lawfulness of rational nationality demands and the nation will apply its liberal views to ethnic groups who will receive equal shares from the benefits of the constitution. Further, these groups will not forget the invaluable benefit of being endowed by legal protection to keep and maintain their national identity." He thought that "presently Hungarians are not under suspicion of demanding sacrifice from national freedom as in 1848."[9]

József Eötvös held a similar view: "If we Hungarians only lure our kindred people under promise of liberty and do not want to keep our promises of honoring their national interests; if we again face times when people of this homeland will have to make a choice between liberty and nationality and by giving up the former or the latter they become devoid of one of them, then a healthy development of people cannot be expected. And we will have to forsake hope and be assured that the perils directing our land to the brink of the grave twelve years ago will surface again." We have to understand that "the principles applied to individual human beings are also to be applied to relations among peoples, and are not ever to be revoked." Thus, "satisfying the various different nationalities in this homeland does not depend on our will and cannot be expected from the generosity of the nation. Rather, it is fundamental for our future because to the extent that every human being of this land is extended constitutional liberty and that all the reasonable demands of every nationality are satisfied, to such an extent do we assure the preservation of our own nationality and constitutional liberty." He also posed the question: "Is there really a contradiction between liberty and nationality interests?" He thought it was possible "to unite the different nationalities under the Hungarian crown on the basis of common liberty while satisfying all the nationality demands."[10]

Móric Lukács also criticized mistakes committed in the language laws of the Reform Age. He noted that "legislation corrected these mistakes in 1848 when it terminated political privileges and extended both political and civic rights to every citizen of our country. An obvious consequence of the extension would have been the termination of the rule of Hungarian ethnicity and language and the enforcement of the fair rights of every living language in the country." That is why "it is inevitably needed that the Parliament would correct or cancel those 1848 laws which are adverse to our time and progress and which limit equal rights of citizens of different races and religions....The period of blanket statements and promises is over. Our fellow citizens of various different ethnic backgrounds are justified in expecting the Hungarian Legislature to fulfill their fair demands and wishes."[11]

The chief dilemma of the liberals was how to organize a multiethnic state that would guarantee the free national development of all the people living within its borders. To empower the nationalities as legal entities with collective political rights and territorial autonomy contradicted bedrock liberal principles according to which political rights focus upon individual citizens. Due to the fact of mixed settlements, territorial separation of nationalities was not considered feasible in Hungary although, according to his diary notes, Eötvös entertained the possibility of territorial autonomy and federation. Even Deák was not averse to a certain degree of territorial autonomy, and in the case of the Serbs, did not oppose rounding-off county areas in accordance with ethnic distributions.[12]

The concrete proposals of the liberals, especially those of the former centrists, were in many ways similar to Kossuth's earlier draft constitution. They posited equal rights for the individual; the right of assembly; communal, county, and church autonomy; that the official language would be determined everywhere by the majority while retaining the rights of the minority; the free use of one's native tongue in every forum (according to some, even in Parliament); and unlimited care and development of nationality interests through freedom of social assembly. The major difference was the 1868 liberals' rejection of universal suffrage–an important diversion from Kossuth's draft. Liberals, in concordance with the prevalent trend all over Europe, were advocates of census voting, although adjusting the census and extending voting rights for the sake of political predominance were considered necessary. They also stressed that the Hungarian nationality leadership should resign from its exclusive rule, from a major part of its historic rights, and from its political supremacy. Although Hungarians ought to exert leadership on social, cultural, and moral levels, they should not possess institutionalized, legalized privileges, and should only be first among equals.

EÖTVÖS AND DEÁK ON THE NATIONALITY PROBLEM

József Eötvös expressed classic Hungarian liberal views concerning the nationality problem in his political science work, "The Influence of Prevailing 19th Century Ideas on the State,"[13] in his German language pamphlets on the nationality problems of the Habsburg Monarchy, in his book *The Nationality Question* (published in 1865), and in his diary.[14]

In the 1850's Eötvös both theoretically approached the nationality question and searched for a practical solution to it within the framework of the Habsburg Monarchy. He explained that, in addition to equality and freedom, nationality was the third prevailing idea of the 19th century, and that he understood the underlying antagonism. He also realized that the continued existence of the Habsburg Monarchy depended on the settlement of the nationality problem and thought that the unity of the empire was reconcilable with fulfilling the just demands of nationalities. The solution for him lay in providing individual freedom and equality, and in establishing provincial and municipal self-governments. It was in the 1860's that his attention turned towards the nationality problem in Hungary when he recognized that "in our present situation nothing is more important than this issue. Setting people's mind at ease, the existence of our constitutional freedom, even the existence of our state mostly depend on the solution of this question–it is obvious."[15]

He emphasized that "the nationality movement is not the result of propaganda" as many thought. "I am convinced that the nationality question is only one area of the great freedom movement of our era that has already led to great results." That is why it cannot be oppressed by force or be appeased by fake concessions. "Instead the needs that bore it should be soothed. Thus, in this situation, if the obstacles preventing the citizen from exercising his/her ethnic rights are discarded, then the citizen will feel free in every way, just as much as in his/her nationality."[16] Therefore the solution is to grant "the most perfect freedom as regards language and nationality" and to create a state that assures that "the law permitting the individual to exercise his/her nationality will not remain a dead letter."[17]

Similar to other liberal politicians of the period, Eötvös also argued that it was in the interest of all the small peoples in the Carpathian Basin to maintain a common and united homeland to guard their freedom and national existence against the ambitions of neighboring empires. Hungary, however, could not be transformed into a West European type nation state because the non-Hungarian groups had already awakened to their national consciousness and could not be melted into one nation. He rejected a new Hungarian state where "keeping barely the historic rights in mind, the demands of certain ethnic and language groups are not satisfied." He was convinced "that the nationality problem may only be finalized if the solution satisfies the justified political and linguistic demands of the nationalities." That is why "a peaceful solution of our ethnic conflicts depends on solving the antagonism between the terms of unity of the country and the demands of different ethnic groups."[18] It is not in the interest of the Hungarian nation to oppress the nationalities. "It is rather in Hungary's interest that the nationalities develop to their potential on their own and acquire their own characteristic features" because "it is the common freedom, not the rule of one nationality, that keeps this state together."[19] "Whether we should reject the demands of the nationalities is not a question to ask since it is not in our power any more. We should fulfill their demands so that the country will not be damaged...and this can happen only if we disagree on the ethnic division of the country and instead we work according to the principle of individual freedom and extend the most perfect freedom and equality to reassure the nationalities."[20]

Eötvös did not think that "ethnic division of the country," federation, or even any kind of territorial autonomy was feasible "since in our country six ethnic groups are so much mixed that outlining the nationality areas is impossible."[21] Non-Hungarian citizens, however, are justified in wishing that "their own nationality be respected and cultivation of their language and expression of their nationality be granted. In other words, all the nationalities living in the country demand equal freedom and an establishment that allows them to use their freedom."[22] The new Hungarian state ought to offer guarantees for ethnic existence. The only way is "to assure a higher degree of welfare and freedom than they would have in neighboring countries."[23] Therefore, centralization should be limited to the bare minimum and administration ought to be based on self-governing principles. "Our country cannot be transformed into a Prussian or French type centralized state...because under that form of administration even the most moderate demands of the nationalities cannot be satisfied."[24] The demands of non-Hungarian nationalities will be best satisfied in the framework of communal, county, and municipal autonomies and within the framework of autonomous churches. For that reason "nobody in his senses can oppose...the ethnic division of certain counties."[25]

Notwithstanding this argument, in 1868 Eötvös himself rejected this solution. He opposed the new language rule because county and state offices, dignities, and even parliamentary positions would be allotted according to nationalities, a system which imperiled individual civic liberties.

Eötvös knew that if one wanted to achieve a permanent solution to the ethnic issue then "we can give very few national privileges to the Hungarians...."[26] He fully opposed the compromise known as the German–Hungarian handshake, a mutual advantage "to unite against the demands of other nationalities of the empire." The compromise opened up possibilities for enacting laws "to assure the supremacy of the Hungarian element....I am convinced that such a national supremacy is the gravest possible disaster.... Hungarian nationals need freedom to be satisfied and this is impossible if the demands of different other nationalities are rejected, in which case the created situation could only be sustained by repressive rule."[27] He clearly saw that there were many "who give priority to nationality interest over freedom and the majority might think this way in our country. I hear from many that nothing is of our greater interest than a good absolutism, even if it comes along with a little despotism as long as that despot is Hungarian."[28] These people wanted to assure Hungarian hegemony by way of special privileges and prerogatives. One can aim for the predominating influence of the Hungarian element "not by preventing others from their full development, but instead by establishing our own nationality on a higher level."[29] That is the reason why he suggests that the Hungarian nation should resign from its political supremacy. "The empire that we create should be founded on freedom and not on oppressing other peoples. Thus we should strive to get more credit for public purposes and to become first among equals."[30]

In his great address in the parliamentary debate of the nationality question on November 25, 1868, Eötvös summarized his political testimony: "In my view the nationality question is not an issue of one or the other ethnic group, it is our common issue. If you believe that the unity and the existence of this homeland is only in the interest of Hungarian speakers or think that the civilization and welfare of Serbian, Romanian, and Slav compatriots are only Serbian, Romanian, or Slav issues, then you do not understand the question. I am convinced that the solution of the nationality question is our common task, and our common interest....We have to solve this question also in the spirit of this century and this is the century of liberty. There is no rhetoric or power that will make us retreat from the grounds of free competition and freedom into the entrenchment of privileges once again."[31]

It is essential to discuss Eötvös' nationality ideas in detail because his thoughts greatly contributed to the creation of the Nationality Act.

Ferenc Deák, the highly respected Hungarian liberal politician of the 1860's, raised objections to the administrative propagation of the Hungarian language in the 1840's. At the end of August 1848 Deák, as Minister of Justice, brought a Bill before Parliament about the Croat question. This was a precursor to the most significant points of the 1868 Croat-Hungarian compromise. Deák's text also mentioned that "if the conciliation cannot happen, separation, thus a federation, can also be acceptable."[32] In 1861 he took further steps to deal with the Croat question by revoking Hungarian demands for Eastern Slavonia and preparing to modify those 1848 laws objectionable to the Croats. He also recognized a territorially and politically separate Croatia—within the Austro-Hungarian Empire—with separate municipal rights and asserted that Hungarians wished to discuss new conditions of the union between Hungary and Croatia within the Empire. "If Croatia wants to unite with us, they are welcome. If they want to stipulate conditions in their own ethnic interest or autonomy, or want to extend the authority of their national parliament or want to participate with us in the common legislation in a different way or in a different proportion, we will not reject their terms and will not oppose their modifications....If Croatia wants to terminate every constitutional relationship we ever shared and wants to sever all ties, we cannot declare that we agree to a final separation, rather it is our duty to lodge a protest and to vindicate our rights. However, we will not take any steps to hinder separation and will not apply force even if it were in our power. Whether union or separation, it is mostly up to Croatia."[33]

In March 1861 Deák was ready to satisfy ethnic aspirations saying, "We are not taken aback by the demands of our compatriots of different ethnic backgrounds because it is our strong will to fulfill anything possible, as long as it is not the political disintegration of Hungary. We are convinced that our compatriots of different ethnicity will not raise demands which are impossible to satisfy."[34] Nevertheless in reality Deák was rather pessimistic about the solution to the nationality question. In a private letter he stated that "the effective solution of four important questions is almost impossible." One of them was the nationality problem. In his view, the nationalities put forth impossible demands. Fulfilling their demands "would dismember the country, would dissolve Hungary, and would at best create a new federal state with the Hungarian ethnicity in the middle without any defensible natural borders, fragmenting the population."[35]

That was why he considered it vital to defend and declare the unity, integrity, and the leading role of the Hungarian majority. But beyond this, he conceded that civic rights to allow minority languages should be expanded. "On county, municipal, church levels I am not reluctant to extend equal rights on an unlimited basis....It would be my wish that the language of litigation would be the language of the native population." Privately he realized that the prospect was not promising.[36]

Relating to a real case in November 1869, Deák explained his views on the tasks of the state in a multi-ethnic society. The government had included the subsidy of the Pest Hungarian National Theater into the budget. Immediately a Serbian representative requested the Serbian National Theater in Újvidék (Novi Sad) to receive a similar subsidy. Deák supported the request. "It is not fair that the state...merely and exclusively would support only one language and nationality [in this case Hungarian] from the common tax. In my view, either all or none."[37]

In 1872, in his last parliamentary speech relating to the nationality problem, Deák's views were summarized in a political testament for those contemporaries who had been moving away from his brand of liberalism. His views were fully concordant with Eötvös's quoted statement "...if we want to win the nationalities it is not to be done by Hungarianization, but by popularization. Because I can see clearly two things: extirpating them would be barbaric even if they were not so numerous; hence extermination is impossible. To create enmity is not in our interest. They are in a similar situation. If they seceded to form a big nation, I would understand the aspiration. But in the European situation it is impossible. Consequently, both parties should strive to live together and next to each other in greater harmony."[38]

It is evident from the above that in spite of minor differences the Hungarian liberal elite of the 1860's saw clearly that the predominance of civil rights, an autonomous administrative system, and free competition of the individuals and peoples within the framework of a multi-ethnic liberal state were the keys to dealing with the nationality question. In their mind the state was not solely Hungarian, but rather a neutral institution beyond peoples and nations—a "common homeland" that ensured and fostered a free national development of every citizen and nation living within it. This liberal concept, however, did not prevail without adulteration as the legal solution to the nationality problem. The parliamentary session of 1861 was dissolved and not reconvened again until 1865.

THE FIRST NATIONALITY COMMITTEE

When the Hungarian Parliament reconvened in the spring of 1861, the majority of the political leadership unanimously opted for the legislative regulation of the nationality question. Deák's address recognized that "our non-Hungarian compatriots have demands concerning their own status and concerning the constitutional status of Croatia which cannot and will not be ignored. We are determined to do our utmost to overcome misunderstandings without dismembering the country and sacrificing our independence, so that all the citizens of every ethnicity will be united in interests and sentiments."[39]

At the recommendation of Eötvös, the Parliament commissioned a 27-member committee to draft a Nationality Bill. Besides eminent Hungarian politicians as Eötvös, Andrássy, Szalay, and Imre Madách, there were also twelve non-Hungarian representatives selected. Referee György Bartal presented the Bill on August 8, 1861. Eötvös had had a substantial role in drawing it up. While propounding on the Bill, the committee had to take a stand on the wishes of non-Hungarian nationalities. The Serbs formulated their demands at their 1861 national conference in Karlóca, while the Slovaks did the same at their Túrószentmárton meeting. Both the Serbs and the Slovaks wanted territorial autonomy, within the Serbian Voivodina and "the Slav district of Upper-Hungary" respectively. The Serbs wanted to be recognized as a nation state. The Slovaks viewed both the Slovak and other nationalities as legal entities entitled to corresponding rights, as opposed to individual citizens to be endowed with linguistic rights.[40]

In accordance with prevailing liberal views, the parliamentary committee wanted to settle the nationality question on the bases of equal rights and individual freedom, but also recognized the nationalities as freely developing national entities. As the Bill read the nationality question ought to be solved when "the legitimate demands of individual citizens" prevailed. The second function of the Bill was "to ensure the free development of each nationality as an entity by way of free union." This was going to happen within the municipal and county self-governing bodies and through the church and school autonomy of various different denominations. The Committee did not consider the demand for territorial autonomy viable because "some nationalities are scattered and mixed in this homeland." Thus, autonomy would present the opportunity to oppress minorities on nationality territories.

As a theoretical principle the Committee decreed that "politically, all the ethnicities, corresponding to the different languages of Hungary, establish one nation, a unified and indivisible Hungarian nation corresponding to the historic notion of the Hungarian state," but with all the nationalities as equal members. "All the peoples living in the country–Hungarian, Slav, Romanian, German, Serb, Russian, etc.–are to have equal rights. They assert their separate nationality rights freely and without any restrictions within the limits of the political union of the state, on the basis of individual freedom and the freedom of union." In this wording the Hungarian political nation was the sum total of all citizens, with ethnic Hungarian people simply one of the equal nationalities of the country having no additional privileges beyond what they were entitled to as a nationality of the relative majority. Hungarian was to be the language of legislation, government, and national authorities.

According to the Bill, national languages could be used in local communities, in petitions to municipal and state authorities, and in addressing community and municipal meetings. Communities were to make their own decisions about the official, administrative language, but at the request of a local minority, that language could also be used. Parishes and congregations were also free to determine the language of administration, school, and registration. The language of municipalities (counties) was to be determined by the general assembly. It might be non-Hungarian but in that case the minutes should also be kept in Hungarian (for government control). In addition, all the national minorities living in the county had the right to demand the minutes to be kept in their own tongue. There were important provisos to assure that community magistrates and county clerks would have to use the native tongue of individual residents and communities under their authority during communications and discussions. There was also a proviso made for counties of the same majority language to correspond in their official language with one another. State laws were to be made public in the language of every nationality, while state authorities were to employ nationality clerks who were able to attend to petitions by non-Hungarian citizens and municipal authorities. The Bill also recognized the right of every religious denomination and nationality to establish secondary and higher educational institutions and to determine the language of education used in them.[41]

Obviously not everybody concurred with the recommendations of the Committee. There were quite a few who wished to follow the pre-1848 guidelines. The conservative János Török, arguing with Móric Lukács, declared that "the Hungarian nation cannot exist without the support of linguistic laws" and was concerned about Eötvös's "anachronistic nationality proposal" (that is, the proposal of the Committee). "We do not agree with those who believe that without the political hegemony of the Hungarian nationality and on the basis of the so-called equal rights, either public freedom or Hungarian nationality can be preserved,"[42] Török declared. Many all over the country shared this view, especially among the country gentry and lesser nobility who wished to retain, by any possible means, their leading roles in the counties.

The Bill was not passed due to the dissolution of the Parliament in 1861.

THE BIRTH OF THE NATIONALITY LAW

The address convening in Parliament December 1865, like that of the 1861 Parliament, declared that "the ever increasing minority nationality consciousness deserves attention and it cannot be measured by old laws of bygone times. We will not forget that the non-Hungarian speaking inhabitants are also the citizens of Hungary and we wholeheartedly wish to assure, by law, everything that their interest and the public interest of this country requires. We are following the principles of justice and fraternity even when we enact laws in the interest of other nationalities."[43]

In April 26, 1866, the Chamber of Deputies elected a 40-member committee to draft the Nationality Bill. As well as Hungarian deputies, Serbian, Romanian, Slovak, and Saxon deputies also participated in the committee having been selected by secret ballot. Pál Somssich was chosen as Chair. The committee commissioned a sub-committee with Pál Nyáry as Chair to draw up the text of the Bill. Their work was drawn out due to the Prussian war, the Austro-Hungarian negotiations about the Compromise, and coronation ceremonies.

After the Hungarian government was formed in 1867, it was empowered by Parliament to invalidate the section of Article 1848:16 that "assigned Hungarian as he only language of discussion of county boards." It was also empowered to permit "the discussions of county boards as well as city and district deputy bodies in prevailing languages other than Hungarian and that these bodies record their proceedings in languages other than Hungarian"—although Parliament insisted that these records should be submitted to the Ministry in the Hungarian language.[44]

The union between Transylvania and Hungary, which had already been declared in 1848, finally materialized in 1867. The traditional Transylvanian constitution with its three nations was declared null and void since this was an incompatible constitutional form with the modern parliamentary state. The union law declared that "according to the 1848 Kolozsvár (Cluj) Article I, all the inhabitants of Transylvania, irrespective of their nationality, language and religion, are declared equal and all the laws contradicting that are nullified, while national territorial divisions, names, privileges and franchises are nullified as long as they concern one nationality to the exclusion of another. Thus the political and civic equality of the citizens of united Hungary and Transylvania is newly assured."[45]

The nationality Sub-committee completed its proposal in June 1867. In its report submitted to Parliament it stated that "its main principle was to consider the equality of nationalities living in the country and that it intends to prepare a Bill that, after passing, assures the enforcement of nationality demands within the nation's borders, which necessarily surround them by the political unity, territorial integrity, the unified legislature and state government." In effect, the latter term alluded to Parliament's refusal to endorse federative reorganization or territorial autonomy beyond county levels. This time the "main principle" of the committee did not include the expression "Hungarian nation state."[46]

The Bill on the "equality of nationalities" discussed communal, church, municipal and state administrative, associative, judicial, and legislative "nationality rights" in seven chapters and 35 paragraphs. In most cases the proposal assumed the provisions of the 1861 version, which were discussed in detail. Thus it closely regulated language use in municipalities and counties stating that municipal and county proceedings should be recorded in the languages of minorities above 20% of the population. The chapter which permitted the use of native languages in municipal, district, and county courts was completely new. It proposed Hungarian as the official language of higher and commercial courts (which were dependent on government nomination), but obligated the government to provide "expert judges of every nationality at higher and supreme courts in adequate numbers."

In addition, municipal and county clerks would be obliged to communicate in the language of their clients. The proposal also ordained that "the government is obligated to employ ample numbers of different people of ethnic origin as high dignitaries of the land–state officials, especially for Lord Lieutenants of the counties, who would be knowledgeable enough to handle issues with individuals and associations." Private individuals, societies, and churches had the right to establish schools of any level and to choose the language of education. The state was also obligated to establish non-Hungarian speaking primary and secondary schools. The statutory provision for the right of assembly was also completely new in the Bill, compared with the 1861 proposal.[47]

In response to the Hungarian majority proposal, the minority (mostly Serbian and Romanian) deputies also drew up theirs. While the Hungarian proposal generally assured language, association, and educational rights for individuals, the proposal of the nationality leaders recognized the five largest ethnic minorities as "political nations" and granted these national communities political rights as legal entities. According to the first proposal, the individual citizen was the subject of national rights, while according to the other, it was the national community. The minority proposal began with the statement that "in Hungary, Hungarian, Romanian, Serb, Slovak, Russian, and German are all recognized as equal political nations for whom the political equality of nationality and language is assured by law within the territorial integrity and political unity of the country." The six nationalities would have the right to use their own national banners and each "will be appropriately represented in the upper house of the parliament, at the central authorities, higher courts, at the head of counties and districts, and in all the high ranking positions and offices to be nominated by the crown or the executive authority." This time territorial autonomy, similar to the one requested by the Serbian and Romanian national assemblies in 1861, was not demanded. However, they wished to round up the areas of counties and constituencies so that they would mainly constitute one nationality.

The official language in every municipality, county, and city would be the language of the majority "provided the majority belongs to one of the six political nationalities." (Significant ethnic groups such as Croats, Catholic Serbs, Slavonic sokács, Slovenians, or the Gypsies would not have shared these rights). The minority language would have been used as a second official language everywhere. Counties and cities would have corresponded and received correspondence with superior and state authorities in their own language. The proposal also stipulated for addressing Parliament in nationality languages and for the use of minority languages at central authorities. Teaching nationality history at schools–in courses beyond the mandatory state history course–as well as lectures and examinations at universities and schools of law, were also requested in the minority languages. Similar to Kossuth's constitution, the proposal was meant to "form and organize national unity in the national assembly or congress in order to promote public and national education, national development, and the liberty of each national minority."[48]

The Bill of the sub-committee stirred protest not only in the national minority press but also among the Hungarian leadership, especially among the nobility of national minority or mixed counties. All over the country the alarm-bell rang from fear that "under nationality pretexts, our homeland is to be dismembered." Municipal meetings sent protests asserting that "a nationality Bill on such a wide basis...would strip the counties of their Hungarian character." Further, they objected to the proposal that the official language of each county be the language of the majority since it often would turn out to be non-Hungarian. To avoid this they demanded that Hungarian remain the official language of all the counties. "A law that would strip the great political bodies of their Hungarian character would create a polyglot state. That state might be free and even flourish for a while, but would not be Hungarian by any means. Later, by its polyglot nature, it would necessarily dissemble."[49] Hence, the gap between the liberal elite and the country nobility, the main body of the political leadership, widened further.

Almost one and a half years passed before the nationality committee, after considering the sub-committee's proposal and the incoming reports, prepared a new Bill. In the meantime the committee's composition changed considerably. Everybody whose state office was incompatible with the mandate or who became a government official had to resign. This change, and especially Eötvös's absence, greatly influenced the fate of the Bill.

"What are the interests of non-Hungarian speaking citizens to be furthered by the Law?" and "What impact would the Law have on the common homeland?" were two important questions needing answers reported the Committee on October 28, 1868. In response the report asserted that "non-Hungarian speakers of the country are fully recognized by existing political and social laws since the law does not prioritize among citizens...and having political, official, and property rights are not contingent upon nationality. It is the use of their native tongues that non-Hungarian speaking citizens of the country are somewhat limited by existing laws." For that reason the committee tried to regulate the use of native languages. First and foremost they declared "the complete equality of native tongues as far as the individual is concerned. Thus,

—every citizen is free to communicate in his/her native language with officials of national government, church, school, municipal authority, and community while seeking information or doing business;
—communities, associations, private agencies, and churches are free to choose the language of record-keeping and administration;
—municipal authorities may keep records in languages different from the official language of the country;
—everybody may speak in his/her native language at community, municipal, church, and association meetings;
—equal rights are assured with respect to associations, public education, church governments so that non-Hungarian citizens of the country will develop their ethnicity in each area."[50]

The most significant change in the 1868 Bill, compared with the sub-committee proposal, the 1849 Szeged Resolution, and the 1861 proposal, was the regulation concerning Hungarian record-keeping obligations and the option of using a nationality language as a secondary language in case of a majority of one fifth. Hungarian was also to be the language of administration of municipal authorities with an exception for ethnic clerks for whom use of Hungarian would have caused unsurmountable difficulties. These clerks were permitted to use one of the other record-keeping languages. Hungarian was also compulsory in inter-municipal communication, albeit with a secondary language permitted. The committee allowed for pressure and essentially made Hungarian the primary language of all municipal authorities. A short introduction preceded the Bill stating that "citizens of different ethnicities have equal language rights" and the goal of the Bill is to regulate the practice of these rights with respect "to the unity of the country, to the practicability and feasibility of public administration, and to the demands for fast and accurate judicial service."[51]

The central committee (draftsmen of statutes) also slightly modified the Bill submitted by the nationality committee. The most significant of these modifications was to remove the compulsory obligation of municipal clerks to use the native tongue of the client, instead stating that clerks should use the client's preferred language "*as much as possible*."[52]

At the beginning of the parliamentary debate over the Committee's Bill, Ferenc Deák presented an alternative Bill. Its content was almost identical with the Committee's proposal, although Deák significantly restructured the text using dissimilar legal language. The Committee's Bill repeatedly spoke about the official language of the state, although Hungarian was never explicitly mentioned. Deák, however, started with the statement that Hungarian was the national language of Hungary and was principally valid for use in Parliament and in the government. Then he moved on to specify language use at each governmental level starting from supreme state bodies and institutions and moving down through municipal authorities, courts, church bodies, schools, and communities. Significant differences occurred only on two areas. First, Deák allowed municipal clerks to use their clients' language "if the clients so wish." He did not accept the loop-hole hidden in the "as much as possible" statement recommended by the committee. Second, Deák proposed to maintain the established practice of the lower courts as they were to be revised by the legislation anyway.

Put against the three committee proposals, the novelty in Deák's proposal lay in its introduction which stated, similar to the committee proposal of 1861, that "all the citizens of Hungary constitute one political nation, an indivisible Hungarian nation, and that every citizen of the homeland is an equal member of this nation. With respect to the official use of languages prevailing in the country, this equality may be separately regulated as long as the unity of the country, the practicability of government and public administration, and an accurate judicial service make it necessary."[53]

During the ensuing parliamentary debate the most important modification made to Deák's Bill dealt with the Committee's text that required municipal clerks to use the client's language "as much as possible."[54]

THE NATIONALITY ACT OF 1868

In November 1868 after tempestuous debates and despite nationality protests the Nationality Bill passed. First and foremost, it assured an extensive use of the native language by individual citizens in every forum of public life. All citizens could address communal, municipal, and church meetings and submit petitions and receive responses to and from every authority in their native language. All could engage in litigation in their native languages in lower courts. Hungarian became the official language of supreme courts and non-Hungarian documents submitted to them through appeals would be translated into Hungarian by publicly paid translators. Sentences, judicial decisions, injunctions of supreme courts had to be announced and documented in the respective language.

Communities had the right to choose their language of registration and administration. Community officials were obligated to communicate with clients in their native tongue. Communities were free to use their own administrative language when submitting petitions to county and state authorities. Parishes were also free to determine the language of registration, administration, and education.

County and city municipal authorities were to keep records in Hungarian and in any other language that one fifth of the deputies wished. Internal administration of municipal authorities was in Hungarian, but if it met with difficulties "respective officials may use any record-keeping language of the municipal authority as an exception."

"As much as possible officials of municipal authorities should use the native tongue of their clients during official interaction with communities, associations, and institutes." Documents of municipal authorities sent to state authorities were permitted to be in any record-keeping languages in addition to Hungarian, with the text arranged in columns side by side. The same applied to superior church authorities who could determine their own language of discussion, record-keeping, and administration, although a certified Hungarian translation of their records had to be attached to copies sent to the national supervising authority.

The official language of the parliament and the government was Hungarian, but Bills had to be presented in all the languages of the nationalities living in Hungary. In response to petitions the government was obligated to issue injunctions in the language of the petition as well as Hungarian. Churches and communities were allowed to determine the language of education in their schools. The Act also regulated that in public schools "instruction is to be provided in native tongues so that minority, nationality citizens who live in large numbers in close proximity are able to educate themselves in their national languages, below the level of higher education." University linguistic and literary departments should be established for the nationalities.

Statutory law regulated distinct ethnic citizens' rights to establish nationality schools and associations. "For establishing institutes for the advancement of language, art, science, economy, industry, and trade individual citizens can establish societies or associations under state supervision as determined by law. They may lay down rules and act upon those rules, raise funds, and administer them according to their lawful national needs." The language used by institutes and associations was to be decided by the founders.

Finally the law stated that "ability remains the only guiding principle for holding offices and nationality status will not be considered an obstacle to rising to any office or position in the country. Furthermore, the national government will make sure that in the national offices of judges and public administration, and first and foremost, the offices of Lord Lieutenants, various nationalities will be employed who are proficient in the required languages, and are suitable otherwise also."

In certain special fields the provisions of the Nationalities Act were supplemented by contemporary laws which regulated language use according to the Nationality Act. Eötvös' personal creation, the Public Education Act (Article 1868:XXXVIII) was one of them. It stipulated that churches, associations, communities, and private people had the right to establish and run schools. The right of churches to establish schools was especially important for national minorities because Serbs, Romanians, Ruthenians, and the Transylvanian Saxons all had their own church organizations. Churches were permitted to select their own teachers, to choose their textbooks, and to design curricula. The Act stated that in public schools "all students will receive instruction in their native language as long as it is among those predominant in the community. For that reason mixed communities ought to employ teachers who are able to teach in the predominant languages. In more populous communities where people of several languages live, they can employ assistant teachers of different languages, if it is financially feasible." The Nationalities Act complemented this provision by stating that the state was obligated to establish primary and secondary schools where the language of education was that of the national minority. Hungarian was not to be taught even as a subject (although Eötvös's 1848 Public Education Bill still included that). It was only a decade later, in 1879 that teaching Hungarian as a subject was instituted (Article 1879:XVIII) and after a four-year grace period for teachers to acquire the language, it went into effect universally in 1883.

As noted, the Nationalities Act indicated that it was the obligation of the state to provide secondary education in national languages. One of the last significant addresses of the great liberal generation was connected to this. When in 1872 the establishment of a new Serbian Secondary School was on the agenda, Ferenc Deák said the following: "every nationality, even the non-political nationality has the right to educate and cultivate its children in its native language. Even if there are 300 secondary schools in the nation...if one of the secondary schools in the country does not teach in the language predominant in the area, then the advancement of education will be troublesome." If non-Hungarian citizens "are forced to learn everything and everywhere in Hungarian, even if they are only a little or not at all proficient in it since public schools have taught them in their own languages, the advancement of these young people will be impossible, their parents will have wasted money, and the children have spent their time in vain."[55]

Article 1868:IX concerning the Greek-Orthodox issue was an important complement to the rights enacted in the Nationalities Act. This Article assured extensive internal autonomy for Serbian and Romanian orthodox churches. "They are entitled to independently administer and organize their churches, schools, and connecting foundation issues in their periodically convened church congresses, where they are to pass regulations to be sanctioned by the Emperor and to be administered and managed independently through their own media."

The Nationalities Act allowed that in the lower courts every citizen could engage in litigation either in his/her mother-tongue or in a selected language, could follow the legal proceedings in his/her language, and would receive any document relating to legal proceedings in his/her language as well. Around the period of the Compromise lower courts belonged to local governments (communities, districts, and municipalities). In the following years, however, a radical transformation and modernization of the court system took place. Article 1869:IV separated jurisdiction and administration, and nationalized the whole court system. It reinforced the rule that Hungarian was the official language in higher and appellate courts. Lower courts were still regulated by Article 1868:XLIV, paragraphs 7–11. The same Act stated that "at appointing judges special attention should be given to lower court appointment by considering different nationality candidates from the judicial district." The office of judge can be held only by someone "who meets the requirements of Article 1868:XLIV, paragraph 13. The official language of every court appointed by the state government is exclusively Hungarian–refers to higher courts only." Article 1871:XXXIII decreed the same about Prosecution officials and Article 1874:XXXV enacted it about Royal Notaries. Articles 1870:XLII and 1886:XXI, about municipal officials, and 1886:XXII, about community officials, decreed that the provisions of the Nationalities Act applied to personnel appointments. Article 1908:XXXVIII, about organizing public health, obligated community and district physicians to acquire the common language spoken by the majority of the population in their area of professional activity.

The above enumeration contradicts statements made by contemporary publications and some historical literature that the Nationalities Act papered over the language issue and was never meant to be executed by Hungarian governments. Execution of provisions of the Act mostly belonged to autonomous, municipal, communal, and parish bodies. Thus the situation varied from county to county and from community to community. Undoubtedly the tendency, especially after 1875, seemed to be that official use of the Hungarian national language surpassed the limits enacted by the Nationalities Act. Nevertheless, even in the early 20th century in the period of coalition governments with more intolerant nationality policies than the liberal ones, decrees by the Minister of Interior stressed that "county officials, primarily chief constables and district administrators, who continuously and frequently interact with the population, should know the language of the respective district."[56]

In the preamble to the 1913 Bill on universal suffrage the Minister of Interior stated that knowledge of Hungarian was not a prerequisite of the franchise. "The historical tradition of the one thousand-year-old Hungarian state does not acknowledge privileges relating to knowledge of the national language. Hungarian legislation never excluded anybody from the political nation for lacking the knowledge of Hungarian."[57]

Concerned contemporaries also recognized the change in the approach to and the administration of the nationality question by the Hungarian political elite in the 1850's and 1860's. In 1866 Eugen Kvaternik, one of the founders of the Croat Justice Party, wrote about Kossuth to the Italian Foreign Minister, "When Mr. Kossuth acknowledges the Croat state and national existence, and the national autonomy of the Croats, he takes a giant step forward in a gigantic spiritual battle and in reality finally conquered poetry!" *(„C' est un pas immense qu'il vient de faire...Dans un gigantesque combat d'esprit, la réalité a enfin vaincu la poésie!")*[58] All the outstanding personalities of the Hungarian liberal élite took the "giant step forward" in their own way. They trusted that there was a solution and there was sense in making the effort. Even by European standards the effort produced several valuable writings and documents written by liberal political theorists. All this work and mental effort were included in the 1868 Nationalities Act, but as with other enacted statutes this one was also the result of compromise between opposing, polemicizing political powers. Obviously the "gigantic spiritual battle" mentioned by Kvaternik was fought to the finish by only a few Hungarian political leaders. Few came to recognize those truths, which, if put into practice, might have turned the co-existence of the peoples in the Carpathian Basin in a more favorable direction.

Nevertheless, the Nationalities Act even in its limited form was an outstanding creation of Hungarian and East Central European liberalism. Although it did not have provisions for territorial autonomy or collective political rights, the codification of free language use in every forum of public life, the right to establish schools, and the right to free association are still examples to follow in many ways at the end of the 20th century in settling the unsolved nationality problems of the area.

Finally, the following neutral, objective evaluation by the eminent American historian Arthur J. May called the Act "prudential, enlightened legislation." He went on to say, "All in all, the Nationalities Act of 1868 was one of the most enlightened measures of its kind ever adopted, even more liberal than the minority safeguards incorporated in the peace settlement of 1919–20, which, indeed, were very largely modeled on the Hungarian precedent of 1868."[59]

NOTES

1. Editor's note: The elementary and secondary schools, however, were maintained by the various churches and the language of the church was the language of the school, too. Thus, e. g., Orthodox Romanian children were taught in Romanian language.

2. For language laws see Gyula Szekfű, *Iratok magyar államnyelv kérdésének történetéhez 1790–1848.* [Documents to the History of the State Language of Hungary 1790–1848] (Budapest, 1926); Imre Mikó, *Nemzetiségi jog és nemzetiségi politika* [Nationality Rights and Nationality Policy] (Kolozsvár, 1944), 20–37.

3. László Katus, *Multinational Hungary in the Light of Statistics*, in Ferenc Glatz, ed. *Ethnicity and Society in Hungary* (Budapest, 1990), 117.

4. Lajos Kossuth, *Irataim az emigrációból, II.* [My Documents from Exile, II.] (Budapest, 1881), 143.

5. Edmund Bernatzik, *Die österreichischen Verfassungsgesetze. 2.* (Wien, 1911), 151, 159; Gerald Stourzh, Die Gleichberechtigung der Volkstämme als Verwaltungsprinzip 1848–1918, in *Die Habsburgermonarchie 1848–1918.* ed. Adam Wandruszka Bd. III/2. *Die Völker des Reiches* (Wien, 1980), 990–991.

6. László Teleki, *Válogatott munkái*, II [Selected Works II] (Budapest,1961), 19–28.

7. Aurél Kecskeméthy, *Vázlatok egy év történetéből* [Sketches of the History of One Year] (Pest, 1860). 109.

8. Lajos Mocsáry, *Programm a nemzetiség, s a nemzetiségek tárgyában* [Program in the Issues of Nationality and Ethnicity] (Pest, 1860), 109.

9. *Pesti Napló* (December 6, 1860 and January 1, 1861).

10. *Pesti Napló* (November 22, 1860).

11. *Pesti Napló* (April 10, 1961)

12. In March 1861, Serbian Prime Minister Garasanin, and Foreign Secretary Ristic met Hungarian leaders in Pest and Deák agreed with their proposal of rounding-off counties according to nationalities. See, János Risztics, *Szerbia külügyi viszonyai az újabb időben. II. kötet* [Serbia's Foreign Relations in the Most Recent Times, Vol. II.] (Nagybecskerek, 1892), 37–38. On June 8, 1861, the emissary of the Serbian government Nicola Krstic met Deák in Pest. Deák, according to Krstic's hand-written diary, "agrees that Bácska and Bánát (Backa and Banat) would become Serbian counties" but is adverse to the name Vajdaság (Voivodina). In Dnevnik Nikola Krstica, *Arhiv Srpske akademije nauka i umetnosti* (Beograd, br.7198, 8. Juni), published in, Vuckovic, Vojislav J, *Politicka akcija Srbije u juznoslovenskim pokranijama Habsburske Monarhije 1859–1874* (Beograd, 1965), 46. Scovasso, the Italian consul to Belgrade, also reported on February 12, 1863, that "some Hungarian dignitaries assured him that Deák would be willing to extend 'administrative autonomy' to the Serbs, ("alcuni distinti Ungheresi mi assicurarono che il Deák darebbe la sua adesione a tale progetto di autonomie") (Archivio storico del Ministero degli Affari Esteri, Roma. Consolato in Belgrado, 225 (863)). For Eötvös' opinion, see József Eötvös, *Naplójegyzetek–gondolatok, 1864–1868* [Diary Notes–Thoughts 1864–1868] (Budapest, 1941), 176.

13. Editor's note: See József Eötvös, *The Dominant Ideas of the Nineteenth Century and Their Impact on the State.* Two volumes. Translated, edited, annotated, and indexed with an introductory essay by D. Mervyn Johns (New York, 1997–1998).

14. For Eötvös, see Johann Weber, *Eötvös und die ungarische Nationalitätenfrage* [Eötvös and the Hungarian Nationality Question] (München 1966), in Südosteuropäische Arbeiten 64; Paul Bödy, *Joseph Eötvös and the Modernization*

of Hungary, 1840-1870 (Philadelphia, 1972); István Schlett, *József Eötvös* (Budapest, 1987)

15. József Eötvös, *Reform és hazafiság* [Reform and Patriotism] ed. István Fenyő, *Eötvös József művei* [József Eötvös's Works] (Budapest, 1978), III. 341.

16. Eötvös, III. 442.

17. Ibid., 443.

18. József Eötvös, *A nemzetiségi kérdés* [The Nationality Question], in *Báró Eötvös József összes munkái, XVI.* [Collected Works of Baron József Eötvös. XVI] (Budapest, 1903), 25, 29, 45.

19. József Eötvös, *Vallomások és gondolatok* [Confessions and Ideas], ed. Miklós Bényei, *Eötvös József művei* [Works of Eötvös József] (Budapest, 1977), 669, 706.

20. *Eötvös József levele Bánó Józsefhez 1865. május 5.* [József Eötvös' Letter to József Bánó on May 5, 1865], in József Eötvös, *Levelek* [Letters], ed. Ambrus Oltványi, *Eötvös József művei* [Works of József Eötvös] (Budapest, 1976), 395.

21. József Eötvös, *A nemzetiségi kérdés* [The Nationality Question], 68.

22. Ibid., 57.

23. József Eötvös, *Vallomások és gondolatok* [Confessions and Ideas], 670.

24. József Eötvös, *A nemzetiségi kérdés* [The Nationality Question], 51.

25. József Eötvös, *Vallomások és gondolatok* [Confessions and Ideas], 672.

26. Ibid., 671.

27. József Eötvös, *A nemzetiségi kérdés* [The Nationality Question], 30-31.

28. József Eötvös, *Vallomások és gondolatok* [Confessions and Ideas], 574.

29. Ibid., 671-673.

30. Ibid., 707.

31. *Az 1865.évi december 10-ikére hirdetett országgyűlés képviselőházának naplója* [The diary of the Chamber of Deputies of the Parliamentary meeting convened on December 10, 1865], XI. 34.

32. *Az 1848/49. évi népképviseleti országgyűlés* [The 1848-1849 Parliament with Popular Representation], ed., János Beér, (Budapest, 1954), 681-684.

33. Ferenc Deák, Zágráb megye körlevele és az egyesülés [Circular of Zágráb County and the Union] (*Pesti Napló*, March 24, 1861)

34. Ibid.,

35. *Deák Ferenc beszédei* [Speeches of Ferenc Deák], collected by Manó Kónyi, 2nd ed., (Budapest, 1903), II. 257-262.

36. Képviselőházi Napló, 1865-1868 [Diary of the Chamber of Deputies, 1865-1868], XI. 6.

37. *Deák Ferenc beszédei* [Speeches of Ferenc Deák], VI. 93-94.

38. Ibid., 339-340.

39. *Papers of the Chamber of Deputies of the Parliamentary meeting convened in Pest April 2, 1861.* Hereinafter, Writings, 1861, No. 16, 53.

40. Writings, 1865-68, II, 251-261.

41. *Report of the Committee Commissioned in the Nationality Question,* in Writings, 1861. No. 48, 345-48.

42. *Pesti Hirnök*, January 8, June 11 & 23, 1861.

43. Writings, 1865-68, I. 27.

44. Gábor G. Kemény, *Iratok a nemzetiségi kérdés történetéhez Magyarországon a dualizmus korában* [Documents about the History of the Nationality Problem in Hungary during Dualism], I. 1867-92. (Budapest, 1952), 21.

45. Article 1868:XLIII. Par 1.

46. Jelentése az 1865-dik évi magyar országgyűlés képviselőháza által kiküldött bizottság alválasztmányának. [Report of the Sub-committee Delegated by the Committee Selected by the Chamber of Deputies of the Hungarian Parliamentary Meeting of 1865] in Writings, 1865-68. II. 251.

47. Writings, 1865-68, II. 272-76.

48. Ibid., II. 261-4.

49. Hungarian National Archive. Presidential Archive. 1867-Ib-156.

50. Jelentése a nemzetiségi kérdés tárgyában kiküldött bizottságnak. [Report of the committee delegated in nationality problem] in (Writings, 1865-68. VI. 129).

51. Ibid., VI.130-34.

52. Ibid., VI.249-53.

53. Ibid., VII.11-15.

54. Volume XI of the journals of the Chamber of Deputies (of the parliamentary session of 1865-68) and the first volume of the journals of the Upper House contain the parliamentary debate of the nationality law. See Kemény, Writings I. 129-62; Mikó, 184-243; Iván Nagy, *A nemzetiségi törvény a magyar parlament előtt* [The Nationality Law in the Hungarian Parliament] (Budapest, 1930).

55. Képviselőházi Napló 1868-72.XX.388-9. [The Journal of the Chamber of Deputies], 1868-72.XX.388-9.

56. Rendeletek Tára [Gazette of Statutes], 1907, 2108-9.

57. Az 1910. évi június hó 21-ére hirdetett országgyűlés képviselőházának irományai [Papers of of the Chamber of Deputies of the Parliamentary Session convened June 21, 1910], XXIII.53.

58. Archivio Storico del Ministero degli Affari Esteri. Roma. Gabinetto e segretariato generale. Carteggio confidenziale e riservato. Busta 212. Fesc.2,62.

59. Arthur J. May, *The Hapsburg Monarchy 1867-1914.* (New York, 1968), 82-3.

LAJOS MOCSÁRY'S POLITICAL THEORY OF NATIONAL MINORITIES

ISTVÁN CSUCSUJA

In the spring of 1888 a sensational political event took place in the Austro–Hungarian Monarchy. Nothing could have been more surprising and unexpected than 5,000 Romanian constituents electing a Hungarian politician Lajos Mocsáry to represent Romanian minority interests in Parliament. It happened on behalf of, and with the support of, the Romanian National Party in predominantly Romanian Karánsebes, one of the most important electoral districts of the Banat.

Deputy Lajos Mocsáry, a well-known politician of the country, first rose to prominence as a publicist of articles and studies on nationality issues, and later as a parliamentarian and the leader of the largest opposition party, the Independence Party. Mocsáry was one of the politicians who remained true to the revolutionary heritage and democratic ideology of 1848, and asserted its tragic moral in public life. He was known to have formulated policies and proposals concerning many of the demanding political and social issues, notably the nationality question and related policy, ideas which were frequently contradictory to the expectations of the public sentiments. At the beginning of his career Mocsáry had formulated that "Hungary is not a compact but a polyglot country," and professed that acknowledging this was vital to national policy. Hungary was obligated "to allow for a free development of every language and nationality by its 1848 revolutionary heritage." Although this was not the only reason. An unsolved or inappropriately stated nationality question would have disastrous effects upon the country, so reconciling conflicts among nationalities had to become a major issue on the national agenda.[1] Reconciliation and equality were the starting points for the co-operation of various peoples in the Danube Basin, and their advancement was the historical mission of the Hungarians. These objectives, and his dedicated fight for them, encouraged divergent nationalities to consider Mocsáry's stance as the correct political approach for acquiring justice. His election as deputy of Karánsebes was an endorsement of these stated ideas. According to him, if the Hungarians seriously wanted to achieve independence, harmonious co-existence with the nationalities and a peaceful co-operation with their neighboring mother countries were essential precursors.

In his public roles he strove to achieve complete independence for Hungary, to solve the nationality problem, and consequently to establish good relations with neighboring countries. All these factors were dialectically connected. Mocsáry became a leading politician of independence by recognizing that without a satisfactory solution to the nationality problem there would be no up-to-date Hungarian independence policy. Consequently, his nationality policy and efforts to advance minority rights were indispensable features of his independence policy.

Struggles for power and freedom characterized the nationality tensions throughout this whole period. Nurtured on French revolutionary ideas of liberty and equality, Mocsáry rejected any autocratic solution to social issues. Yet, despite his erudition, he was not a theoretician of the nationality problem, but rather approached it from a pragmatic perspective, in contrast to Eötvös. Eötvös's ideas had provided the foundation for the 1868 Nationalities Act as amplified by Ferenc Deák's motion about the Hungarian political nation. Mocsáry did not cease to praise Eötvös's elevated morality since he subordinated "nationality sentiments" to the desire for freedom. Eötvös viewed nationality rights as individual rights, and thought that "nationality sentiments" and the whole "nationality question" would gradually disappear with the liberal state. "...With the development of civilization, the number of nationalities decreases step by step."[2]

Mocsáry's approach was more assertive. In the *Hungarian Social Life*, which started his career as a publicist and public figure, he wrote, "National identity is deep, natural, and instinctive. That is how a nation lives. As long as a nation exists, it inherently contains national sentiments. As soon as a nation's life is charged with vitality and a desire for advancement awakens, devotion to national identity increases. To maintain and develop this devotion is a nation's primary task. This sentiment supplies strength and ability to the grand work of advancement."[3]

The above quote attests to the fact that Mocsáry did not deny the civilizing role of the state and that he acknowledged the validity of this liberal civil doctrine. He averred that civilization and human advancement were of primary importance in the life of a nation. However, in his idea of a state, reconciled nationalities that are content with their own nationality rights would fight for advancement.

Contrary to Eötvös, Mocsáry professed that nationality divisiveness was a problem of primary importance. While Eötvös viewed it as only a basic individual freedom issue, Mocsáry considered it as a problem endemic to different ethnic groups. His approach was substantially different from those politicians who sought only historical causes. He vehemently disagreed with Eötvös that "a sensation of superiority is the basis of every national ambition and its goal is domination."[4] According to Mocsáry "natural instinct is the basis of every national ambition and its goal is subsistence."[5] "A basic tenet is that in our time national domination, annihilation, and oppression of others are not acceptable. In our world, infinite rule is not the ideal. The ideal is rather freedom and civilization with all their benefits. Freedom can be achieved without subjugating and restraining others. Furthermore, the main guarantee of freedom for a nation is freedom of other nations, that is general freedom. Civilization is contradictory to conquest and genocide."[6]

Mocsáry also posited that the desire for domination was not a natural or necessary concomitant of either of the nationality movements. This was a new perception of relationship between Hungarian and Slav nationalities. Anxiety over the nationality issue had always been driven by the fear of Russian and German ambitions. Thus the fear of Pan-Slavism mostly stemmed from a perceived strong connection between Slav and Russian movements. Unfortunately, the essential difference between democratic national ambitions of small Slav peoples and the czarist imperialistic policy of Pan-Slavism was not recognized by Hungarians, or Germans/Austrians.[7]

Mocsáry as well as representatives of Czech movements for progress and democracy, contested the idea that Russia's national character was exclusively Slav. He stated that there were many foreign elements in the czarist empire and that the history of the empire was also imbued with foreign historical influences. He denounced only absolutism, which prevailed in czarism, just as K. Havliček-Borovský, F. Palacky, and T. G. Masaryk had done earlier. Adherence to one's nationality was one of Mocsáry's natural law arguments. On moral grounds he rejected any ambition to forcibly change this trait. He viewed assimilation of dubious outcome. When contemporary politicians asserted that linguistic and spiritual assimilation met the interests of the country, he furiously insisted that even the most adamant absolutism and tyranny failed at that. Moral and intellectual cultivation and the education of nationalities should supercede such a policy. According to these principles Mocsáry outlined the political framework which "would result in the improvement of the nationality problem." In the *Program on the Subject of Nation, and Nationalities*, he cautioned that the nationality problem was still present and had not been "silenced." "Our approach to this problem will be the touchstone of our political maturity."[8] Passion should not decide this issue. The existence of various nationalities and their devotion to their nation/communities, even occasional militancy, should be accepted. Western countries were aware of the situation and would follow the outcome closely.[9] "Full emancipation of nationalities living in this country is inescapable. To avoid or to postpone it is out of the question. The question is how to do it?"[10] He offered the following four-point program for the non-Hungarian speaking population:

"(1) The language of discussion in Parliament to be Hungarian.
(2) At county meetings, all the prevailing languages in the county to be used.
(3) All the living languages of the country to be the languages of the government and administration.
(4) Separate schools to be established for each nationality."[11]

This was meant as a minimal program, to be succeeded by further positive steps as safeguards to a completely new approach taken by Hungarian politics. Nationalities needed to be reassured that Hungarianization was not to be feared.

Mocsáry was aware of the spirit of rapprochement that followed the 1848–49 revolutions and oppression. There were manifestations of solidarity and friendships, but a clear settlement was urgently needed.

Whatever the settlement, the integrity of the country had to be preserved. He advocated fellowship of people within the unity and indivisibility of the country. The settlement should assure that Hungarian would remain the national language of the country, facilitating communication among the various ethnic groups, even while the linguistic emancipation of nationalities was taking place.

Hungarian was to be an administrative, not a dominant language, since if it were the latter, emancipation would be questionable. Although Mocsáry was aware that Hungarians had concerns, he trusted that the vitality and political literacy of the Hungarians would preserve their leading status.

What were the options Mocsáry offered within his four points?

Since a polyglot parliamentary meeting was not a viable option, Hungarian was offered as the language of discussion. However, an authentically translated journal should be released in each language. The items summarized in the following two points stipulated autonomous governments and recalled the constitutional draft which Kossuth wrote in exile. In Mocsáry's view respective nationality languages should be freely used at county and church meetings, just as much as at different forums of government and administration since nationality languages spoken in the country were widely known. Governmental decrees were to be released and minutes recorded in several languages.

The fourth point of the program emphasized the importance of nationality education where everybody in public and higher education would study in his/her language. Nationality languages were to be the means of education, not merely subjects of study. Mocsáry was convinced that education in ethnic languages and development of nationality culture would contribute to the civilization of the whole country. Increasing the level of education was both a social and state objective. Thus nationality schools and cultural institutions were to be extended state funds. He would also encourage young people to learn languages of different nationalities to get aquainted with one another and other cultures. Since there were several peoples and languages living side by side, national interest and love of country should motivate interactions between them.

Despite his criticism of certain aspects of the 1868 Nationalities Act, Mocsáry viewed that "a complete, honest, literal, and spiritual execution of the Act"[12] was the best tool to approach the nationality problem. Before the parliamentary debates of both the majority and the minority proposals, a short paragraph-long temporary Article was needed that "would declare language equality for each citizen, when each prevailing language of this country is accessible in administration and jurisdiction."[13] It can be inferred that he wanted to extend the language use section of the majority proposal and the language stipulations of the Act. He disapproved of the section of the minority proposal which advocated rounding up the counties according nationalities since this would be dangerous to the unity of the land and it might lead to the dismemberment of the country.

Nevertheless, it was obvious for Mocsáry that Article 1868:XLIV included a whole series of rights which could have favorably influenced the relationship of the peoples living in the country despite the failure of the Article to declare nationalities as legal entities.

Mocsáry fought for the enforcement of the Nationalities Act. However, the outcome was doubtful since the Act, especially following the period hall-marked by Deák and Eötvös, was not adhered to. Even during its debate, opposition nationality leaders conspicuously left the meeting. Caught in the teeth of nationality intentions was Mocsáry's fight futile?

Nationality deputies did not oppose the original Eötvös Bill nor certain passages of it. Ferenc Deák's motion was included into the first paragraph of the Act, the passage declared that all citizens were equal and constituted one political, unified, indivisible Hungarian nation irrespective of the nationality of an individual citizen. Otherwise the majority would not have passed the Bill. However, the Bill spoke of "historical nations inhabiting the country" in addition to the proposal of rounding up the counties according to nationalities. Obviously, there was no mutually satisfactory solution between the two versions.

The approach to the Act changed during the Kálmán Tisza era when ambitions to restructure the country on western models surfaced. Nationalities recognized the advantages of the Act which could potentially strengthen their goals and entities in a period when their neighboring national states had consolidated.

Between 1868 and 1914 Mocsáry, a protector of nationality rights, battled for the Nationalities Act to be observed as fundamental law. He fought for the enforcement of a law which could have a turning point in the ethnic question.[14]

For the implementation of his nationality program, Mocsáry had to fight daily political battles. He declared both in Parliament and in other forums of public life that nationality rights should be respected, their institutions should be subsidized, non-Hungarian speaking citizens should be considered for high office, and electoral district divisions and the census should be revised. His pamphlet called for institutes of public education to relinquish assimilation policies. He raised an outcry against the Hungarianization of public education and passionately argued with Béla Grünwald, who opted for centralized administration as opposed to county autonomy, on the nationality question. Mocsáry argued that county autonomies were essential to balance power against Vienna and also for national equality.

He was active in the foreground of domestic and European public interest which brought him recognition among the nationalities, and even in Romania. He was praised by Josif Vulcan, a well-known Romanian writer, who wrote in *Gazeta Transilvaniei* that "Nobody can claim that Mocsáry is not the most respected Hungarian."[15] Following his 1886 speeches in the interest of Romanian nationalities, he was presented with a memorial album containing signatures of Transylvanian Romanian intellectuals, even that of the Metropolitan of Nagyszeben (Sibiu), Miron Romanul. Corneliu Diaconovici, the author of *Enciclopedia Română*, eulogized him while the Croat and Romanian press repeatedly called him an outpost of understanding among ethnic peoples.[16] In 1878, in connection with the Miletič-trial, he managed to win the Serbian public opinion irrespective of party differences. In the political circles of Transylvanian Saxons he was hailed as a judicial sage. Edmund Steinacker, who was both a politician and a scholar of nationality issues, called him an asset of future collaboration among the peoples of the area.[17]

It was of crucial significance that in 1887 the Hungarian–Serbian–German opposition ran Mocsáry as its candidate for election in Újvidék (Novi Sad). However, official electors detailed there by the Tisza Government prevented Mocsáry from winning a seat in Parliament. Nevertheless his candidacy and support by an enthusiastic populace demonstrated the possibilities for abiding friendship between Hungarian and neighboring peoples. Finally, when the Karánsebes deputies General Traian Doda and Mihai Popoviciu did not attend the Parliament due to nationality policy reasons, the Romanian National Party handed its mandate to Mocsáry in 1888.

Mocsáry faithfully represented both his country and his Romanian electors.[18] At the end of his parliamentary service he said, "the mere fact that I represented Karánsebes will not vanish without a trace. It will make a mark...In a period of prominent differences the Romanian Party gave the parliamentary mandate to a Hungarian man...Where opposition parties are able to act and speak this way, the connecting tissues of mutual understanding and reconciliation are not cut yet."[19]

Mocsáry's stand on the ethnic issue were unpopular in his own party. Opposition arose within his Independence Party in 1874 because his program was perceived as an obstacle to gathering votes. This was despite the fact that the 1848 Party had a theoretical commitment, declared in its Party Manifesto of 1868, that it would fight for a solution to the nationality issue in the name of equality and freedom, while still preserving the integrity of the country.

Early in 1870 there were discussions between Dániel Irányi, spokesman of the leftwing of the 1848 Party, and the national Romanian–Serb club of deputies (Alexandru Mocioni, Svetozar Miletič, and Iosif Hodoşiu). A Parliamentary Bill, passed by the Romanian–Serb club as a probable statute of the land, went well beyond the 1868 Nationalities Act and showed similarities with the original Bill of the same year. It recognized Hungarians, Romanians, Serbs, Slovaks, Ruthenians, and Germans as politically equal. And the language of the legislature would remain the language of the majority—Hungarian. Irányi's statute resembled Kossuth's draft constitution and the Union of the Danube States.[20] Although the discussions on the Bill had several favorable effects, it was never brought to the floor of Parliament. This was followed by a period of mutual isolation begun by an 1869 proclamation of the Romanian National Party.

The change in national policy had its effect within the Independence Party as well. In the Kálmán Tisza period the nationality issue became secondary, and by the 1881 Annual Meeting, after accepting the Party's Transylvanian Committee Program, the nationality issue was completely removed from the Party's official program.

The Party accepted Mocsáry's April 1879 speech on educational issues, but completely rejected his speech on behalf of nationalities in February 1886.[21] Soon afterwards, Mocsáry was compelled to resign from the Deputies' Club of the Independence Party.

Mocsáry, a politician of Hungarian independence from Austria, who followed closely the nationality problems of the Empire, did not believe in Austria's stabilizing mission among the Danube nations. In this he differed from the Czech J. Palacky and other politicians of the extreme opposition. Mocsáry, the shrewd pragmatist, considered it essential to establish good connections with the Danubian and Balkan states, since he viewed the area in its historical context and in its uniqueness.

In a series of articles[22] written in 1870 he stated that the Danube Basin was inhabited by small nations, some of which would have to live in several states during their lifetime. Therefore small nations should work to improve mutual support, providing both domestic and international benefits. As he suggested in the book, *Some Words about the Nationality Issue*, an independent Hungary should turn towards the Danubian states and increase its commitments to Serbs and Romanians. Legally recognized nationalities would form bridges between Hungary and Serbia and Romania allowing the pursuit of common policies, something necessary since an alliance with these countries seemed to be Hungary's historical destiny. Earlier it had been a common danger that had brought these countries together; now the protection of freedom and independence. "Common interests, the need of friends and allies, will prevail despite frictions and antagonisms." One of his insightful observations was that the development of national consciousness would bring peoples into closer connection. "...Good relationship with nationalities is a requisite for good connections with neighboring states."[23]

Yes, peaceful political connections could be maintained with neighboring countries even if the nationality question was not well regulated; international pressure might lead to acceptable political connections. But permanent friendly relationships and mutual support could evolve only through a modus vivendi with the nationalitites.[24]

Mocsáry's ideas about Eastern Europe and his anti-Austrian stand undoubtedly stemmed from Kossuth's statements in exile.[25] So did his disagreement with the foreign politics of the Compromise Era reflected Kossuth's ideas. Freedom and political independence of neighboring countries would constitute assurance for all the Danube Basin peoples including Hungarians against expansionism. Because Hungary was surrounded by a Slav ring, it felt threatened by Pan-Slavism. However, free nations minimized dangers. Thus, the battles for national independence by neighboring peoples coincided with the interests of Hungary since it was the realization of "natural and just aspirations." The result would be independent national policies leading to useful alliances.

Mocsáry did not consider Kossuth's much debated Danube Confederacy obsolete, even in the 1870's. On the contrary, in his view it was going to be an inevitable part of European development. Parts of the plan might be modified according to the future international political situation, but the basic outlines and premises still stood. As part of the resolution of the nationality question, the confederation would be constituted by a number of independent states "as a purely international alliance" in unison with the common interest. The confederation would not operate by alternating parliamentary sessions in Pest, Bucharest or Belgrade, nor would it have common Kossuthian coordinating bodies. Instead, Mocsáry conceived of a looser "alliance of states" and allocated more time for the confederation to develop. Because Austrian and Turkish imperial ambitions persisted in South-Eastern Europe, political absolutism confounded and complicated connections among future states. "There is a historical, ethnographic, ethnic, and cultural chaos here."[26] Consequently the primary task of Hungarian policy would be to assume that Hungary and Hungarians would come forward as independent factors on behalf of themselves and of neighboring peoples. Mocsáry said about the direction of Hungarian foreign policy, "Our neighborhood ought to be the center of our attention." Hungarians must be ready to fulfill their mission to avoid external rule and to lay the foundation for the future.[27]

The idea of alliances among neighboring populations defined his stance during the period of the flare-up of the Eastern issue just before and during the Russo–Turkish War of 1877–78. The War finalized the liberation movements of the Balkan peoples and those of the Romanians when the Czarist Empire sided with the South-Eastern nations. However, the Hungarian still remembered the czarist forces which overpowered the Hungarian revolution of 1849 foaming suspicion ever since. Turkey, on the other hand, granted asylum to the exiled revolutionaries, just as it had done before to Ferenc Rákóczi II and his fighters in the early 18th century.

Mocsáry's statements are a testimony to his consistency during that controversial period. Being aware of the strength and power of ethnicity, he could differentiate between czarist imperial interests and ethnic liberation movements and his sympathy was with neighboring peoples. "I declare that I fully recognize those peoples' aspirations for freedom."[28]

Both Kossuth and Mocsáry professed that Hungarians owed gratitude to the Turks for protection in 1849. However, both of them rejected any kind of external political rule and expansionism from that direction. That was why Mocsáry defended nationalities and national political leaders who openly or secretly identified themselves with their mother-country. Many shared his view that any "declaration of solidarity between our nationalities and their relatives in a different country is natural and justified."[29] Mocsáry went beyond making theoretical statements. Early in 1878 there was a sentence brought against Svetozar Miletič, a Serbian politician and publicist. Miletič, whose legal immunity was violated, was arrested and indicted for high treason by the Tisza Government. He was charged with conducting secret recruitment on behalf of Serbia during the 1876 Serbo-Turkish war and was sentenced to five years in prison. Mocsáry contested the sentence, which he considered unlawful, and wrote an article of appeal–*"In the Miletič case."* The document ignited a great storm in politics and the press. "I openly declare and repeat that I fully appreciate the sympathy Miletič feels towards his relatives in Serbia," Mocsáry wrote. Miletič's call for the Serbs to help their "racial relations" did not constitute high treason. Furthermore, he would not be guilty even if he made plans and campaigned for Greater Serbia unless he violated some law. Law and justice should be the shields of freedom.[30]

Mocsáry was one of the few Hungarians who recognized the turning point in the lives of South-Eastern European peoples with respect to the nationality movements–the occupation of Bosnia-Herzegovina by Austria-Hungary. In the wake of the 1878 occupation many feared the conflicts would become permanent.

Mocsáry consistently referred to the occupation of Bosnia-Herzegovina as annexation. He openly turned against the claim that rebels had resisted the Austro-Hungarian army. He condemned the official policy that declared that the authorities of the Monarchy in Bosnia were lawful. When in Parliament he was accused of "fraternizing with the South Slav states," he stated that since the Austro-Hungarian authorities marching into Bosnia were not Bosnian, it would be unreasonable to expect Bosnians to accept them. "They cannot be required to do that because, for them, the authorities are tools of aggressive occupation, not of legitimate authority and European common law allows for resistance in such a case....The occupation was done for the sake of the reigning royal family as it suited their traditional ambition to expand territorially and to increase population."[31] He recognized that the common army had permanently taken up quarters in the occupied provinces and demonstrated foresight by arguing that the annexation of Bosnia-Herzegovina was a political ploy. Since rule in Bosnia-Herzegovina would be "absolutist," it might further damage the authenticity of democracy within Hungary.[32]

Mocsáry was aware of the ethical and political problems that the Bosnia-Herzegovina situation raised for Hungarian society quite apart from financial and human disadvantages. He urged Hungarians that it was in their future interest to support the people of the occupied territories and not to stand by Vienna's expansionism. Hungarians should speak out for public law because this would be "beneficial for the Hungarian nation because nations who are destined to be good neighbors will say that the occupation was the policy of the Austrian royal family, not that of the Hungarian nation. Hungarian policy will always have the right to expect friendly relations."[33]

He tried to reassure those who struggled with the threat of Pan-Slavism. "Movements in Bosnia-Herzegovina do not anticipate a future Slav state. Bulgaria, Montenegro, and Serbia are focal points reflecting the direction of development." He did not perceive any danger in Bosnia-Herzegovina joining Montenegro or Serbia since an enlarged Serbia would not threaten the Austro-Hungarian Monarchy.

His objections to the Austro-Hungarian military occupation of Bosnia-Herzegovina were endorsed by Kossuth. In a letter of March 9, 1882, from Turin, Kossuth encouraged Mocsáry to stay resolute in these issues since "the nationality question literally evolved into a foreign affair issue. Therefore it cannot be solved with any domestic measures or concessions."[34]

Mocsáry supported and appreciated the aspirations and manifestations of nationality movements as long as they were reconcilable with Hungarian vital interests and capacity. His Újvidék (Novi Sad) candidacy for Parliament, his Karánsebes mandate, and his documents of a long correspondence with Andrej Kmet attested to his abiding support of nationality movements within his country.

He pursued public or friendly relationships with such nationality politicians and writers, as the Slovak Andrej Kmet, the Serbian Mihajlo Polit and Jasa Tomič, the Romanian Gheorghe Pop de Băseşti, and other dedicated nationalists provided that they were not enemies of the Hungarian people. He did not commit the mistake of less well-informed politicians who pontificated about democratic principles while inadvertently encouraging anti-Hungarian propaganda abroad. Anti-Hungarian propaganda intensified his voice. When Björn Björnson made a frontal attack against the Hungarians in his Paris paper, Mocsáry reacted to Andrej Kmet, the Slovak politician, saying "I have stated several times exactly in the *Courrier* that I disapprove of our prevailing nationality policy. Still, I will not allow insults against Hungarians."[35] When Björnson did not content himself with criticizing the government's school policy, an issue which Mocsáry also opposed, and extended his attacks, Mocsáry wrote to the Slovak intellectual politician "...exactly because I honor nationalities' true devotion to their kind and language, *hanc veniam damus petimusque vicissim*, nobody has the right to insult a nation..."[36]

Throughout this period he supported the notion of "integer Hungary" and that was the reason why he could not win over Mihajlo Polit to his federative-liberal ideas and also why he refuted the statement of a *Pester Lloyd* article in January 1908 which described him as federative and as a devotee of "Eastern Switzerland."[37] As a Hungarian, he fought for nationality rights and for the improvement of the national question while enjoying a substantial support of the Hungarian people. When, after the 1886 budget debate, he was excluded from his party and became isolated, his constituents and Independence Party organization declared solidarity with his policy.[38] Reassured by this trust he asserted "I am not alone with my views."[39]

How far did Mocsáry get with respect to nationality rights and consensus with neighboring nations? How much did his struggle coincide with the goals of nationality movements? As a politician who respected his people, nation, and minority nationalities, he went farther than any other politician under the circumstances. In his concept, however, as much as in the general mentality of the time, the national question did not have separate directions or internal regularity. He understood that the nationality movements were innately democratic, although he did not perceive that each of them had separate territorial and political characteristics including striving for total territorial, national, and political integration. He did not see that their program of separate political-administrative territories and autonomy within Hungary, demanding equal rights for all the nationalities, was a first step towards secession. Nor did he recognize that the nationality rights and laws he referred to were no longer considered by these nationalists extending assurances for autonomous development, but rather were assurances for eventual secession by new generations of nationality movements.

NOTES

1. Lajos Mocsáry, A vármegye ostroma [The Siege of the County] (*Ellenőr,* June 10, 1969), 83.

2. *Képviselőházi Napló* [Journal of the Chamber of Deputies] 1865–68. XI. 31–34, cf, József Eötvös, *A XIX. század uralkodó eszméinek befolyása az álladalomra,* I. [Influence of Prevailing 19th Century Ideas on the State] (Budapest, 1892), 63–78.

3. Lajos Mocsáry, *A magyar társasélet* [Hungarian Social Life] (Pest, 1855), 64.

4. Eötvös, 65.

5. Lajos Mocsáry, *Nemzetiség* [Nationality] (Pest, 1858), 87.

6. Ibid., 87–88.

7. Ibid., 198.

8. Lajos Mocsáry, *Programm a nemzetiség és a nemzetiségek tárgyában* [Program on the Subject of Nation and Nationalities] (Pest, 1860), 87.

9. Ibid., 1–2.

10. Ibid., 109.

11. Ibid., 72.

12. Mocsáry Lajos nyilatkozata [Lajos Mocsáry's statement] (*Egyetértés,* January 19, 1908), 17.

13. A nemzetiségi kérdés [The Nationality Problem] (*Hon,* November 11, 1868, 26).

14. Mocsáry Lajos nyilatkozata [Lajos Mocsáry's statement] (*Egyetértés,* January 19, 1908, 17).

15. *Gazeta Transilvaniei,* February 13/25, 1887. No. 33.

16. Budapest'a, 15 aprilie 1886, Luminatorul, April 21, 1886. No. 29.

17. E. Steinacker, Eötvös and Mocsáry (*Nation und Staat,* 1928), 928–934.

18. *Tribuna,* January 15/27, 1891. No.11.

19. Mocsáry's farewell note to his Karánsebes electors (*Egyetértés,* January 3, 1892), 3.

20. A nemzetiségi törvényjavaslat [The Nationalities Bill] (*A Hon,* April 23, 1870), 92.

21. *Képviselőházi Napló* [Journal of the Chamber of Deputies] 1884–87. IX. 38–39.

22. A magyar külpolitikáról [On Hungarian Foreign Policy] (*Ellenőr,* October 22–23, 1870), 37–38.

23. Lajos Mocsáry, *Néhány szó a nemzetiségi kérdésről* [Some Words about the Nationality Question] (Budapest, 1886), 65.

24. Ibid.

25. Lajos Mocsáry, *A közösügyi rendszer zárszámadása* [Balance of the Joint System] (Budapest, 1902).

26. *A magyar külpolitikáról* [On Hungarian Foreign Policy] (*Ellenőr,* October 22–23, 1870), 37–38.

27. Ibid.

28. *Képviselőházi Napló* [Journal of the Chamber of Deputies], 1879–81. XIV. 136–137.

29. Lajos Mocsáry, *Néhány szó a nemzetiségi kérdésről* [Some Words about the Nationality Question] (Budapest, 1886), 78.

30. Lajos Mocsáry, *Miletičs elitéltetése* [Miletič's Conviction] (*Egyetértés,* January 20, 1878), 20.

31. *Képviselőházi Napló* [Journal of the Chamber of Deputies], 1881-84. VI. 43-44.

32. Ibid.

33. Ibid.

34. Kossuth's letter published in *Mocsáry Lajos válogatott írásai* [Lajos Mocsáry's Selected Writings], collected and introduced by Gábor G. Kemény (Budapest, 1958), 507-508.

35. Ibid., 579.

36. Ibid., 580.

37. Mocsáry Lajos nyilatkozata [Lajos Mocsáry's Statement] (*Hon,* January 19, 1908), 17.

38. Mocsáry Lajos nyílt levele [Lajos Mocsáry's Open Letter] (*Egyetértés,* March 11, 1887), 69.

39. Lajos Mocsáry, *Néhány szó a nemzetiségi kérdésről* [Some Words about the Nationality Question] (Budapest, 1886), 63.

THE HUNGARIAN-CROAT COMPROMISE OF 1868

IMRE RESS

The bourgeois revolutions of 1848 whose aims were to dismantle the feudal society were accompanied by a series of nationality clashes throughout the Danube Basin. This period saw signs of newly awakened national communities all demanding to restructure the intertwining connections and positions they shared in the Habsburg Monarchy. The Hungarian-Croat relationship was an integral part of the decades-long process of evolving national emancipation within the Monarchy, influenced by such factors as power relations, ethnic ratios, and the relationship between the great powers.

The Hungarian-Croat Commonwealth originated in the Middle Ages and retained into modern times such feudal elements of Croatian separation as the Provincial Diet (Sabor), the Ban (viceroy of Croatia), and the county system, even though Croat territory itself did not constitute a separate political and administrative unit. However, within the Habsburg Monarchy the Dalmatian-Croat-Slavonian Triune Kingdom implied a virtual Croat state and included at least four different territorial units. The authority of Croat feudal institutions was limited and affected only three counties of Croatia proper. Yet, this central area was separated from the three Slavonian counties by the Military Border which was under the auspices and directions of the Vienna Court War Council (*Hofkriegsrat*). The Slavonian counties, which had representatives both in the Hungarian Diet and the Croat Provincial Diet, were claimed by both Hungarians and Croats. Furthermore, Croat constitutional theory also claimed Dalmatia, an Austrian province (governed from Vienna), Fiume (an old German imperial seaport annexed in 1779 by the Holy Crown of Saint Stephen), and Turkish Croatia (belonging to the Ottoman Empire) to be part of the Triune Kingdom.

Among the issues which generated permanent controversies were interpretations of centuries old laws regarding the parliamentary rights of the *Sabor* delegates, and the exact degree of Croatian autonomy. Applying language laws often conceived to be rational administrative tools, was an additional difficult issue. The use of Hungarian instead of Latin in the common Diet, and between Hungarian and Croat authorities, was perceived by the Croats to be a severe constitutional grievance. In addition, Croats adhered to a political concept that considered Hungarian jurisdiction over Croat territories as only temporary until a territorial resolution was completed, a concept also the source of latent conflicts. In Croatia and Slavonia there was no significant Hungarian population, apart from a few sporadic groups. Therefore the Hungarian–Croat relationship was not burdened by those Hungarian-landowner vs. nationality-peasant conflicts which afflicted other areas.[1]

Croatia's political relationship with Hungary was a central issue of Croat politics, and had a basic impact on the development of the system which began in the Reform Era and lasted until the end of the 19th century. A pro-Hungarian faction composed of landowning aristocrats, government officials, county officials, and overseers, all perceived Croatian national development best served within the Kingdom of Hungary. In addition to safeguarding their autonomy and the traditional county system, they endorsed participation in the Hungarian Parliament, and supported the introduction of liberal economic and social reforms urged by the Hungarian liberals in Croatia.

Another grouping, oriented towards Vienna, became a significant political factor from the 1840's onward as the National Party. Their program blended Croatian feudal traditions and Slavic cultural ideas. Their primary goal was to establish a united Croat political nation and to achieve equal political status for the Triune Kingdom.

By the use of the name 'Illyr' as a symbol of national self-identification they professed the ethnic unity of the Southern Slavs and encouraged cultural and political unification. This intellectual movement created considerable distrust in Hungary since the future prospects of a Southern Slav Union led by Croats would threaten the integrity of of the countries of the Crown of St. Stephen.[2] To sum up, Hungarian–Croat antagonisms were of feudal and political origin and were caused, to some degree, by the fears and intimidations of a small nation within a multi-national state.

CONFRONTATION IN 1848

In the spring of 1848 the Hungarian Diet, under pressure from revolutions in Europe and Hungary specifically, passed a series of laws which laid down the foundations of the bourgeois and national transformation of the country. The April Laws of 1848, however, did not include comprehensive reform of Croatian autonomy according to the needs of the newly adopted representative governing system. Instead, Croatian autonomy was reinforced, albeit with the earlier political and territorial status quo remaining intact. As was usual in constitutional monarchies the appointment of the Croat *Ban* by the monarch had to be ministerially approved. The laws proclaimed the principle of popular representation including the means for Croatian representation in the Hungarian Parliament. Accordingly, representatives from the Slavonian counties were individually elected while deputies from Croatia to the Hungarian Parliament were delegated by the *Sabor*.[3] One result of this practice was that Croatia and Slavonia remained legally divided.

Based on direct negotiations between the Hungarian Parliament and the Croat *Sabor*, legislators in Pozsony (Bratislava) planned to discuss the content of Croatian autonomy at a future date.[4] However, due to the rapid events of the revolution, the ideas upon which this autonomy was to be based became obsolete. In March 1848, the national revolutionary action program, accepted at a mass-meeting in Zagreb, demanded equal political status for Croatia with Hungary within the Habsburg Monarchy and the immediate establishment of independent legislative and executive authorities for Croatia. The Croatian demands submitted the Hungarian–Croatian relationship to a decisive test since their realization opposed the Hungarian political strategy and depended on the centralization of the Habsburg Empire. Colonel Josip Jelačić promoted within two weeks to Lieutenant General and who was appointed to the position of *Ban* by the Monarch during the revolutionary days, played an important role in the ensuing events. This border guard officer was the first born Croat to serve in the position of the *Ban*, the symbol of Croatian autonomy for a long period of time. His connections with the Illyr political movement established his reputation which he increased with social and nationality measures. Under the pretext of protecting Croat autonomy, he openly turned against the Hungarian government. Since

Jelačić contested the legality of the April Laws–he objected to limiting the Monarch's power–the prospects for a settlement through negotiations were doubtful.[5]

The differences stemming from the bilateral relationship and the unsettled political connection were not the only reasons why the Croatian national movement turned against the Hungarian government. The prospects for national transformation and political separation in the wake of European revolutions reinforced Croatian interests in the survival of the Habsburg Monarchy. The prospects of triumphant national, German, Italian, and Hungarian, revolutions threatened the existence of the Monarchy and created more fear than hope in the Croats, mostly due to their inferior demographic and geographical situation. The central question of the European revolutions had to do with the constitution and territorial scope of Germany, as debated by the Frankfurt Parliament. Although the Croats were not directly effected by the German unification, indirectly it limited their scope in many ways. The Croats rejected a Pan-German state because the German-Austrian provinces might join it, strengthening the Eastern successor state of the Habsburg Monarchy–"Kossuth's Great Hungary" including Transylvania and Hungary.[6]

The nature of prospective national states in Central Europe compelled the Croats to opt for a Habsburg Monarchy separated from Germany and an Austro-Slav constitutional federation. In the hope of a federation that would endow the Slavs living within the Habsburg Empire with equal rights, the Croat *Sabor* declared the secession of the Triune Kingdom from Hungary and the establishment of a new political connection with Austria including representation in the Vienna *Reichstag*.[7]

Of course, unilateral declaration of separation or secession gravely impacts relationships between respective parties. However, Croatian Austro-Slavism was not just a nationalist idea to restructure the Hungarian-Croatian relationship; it was also a Southern Slav integrating effort to restructure the whole Empire. Its realization would have limited the far-reaching Hungarian autonomy within the Empire and would have violated Hungarian territorial integrity. Croat political emancipation within the Austro-Slav context would have required a constitutionally centralized government of the Habsburg Monarchy, which would have required the elimination of an independent Hungarian national defense and finance. Moreover, Croat political emancipation program envisioned large-scale territorial restructuring. Beyond separating historical Croatian territories the Serbian Voivodeship in Southern Hungary and the areas of the Austrian provinces inhabited by Slovenes would have been united with the Triune Kingdom. In the summer of 1848 a wide-scale Croat mobilization gave emphasis to these demands and when Vienna infringed upon Hungarian autonomy the opportunity for an attack arrived.

Whenever there was an open confrontation between the Imperial and the Hungarian government, the Croats made assertions on three issues: to restore the rights of the Emperor-King, to protect Imperial unity, and for nationality emancipation. In order to ward off the Croat threat, Hungary issued a peace initiative which included the possibility of a political dissolution of the bilateral connection—the separation of Croatia.[8] This initiative was not successful but not because it was belated or because there were unacceptable conditions attached to surrendering the Slavonian territories. Rather, bilateral separation which granted autonomy and equal status to Croatia was not of interest to the Croats. In September 1848 Croatia attacked Hungary to eliminate Hungarian political separation, which in Croat eyes was the greatest obstacle in the way of an Austro-Slav federative transformation of the Monarchy. Neither the failure of the Croat intervention nor their contribution to the suppression of the October Revolution in Vienna diminished the support in Croatia of military obligations for the Monarch. In the spring of 1849 the Croat national consensus was broken when limitations were imposed both on the constitution and the free press. Signs of an absolutist restoration and the military successes of the Hungarian army forced some Croat liberals to reconsider their relationship with Hungary but they did not go beyond careful orientation. After the defeat of the 1848–49 Hungarian War of Independence, the Habsburgs imposed a neo-absolutism in the form of the same rules on both the Croats and the Hungarians. For the Croats, these were rewards; for the Hungarians, they were punishments.

IN A COMMON FRONT IN 1861

By the end of the 1850's, the Habsburg experiment in hindering Italian national unification had ended in a lost war which, however, also marked the beginning of a series of reforms to transform and restructure the government. Neo-absolutism was in a crisis and, so, was exchanged for constitutional centralism in an attempt to preserve German hegemony. It was supposed to consolidate the Monarchy by sustaining a central government and by the establishment of a Central Parliament (*Reichsrat*). Both the Hungarian Parliament, convened in the spring of 1861, and the Croat Provincial Diet rejected this governing system. Instead of observing the authority of the Central Parliament in Vienna and electing delegates to it, both national parliaments reaffirmed their autonomy by retaining the old constitution and by enforcing the political achievements of 1848.

From a Hungarian perspective, the political legacy of 1848 rested in the territorial and legislative restoration of the countries of the Holy Crown and a constitutional representative government of the country based on the April Laws. It would have included the renewal of political connections directly between Hungary and Croatia, which was governed as a separate province during the neo-absolutistic period. However, Hungarian policy, which insisted on the principle of legal continuity, was inclined to agree to major changes in the substance of Croat autonomy. Supported by the Hungarian leadership, Ferenc Deák distanced himself from the "conquest theory" of Hungarian romantic nationalism of the Reform Era, a theory which would have contested Croatian autonomous rights.[9] In two of his addresses to Parliament, Deák stated that Croatia was a separate political nation with its own territory and that based on the mutual agreement between the two nations' parliamentary bodies it was possible to expand autonomy in Croatia. Moreover Deák would acquiesce if Croatia decided on total separation and on joining the Central Parliament. The Hungarian position was to achieve mutual compromise even on controversial territorial issues. One of the sources of discord in the Reform Era and in 1848 was the status of the three Slavonian counties and Deák declared them to be parts of the Triune Kingdom. However, he was not willing to give up Muraköz (Medimurje), which was annexed by Croatia after 1849 and re-attached to Hungary in 1860, and Fiume, which was majority Italian.[10]

Croat political trends of the 1860's were still divided by both the substance and type of political connections with Hungary. As a result of negative experiences during the period of neo-absolutism, such as regulations limiting Croatian autonomy, and those promoting Germanization, the political program of Croat liberal nobility, which had sought Croatian national existence within Hungary, was revived. In the 1860's as before, still mostly aristocrats and landowners represented this trend. However, their social support was greater than before 1848.

Several aristocratic and intellectual followers of the Illyrian movement also concluded that the constitutional Hungarian state, and not Imperial absolutism and centralization, would assure extensive Croatian autonomy. The election of a pro-Hungarian representative from Zagreb for a decade after 1861 demonstrated the changed perspective of the city bourgeoisie. [11] The pro-Hungarian, i.e. unionist political program recognized the validity of the April Laws of 1848 in order to safeguard against imperial centralization. At the same time, the resolutions of the Croat Provincial Diet of 1848, which established Croatia's administrative independence, were considered as an equal source of law. Declaration of a Croat *de facto* independence was connected to a voluntary union with Hungary based on historical law and the present mutual interests of both nations in protecting constitutional freedom.[12] The liberals claimed not to have any prerequisites. However, constitutional representative government, restoration of autonomous institutions, and territorial integrity were their basic requirements. Despite its increasing popularity the National Constitutional Party, which advocated union with Hungary, did not become a significant political factor. The unionists remained in minority in the Provincial Diet both during the 1861 constitutional transformation and during the preparation for the Hungarian–Austrian Compromise in 1865–1867.

From the 1860's on, the dominant trend of the Croat national movement was represented by the National Party, constituted of the Catholic clergy and the mainly non-aristocratic intelligentsia holding office during the Bach period. The National Party adopted and improved the legacy of the Reform Era and that of 1848 in several areas. This Croat national liberal ideology was made of two stable elements: an integrative Southern Slav ideology, renewed in the form of Yugoslavism, and the federative transformation of the Habsburg Monarchy. They were, however, distant goals. Political emancipation of the Triune Kingdom and territorial restitution according to historical political law were regarded as the main immediate tasks by the national liberal majority of the 1861 *Sabor*. As a consequence of the Revolution of 1848, the Croatian Provincial Diet declared the Croatian commonwealth with Hungary null and void. In the absence of the pro-Hungarian minority, who had left the session in protest, they passed Article 42:1861 which codified the separation and political autonomy of the Triune Kingdom. They were not averse to renewing political connections with Hungary as long as Hungary accepted Croatian political equality and territorial integrity according to political law. In return, they would restore common legislation and government with Hungary while public administration, religion, education, and jurisdiction would remain within the sphere of Croat autonomy. The Imperial government supported Croat political emancipation in order to break Hungarian opposition to constitutional centralism, but was less inclined to accept territorial integrity. The question of constitutional centralism divided the National Party considerably. By a narrow margin, the Provincial Diet rejected common affairs with Austria and participation in the Central Parliament.[13]

There was a split in the National Party after the Sabor was dissolved and absolutism was restored. The office holder intelligentsia, gathering around Croat Court Chancellor Ivan Mažuranić, strove to achieve autonomy and the unification of divided Croatian territories by adopting common affairs with Austria and by participating in the Central Parliament. However, a substantial Croat opposition sprung up against the compromise with the centralist system. All of the pro-Hungarian unionists and the majority of national liberals turned against this idea of compromise. During the Schmerling Government the alliance of the two parties for the defense of Croat historical political law crosscut attempts to generate a parliamentary majority in support of constitutional Imperial centralism.[14]

THE COMPROMISE ON ITS WAY

In the mid-1860's a series of crises signaled that the Vienna government was unable to stabilize Imperial internal politics and finances. Owing to its unsuccessful Hungary policy the Schmerling Government lost both the confidence of the Emperor-King Francis Joseph and the support of the Central Parliament. The vital interests of the Empire required a settlement of the political situation in the countries of the Holy Crown and both sides showed increased propensity towards a compromise. The Hungarian political leadership was ready to adjust the April Laws of 1848 for the sake of the security and stability of the Monarchy, and they would accept "common affairs. For his side, Francis Joseph was inclined to restore the territorial, legislative, and administrative unity of the countries of the Crown of Saint Stephen.

The constitutional dualism that replaced a centralist Monarchy significantly rearranged Croat political power relations. The alliance of the unionists and the national liberals broke up. On the one hand the unionists approved of the dualist transformation of the Monarchy and, as a result, of the Croat autonomy within Hungary. On the other hand the goal of the national liberals was the emancipation of the Triune Kingdom and the federalization of the Empire. Joining forces with the earlier supporters of the centralist government they created a majority in the Provincial Diet convened in the fall of 1865.[15] Their success, however, was not complete since the significance and influence of the pro-Austrian group significantly decreased after Schmerling's defeat and the resignation of the Croat–Slavonian Court Chancellor Ivan Mažuranić, who had opposed compromise with the Hungarians. The national liberals' reversal revealed the dilemma of the Croat national movement. It had sought protection within Hungary at the appearance of German centralism but had then sought protection at the Imperial Court against dualism. Political emancipation and territorial integrity were the prices set by the Croats for either an alliance with Hungary or cooperation with Vieanna. But the dualist system was not advantageous for wide-scale Croat emancipation. Vienna still attached high significance to Croatian aspirations, but from the fall of 1865 onwards they considered them as tools of pressure and concessions to promote the Hungarian compromise. In order to expand the spheres of mutual interests with the Croats the address of the Hungarian Parliament passed in February 1866, alluded to Croat territorial integrity within Hungary as a requirement of the compromise with the Monarch.[16] These were only sufficient to initiate talks, supported by the Imperial Government, between the delegates of the Hungarian and the Croatian parliaments.

In April 1866 Croat delegates of the Sabor including national liberals and followers of the pro-Austria National Independent Party, arrived in the Hungarian capital with a maximal program of seeking political emancipation and recognition of Croatian state territory as outlined by historical law and the ethnic principle. The Hungarians refused the "personal union" interpretation of the

Croat Article 42:1861 but were willing to recognize the scope of authority outlined in it. Territorially, the Hungarians recognized the Slavonian counties as integral parts of the Triune Kingdom, but refused to give up Muraköz (Medimurje), and Fiume. Talks broke up at the news of the Austro-Prussian War and were not resumed even after the conclusion of peace.[17]

After the defeated Austria left the *Deutscher Bund,* the Croat National Party again hoped that under the changed circumstances Vienna would be forced to abandon both centralism, based on the German population, and dualism, based on German-Hungarian supremacy. This development would open the way to federalism and thus the Slavs of the Empire would gain more political influence. Besides uniting the Croat territories the establishment of a Southern Slav state led by Croatia would counter-balance the demographic and territorial superiority of Hungary. The National Party planned to unify the Slovene territories of the Austrian provinces and the districts inhabited by Serbs in Southern Hungary with the Triune Kingdom. While guarding against dualism, the National Party politicians pressed for an increased influence of the Southern Slavs through territorial expansion in the Balkans, first of all, through occupying Bosnia-Herzegovina.[18] According to this logic Balkan expansionism might assure a successful and permanent federalization of the Monarchy against dualist attempts. Their chances were diminished by the Pentarchia Plan developed by Austro-Slav federalists like Bishop Strossmayer, Frantisek, and the Czech Rieger in August of 1866. It envisaged the autonomy of five historical groups of countries and stated that regulating the Southern Slav territories was contingent upon the Hungarian-Croat agreement.[19] Another branch of the Southern Slavs, the Serbs of the Monarchy, vehemently opposed federative objectives and Croat aspirations towards Bosnia. From their point of view, a Southern Slav integration within a federative Habsburg Monarchy might threaten the existence of a would-be independent Serbian Principality.[20]

Croat national liberals hoped for a separate agreement with the Crown to realize their ideas. The address of the December 1866 *Sabor* demanded the unification of Croat territories and the appointment of a representative provincial government. In return, they offered the recognition of common affairs with the Empire and the principle of a central government. Vienna had serious reservations about the change of course the Croatians took. In their view it questioned the principle of the Hungarian compromise (already endorsed by Francis Joseph), dualism, and the legislative-administrative unity of the countries of the Holy Crown. Before successfully completing the Compromise the Provincial Diet was adjourned without date.[21]

The 1866-67 strategy of the Croat National Party made allowances to gain the support of the Monarch and for a successful anti-dualist intervention by the Austro-Slav federalists. Besides this strategy was built on secret cooperation with the Serbian Principality as well. The national liberals assumed that in the extraordinary central parliament planned by Prime Minister Belcredi, which would convene the delegates of the Provincial Diets to discuss common affairs and constitutional questions, cooperation between the opponents of the Hungarian Compromise and the Slavs could obstruct the dualist transformation of the Empire. The February 1867 change in the Austrian government policy upset these plans. The Austrian government suspended the various provincial diets then convening and took the issue of the Hungarian Compromise to the regular Central Parliament, ensuring an Austrian-German parliamentary lead.[22]

Enlivened activities of the Serbian Principality in the Balkan did not bear any useful advantages either. The Croat national National Party politicians secretly supported the Belgrade government in preparing a Bosnian anti-Turkish uprising. In this way, the Croats expected to improve the political position of the Austrian Slavs and, consequently, the conditions for federalism. However, the Serbian government dreaded the risks of an armed uprising and also had reservations about both an Austrian absolutistic-centralist restoration and the federalization of the Monarchy. Hence, the Serbian-Croatian rapprochement did not become an effective political alliance against dualism.[23]

The Croat National Party politicians wanted to achieve simultaneously political emancipation, territorial integrity, and federalization of the Monarchy. However, they finally landed themselves in a vacuum because there was no external support; the Austro-Slav federalists were divided, and they became far removed from the basis of a possible compromise with the Hungarians. Namely, the Hungarian dualist program was quite the opposite of the federalization of the Monarchy and contrary to the idea of a territorial expansion in the Balkans. Therefore dualist Hungarian liberals never did consider the recognition of the Triune Kingdom as a completely separate country between Austria and Hungary. The first Hungarian Prime Minister of Dualism, Gyula Andrássy, perceived a direct connection between the recognition of a politically separate Croat–Slavonian–Dalmatian Kingdom and the federalization of the Monarchy.[24] It was the interests of the Vienna government and Hungarian liberal aspirations which influenced the content and the nature of the Croat compromise. This interconnection was symbolized by the composition of the Crown Council which decided on the political status of the Triune Kingdom. The Monarch, the Austrian Prime Minister Benst, and the Croat–Slavonian Court Chancellor Kusević participated in the decision about the Hungarian Prime Minister's plan to settle the Croat question. The Crown Council adopted Andrássy's draft which projected a sub-dualist legal status for Croatia. That is, there would be a Hungarian–Croat union subsumed under the Austrian–Hungarian union of the Monarchy. However, Hungarian legislative and executive power, with respect to Croatia, would be limited to certain areas. It recognized the authority of the Croat legislature and government as defined by Article 42:1861. It was a sign of the strengthening of the Hungarian position that Francis Joseph consented to appointing a Royal Commissioner for Fiume. Thus the seaport fell under Hungarian administration. There was no territorial compensation for the Croat loss because Benst cautioned against supporting Croatia's claim on Dalmatia.[25]

The coronation of Francis Joseph as King of Hungary was the solemn occasion to recognize the sub-dualist legal status of the Triune Kingdom. Complying with the decision of the Crown Council in April 1867, the Hungarian Parliament invited the delegates of the *Sabor* to compose a joint coronation diploma stating the legal status of Croatia–Slavonia and Dalmatia and to participate in the coronation ceremony. For its part, the Hungarian Parliament pledged to grant the most extensive autonomy possible.[26] At the same time Parliament applied the personal prestige of the Monarch and a series of political concessions to change the opinion of the majority of the Provincial Diet which had demanded political emancipation. Francis Joseph unsuccessfully called upon influential Bishop Strossmayer to support autonomy. Andrássy offered the majority National Party the right to form an autonomous government and he also followed through with an important demand by Croat Parliamentarians, expecting royal confirmation since 1861, to grant parliamentary immunity to the *Sabor* representatives. In spite of these efforts the majority persevered with the December 1866 address and made Croatian participation at the coronation conditional on recognition of political emancipation and territorial integrity, and of having the *Sabor* sanction the Austrian-Hungarian compromise. In response the Monarch dissolved the *Sabor* and the coronation took place in the absence of the Croats.[27]

The absence from the coronation, a spectacular political demonstration, aroused the disapproval of the Imperial Court. Even some Slav allies of the Croat national liberals considered the rigid rejection of the Hungarian compromise as manipulation by reactionary and military circles dissatisfied with the constitutional transformation and the parliamentary government system.[28] General distrust, owing to the Croat cooperation with anti-dualist military circles, deeply permeated the Hungarian political leadership and, from then on, the plans to establish a Croat compromise was built on the advocates of the Hungarian–Croat union. In Croatia and Slavonia new elections were held and, in the course of preparation, significant structural and personnel changes occurred both in the government and in the higher levels of county administration. Owing to the dualist transformation General Josip Šokčević, an influential opponent of political connections with Hungary, resigned from the position of *Ban* he had occupied since 1860. According to absolutist practice the *Ban* disposed of the civil governance of Croatia and of the tasks of the commander-in-chief of the Croatian–Slavonian Military Border Area. After his resignation the civil and military functions of the Ban were separated. The Military Border, falling under the auspices of the Imperial Ministry of Defense, remained separate but with a German General appointed to it.[29] A unionist landowner, Levin Rauch, who enjoyed the full confidence of the Hungarian government, became Ban Governor and took over civil administration of Croatia and the preparation for the elections. With the support of the Hungarian government, the Unionists were in a more favorable position than the National Party, which had lost its former imperial support.

The advocates of the compromise with Hungary were mostly landowning aristocrats. Their Hungarian orientation had been motivated by historical feudal traditions, social views close to those of Hungarian liberals, and opposition to the consequences of absolutistic modernization. Within the Hungarian state they perceived better opportunities to remedy the shortage of capital obstructing agricultural modernization, to extend agrarian markets, and to develop a missing transportation infrastructure. Renewed political connections with Hungary would facilitate restoring county autonomy by reinstating the nobility to their traditional positions which civil servants mostly of non-aristocratic origin had occupied during absolutism. Even during the period of preparation for the election the *Ban*-Governor carried out these ambitions, gradually dismissing county officials who had been appointed by the centralist government in Vienna and who opposed dualism. The pro-Hungarian atmosphere was reinforced by a general dissatisfaction with the post-1849 absolutistic and centralist government system which had prevailed in Croatian society. Ever increasing taxation and the omnipotence of the police-official bureaucracy irritated all the layers of society. Not only the landed gentry, but even the peasants, who often clashed with the landowners in lawsuits over land distribution, placed their hopes in the unionists to get rid of the burdensome legacy of absolutism. By lowering the property requirement of the census, these strata of society became franchised and so counter-balanced the influence of the national liberal city bourgeoisie, church, and intelligentsia (of non-aristocratic origin). The unionists, who managed to utilize the advantages of administrative and governing positions, claimed a landslide victory at the December 1867 elections. In protest the National Party deputies resigned from their mandates and, in this way, the delegates to the Compromise discussions were selected again from one party, the pro-Hungarian Unionist. [30]

The Unionists also demanded extensive autonomy and the unification of Croat territories based on historical law. For several months from April 1868 on the delegates of the Hungarian and Croat Parliaments worked on the draft of a Bill to regulate the relationship between the two parties. As with the Austrian–Hungarian resolution, the Hungarian–Croat settlement was based on historical claims, primarily on the Pragmatica Sanctio adopted by the Hungarian Diet in 1723. They reached back to the one and a half centuries old law to circumvent the mutually exclusive laws of the two national movements, namely, the April Laws of 1848 and the Croat Article 42:1861. Notwithstanding this, several elements of these laws, such as the political unity of the countries of the Holy Crown and the institutionalization of Croat autonomy, were included in the 1868 Hungarian–Croat Compromise.[31] The Compromise declared an indivisible political alliance between Hungary and Croatia–Slavonia–Dalmatia. It codified the partial division of national sovereignty, the territorial autonomy of the Croat political nation, and independent internal administration in such areas as public administration, religion, public education, and jurisdiction. In Croatia-Slavonia the Croat language became the official language and it also affected the representatives of the common government. The law mandated that Croatian become the language of command of the Croat territorial army *(domobranstvo)*, established within the Hungarian military.[32] Croat autonomy was manifested in ceremonial formalities as well. Autonomous authorities and the Croat military wore their own national colors and the Croat coat of arms, although with the Hungarian Holy Crown placed above it.

The Croatian-Slavonian budget was based on national revenues calculated according to a rate and appropriated by the *Sabor*. The ratio of the costs of the autonomy, the Hungarian-Croat commonwealth, and the common expenses of the Monarchy was stated in a financial agreement and planned to be revised in every ten years. The Croat contribution was 6.4% of all common expenses. This was beyond the capacity of economically backward Croatia and leftover finances did not cover the expenses of the autonomy. Therefore a lump sum of annual 2.2 million forints or after 1873 at least 45% of all the Croatian revenues was set aside for the budget of the Autonomous Area. The Croats had to spend only the surplus (whatever was left beyond the 45%) on common expenses even if it did not cover actual expenses. Nevertheless, the issue of the quota, i.e., the rate of contribution to common expenses, remained a sensitive issue both in Hungarian-Croat relations and in the post-1867 Austrian-Hungarian relationship. The Hungarian side found their actual contribution to the costs of the autonomy too high while the Croats found common finances disadvantageous and they blamed the Unionists for it. In truth, at the time of the Compromise no complete Croat financial plans existed. Originally the National Party had also not claimed independent finances as a condition of political emancipation since finances belonged to the Austrian Central Government both in Centralist practice and according to the Austro-Slav federalist program. During the negotiations preceding the Compromise, Ferenc Deák asserted that the Croats would have full financial autonomy, except for the indirect taxes uniformly imposed on everyone in the Monarchy, because bilateral frictions could be decreased by fewer common affairs. He also advocated the elimination of Hungarian "guardianship" of the Croats because it irritated their national pride. However, neither the Croat nor the Hungarian majorities supported his views. The Croats were discouraged by the financial burden attached to autonomy, while on the Hungarian side Prime Minister Gyula Andrássy's views protecting the interests of the dualist partner prevailed. Andrássy opposed Croat financial independence fearing that it would serve as a precedent for the Czechs and the Poles and eventually it would threaten German hegemony in the Austrian half of the Monarchy. Another important consideration was that, under financial autonomy, modest Croat revenues would not offer a sufficient guarantee for foreign investors who were expected to develop missing transportation, mainly railroad, infrastructure.[33]

In addition to general political and economic factors, demographic differences, territorial size, level of economic development, and the leftovers of absolutist government influenced the character and institutional system of Hungarian-Croat sub-dualism. These differences were also reflected in the structure of the autonomous government and in the relationship between Croatian autonomy and the Hungarian central government. The head of the Croat autonomous government was the *Ban*, appointed by the Monarch at the recommendation of the Hungarian Prime Minister. The *Ban* was responsible to the Sabor but his position was dependent on the common confidence of the Hungarian Prime Minister and the Monarch. However, he needed the majority support of the *Sabor* in administration. The institutional structure of the autonomous government was defined by the *Sabor* but decisions needed royal assent like in Hungary. Legislation also required royal pre-assent and every Bill was tabled in the *Sabor* after the Monarch gave his royal assent to it.

The Croat *Ban* did not have direct access to the Monarch but acted through the common government in Budapest with the contribution of the Minister for Croat-Slavonian-Dalmatian Affairs. The latter was considered to be a constitutional Court Chancellor, responsible to the common Parliament in Budapest and having voting rights in the Hungarian government. His authority consisted of advancing and protecting Croat interests and supervising the autonomous government. His supervisory rights were modified by the 1873 revision of the Compromise which stated that he could not turn away the *Ban's* proposals. Instead he had to submit them—with his opinion attached—to the Monarch.[34] In this way the

Monarch was able to counter-balance Hungarian central governmental aspirations to curtail Croatian autonomy.

In contrast to autonomous affairs, Croat influence was rather limited in common affairs managed by the central government in Budapest and the common legislature. In the Hungarian-Croat relation common affairs comprised two groups: (1) imperial affairs (foreign affairs, military affairs, and their budgets) deduced from the *Pragmatica Sanctio* and the so-called non-pragmatic common affairs (the trade and tariff union, appropriation of common expenses, etc.); and (2) commonwealth related special Hungarian-Croat common affairs (e.g., expenses of the Royal Court, conscription legislation, state finances, different questions of industry and transport, etc.). The *Sabor* sent deputies to the Parliament in Budapest from among its own representatives in proportion to the population of Croatia. In 1868 it sent 29 deputies, while it sent 40 in the early 1880's when the Croatian-Slavonian Military Border Area was joined to Croatia. In common affairs, the delegates enjoyed individual voting rights. The delegation supervising Austrian-Hungarian common affairs had the same proportionate representation, with four Croat representatives and one member of the Upper House. The Croats were free to use their language in both bodies.

With ten times more Hungarian than Croat representatives majority rule limited their influence in Parliament in enforcing their interests in common affairs, and in controlling the central government. However, the Act of Compromise contained several elements in the area of common affairs which protected Croat autonomy. The Act could be revised only by the mutual assent of the Hungarian Parliament and the Croat *Sabor*. In a period of expanding government activities it was of great significance that the Act of Compromise precluded the possibility of increasing the number of common affairs. Every issue that fell beyond the authority of the common parliament and the central government was transferred to the authority of Zagreb. The consent of the *Sabor* was necessary for certain transactions, such as the sale of Croat state property. In Hungarian Ministries having authority that included Croatia, Croat departments with Croat officials had to be established. Due to the allegedly low proportion of Croatian officials in common authorities and the fact that Hungarian was substituted for a supposedly exclusive use of the Croatian language in official contacts with common authorities in Croatia, especially in the common management of the railway and the post office, did much to perpetuate Hungarian–Croat animosities over the interpretation of the Compromise.

On territorial issues, Croat unionists gave up on the simultaneous enforcement of ethnic and historical principles during the negotiating phase of the Compromise. Unlike in 1866, the Unionists now relinquished demands on Muraköz (Medimurje), Istria, and the Northern Adriatic Islands, all of which were beyond Croat historical state territories. However, they now tried to place claims on the Bosnian territories of the Ottoman Empire. The Hungarians, however, refused to consider it due to its consequences in international politics.[35] Hence, the Compromise acknowledged Croat integrity relating to the area within the Habsburg Monarchy and acknowledged the unity of Croatia proper, Slavonia, eleven border regiments, and Dalmatia, but did not change the political status of Austrian Dalmatia. Hungary declared that it would promote the unification of Croatia and Dalmatia but did not put much dedication nor interest in the implementation of the pledge since annexation would have entailed conflicts between Hungary and its Austrian dualist partner.

Hungarian and Croat interests coincided in the issue of the civil transformation of the Military Border. Hungarians intended to eliminate it as a military zone and place it under a civil government since the Military Border was considered to be a possible base for centralist restoration. For the Croats the possibility arose to integrate these districts with a substantial Serbian population into Croatia. Initiated by the Hungarian government in 1869, the dissolution of the Military Border took more than ten years to complete. After this the population and size of Croatia–Slavonia doubled and included almost two thirds of the Croat ethnic population and territory within the Monarchy.

Still, there was no agreement reached about Fiume. The Croats had hoped for concessions about the seaport in return for the recognition of the commonwealth, while the Hungarians intended to compensate themselves for the loss of Slavonia with Fiume. The Italian population saw their economic interests, use of their own language and administrative autonomy as a privileged seaport status better protected under Hungarian authority than by belonging to an economically backward Croatia that fiercely enforced its own language dominance on its own territory. Finally, in 1870 the Fiume Provisory was issued and held throughout the period of

Dualism. It placed the administration of the seaport under the authority of a Governor appointed by the Hungarian government.

Historiography describes the 1868 Hungarian-Croatian Compromise in pessimistic terms.[36] This tone arises partly from the approach most observers adopt of comparing the Compromise to the optimal outcome possible for the national movement—an independent state. Others blame sub-dualism with causing the failure of Austro-Yugoslavism, a Southern-Slav unity led by Croats and political emancipation within the Monarchy.

It is evident that the Compromise provided only a limited form of a political state for the Croats. However, the politics of the Compromise did in fact correspond to one of the characteristic tendencies of Croat nationalism and did match the social conditions and economic development of the Croats. At the time of the Compromise Croat territories were considerably divided and the region was extremely backward economically. The Compromise facilitated the administrative unification and economic integration of the area and encouraged the Croat leadership to further the process of modernization and development. Croatian autonomy contained several prerequisites of statehood and its administrative-legislative authority was much more extensive than either before 1848 or what was forecast by Austro-Slav programs, let alone during the constitutional centralism of the early 1860's. Following the 1868 Compromise, Croatia established its own civil and penal legal systems, administrative institutions, and school system from elementary schools through university. Within sub-dualism Hungarian sovereignty over Croatia was retained but the latter enjoyed an institutionalized autonomy unparalleled in Europe. English liberal politician Gladstone, who acted to satisfy the Irish Home Rule movement, considered the Hungarian-Croat Compromise a model to follow when in the 1880's he worked on his Home Rule Bill. The British Parliament, attempting to protect the integrity of the state, did not pass the Bill.[37] The Croat constitutional compromise has always been much more appreciated externally than internally.

The Croatian public could never come to terms with the limitations of the Compromise, especially with the lack of political and financial independence. As a result, pro-Compromise unionist liberals quickly lost their national legitimacy. As a government, they held out through only one parliamentary cycle. However, the system of the Croat autonomy inherently guaranteed unionist liberal participation in legislative and executive powers until the end of Dualism because 50 % of the deputies of the *Sabor* were great taxpayer landowners, who became members of the legislative system without election. Positions of the autonomous government dependent on Hungarian government appointment like the *Ban* or the Minister of Croatia-Slavonia-Dalmatian were filled mostly by Croat landowner aristocrats. The influence of unionists, who limited themselves to protecting the political and social status quo, gradually decreased in Croatia's political life during the 1870's. The failure of the endeavor to transform the dualist structure connected to the Hohenwart Ministry in 1871, compelled the National Party to give up its political opposition. Both in the new government party, established by the fusion of the Unionist and the National Party, and in the autonomous government, former National Pary leaders received decisive roles. The ensuing parliamentarism in Croatia expedited the liberal modernization of legal, administrative, educational, and cultural institutions and through the demilitarization of the Border, the partial restoration of Croat territorial integrity.

NOTES

1. Gyula Miskolczy, *A horvát kérdés története és irományai a rendi állam korában, I.* [The History and the Writings of the Croat Issue in the Period of the Feudal State] (Budapest, 1927); György Szabad, Hungary's Recognition of Croatia's Self-Determination in 1848 and its Immediate Antecedents. (*Annales Universitatis Scientiarum Budapestinensis de Rolando Eötvös Nominatae. Sectio Historica, 21,* 1981), 23-38; János Varga, *A Hungarian Quo Vadis: Political Trends and Theories of the Early 1840s.* (Budapest, 1993), 89-109.

2. Wolfgang Kessler, *Politik, Kultur und Gesellschaft in Kroatien und Slawonien in der ersten Hälfte des 19. Jahrhunderts. Historiographie und Grundlagen* (München, 1981), 89-96, 269-287; Jaroslav Šidak, Stranacki adnosi u Hrvatskoj prije 1848 [Croatian Party Relations before 1848] in *Studije iz hrvatske povijesti XIX stoljeca* (Zagreb, 1973), 125-151.

3. For the 1848 laws, see *Magyar törvénytár. 1836-1868. évi törvénycikkek* [Hungarian Legislative Records: Laws of 1836-1868] (Budapest, 1896], 216-260.

4. Árpád Károlyi, *Az 1848-diki pozsonyi törvénycikkek az udvar előtt* [The 1848 Laws Before the Royal Court] (Budapest, 1936), 110-114, 272.

5. Ernest Bauer, *Joseph Graf Jellachich* (Wien-München, 1975); Jaroslav Šidak, Seljacko pitanje u hrvatskoj politici 1848 [The Peasant Question and Croatian Politics in 1848] in *Studije iz hrvatske povjesti za revolucije 1848-49* (Zagreb, 1979), 153-162.

6. E. I. Ignatijewitsch [Tkalac]: *Croaten, Serben, Magyaren, ihre Verhältnisse zu einander und zu Deutschland.* (Wien, 1848), 20.

7. Jaroslav Šidak, Poslanstvo hrvatskog sabora austrijskom parlamentu god 1848. [The Delegation of the Croat Sabor to the Austrian Parliament in 1848] in *Studije iz hrvatske povijesti za revolucije 1848-49.* (Zagreb, 1979), 175-195.

8. Documents of the Hungarian peace initiative: *Kossuth Lajos összes munkái, XII.* [Complete Works of Lajos Kossuth, XII] ed. István Sinkovits (Budapest, 1957), 800, 805-806; For the development of Hungarian government policy, see György Szabad, 30-38.

9. László Katus, A magyar politikai vezetőréteg a délszláv kérdésről 1848 és 1867 között [Hungarian Political Leadership on the Southern Slav Question between 1848 and 1867] in *Szerbek és magyarok a Duna mentén II. Tanulmányok a szerb-magyar kapcsolatok köréből, 1848-1867* [Serbs and Hungarians along the Danube, II: Essays on Serbian-Hungarian Connections] ed. István Fried (Budapest, 1987), 166.

10. *Deák Ferenc beszédei 1842-1861. II.* [Ferenc Deák's Speeches 1842-1861, II.], collected by Manó Kónyi (Budapest, 1903), 605-616.

11. Mirjana Gross and Agneza Szabo, *Prema hrvatskome gradjanskom društvu* [On the Way to Bourgeois Society] (Zagreb, 1992), 250-251.

12. Emerich Bogovich, *Politische Rückblicke in Bezug auf Kroatien* (Agram, 1861), 74-75.

13. Gross and Szabo, 129-140.

14. Jaroslav Šidak, Ivan Mažuranić kao politicar [Ivan Mažuranić as a Politician] in Šidak (1973), 297-300; Gross and Szabo, 170-180; Vasilije Dj. Krestić, *Horvatska-ugarska nagodba 1868* (Beograd, 1969), 177-196.

15. Gross and Szabo, 192-198; Krestić, 214-219.

16. *Deák Ferenc beszédei 1861-1866, III.* [Ferenc Deák's Speeches, 1861-1866, III.], collected by Manó Kónyi (Budapest, 1903), 556.

17. *Csengery Antal hátrahagyott iratai és feljegyzései* [Antal Csengery's Posthumous Writings and Notes] (Budapest, 1928), 179-184; Gross and Szabo, 200-203; Krestić, 220-225.

18. Peter Korunić, *Jugoslavenska ideologija u hrvatskoj I slovenskoj politici* [The Yugoslav Ideology in the Croat and Slovene Politics] (Zagreb, 1986), 278-318.

19. Éva Somogyi, *A birodalmi centralizációtól a dualizmusig* [From Imperial Centralization to Dualism] (Budapest, 1976), 149.

20. Korunić, 311-312.

21. Gross and Szabo, 207-208; Krestić, 235-236.

22. Somogyi, 178-182.

23. Imre Ress, A szerb külpolitika és a Habsburg monarchia dualista átalakulása, 1865-1867 [Serbian Foreign Politics and the Dualist Transformation of the Habsburg Monarchy, 1865-1867] in *A magyar polgári átalakulás kérdései* [The Questions of Hungarian Bourgeois Transformation] ed. András Gergely, Iván Dénes and Gábor Pajkossy (Budapest, 1984), 381-402.

24. Haus-, Hof- und Staatsarchiv Wien, Kabinettsarchiv, Geheimakten. Karton 21. (April 1, 1867).

25. Hungarian National Archives, Budapest K 26 and records of Hungarian Council of Ministers (April 1, 1867). Miklós Komjáthy, Két ismeretlen minisztertanácsi jegyzőkönyv [Two Unknown Minutes of the "Common" Ministerial Council] (*Levéltári Közlemények,* 1974), 44-45, 273-295.

26. *Deák Ferenc beszédei 1861-1866, IV.* [Ferenc Deák's Speeches, 1861-1866, IV.], collected by Manó Kónyi (Budapest, 1903), 482-490.

27. Gross and Szabo, 209-211; Krestić, 253-261.

28. Vojislav V. Vučković, *Politička akcija Srbije u južnoslovenskim pokrajinama Habsburske monarchije 1859-1874* [The Political Activities of Serbia in the Southern Slav Provinces of the Habsburg Monarchy, 1859-1874] (Beograd, 1965), 297.

29. Mirko Valentic, *Vojna krajina i pitanje njezina sjedinjenja s Hrvatskom 1849-1881* [The Military Border and its Reunion with Croatia, 1849-1881] (Zagreb, 1981), 141-144.

30. Gross and Szabo, 221-223; Krestić, 264-278.

31. Csengery, 185-239; Hungarian-Croat Compromise, Act 30:1868, see *Magyar törvénytár, 1836-1868. évi törvénycikkek* [Hungarian Legislative Records, Statutes of 1836-1868] (Budapest, 1896), 422-432.

32. Josip Horvat, *Kultura hrvata kroz 1000 godine. II.dio* [A Thousand Years of Croat Culture, Part II.] (Zagreb, 1942), 450-451.

33. For different concepts of Deák and Andrássy, see Csengery, 218-224, and Josip Zivkovic, *Kako je postala hrvatsko-ugarska nagoda* [How the Croatian-Hungarian Compromise Came into Being] (Zagreb, 1892), 56-74.

34. Revision of the Hungarian-Croat Act of Compromise, Act 34:1873, see *Magyar törvénytár, 1872-1874. évi törvénycikkek* [Hungarian Legislative Records, Statutes of 1872-1874] (Budapest, 1896), 222.

35. Csengery, 210.

36. For evaluation of the Hungarian-Croat Compromise, see Vasilije Krestić, Über einige politisch-historische Bedingungen der Entstehung des kroatisch-ungarischen Ausgleichs 1868, in Der österreichisch-ungarische Ausgleich 1867 (Bratislava, 1971), 783-829; Waclaw Felczak, *Ugoda wegiersko-chorwatska 1868 roku* [The Hungarian-Croatian Compromise in 1868] (Warszawa, 1969); Ferdo Hauptmann, Der kroatisch-ungarische Ausgleich von 1868, in *Der österreichisch-ungarische Ausgleich von 1867. Seine Grundlagen und Auswirkungen* (München, 1968), 36-48; Branko M. Peselj, Der ungarisch-kroatische Ausgleich vom Jahre 1868. in *Der österreichisch-ungarische Ausgleich vom 1867. Vorgeschichte und Wirkungen,* ed. Peter Berger (Wien, 1967), 169-185; Mirjana Gross, The Character of Croatian Autonomy in the First Decade after the Hungarian-Croatian Compromise of 1868, in, *The Mirror of History: Essays in Honor of Fritz Fellner* (Santa Barbara-Oxford, 1988), 275-294. For positive references of the Compromise, see Josip Horvat, endnote 32.

37. Anton Radvánszky, Das ungarische Ausgleichsgesetz vom Jahre 1867, in *Der österreichisch-ungarische Ausgleich vom 1867. Vorgeschichte und Wirkungen*, ed. Peter Berger (Wien, 1967), 109.

ERA OF UPHEAVALS (1918–1998)

CONCEPTUAL CHANGES IN CENTRAL EUROPEAN INTEGRATION IN HUNGARIAN POLITICAL THINKING, 1920–1948

GYÖRGY GYARMATI

THE INTER-WAR PERIOD

Revisionism prevailed in Hungarian political thinking between the two world wars. Successive defeat in war, revolutions, dismemberment of the country sanctioned in the Trianon Treaty, hundreds of thousands fleeing over the border, and heavy war reparations all caused socio-political trauma with a general existential insecurity. Both the citizens of the Hungarian Kingdom, which had lost almost three quarters of its former territory and two thirds of its population, and political thinkers considered Trianon unviable. Successive governments, hall-marked by Regent Miklós Horthy, proclaimed revisionist demands under the slogan of "reverse everything," forming the nation's foreign policy during the inter-war period. In 1921 when King Charles IV attempted twice to reclaim the throne, Hungary experienced a revived push for the Habsburg dynasty prompting Czechoslovakia, Romania, and Yugoslavia to establish a political-military union—the Little Entente.[1] This, in turn, further deepened fears among Hungarians. As a consequence, Hungary rejected all non-revisionist plans, such as Richard Coudenhove-Kalergi's Pan-Europe movement. Government circles and the right wing opposition suspected further dismembering motives by the Pan-Europe movement. In addition, social democrats viewed it as a form of "intra-continental colonization," beneficial for the stronger powers.[2]

Yet curiously enough there remained a few people who acted to carry on the idea of cooperation and reconciliation among the small states of the region. There were not many of them and even fewer forcefully pursued the idea. Yet among them in the 1920's were Elemér Hantos,[3] Gusztáv Gratz,[4] and Miklós Makay.[5] Elemér Hantos and Gusztáv Gratz authoritatively analyzed programs and international conferences which aimed to make acceptable the

Paris Area Treaty System. They even appreciated the liberal social reformer Friedrich Naumann's *Mitteleuropa* concept after it had been adjusted to changed circumstances. According to the new interpretation of the Mitteleuropa concept, economic and social recovery of the region were to be achieved by cooperation among the Central European countries and not by subordination to German hegemony. Preferential contracts, co-ordination of productive industries, and the gradual elimination of the customs frontiers would be the initial goals of a new Central European cooperation. The concept was based on the idea of "mutual assurance." Gradual integration would protect comparative benefits by which individual national economies and, hence, the whole region would be stabilized.

In their theories, the reconciliationists held no differences in terms of goals and none of them even considered restoration of the pre-war status quo. However, there were differences among them in terms of reasons for supporting reconciliation. Elemér Hantos[6] mostly approached his topic from the perspective of the effects and consequences of economics. He circumspectly tried to avoid offending Hungary's neophyte national consciousness, which was protective towards internal self-determination and external sovereignty. Former Foreign Secretary and historian Gusztáv Gratz[7] often applied historical allusions to the situation of Hungary and Austria. He presented the two states, politically separated after World War I, as an economically complementary unit. To utilize the complementary characteristics of industrial Austrian and agrarian Hungarian territories, they should be integrated to create an "economic Danubian confederation" and then integrate surrounding states into the confederation.[8]

Miklós Makay reinvented the concept of Central Europe with the idea of dividing East Central Europe into separate subregions. He drew a line between the historically changing political states of the German language area and those areas which briefly or extensively had lost their sovereignty due to Russian, German, or Ottoman occupation. Makay applied the term East Central Europe to the non-German speaking area regarding the experience of "subjugation" as a foundation for "a common fate." He proposed a union of states along the northern-southern meridian between the Baltic Sea and the Balkans. This subregional union would form a part of a future Central European or continental "United States."[9] The primarily mercantilist economics of Hantos, the historically oriented ideas of Makay, and Gratz's ambitious work to apply both approaches did not greatly influence contemporary thinking. Instead, both the majority of political thinkers and common people all envisioned prosperity within the restored "Greater Hungary."

By the end of the 1920's regional reconciliation had not developed. Rather, things had gone in a different direction. The fundamentals of newly formed or restructured small states were all terrible. Organizing the state administration and creating an economy under changed circumstances was a difficult challenge. A sense of vulnerability gradually turned into an inferiority complex. As a result, these small states came to expect protection by outside powers to enforce and safeguard their interests.

The new geopolitical situation in postwar East Central Europe presented the states there with several different alternatives. With no big powers in the region, World War I had left a power vacuum. Some saw this as an opportunity to establish an "internal" regional bloc. One version of this occurred when several states formed the Little Entente, under the French *gloire*, in opposition to Hungary, hoping that this subregional union would externally stabilize their states. However, French power was enough to maintain the formalities of a vanishing *gloire*, but not enough to construct a continental or even just a regional security system.[10] Western stabilization loans helped the small states of the region to get themselves afloat economically, but they proved to be insufficient for an extended and balanced development in the absence of markets.[11] French President and Foreign Minister A. Briand's Pan-Europe Memorandum and the Tardieu Plan both recognized this. Yet both also failed due to the resistance of rival great powers intimidated by French predominance in the subregion. In addition, the initiative of the small states of the intermediate region, the so called *agrarian bloc,* also failed.

The agrarian bloc held a series of talks among agrarian Poland, Hungary, Romania, Yugoslavia, and Bulgaria during 1930–31. (Czech representatives appeared intermittently.) The goal was to foster cooperation in order to benefit from Western European markets. The initiative was motivated by the global depression and by the recognition that, in spite of surpluses of the same goods (wheat, rye, corn), it would be beneficial to represent their interests as an inter-state cartel. However, the experiment failed. As a consequence, the weak national economies of the region further deteriorated. Losing their earlier credit rating in the West was another, equally grave, consequence. As a result, an opportunity opened up for the "new Central European order" embodied in the German *Grossraumwirtschaft*. According to György Ránki, the 1920's "was only a momentary break in the several centuries-long historical process in which the fate of the Danubian peoples was decided by one or several dominant powers of the region." When the intermezzo ended, the small nations again moved to fulfill their destiny. The course came full circle when the small states who failed under French hegemony came under the sway of Hitler's dictates resulting in increasing defenselessness, diminishing political independence, and the eventual apocalypse of war.[12]

Emma Kövics regretted the rejection of Briand's Pan-European Plan. "The plan itself is a crisis strategy and it offered an alternative against German economic and political influence on Austria and South Eastern Europe."[13] The question is whether contemporary politicians of the intermediate region or French statesmen, who wished to combine French *gloire* with security, should have foreseen what was coming a decade later. Based on hindsight, we might be criticizing statesmen who had governed their countries before Hitler came to power and tried to influence the international scene, for not having "envisioned" the continental devastation of Hitler's national socialism.

An unusual example is Pál Teleki, Prime Minister of Hungary between 1920–21 and 1939–41, who also joined the 1931 public debate about Briand's Pan-European Plan. Count Teleki, a university professor in 1931, considered the compromises of the Plan virtuous–contrary to its critics–and argued that "any union implies a certain limitation on state sovereignty. It is inescapable. Natural political development progresses towards a continuous and accelerated enrichment of associations, as it has been proven so far. If the limitation on sovereignty applies to both large and small states, individual state sovereignty is not violated. As far as the violation of internal affairs, that is, the internal limitation or partial termination of sovereignty, is concerned–who cherishes the illusion that actual powers had not done so a long time ago, both politically and economically?"[14] Those concerned with the issue of sovereignty generally opposed the Plan on principle, which concealed the fact that they really feared strengthening a new continental French dominance.

Only a "sterile logic" could blame the governing political elite of the small states of the intermediate region for not utilizing the greater scope created by the power vacuum to push for regional integration which would have entailed limitation of sovereignty but would also have assured an even development and security for both individual states and the whole region. Such a logic assumes that new small states struggling to stabilize and enforce sovereignty should come up to expectations which even much older and more stable great powers had been unable to fulfill. In the 1920's small states of the intermediate region were absorbed with the divergent tasks of consolidating their new states and were not in the position to see beyond their immediate reality.

After Hitler came to power, new elements were added to the various theories about the intermediate region. New naming conventions were used in order to stipulate separation from the German *Mitteleuropa* concept. The term Central Europe was still in use. However, new terms such as the Danube Valley States, Danubian Europe, Carpathian Europe, and "The Zone of European Buffer States were used." The term "pagan powers," which alluded to the confinement between the Nazi and the Bolshevik, was used to define and reinforce the inter-dependence of the "intermediate region" more than to declare a conscious separation from the German *Lebensraum*.

Following the global depression, both the Hungarian political parties and the profile of the governing elite underwent a transformation. After István Bethlen's decade-long consolidation policy, the government shifted to the right. Because of an increasing right-wing etatism, influenced by Hitler, the opposition also changed considerably. A loose conglomerate of conservative constitutionalists, bourgeois or national democrats, and social democrats represented the anti-fascist faction. Even during the war years the representatives of earlier governments sought reconciliation with neighboring states by means of an anti-German stance.

After the Nazis came to power in Germany the Hungarian Social Democrats hastened to translate and publish the Austrian Social Democrat, Karl Renner's brochure, which discussed the Danube Basin problem and advocated close cooperation among those neighboring states laboring under the shadow of a newer German *Drang nach Osten*.[15] The Hungarian *Sarló* (Sickle) movement, with cells in Czechoslovakia, Hungary, and Romania, held a similar orientation. The majority of populist writers also argued the necessity for reconciliation among neighboring countries ("foster siblings" as László Németh put it) of Intermediate Europe.[16] The political coalition of the left-wing opposition, the March Front drew up a 12-point program for the democratic transformation of Hungary. The closing points of the Manifesto, first published in 1937 with an extended version in 1938, promulgated the idea of a Danube Basin Federation. Writer Imre Kovács, a leading personality of the March Front and later of the National Peasants' Party, openly declared the geopolitical goals of regional integration to be a fifty million strong confederation that "would impede German colonization in the Danube Basin."[17]

It was in the inter-war period when politician Endre Bajcsy-Zsilinszky, who later became a strong oppositionist, published his topical writings. In the late 1920's he became increasingly independent and even antagonistic to those who wished to gain territories under German revisionism. In his paper *Előörs* (Vanguard), launched in 1929, he stated that "Hungarians...within a wide and organic Danube plan...will have to find a *modus vivendi* followed by close cooperation, and an eventual tight association with other Danube peoples."[18] A year later he formulated similar thoughts in his party program, discussing the natural solidarity among the Danube peoples that "is embedded in the Central European community of interests....We have to brace ourselves in the neighborhood of the German empire and protect ourselves against its excess political weight on the Danube Valley and its biased cultural influence."[19] A decade later these views were summarized in *Helyünk és sorsunk Európában* (Our Place and Destiny in Europe) where he discussed how to settle the Danube Basin situation via consensus. After the division of Poland, Hungary's regional importance and increasing historical responsibility dictated that it ought to deal with the "political and administrative independence of the Central Danube Basin."[20] The book was published in the spring of 1941, a few months before Hungary entered the war. Because of German protests, the government banned the book, thereby greatly increasing people's interest in it.

There are quite a few more people and relevant passages to quote. However, moderation is a cherished characteristic as András Rónai, Pál Teleki's colleague, said when the program of the *March Front* was released in 1937. "Kossuth's confederation plan is a more and more frequently used catchword by young movements. But it is only a catchword. There are no concrete, underlying ideas or realistic political constructions."[21] However, "a realistic political construction" is an obscure term. Human history is abundant with rational thought which never materialized, while extreme irrationalism prevails in everyday political reality.

After World War II broke out, censorship became stricter. Free thoughts prevailed only in diaries, confidential memoranda, and circles in exile. By then Count István Bethlen, the Prime Minister of the 1920's, had not had any government assignment for a decade but was still Hungary's "grand old man," considered to be the leading personality of the anti-German, Western-oriented policy.[22] In March of 1940 Bethlen sent a memorandum to Prime Minister Pál Teleki. It contemplated Hungary's postwar peace prospects and predicted the German defeat.[23] Bethlen's views markedly changed concerning a federative reconstruction of the intermediate region. While in the 1930's Bethlen had rejected a possible federative reconstruction, lashing out on Mihály Károlyi's "irrationality,"[24] by 1940 Bethlen himself considered different types of federalism. Similar to Teleki, Bethlen also held revisionist views. However, both men recognized that not only Hungary, but the whole region was geopolitically vulnerable. Bethlen modified his standpoint so that it would be compatible with regional integration, in order to serve geopolitical security concerns–especially in the case of Transylvania. Reclaiming Transylvania was a question more important than just the Hungarian-Romanian relationship; it had an overall European significance. Beginning from the premise of a German defeat, Bethlen argued that a Hungarian-Austrian federation would not be desirable, if Germany remained unified, because that might lead to another *Anschluss* and then Hungary would share Poland's fate. However, if the democratic powers, England and France, insisted on a federation, it should entail a modified reconstruction of Greater Hungary. Another option would be a situation so that "all Hungarians and Romanians were within a federative state with three members: (1) Hungary extending to the Király Pass, (2) Transylvania with Krassó-Szörény (Karaş-Severin) County, and (3) Eastern part of Temes (Timiş) County not including the Regat, Bessarabia, and South Dobrudja–that is, whatever was left of Romania by the Russians."

There are two relevant, voluminous memoranda from Prime Minister Miklós Kállay's period in power (March 1942-March 1944). When the war took a turn against the Axis powers after the battles of El Alamein and Stalingrad, Kállay initiated secret diplomatic connections with the Anglo-Saxon powers[25] and organized an informal peace initiative group within the Ministry of Foreign Affairs. Aladár Szegedy-Maszák's appointment as head of the Political Department was among the preparatory steps. Before he occupied his position, he had been asked to prepare a confidential memorandum of postwar peace objectives for the Hungarian government. The last two chapters of the large document, secretly sent to London,[26] discussed the prospects of a new postwar international reconstruction and the place of Hungary within the system. "... It has become common knowledge that a system of rivaling and intriguing nations cannot be maintained on the area between Germany and Russia. The system thrived between the two wars and collapsed under the first blows of its mighty neighbors.... A federation or a confederation would help this weakness and consequently several small weaknesses would unite into one or two powers." The memorandum listed all the historical traditions and mixed ethnicities to be taken into consideration and declared that "the future of Transylvania is within a Danube Basin federation."

In December of 1943 Gusztáv Gratz drew up a similar study within the same confidential peace initiative project, also envisioning a Central European confederation. Gratz emphasized that mutual economic interests were prerequisites for a federation. Its constitutional, administrative, and social conditions are listed in the closing chapter:

> It would be advisable if each people of a Central European federation would define their autonomous territories in a way so that unilingual areas are connected to one another. This is extremely important even if we reach the unlikely stage where language and origin do not matter any more. The administration would be simpler and more cost effective; civic representation to authorities would be more comfortable; and friction among ethnic groups (which will still prevail in the foreseeable future) would diminish. The remaining ethnic minorities should take charge of their own cultural and economic development with the help of state support, but their activities should never be paralyzed by opposing wills.[27]

István Bethlen, who had been approached to co-ordinate the work of the confidential peace initiatives by the Prime Minister, was considered to be the likely head of an eventual peace delegation. Early in 1944, before the German occupation of Hungary,

Bethlen rewrote his reorganization plan of four years before. He was undoubtedly influenced by information about foreign reaction to the initiatives. The new memorandum continued to envision a federative reorganization plan of the region, but Bethlen rejected Tito's and Benes's proposals for integration. Bethlen's concept had Intermediate Europe—extending between the Baltic states and the Balkans—comprising three distinctly separate zones divided by geographic, historical, and cultural differences. The first is the zone north of the Carpathians including Poland and Lithuania, if it remains independent. The second is south of the Carpathians and the Sudetenland including the former Austro-Hungarian Monarchy and Romania, with eight nationalities: Czechs, Slovaks, Ruthenians, Austro-Germans, Hungarians, Romanians, Croats, and Slovenians. The third is the Balkans, with five nationalities: Serbians, Bulgarians, Romanians, Albanians, and Greeks.[28]

In all the three zones, adherence to the idea of federalism would be the guiding principle.

Bethlen proceeded to elaborate on the middle zone. The envisioned "Danube Federation...would include the following states: Austria, the Czech state (with an autonomous Sudetenland), Slovakia, Hungary (with the three autonomous territories of Ruthenia, Transylvania, and the Banat), Croatia, and Slovenia, although the latter two might form one state. These five or six states would form the United Danubian Federative State."[29]

Endre Bajcsy-Zsilinszky's proposals were also sent abroad with the assistance of the Foreign Ministry before the 1944 German occupation. The basic concept of "Transylvania's Past and Future"[30] fit well with Bajcsy's earlier thinking on foreign affairs—the mission of the Hungarians, based on their historical calling, was to reclaim their leading role in the Danube region of Central Europe.[31] Transylvania would gain extensive autonomy or even independent statehood within the Holy Crown as a partner state.[32] Both Bajcsy and Bethlen were inclined to sustain the monarchy, although Bajcsy supported it within the "Hungarian Kingdom" while Bethlen would accept even a Habsburg ruler under certain circumstances. "The constitution of the federation should more imitate that of the British Commonwealth than the constitution of the dualist monarchy since the former is much more flexible and has a larger scope to include individual national characteristics."[33] Unfortunately, neither Bajcsy nor Bethlen was able to participate in the reconstruction. When the Germans occupied the country, Bajcsy was arrested and then executed during the Christmas of 1944. In the spring of 1945 the Russians arrested Count Bethlen and transported him to Moscow. He died in the Butyirka Prison one and a half years later.

Different Hungarian groups in exile living in the "free world" all envisioned a postwar federative restructuring of the intermediate region. They also would advise Hungary to join various regional associations developed with British assistance during the war. Greek, Yugoslav, Polish, and Czech governments in exile all signed agreements for postwar development during the winter of 1942–43. Although the Hungarian groups in exile never established governments, they advocated for a federative solution. The *Hungarian National Independence Front* in Switzerland repeatedly argued for it. The London-based movement *For Democratic Hungary*, led by Mihály Károlyi, also endorsed it.[34] The *Magyar Fórum* (Hungarian Forum) and the *Harc* (Fight) published in New York never failed to include a federative topic as its central theme.

Oszkár Jászi, the doyen of the federative idea, repeatedly published works dealing with some aspect of the issue in both papers.[35] He also discussed the issue at different public forums in America. The following two quotes highlight how his understanding of the chances for a regional federation changed with the approaching end of the war. At the outbreak of the German–Soviet war, Jászi summarized his views on settling the Central European issue at the request of the Council on Foreign Relations.

> Under the guidance of the victorious states a system of local federations should be developed as parts of a larger European Union. The ideal aim would be the federal organization of the whole Danube–Vistula region consisting of Poland, Czechoslovakia, Hungary, Rumania, Yugoslavia, Greece, and Bulgaria, which would include a territory of about 540,000 square miles with more than 100,000,000 inhabitants....An economically reconstructed and federated Central-Eastern Europe would lead inevitably to the solution of the vexed nationality problem. It is stupid and demagogic to speak of the innate hostility of the various tribes. Human nature in the Danubian region, or elsewhere, is essentially the same as in Switzerland...The cure of the nationality rivalries is neither the barbaric expulsion of minorities carried out by the dictators, nor

> forced migration advocated unfortunately even by liberal statesmen, nor new strategic frontiers, but federalism, decentralization, and equality of private and public rights.[36]

At the end of December 1944 he delivered the paper "Central Europe and Russia" at the Modern History Section of the American Historical Association. By then he seemed to be quite skeptical about the prospects for a Central European federation.

> Whether a division into spheres of influence was contemplated or not at Teheran, no realistic student of politics will question that the Russian influence in that territory, whether we like it or not, will be preponderant.[37] Russia will come out of this war as the greatest continental power of Europe. This control will be the more dominant because, since the days of Czarist imperialism, this region has been regarded by the Russians as belonging to the sphere of their natural expansion and as a precondition of the security of the Empire...One can scarcely doubt that Russia will be adamant concerning her so-called strategic frontier from the Baltic to the Black Sea, with the further claims that she should annex a part of East Prussia with Königsberg, and that Poland should occupy parts of East Prussia as well as Danzig and Pomerania, including Stettin, and perhaps a part of the Breslau region.[38]

Jászi's prognosis was quite accurate considering that his talk was delivered before Yalta or Potsdam. Eventually his concerns about the fate of the federation were also justified, but this Central European drama still had an act full of surprising turns.

AFTER WORLD WAR II

For most governments involved in East Central Europe, postwar projects deviated substantially from earlier assumptions, initiatives, and ambitions. The idea of regional integration was primarily advocated by oppositionist or exiled theoreticians, politicians, and others who were of marginal power compared with the ruling political elite of the period. However, after World War II various governments in the region reversed themselves and included elements from different versions of integration in their official policies. Where continuity lay was with the great powers' reception of the initiatives. The attitude of the war winners who sliced up East Central Europe depended on their own interests.

The project Tito initiated in the spring of 1944, running throughout the war, also made references to Hungary. It was originally a draft of a Balkan Federation to include Yugoslavia, Bulgaria, and Albania. Edvard Kardelj carried on negotiations in this matter in Sofia in December 1944. Belgrade and Sofia had quite different positions, but it was not the dissimilarity that stymied the talks. At that point in time the Soviet Union supported the integration of the Southern Slavs, whereas Great Britain vehemently opposed it. Great Britain contested whether Bulgaria, which had just lost the war and was under the control of Allied Control Committee, had the right to take a political step which assumed its sovereignty. However, the British veto was likely motivated by something else entirely. Their influence in the Balkans would have been severely damaged if the proto-communist Yugoslavia were integrated with Bulgaria, a country regarded as being in Moscow's sphere of interest.[39]

In March of 1945, with the war still going on in Hungary, the Provisional Government of Debrecen sent an envoy to Bucharest authorized to inquire about restoring relations between the two countries. According to the report sent to the Hungarian Foreign Minister, Romanian Prime Minister Petru Groza had anticipated more than merely re-establishing connections. " Petru Groza has the image of a united bloc between the River Leite and the Black Sea in view, with a Hungarian–Romanian Union as a central part, where customs borders disappear, the currency is uniform, and a full political cooperation is established."[40] Although the Hungarian diplomat was not aware of the Bulgarian–Yugoslav precedent, he did raise the issue of the expected reaction of the Great Powers. In this case there were two defeated countries involved, both under the control of the Supervisory Committee. The Romanian Prime Minister had already had discussions with the Soviet Foreign Affairs Commissar Visinki and Colonel-General Susaikov,[41] and both supported immediate direct discussions.[42]

In the spring and summer of 1945 different re-established news organizations discussed the federative alternative in the context of a Romanian–Hungarian "historical reconciliation." However, an official declaration was issued only in September. The Allied Control Committee called on the Hungarian government to discuss how to settle its relationship with the neighboring countries. The memorandum sent to the American, British, and Soviet delegates of the Allied Control Committee stated that

> "In a prospective peace treaty the Hungarian government does not intend to place special Hungarian interests in the foreground. However, its wish is that the Hungarian question would be settled as part of world peace and in the interest of all the peoples of Central Europe. From the Hungarian perspective, the best peace agreement brings resolution to nations tormented by war, gives satisfaction to many, and makes peaceful cooperation with foreign countries, especially with our neighbors, possible....
>
> The Austro-Hungarian Monarchy was politically obsolete yet, within its area extending from Passau to Pola and Predeal,[43] it had proved to be economically more viable in assuring prosperity for all its citizens than the states created on its territory. Successor states, incited by extreme chauvinism, strove for an unhealthy autarchy and pursued an isolationist economic policy that damaged the prosperity of the peoples of the region.
>
> Consequently, peace treaties should institutionally sanction that naturally complementary and mutually dependent Danubian states would pursue close economic cooperation and would not abide by a policy of economic isolation. Close economic cooperation would significantly decrease political contradictions and frictions and would benefit the world economy since an economic upswing in the Danube Basin would increase its significance as a market."[44]

Hungarian foreign policy had no information whether the Danube Basin reorganization proposals prepared by the American State Department showed any similarities with the Budapest ideas.[45]

The election program of the Hungarian Communist Party released on September 23, 1945 went well beyond economic rationalism, "The main goal of Hungarian foreign policy is to secure the peace and understanding of Danubian peoples and to achieve the Kossuthian ideal of a Danubian Federation. To achieve intensive trade, a Romanian-Yugoslav-Hungarian customs union should be established."[46] It has not been established yet what negotiations led to extending the Groza proposal to include Yugoslavia. However, knowing Mátyás Rákosi's situation, the leadership of the

Hungarian Communist Party could not have released an initiative of such a scale without the Kremlin's consent. It has come to light that during the war, even in Moscow, there were drafts prepared describing some kind of integration in the Danube region in order to achieve a consensus on the status of Transylvania.[47] Nevertheless, Moscow never openly supported these initiatives. Sometimes they were not opposed, while at other times they were vetoed.

During 1946 the mass media heavily promoted different variations on the theme of integration. Certain party organs and different newspapers kept the issue on their agenda. When after a quarter of a century in exile, Prime Minister of the 1918 Republic Mihály Károlyi returned to Hungary, the federative idea gained even more ground. The Hungarian political leadership at the time had intentionally avoided inviting Károlyi back to his post as Prime Minister of the Republic and had difficulties finding an appropriate position for him. For a while, the idea of a Danubian Ministry was considered. Headed by Károlyi, it would have "to set the path for a customs union...in the spirit of a confederative plan." However, this "regional Foreign Ministry" was never established[48] even though Károlyi launched the paper *Köztársaság* (Republic) to serve this idea. The *Danube Colloquium*, organized around the paper and inspired by Yugoslav initiatives, further extended the circle of those favoring a federation. In July of 1946 the *Köztársaság* initiated a several weeks-long brainstorming session to perfect and propagate the idea of a Danubian Federative Republic. "First, Hungary would form a common customs union with Romania while Bulgaria would set up a union with the Yugoslav federation. And finally, the two alliances–on the right and left banks of the Danube–would enter into a customs and political union."[49] It is of significance that contrary to the 1944/45 initiatives, the Balkan Southern Slav and the Danubian Romanian-Hungarian integration projects seemed to have been inter-connected–at least according to the press releases.

In the same year several versions of a regional integration plan were presented at the Peace Initiative Department of the Ministry of Foreign Affairs. There were several people involved whose names had come up during the discussion of the war years. Quite a few members of the informal peace initiative group, which used to gather around István Bethlen, were reinstalled in the Ministry of Foreign Affairs following postwar political screening. Aladár Szegedy-Maszák was one of them. "Secretary" of the former confidential peace initiative, István Kertész became the director of the Peace Initiative Department. He collected all the contemporary reorganization plans which he himself had hidden in March of 1944 when the German occupation took place. Kertész, the President of the National Bank Artúr Kárász, and the co-workers of the Hungarian Economic Research Institute prepared a series of preliminary economic and political studies. The chances of a customs union were evaluated in a country-to-country (Hungarian–Yugoslav, Hungarian–Romanian, Hungarian–Czechoslovak, and Hungarian–Austrian) break-down in order to consider the benefits and disadvantages. Individual studies statistically outlined the inter-war economic structures of the respective countries and the volume and distribution of trade with one another. Finally, a separate study examined the idea of a comprehensive "South-Eastern European customs union."[50] All the studies pointed towards the advantages of an Austro–Hungarian customs union. However, they were negative about including Czechoslovakia in regional integration, presumably owing to the conflicts of 1946 created by forced resettlements, population exchanges, and the disfranchisement of Hungarian minorities in Slovakia.[51]

The summary indicated that the initiation of such a comprehensive and close regional co-operation needed the approval of the Great Powers.

> When agreed upon, South-Eastern European states need to seek the permission of the Allies for the creation of a South-Eastern European economic union and ask for their support of this initiative. The Allies will decide from a political perspective...Considering economic aspects, it is in the interest of the Allies that the economic union be created. Difficult living conditions in the South-Eastern European states have caused grave problems to global politics for decades. World peace would be served if these countries found a solution to improve their welfare. Therefore the threat of economic difficulties, which upset the peace of this continent and consequently that of the whole world, would be eliminated....South-Eastern Europe would stand on its feet owing to the planned economic union. Economic problems which inter-war politicians and economists failed to solve would come to an end.[52]

In line with postwar peace propaganda, Bibó's *Misery of Eastern-European Small States* was published. Bibó did not reject the widely publicized initiative. However, he tried to save his contemporaries from rushing into an unfounded euphoria of reconciliation while ignoring the tensions caused by the recent world-wide catastrophe. He did not reject the plan, but tried to face and confront the chaotic legacy facing the peoples and states of the region.

> It is a dangerous superstition to say that it is not worth drawing up the borders of this area, claiming instead that the solution is not to arrange border disputes but to establish a supra-national federation where borders between individual nations lose their significance. This is a dangerous idea because there has already been a supra-national federation here in the form of the Habsburg Empire. It exploded and sank the whole area in waves of miserable uncertainty because it had not been able to provide satisfying internal demarcation lines between the nations unified in it. A federation is like a marriage. One should not enter into with unsettled problems since its essence is to create new perspectives with several new problems and one does not save on an unsettled issue. Any kind of future federation will only function if a minimal stability is created in the area of border issues, which is the psychological prerequisite of a federation. Nations will only unite in a federation if every one of them has something to defend within the security of the federation.[53]

In another of his articles from the same period, Bibó pointed out the relatively new political narrow-mindedness that utilized the grave injuries of the post-World War I Trianon Treaty to legitimize an ideologically and functionally anti-democratic political system. Since Bibó could not exclude the possibility of the occurrence of a similar development now and since he found the parties, which mostly concentrated on discrediting one another and excluding one another from the government, unsuitable to devise and represent a balanced standpoint, he himself summarized the principles for Hungary to follow after the peace treaty was accomplished "in a way it can be said on behalf of the whole nation." In his peace manifesto Bibó concentrated on tasks which could be and should be solved according to the competence of individual states.

In connection with Hungary, he claimed that:

> However severe the peace treaty might be, once it is signed it will be implemented. It would not be sincere to pretend

that we are enthusiastic devotees of the severe regulations of the treaty. But we will not create an ideology or a program for changing the borders either and will not pursue a policy which speculates on international crises or catastrophes to obtain redress for territorial injuries. We will adjust to conditions created by the peace treaty without reservation....However, Hungary cannot give up its political interest in the fate of Hungarian minorities in neighboring countries. This is not to be done by noisy demonstrations, but by assuring the vital interests of the Hungarian minorities. Finally, Hungary declares that the severity of the peace treaty cannot be an excuse to give up the policy of our European integrity, democracy, benevolence towards our neighbors, and adaptation to the political and cultural community of Eastern European nations.[54]

The peace preparatory conference organized in Paris in the summer and fall of 1946 put various publicly held positions in a new context. Some people changed their positions accordingly. In the preceding one and a half years the alternative of an "historical reconciliation" with Romania was discussed primarily in historical context, that is relating to Kossuth's plan. While it is clear why Kossuth's plan was often evoked, it was also apparent how methodically Oszkár Jászi was neglected. By then Jászi, who sympathized with socialism in his youth but intransigently rejected Bolshevism, became persona non grata with the Communist Party, which predominated in internal politics. The communist party's influence in the postwar coalition period was so strong that an earlier friend and comrade, Mihály Károlyi, avoided publicly mentioning Jászi's name even while he himself tirelessly worked to realize their common ideals.

Historical analogies were replaced by actual political arguments owing to the proximity of the Paris Peace Conference. Hungary's governing parties tried to lessen public disappointment with a "second Trianon" by promising the establishment of a federation. In this context Mátyás Rákosi's elaboration was understandable when, at the September 1946 Congress of the Communist Party, he repeatedly spoke about regional integration as the main objective of Hungarian foreign policy. "We consider a democratic Danubian federation both possible and desirable. ... The establishment of such a democratic alliance entailing the abolishment of customs borders would ease the bitterness our people feel towards the upcoming peace treaty."[55] According to public opinion polls the idea of regional integration seemed to be appealing to a much wider circle in Hungary than just the Hungarian Communist Party. In May of 1946, 84% of the surveyed sample supported the Hungarian–Romanian customs union and in December 1946, 89% of a representative sample approved of the establishment of an extensive federation.[56]

To sum up, during 1945 Hungary was not a source of foreign policy initiatives, but rather reacted favorably to initiatives of Hungary joining a regional integration plan.

Moreover, during 1946 Hungary also urged a version of *Pax Danubiana* to mitigate the unfavorable consequences of the new territorial settlement being outlined at the Paris Peace Conference.

In 1947, after the defeated states of the region had signed the Paris peace treaties, they regained their *de jure* sovereignty. Diplomatic activity on the issue of regional integration intensified. In May Romanian President Petru Groza and a delegation of over onc hundred held talks in Budapest. Hardly had it been over when the coordinated recovery and development of the regional economy was on the agenda of the Budapest International Conference of the Central-European Social Democratic Parties. However, contrary to prognoses of the preceding period, now caution and postponement were exercised when the topic of a customs union was mentioned. Moreover, the secretary of the Romanian Communist Party, Vasile Luca, released an article following Petru Groza's return from discussions in Hungary in which he concluded that integrating efforts were "tools of imperialist plotting."

The sudden standstill did not prevail in other countries. Following top level talks in Bled in June of 1947, Bulgaria and Yugoslavia signed a preparatory protocol of a customs union. Before the signatures were applied, the document had been presented to Moscow where it was noted that it should remain in force for twenty years. Representatives of both countries' governments convened again in Evxinograd–in the vicinity of Varna–in November of 1947. In ensuing statements, both Tito and Dimitrov declared that the customs union could be implemented in the near future while a federation remained a long-range objective.[57]

Yet after November 1947 there was a twofold conceptual turn in the approach to postwar integrating ideas. Up to that point most of these ideas had predicted "a horizontal integration" of the

Danubian states. Following his talks in Prague, the President of the Hungarian National Planning Office, Imre Vajda, announced that in addition to the countries already involved, Czechoslovakia and Poland should be included "in the more or less contiguous economic system of Eastern-European democracies."[58] Ten days later an article, *Új nagyhatalom* (New Great Power), was released in the *Szabad Nép*, the party organ of the Hungarian Communists, which more extensively outlined the same idea. There were two significant features about the release of the article: (1) it coincided with Tito's arrival in Budapest to sign the Hungarian–Yugoslav friendship and co-operation pact, and (2) it drew up the program of a "vertical integration" instead of a "horizontal integration."

> The New Great Power would be constituted from the new democracies of seven countries (Poland, Czechoslovakia, Hungary, Yugoslavia, Bulgaria, Romania, and Albania) situated between the Ost Sea, the Adriatic Sea, and the Black Sea with a population of almost 90 million. The combined value of their agricultural production ranks second in Europe after the Soviet Union and that of their industrial production ranks third after the Soviet Union and England.[59]

The most pronounced element of the change was the underlying political message. The article described a "united front" with a "defense pact," referring to Czechoslovak Minister of Foreign Affairs J. Masaryk's, earlier declaration. The task of the "united front" was most explicitly defined by Petru Groza following the signing of the Hungarian–Romanian friendship pact, "Here we are in the big family of allied peace-loving peoples who are aware of their mighty power which can even resist nuclear power and the power of the dollar." These declarations were made following the implementation of the Marshall Plan and the establishment of KOMINFORM. The primary task of the "New Great Power," organized in the buffer zone, would have been to form a "*counter cordon sanitaire*" between the Soviet Union and Atlantic Europe when international relationships were immobilized by the cold war.

On January 29, 1948, *Pravda* called the ideas, which had been formulated with Moscow's acceptance and approval, "made up" in reaction to a statement made by Bulgarian communist premier, G. Dimitrov, in Bucharest. In the immediate region it was becoming evident that *Pax Danubiana*, seeking consensus among the concerned small states, would not be an alternative to the Bolshevik

Drang nach Westen, modeled on the earlier German *Drang nach Osten*. Obviously, to establish the federation a multi-lateral consensus was required. This stage was not reached. The multi-layered bilateral discussions were brought to a halt by the prohibitive command of the Soviet political leadership.

NOTES

1. Magda Ádám, *Richtung Selbsvernichtung. Die Kleine Entente, 1920–1938* [Direction Self-destruction. The Little Entente, 1920–1938] (Budapest-Wien, 1988).

2. Emma Kövics, *Az európai egység kérdése és Németország, 1919–1933* [The Question of European Unity and Germany, 1919–1933] (Budapest, 1992).

3. Elemér Hantos (1881–1842), lawyer and economist. Started his university studies in Budapest, continued them in Vienna and Leipzig, and completed them in Paris. In the first years of the 20th century he received a scholarship to Oxford and Cambridge. Returning to Budapest, he worked as a lawyer and became a Deputy to Parliament in 1910. Between 1917 and the end of the War, he was an Under-secretary of State in the Ministry of Commerce. In the same year he started teaching finance at the Law School of the Royal Hungarian University of Sciences in Budapest. From 1924 on he was the economic expert of the League of Nations. He was a founder of the Central European Institutes of Geneva, Vienna, Budapest, Leipzig, and Brno, all of which established close cooperation.

4. Gusztáv Gratz (1875–1946), lawyer, historiographer, and politician, started his university studies in Kolozsvár (Cluj) and gained his doctoral degree in law and political science at the Royal Hungarian University of Sciences in Budapest. Founder and editor of the social science journal the *Huszadik Század.* Gratz became a Deputy to Parliament in 1906 and the executive director of the *National Alliance of Hungarian Industrialists* in 1911. From 1917 until the dissolution of the Monarchy, he was the director of the Department of Commercial Policy of the common Ministry of Foreign Affairs of the Austrian-Hungarian Monarchy—with a few months interval as the Minister of Finance of the Hungarian Government. Gratz participated in the Brest-Litovsk Russian-Romanian peace talks. From the end of 1919 until early 1921, Gratz was the first Hungarian ambassador to Vienna. He was also Hungarian Foreign Minister between January 1921 and Charles IV's second attempt to regain the throne. Following that, he withdrew from active politics. Between 1924 and 1938 he was a board member of several economic enterprizes and social societies, and the founding president of the Cultural Society of Germans of Hungary. Following the Anschluss, when Hungary became more directly threatened by Hitler's Germany, he resigned. In 1941 he was elected member of the Hungarian Academy of Sciences. From 1942 on he belonged to the anti-German circle around István Bethlen, which tried to seek contact with the Anglo-Saxon powers. After the March 19, 1944 German occupation of Hungary, Gratz was also transported to the Third Reich. After his return to Hungary in the spring of 1945 in poor health, Gratz became an advisor

to the peace preparatory talks but could not participate in the 1946 Paris Peace Preparatory Conference. He died a month after the conference. See György Gyarmati, Gratz Gusztáv a Monarchia felosztásának következményeiről [Gusztáv Gratz on the Consequences of the Dissolution of the Monarchy] (*Történelmi Szemle,* 1995.1), 83–85.

5. Miklós Makay (1905–1977), protestant minister and public writer.

6. Elemér Hantos, *Die Kooperation der Notebanken als Mittel zur Rationalisierung der Weltwirtschafts* (Tübingen, 1921); *Das Geldprobleme in Mitteleuropa* (Jena, 1925); *Die Handelspolitik in Mitteleuropa* (Jena, 1925); *Der Zusammenschluss der mitteleuropäischen Wirtschaftssysteme* (Wien, 1925); *Das Kulturprobleme in Mitteleuropa* (Suttgart, 1926); Europäische Zollverein (*Zeitschrift Paneuropa,* 1926); La Cooperation economique en Europe Danubienne (*Revue de Hongrie,* Mai–Juni, 1926), 161–168; *Denkschrift über die wirtschaftlichen Probleme Mitteleuropas. Im Auftrage der Mitteleuropäischen Wirtschaftstagung für die Weltwirtschaftskonferenz des Völkerbundes* (Wien, 1927); Paneuropäische Verkehrsprobleme (*Zeitschrift für Geopolitik*, 1927); La cooperation des Banques centrales D'Emission (Revue de Hongrie, März, 1927), 81–86; *Die Weltwirtschaftskonferenz: Probleme und Ergebnisse* (Leipzig, 1928); *Europäischer Zollverein und mitteleuropäische Wirtschafts-gemeinschaft* (Berlin, 1928); *Das Donauproblem in der mitteleuropäischen Wirtschaft* (Wien, 1928); La Sphere de Civilization de L'Europe Centrale (*Revue de Hongrie,* Mai–Juni, 1928), 193–202; L'Institution de L'Europe Centrale pour le Rarrochement Culturel et Economique (*Revue de Hongrie*, Dezember, 1928), 193–197; Europäische Produktionsgemeinschaft (*Europa-Wirtschaft*, 1930); Neue Frontbildung in Mitteleuropa? (*Europa Wirtschaft*, 1930); Les Idées Conduettrices de la Conference Economique Internationale (*Revue de Hongrie*, Oktober, 1930), 97–109; *Das Mitteleuropäische Agrarproblem und seine Lösung* (Berlin, 1931); Pour une Transformation de L'Union Douamiere Austrie-Allemande en Europe Centrale (*Revue de Hongrie*, Oktober, 1931), 103–112; *L'Europe Centrale. Une nouvelle organisation economique* (Paris, 1932); Une nouvelle organization de l'Europe Centrale (*Nouvelle Revue de Hongrie*, März, 1932), 119–122; *Denkschrift über die Wirtschaftskrise in den Donauraum* (Wien, 1933); *Der Weg zum neue Mitteuropa: Die wirtschaftliche Neugestaltung* (Berlin, 1933); Vers le relevement national (*Nouvelle Revue de Hongrie*, Februar, 1933), 194–197; *L'Europe comme unite economique* (Roma, 1933); La Communaute de sort des Peuples Danubiens (*Nouvelle Revue de Hongrie*, Februar, 1934), 118–121; Die Neuordnung des Donauraums (*Mitteleuropäische Wirtschaftsfragen*, Berlin–Wien, 1935); Die Schweiz und der Donauraum (*Zeitschrift für Schweizerische Statistik und Volkswirtschaft,* 3, 1935); Der regionale Aufstieg Donaueuropas, in *Der gegenwärtige Stand der Donauraum-Pläne. 1. Donauraum. Beiträge zur Frage der wirtschaftlichen Annäherung und Zusammenarbeit der Donaustaaten,* ed. Roman Frhr. v. Prochazka (Wien, 1937); *La regionalisme economique en Europe* (Paris, 1939).

7. Gusztáv Gratz, *A dualizmus kora, II.* [The Age of Dualism] (Budapest, 1934); *A forradalmak kora* [The Age of Revolutions] (Budapest, 1935); *Der wirtschaftliche Zusammenbruch Österreich–Ungarns. Die Tragödie der Erschöpfung,* co-authored with Richard Schüller (Wien–New Haven, 1930); Nemzetközi

viszonyok [International Relations] co-authored with András Frey in *A mai világ képe I.* [The Image of Today's World] ed. András Frey (Budapest, 1940), 143-304; A világháború utáni kor története [The History of the Postwar Era] in *A mai világ képe II.* [The Image of Today's World] ed. András Frey (Budapest, 1940), 21-139.

8. Gustav Gratz, *Die äusere Wirtschaftspolitik Österreich-Ungarns. Mitteleuropäische Pläne,* co-authored with Richard Schüller (Wien, 1925); *Bestrebungen nach einer wirtschaftlichen Annäherungen zwischen den mitteleuropäischen Staaten. Ungarisches Wirtschaft-Jahrbuch, 1925* (Budapest, 1925), 86-89; Business Conditions in Hungary and its Neighbouring States. (*Proceedings of the Academy of Political Science in the City of New York,* 1926. Vol. I.), 174-183; Die ungarische Volkwirtschaft, Sonderdruck aus dem *Wirtschaftsjahrbuch für Industrie und Handel des Deutschen Reiches und der Nachfolgestaaten Österreich-Ungarns* (1928-1929); Die kleine Entente und Ungarn (*Europäische Gespräche,* September, 1928); Handelspolitische Kollektivverträge (*Zeitschrift für Zölle und Verbrauchssteurern,* Dezember, 1928); A páneurópai gondolat és Briand emlékiratai [The Pan-European Idea and Briand's Memoirs] (*Magyar Szemle,* 1930, 7), 210-219; *A német-osztrák vámunió kérdéséhez* [To the Question of the German-Austrian Customs Union] (Budapest, 1931); Az agrárállamok gazdasági együttműködése, 1 [Economic Cooperation of Agrarian States] (*Külügyi Szemle,* 1931), 21-30; A német-osztrák vámunió terve, 3. [The Plan of the German-Austrian Customs Union] (*Külügyi Szemle,* 1931), 277-287; Das Wesen des Präferenzsystems (*Zeitschrift für Zölle und Verbrauchssteuernm,* Äpril, 1931); Meistbegünstigung und Präferenz (*Zeitschrift für Zölle und Verbrauchssteuern,* Äpril, 1931); Ausfuhr-kontingente und Meistbegünstigung (*Zeitschrift für Zölle und Verbrauchssteuern,* Mai, 1931); Nationale und europäische Handelspolitik Sonderdruck aus der *Festschrift für Julius Wolff: Der Internationale Kapitalismus und die Krise* (Berlin, 1932); Cooperation economique et politique des Etats Danubien (*L'esprit International,* Juli, 1932); Középeurópa problémája [The Problems of Central Europe] (*Külügyi Szemle,* 1936, No.2), 114-118; Politique et Economie en Europe Centrale (*Nouvelle Revue de Hongrie,* Juni, 1936), 485-495; and La France et l'Europe Centrale (*Nouvelle Revue de Hongrie,* Äpril, 1938), 302-306.

9. Miklós Makay, *A kelet-közép-európai államrendszer problémája* [The Problem of the East Central European Political System] (Budapest, 1928).

10. Mária Ormos, *Franciaország és a keleti biztonság* [France and Eastern Security] (Budapest, 1969); *Az európai biztonság kérdése a két világháború között* [The Question of European Security between the Two World Wars] (Budapest, 1972).

11. György Ránki, Kredit oder Markt? Zum Wandel der Wirtschaftspolitischen Hegemonialbestrebungen der Grossmächte in Südosteuropa in Deutschland und Europa in der Neuzeit, in *Festschrift für Karl Otmar Freiher von Aretin zum 65. Geburtstag,* ed. R. Melville and C. Scharf (Wiesbaden, 1988), 805-824; Der ökonomische Hintergrund des "Mitteleuropa," in *Economic Development in Hungary and in Finland, 1860-1939,* ed., Tapani Mauranen (Helsinki, 1985), 221-253); The Economic Problem of the Danube Region after the Breakup of the Austro-Hungarian Monarchy, in *War and Society in East Central Europe. Vol.VI. Essays on World War I. Total War and Peacemaking. A Case Study on Trianon,* ed. Béla Király, Peter Pastor and Ivan Sanders (Brooklyn-New York, 1982), 89-105.

12. György Ránki, "Range" and "Constraint"–The Small States of the Danube basin and the International Political and Economic System, 1919-1945, in *Etudes Historiques Hongroises, 1985,* ed. Ferenc Glatz and Ervin Pamlényi, vol. 2. (Budapest, 1985), 225-274.

13. Kövics, 178.

14. Pál Teleki, Az európai probléma [The European Problem] (*Magyar Szemle,* 1931, 3), 209-220.

15. Karl Renner, *A Duna-medence gazdasági problémái és a szociáldemokrácia* [The Economic Problems of the Danube Basin and Social Democracy] (Budapest, 1935).

16. László Németh, *Magyarság és Európa* [Hungarians and Europe] (Budapest, 1935); *Helyünk Európában. Nézetek és koncepciók a 20. századi Magyarországon, I–II.* [Our Place in Europe: Views and Concepts in 20th Century Hungary], ed. Éva Ring (Budapest, 1986); Gyula Borbándi, *Der ungarische Populismus* (Mainz, 1976); Gábor Bátonyi, A Duna-konföderáció gondolata a két világháború közti Magyarországon [The Idea of a Danube Confederation in Inter-war Hungary] (*Alföld,* 1985, 8), 35-42; István Bernát, Utópia, remény, valóság [Utopia, Hope, and Reality] (*Világosság,* 1989, 8-9), 683-689; Gyula Gombos, *Szabó Dezső* (München, 1966, Budapest, 1989).

17. Imre Kovács, Dunakonföderáció [Danubian Confederation] (*Magyar Út,* 1937, April]; Konrád Salamon, *A Márciusi Front* [The March Front] (Budapest, 1980), 77; Gyula Juhász, *Uralkodó eszmék Magyarországon, 1939-1944* [Prevailing Ideas in Hungary, 1939-1944] (Budapest, 1983).

18. Endre Bajcsy-Zsilinszky, Új helyzet–új magyar politika a német impériummal szemben, 1-3. [New Situation–New Hungarian Policy towards the German Empire, 1-3] (*Előörs,* 1929, March 2-9).

19. Endre Bajcsy-Zsilinszky, *Nemzeti radikalizmus* [National Radicalism] (Budapest, 1930).

20. Endre Bajcsy-Zsilinszky, *Helyünk és sorsunk Európában* [Our Place and Destiny in Europe] (Budapest, 1941), 330.

21. András Rónai, A dunai megegyezés lehetőségei [The Possibilities of a Danube Agreement] (*Apollo,* 1937, 2), 127-130.

22. Ignác Romsics, *Bethlen István* (Budapest, 1991).

23. István Bethlen's memoirs about the expected peace conditions, in *Magyarország külpolitikája a második világháború időszakában, 1939-1940. Diplomáciai iratok Magyarország külpolitikájához, 1935-1945, IV.* [Hungary's Foreign Policy during World War II, 1939-1940. Hungarian Foreign Policy Diplomatic Documents] ed. and introduction by Gyula Juhász (Budapest, 1962), 743-761; Many voiced similar views to that of Bethlen's in Hungary. See István Kertész, Az Amerikai Egyesült Államok külpolitikája [The Foreign Policy of the United States of America] in *Külügyi Évkönyv, 1941* [Foreign Policy Yearbook, 1941] ed. György Drucker (Budapest, 1941), 148-163; Iván Lajos, *Németország háborús esélyei a német szakirodalom tükrében* [The Chances of War for Germany Reflected by the Professional Literature] (Pécs, 1939).

24. *The Practical Policy of the Peace Revision* (Congress of the Revisionist League on May 22, 1932 in the Vigadó), in *Bethlen István gróf beszédei és írásai II.* [Speeches and Writings of Count István Bethlen II.] (Budapest, 1933), 376; The change in Bethlen's attitude can be observed from 1937. See *Pesti Napló,*

August 20, 1937, in Ignác Romsics, *István Bethlen,* 271; Bethlen koncepciója a független vagy autonóm Erdélyről [Bethlen's Concept of an Independent or Autonomous Transylvania], in *Magyarságkutatás. A Magyarságkutató Csoport évkönyve* [Hungarian Research: The Yearbook of the Hungarian Research Group] (Budapest, 1987), 49-64.

25. Gyula Juhász, *Magyar-brit titkos tárgyalások, 1943-ban* [Hungarian-British Secret Talks in 1943] (Budapest, 1978).

26. Aladár Szegedy-Maszák (1903-1988), diplomat, entered the Foreign Service in 1927, served in the Berlin Embassy of Hungary between 1932 and 1937, was Deputy Director of the Political Department of the Ministry of Foreign Affairs from 1942, and was Director of the Political Department from 1943. On March 19, 1944, the day of the German occupation of Hungary, he was arrested by the Gestapo and transported to Dachau. From 1946, he was Ambassador of Hungary to the United States. In June 1947, in protest against Prime Minister Ferenc Nagy's forced emigration, he resigned from his position—along with several diplomats of the period—and stayed abroad. The *Memorandum* was first published in Juhász, *Secret Talks*, 190-219. See also Aladár Szegedy-Maszák, *Az ember ősszel visszanéz II.* [One Looks Back in the Fall] (Budapest, 1960), 230-282. The original text is included (any differences with Juhász's version are due to translation back from English) along with comments by the author.

27. Gusztáv Gratz, Az Osztrák-Magyar Monarchia felosztásának következményei [Consequences of the Dissolution of the Austrian-Hungarian Monarchy] (*Történelmi Szemle*, 1995, 1), 99-114.

28. István Bethlen, Emlékirat a dunai föderáció tárgyában [Memoir on the Issue of the Danubian Federation] ed. Károly Urbán and István Vida, (*Kritika*, 1991, 11), 32-38.

29. The potential for the Federative internal organization following the Swiss pattern came up in one of Bethlen's lectures in England in 1933. The last sentence of this lecture is worth attention as it proved to be a Cassandra's prophecy relating to the Ribbentrop-Molotov Pact six years later. "Europe should understand that either the Great Powers manage to reconcile small Danubian nations—depending on the right solution of the Transylvanian question—or a dark and stormy period will arrive. Either the Eastern Slavic giant will clamp down on the small nations of Eastern Europe or the German *Drang nach Osten*—or both in mutual agreement." *Az erdélyi kérdés* [The Transylvanian Question] in Bethlen István angliai előadásai [István Bethlen's Lectures in England] (Budapest, 1933), 86, 91.

30. The book was originally published—with the assistance of the Bern Hungarian Embassy—in Switzerland. Andrew Bajcsy-Zsilinszky, *Transylvania Past and Future, 1944* . For the background of the development and publication of the book, see Loránt Tilkovszky, Bajcsy-Zsilinszky könyve Erdélyről [Bajcsy-Zsilinszky's Book about Transylvania] (*Világosság*, 1990, 10), 767-779.

31. Károly Vígh, *Bajcsy-Zsilinszky Endre külpolitikai nézeteinek alakulása* [The Development of Endre Bajcsy-Zsilinszky's Foreign Policy Concepts] (Budapest, 1979); Vígh, *A küldetéses ember* [The Man with a Mission] (Budapest, 1992); Loránt Tilkovszky, Bajcsy-Zsilinszky programtervezete 1943-ból [Bajcsy-Zsilinszky's Program Draft from 1943] in *Kiútkeresés, 1943* [Searching for a Way Out, 1943], ed., Zsuzsa L. Nagy (Budapest, 1989), 115-123.

32. Similar points are raised in Bajcsy's memoirs, "Federalization of Hungary" written while in German captivity a year later. "I treated the issue of the renewal of an autonomous Transylvania in my book published in Switzerland, 'Transylvania: Past and Future.' According to that work, Transylvania–obviously the whole area–would again become an independent state, a joint union of the Holy Crown modeled after the 1867 Austrian-Hungarian Compromise." See Lóránt Tilkovszky, Bajcsy-Zsilinszky Endre 1944. évi tanulmánya a kisebbségi kérdésről és Magyarország belső föderalizálásáról [Endre Bajcsy-Zsilinszky's 1944 Essay on the Minority Question and the Internal Federalization of Hungary] (*Baranyai Levéltári Füzetek*, 1986, 74), 647-683.

33. Bethlen raised this isssue relating to the Benes versus Habsburg constellation and opted for the latter. Beyond his personal and political aversion to Benes, there were conceptual considerations at work in Bethlen's views. In the January 1942 issue of *Foreign Affairs,* there were two articles published: E. Benes, The Organization of the Postwar Europe, and Otto von Habsburg, Danubian Reconstruction, and both treated the issue of the federative reorganization of the area. Benes seemed to have found support for Czechoslovakia's sovereignty and a leading role in Central Europe in Moscow. On the other hand, Bethlen rejected Benes' plan, just as he had done before with any federative construction which would have assured Soviet hegemony in the area. Especially after the conclusion of the Soviet-Czechoslovak Treaty of Alliance and Mutual Aid, Bethlen viewed Czechoslovakia as the Trojan horse of Soviet penetration into Central Europe. Bethlen expressed similar views in the summer of 1943 when he held secret political discussions with an envoy of the London Polish Government in exile about the chances of future cooperation between the two countries. He considered maintaining a common Polish-Hungarian border to counter-balance a Moscow-Prague axis. See Katalin Szokolay, A londoni lengyel levéltárak magyar vonatkozású anyagaiból [From the Hungarian Holdings of the London Polish Archives] (*Valóság*, 1995,1), 30-54.

34. János F. Varga, An Illusion of Cooperation: Hungarian Emigrants in Britain during World War II, (*Acta Historica Acad. Sci. Hung.*, 1986), 69-96.

35. Oszkár Jászi, Föderációs tervek I-III. [Federative Plans, I-III] (*Magyar Fórum,* New York, 1942), No. 1. 9-11, No. 2. 31-33, No. 4. 79-85; Európa jövendő megszervezéséről [The Future Organization of Europe] (*Harc,* June 19 and November 30, 1943); and The Future of Transylvania (*Harc,* November 21, 1943).

36. Published in Oszkár Jászi, Central Europe and Russia (*Journal of Central European Affairs,* April, 1945, 1), 1-16. However, Jászi indicates in this paper that this section of the article was written three years before. "Three years ago I was asked by the New York Council on Foreign Relations to write a short memorandum concerning the future of Hungary. As this paper had only private circulation, I beg to give you a few of its main conclusions," Jászi, 1.

37. Ibid., 3-4.

38. Ibid., 1-16.

39. *Yugoslavia and the Soviet Union, 1939-1973,* ed. S. Clissold (Oxford, 1975); Edvard Kardelj, *Visszaemlékezések* [Memoirs] (Novi Sad, 1981); and E.R. Goodman, *The Soviet Design for a World State* (New York, 1961), 332; E. Kardelj, 120.

40. Ildikó Lipcsei, Réczei László feljegyzései 1945. márciusi romániai megbeszéléseiről [László Réczei's Notes about His Romanian Talks in March 1945] (*Történelmi Szemle*, 1984, 4), 624.

41. President of the Romanian Control Committee.

42. Lipcsey, op. cit.

43. Passau is at the German border, Predeal is in the Southern Carpathians (today Romania), and Pula is a port on the Adriatic Sea (today Croatia)–thus, denoting the western, south-western, and southern end-points of the Austro-Hungarian Monarchy.

44. Az ideiglenes magyar kormány jegyzéke a három szövetséges nagyhatalom budapesti képviselőihez, Magyarország békecéljairól, Augusztus 14, 1945 [Memorandum of the Provisional Hungarian Government to the Budapest Representatives of the Three Allies about the Peace Goals of Hungary, August 14, 1945] in István Kertész, *Magyar békeillúziók, 1945-1947* [Hungarian Peace Illusions, 1945-1947] (Budapest, 1995), 535-545.

45. Ignác Romsics, *Amerikai béketervek a háború utáni Magyarországról* [American Peace Plans Regarding Post-war Hungary] (Gödöllő, 1992).

46. *Szabad Nép*, September 23, 1945.

47. Iszlámov Tofik, Erdély a szovjet külpolitikában a második világháború alatt [Transylvania in the Soviet Foreign Policy during World War II] (*Múltunk*, 1994), 1-2, 17-50.

48. János Jemnitz, A magyarországi Szociáldemokrata Párt külpolitikai irányvonalának alakulásához, 1945-1948 [To the Development of the Foreign Policy Guideline of the Hungarian Social-Democratic Party] (*Történelmi Szemle*, 1965), 2-3.

49. *Köztársaság,* July 18, 1946.

50. The Impact of a Hungarian-Yugoslav economic cooperation; Expected Impacts of the Hungarian-Romanian Customs Union; The Czechoslovak-Hungarian Economic Union; The Austro-Hungarian Economic Union; and The South-Eastern European Customs Union. Gusztáv Gratz, after returning from German deportation in very grave health, also prepared two drafts on this topic but was unable to participate actively.

51. György Gyarmati, Föderationsbestrebungen nach dem Zweiten Weltkrieg. Vom Mitteleuropa bis zum Ostblock, in *Mitteleuropa-konzeptionen in der ersten Hälfte des 20. Jahrhunderts,* ed. Richard Plaschka, Horst Haselsteiner and Arnold Suppan (Wien, 1995), 369-381.

52. Ibid.

53. István Bibó, *A kelet-európai kisállamok nyomorúsága* [The Misery of Eastern European Small States] (Budapest, 1946), in BIVT, II.247.

54. István Bió, *A békeszerződés és a magyar demokrácia* [The Peace Treaty and the Hungarian Democracy) in BIVT, II. 267-296.

55. *A népi demokrácia útja. A Magyar Kommunista Párt 3. kongresszusának jegyzőkönyve* [The Road of Democracy. Records of the Third Congress of the Hungarian Communist Party] (Budapest, 1946), 68.

56. A Magyar Közvéleménykutató Intézet felmérései [Surveys of the Hungarian Public Opinion Research Institute] (*Közvélemény,* Budapest, 1947), 9-10.

57. V. Dedijer, *J.B. Tito* (Novi Sad, 1953), 447; J.B.Tito, *Beszédek és cikkek III* [Speeches and Articles, III] (Novi Sad, November 29, Novi Sad).

58. *Népszava*, November 29, 1947.

59. *Szabad Nép*, December 7, 1947.

OSZKÁR JÁSZI'S DANUBE FEDERATION THEORIES

GYÖRGY LITVÁN

Oszkár Jászi is often quoted as the authority on nationality issues and the prophet of federative theory. This representation is not unfounded, though improper. Achieving social justice and overcoming hindrances on the way were Jászi's main concerns all his life. His scholarly and political activities focussed on them. He related to the complex national, ethnic, and confederative issues as organic parts of it. As a member of the Hungarian left and as a political thinker, he was the first in the country to recognize the connection between social and nationality problems and was first to try to connect and solve the practical questions of national and social advancement.

From 1904 on Jászi was clear about two issues: (1) Contrary to the doctrinaires of the left he recognized the force and the durability of nationality interests, sentiments, and traditions: "Undoubtedly the history of our near future will be determined by two mighty social trends, nationalism and socialism."[1] (2) He recognized that intellectuals and the middle class of nationalist inclination were primarily concerned about the masses of non-Hungarian nationalities of growing consciousness and the territorial integrity of historical Hungary. These concerns hindered democratic and socialist ambitions, the extension of rights, and the introduction of universal suffrage. In 1907, two years after completing *Socialism and Patriotism* and a field trip in Transylvania, he wrote, "I continuously work on the nationality issue but with altering faith. The Lugos trip was impressive. My work is not solely a theoretical quest as it wants to break off the handcuffs of eight million people in desperate servitude."[2]

In 1912, after five years of work, study, hiking trips, personal experience and data materialized in *The Evolution of National States and the Nationality Question*, Jászi had aspired to summarize the history of the issue and to develop it as a sociological analysis.[3] He pointed out to nationalists and advocates of forced Hungarianization that their aspirations were futile and counterproductive as national awakening and national consciousness were natural processes. He warned enlightened internationalists of the left that nationality oppression existed beyond social oppression and that additional oppression constituted the nationality question.

The greatest poet and most farsighted Hungarian of the period, Endre Ady, claimed in his review of Jászi's book that "he has revealed the Archimedean point of our nationality question, a question of crucial significance."[4] At that point Jászi still sought a solution within historical Hungary and the Monarchy. He was hopeful that a democratic minimal program might satisfy the concrete demands of the national minorities and Romanians, Slovaks, Ruthenians, and the South-Slavs (excluding Croats) would remain within the country.

As Jászi summarized the minimal program: "One requirement is good schools, good administration, and a good justice system in the language of the people. The second is to recognize the right of every ethnic group to freely develop its language and culture."[5] It is almost the exact replica of what international and first of all European norms demand for ethnic minorities. Jászi's proposal met with a varied nationality reception.[6] Some, like the Romanian Emil Babes, appreciated it; others found the proposal unsatisfactory and viewed it as modernized Hungarianization, and the Hungarian nationalists with the historical parties certainly considered it too radical and a looming sacrifice of national interests. That was why R. W. Seton-Watson, whose friendship and appreciation became a major ground for accusation, wrote: "I foresee for your country a very gloomy future, if the efforts of men like yourself should by any unhappy chance (absit omen!) end in failure."[7]

In short, before the end of the war Jászi had not formally left "national consensus" and had not gone beyond the theoretical framework of Hungarian sovereignty. Had he stepped forward with a federative proposal or acknowledged ethnic minorities' secession rights, he would have excluded himself from Hungarian political life. Nevertheless, his writings and activities before and during the war clearly indicate steadfast solidarity with nationalities, several leaders and active representatives of which were accused of high treason and conspiracy and were persecuted during the war years. According to his correspondence, Jászi proved to be the only Hungarian politician they could seek help from. The Romanian writer Emil Isac wrote in an open letter, "In recent months your name has been ringing like a familiar bell, your name has been forceful protection, and through your writings a democratic Hungary has revealed to us, nationalities."[8]

By then the relationship between Hungarian and non-Hungarian populations of the Carpathian Basin had become embittered. Nobody was able to come up with a program which would have satisfied both parties. The problem boiled down to the choice between coexistence and separation. Until the last moment Jászi believed in the saving grace of a democratic turn and the land reform, by which mutual trust would be established and secession could be prevented. He had not counted on the developing anti-democratic feature of the ethnic identity he trusted the democratic spirit of ethnic middle classes, and had not noticed that "the will of survival easily and quickly transforms into tyranny."[9] In the fall and winter of 1918 during his short ministry he bitterly acknowledged this tendency.

Jászi's first federative plan originated from the last year of the war and was published shortly before the complete collapse in the fall of 1918. It had been preceded by an integrating effort which had not threatened the Hungarian sovereignty. On the contrary, the Friedrich Naumann Mitteleuropa plan aspired to save it, too. In 1915–16 the plan had stirred up Hungarian politics and divided unified Hungarian progressives into socialists and radicals. Jászi and his circle opted for the plan. As he reasoned later, "I was for the Central European concept when the Central Powers were on the defensive and to all appearances Russian czarism was going to finish the war unshaken. I was for it because in the given situation this concept would have brought the greatest freedom with the least sacrifice for Hungary and the Danube nations in the face of the Ceasarian pressure and would have offered the most suitable transition towards a complete European integration."[10]

After the 1917 February Russian revolution, which subverted czarism, the situation changed. In Jászi's view "Central Europe can only form as aggressive and militarist, as an exclusive German-Hungarian brotherhood in arms, and not as a free confederation of peoples living here as we had wished." A year later he took the view that "the concentration of the European culture in a common international organization is not a utopia any more. The logical condition to achieve this goal is the new balance of the peoples of the Monarchy and the Balkans, which had been stipulated by Lajos Kossuth with great political intuition over a half of a century ago."[11]

It was also Kossuth's former plan that Jászi renewed when in October of 1918 he published *The Future of the Monarchy: The Fall of Dualism and the United States of Danubia*. In its introduction he related that the book had waited for publication since May and "it might be late as practice is overtaking theory." By then it was clear that his work was for posterity rather than for the racing present. He posed the following initial question: "Is it possible to reconcile Hungary's rational needs for survival with the developmental efforts of the European culture and the whole of mankind? The conclusion I arrived at will invite wrathful criticism both from narrow-minded chauvinism and verbal internationalism thriving on empty clichés and being devoid of ideas. Exactly in this position I can see the need for my book. From a future perspective let posterity see that even amidst a general nationalistic madness there was a public view in Hungary that was aware of the fundamentals and was capable of honoring and even loving our enemies of today. There may still be time left to attract wider circles to a political ideal that can secure Hungary's independence and democratic advancement in a common European culture by setting real goals and outlining rational means."[12]

The first version of Jászi's Danube confederation plan still originated from the existing structure of the Monarchy and aspired to transform it into a democratic federation of states without breaking up viable nation states.

In Jászi's view there are five nations which "meet the criteria of historical-political individualism: Hungary, Germany, Poland, Bohemia, and Serbo-Croatia. Each possesses a more or less defined territory, a population of adequate number and cultural importance to pursue an independent national existence and to sustain historical consciousness." Hence he conceived a United States of Danubia which would consist of five federal states: (1) Hungary without Croatia and Slavonia (2) Austria (3) Bohemia (4) newly united Poland and (5) Illyria, which would unite the South-Slav regions with Croatian leadership.[13] He also stipulated the possibility of Romania joining the union.

Péter Hanák, an authority of the history and literature of the era rightly remarked: "At first sight it appears that the draft is a theoretical construction. Jászi conveniently cut up and joined Polish, Ukrainian, and Macedonian territories unrestricted by reality."[14]

In the same month, October 1918, the second edition of Jászi's book was published. According to the preface, the first edition had sold out within days. The main title changed as the Monarchy had ceased to exist in the meantime. However, *The Future of Hungary and the United States of Danubia* still could not cope with the reality of the end of war. The plan rejected the internal federalization of Hungary and deprived nationalities without history of their own statehood, even though independence had just been granted and eagerly accepted by them.

In 1918–19 just the very opposite materialized of what Jászi had been dreaming of and prepared. His slogan was "freedom and unity" which would come true in a voluntary alliance of free, democratic states converging into growing confederations, first into the United States of Danubia and later the United States of Europe. Neither after the defeat nor later did he acknowledge the total ideological defeat of his nationality policy. In his memoirs published in 1920 he said the following about his activities as a Nationality Minister in late 1918: "My politics could have only three rational goals: to save the idea of the plebiscite and eventually favorably adjust the final borders of the new Hungary; to protect traditional economic and transportation cooperation between the motherland and territories to be disconnected; to prepare an anticipated confederative union of states that would assure the complete autonomy of each state within a vast federation based on territory or personal land-register, whichever is possible. Namely, my policy is rather for the future than for the present."[15]

In the first two years of his exile starting in the spring of 1919, which coincided with the Paris peace talks and sanctioning the new Central Europe, Jászi had to adjust and develop his old ideas to the new situation. In the fall of 1920 after he had conferred with the politicians of Prague, Belgrade, and Bucharest as the leader of the Hungarian democrats in exile represented by Mihály Károlyi, he expressed his views about the situation and the future of the Danube countries. On returning to Vienna he commented that "my Balkan trip put into a grim light the devastating spiritual and moral isolation the cultured humanity of today. Good Lord! Before the war we learnt more and faster about life in Africa and Australia than in Budapest, Vienna, Belgrade, and Bucharest learn from one another today. Monstrous Great Walls of China divide nations; the walls of hunger, hatred, and ignorance." He stressed the necessity of a Central-Europe reorganized in the spirit of understanding and solidarity among its peoples to save a noncompetitive Europe sunk into the present system of economic and political isolation.[16] He avoided the term "confederacy," which was intensively recycled in his vocabulary a year later at Christmas of 1921, when his editorial "The Future of the Danube Union" was published in the *Bécsi Magyar Újság*.[17]

In the first part of the article he analyzed the first few years following the disappearance of the Monarchy and concluded that after achieving their long awaited independent statehood and national self-determination, sobriety and alienation had taken over both the intellectuals and the masses. The general feeling was that "the new system is the El Dorado of the soldiers and the bureaucrats at most," not that of the physical or intellectual workers. "To reconcile a complete independence of state and national existence with the economic and cultural interests of the Danube common fate would be the greatest dilemma of the Danube peoples."

By then Jászi was level-headed and cautious enough not to propose immediate confederative plans in the *Vienna Daily* of the democratic Hungarian community in exile. He first proposed to establish the Cultural Union of the Danube peoples. This task would have been to inform and educate about the history and the culture of diverse peoples, to highlight their economic and social problems, to popularize their cultural values, to publish a common review, and to organize conferences. Moreover, the Union would establish an agency for legal protection "to address every grievance ever committed against national minorities and fight chauvinistic instigation and intrigues...That is how the Danube Cultural Union would ferment the new Danube synthesis."

In the following months Jászi methodically developed his ideas and published them in several successive articles in a Bucharest democratic paper, *Revista Vremii*.[18] The situation and the direction of reasoning fundamentally changed since the end of 1918. It was not the ruling nations, Hungary and Germany of the Monarchy, to be convinced of the need for equal rights. On the contrary, the leaders of new national states had to be impressed that territorial restructuring for their benefit was not an ideal and final solution; furthermore, the internal economic and cultural relationships that had dissembled and repaired old injustices were weakened by new ones. The new rule should acknowledge that the region was not nationally uniform; therefore, ethnical homogeneity could not be created anywhere. With respect to a solution Jászi differentiated between viable steps taken in a given situation and distant goals. With respect to the former the right to peacefully develop "its own ethnic culture and to retain its community with the mother country across the border" ought to be guaranteed to every minority without damaging sovereignty of the state.

The distant goal would be to exceed "the small state"–*Kleinstaaterei*–and to establish a Danube Union of Nations "To break down economic isolation while protecting a perfect political and territorial sovereignty of the new states. This road would take the Danube nations from disarray and disintegration to organization and freedom." His federative plans had a special Transylvanian ramification which connected to Transylvanianism and the idea of an independent or federative Transylvania. At the end of 1918, the idea of a "Switzerland of the East," a Transylvania with cantons, transformed into the idea of a federative Romania or the dream of an autonomous Transylvania belonging to the Danube Union. Árpád Paál, a leader of Transylvanian Hungarians wrote to Jászi during his visit in 1923: "the fate of Hungarians is contingent upon this Union both in Hungary and in the successor states."[19] Jászi also cautioned Romanian and Hungarian public opinion in Romania that not much should be expected from the West since the future could be prepared by the Central European nations themselves. He changed his mind about the center of the Union and the leader of federative ambitions. Obviously, in 1918 and 1919 Hungary would have been the option. Following the stabilization of the Horthy regime he placed his hopes into the most democratic state, Czechoslovakia and its leaders, until he became disappointed in them also.

Most certainly by the mid-1920's Jászi's thinking and mentality had undergone significant changes. Péter Hanák rightly defined this period of his as the developing "Danube patriotism," which abandoned any kind of national hegemony and assumed some kind of common civic conscience, a regional cultural ideal, and ethos.[20] In March 1929 this creed was professed in the preface of his first and most significant book on the dissolution of the Habsburg Monarchy and which was published in the United States: "At present there does not exist for me an isolated Hungarian problem; and, though with an unbroken loyalty to my own, I have the same sympathy for all the suffering peoples of the Danube Basin."[21]

It was not this book that launched Jászi's three decade long "campaign" for the Danube confederacy. As early as 1923, during his first American lecture tour, one of the five talks bore the title *War and Confederation in Central Europe*. In his article "Dismembered Hungary and Peace in Central Europe," published in *Foreign Affairs* at the same time, he described the situation in the area and concluded: "the only way out of this hell is the adoption of the American method or the system of the British Commonwealth–the Anglo-Saxon way of confederation...The only possible cure for Europe's ills is a democratic confederation of democratic peoples, the extirpation of the system of rigid and selfish national sovereignty, peaceful, and rational cooperation between all countries for the common good of all."[22] The sine qua non of this system would be free trade and the national and cultural autonomy of minorities. After 1925, when he settled in Oberlin, Ohio, he regularly published articles and studies in the American press, in *The New York Times*, *The Nation*, and *The New Republic*.[23] One of the reasons of his emigration was the realization that from Vienna he was unable to fight effectively for the democratic and peaceful cooperation of the peoples of the Danube region and hoped to circumvent it by convincing the American public and by influencing the government.

Among all his efforts during the following years, writing and publishing *Dissolution* proved to be the most effective. This passionate book has been in circulation at American universities ever since and has helped generations to learn and understand the past and the real problems of the region.

The Chicago University Press ordered this study as part of a ten-volume civic education series. Jászi was happy to do it and remarked to Mihály Károlyi in early 1926: "the problem is of scientific interest for me and is in the general direction of my work (as all of us broke our necks on this problem)..."[24] With the impartial and unbiassed analysis of the history of the Habsburg Monarchy, Jászi set out to demonstrate that within this multi-national state, which quite successfully overcame nationalism, different ethnicities could have lived and cooperated successfully had the Monarchy been democratized and federalized in time and had its citizens been educated to loyalty towards the common state. He also fully discussed the centripetal and centrifugal forces in operation in the Monarchy. The dynasty, army, aristocracy, the Roman Catholic church, bureaucracy, capitalism, the Jewry, and the socialist movement were enumerated as centripetal forces. Feudal survivals, national antagonisms, awakening and strengthening nationalism, and irredentism belonged to the disruptive, centrifugal forces. He drew a distinction between real and pseudo-irredentist movements and hence only the Italian, Romanian, and South-Slav movements within the attraction of the nation state across the border, were real. Subsequently, he was more optimistic about the coexistence of the peoples of the Monarchy than the majority of contemporary politicians, posterior observers and historians.

Completing the study he gave the following account to Mihály Károlyi: "this book could have been much better if two years had been at my disposal instead of one. Nevertheless, I am pleased with the architechtonic organization of the book and the steady and consistent delivery of the fundamental message, that the Monarchy failed because it failed to federalize."[25] *Dissolution* was the historical ground-work for the idea and possibilities of the Danube confederation. As he remarked in one of his methodological notes: "the chief utility of all historical and sociological investigations is... to admonish us of the alternative possibilities of history."[26]

After completing this magnum opus Jászi followed his path undauntedly to get the idea of federation adopted, although from the early 1930's on the darkening European horizon brought more and more concern.

In 1929 he wrote to Iuliu Maniu, the new Prime Minister of Romania and a decade long acquaintance, and reminded him of their end of 1918 conference when Maniu, on behalf of the Romanian National Committee, politely and firmly refused the Károlyi Government's peace offer towards a federal Hungary. "Then you spoke on behalf of the new Greater Romania, still finally added that the idea of a peaceful alliance of the Danube peoples, which lived in my soul, incited you also. Until this remote idea was realized, you assured me that the Romanian nation would consider the Hungarian minority as a free and equal nation in every area of state and cultural life. Mr. Prime Minister, I trust the earnestness and honesty of your promise."[27]

On another occasion his historical reasoning was extended to a Hungarian national direction. In his study "Kossuth and the Treaty of Trianon," published in October 1933 in *Foreign Affairs,* he recalled that Kossuth, a dedicated enemy of dualism, had predicted the prospective dismemberment of Hungary and Kossuth and Teleki developed the concept of confederation during the process of an exciting correspondence.

In 1934, which was his sabbatical year, Jászi went on a lengthy trip in the Danube region and summarized his experiences in a four-part series called "War Germs in the Danube Basin" in *The Nation*. In the introduction he outlined the changes and a few of their positive outcomes, primarily in the Masaryk-led Bohemia, since the dissolution of the Monarchy. "For a time it was possible to be reasonably optimistic about the outcome....Last summer when I visited the successor states after several years of absence, I found a situation which convinced me that the nationality problem is not solved and that the methods now followed are inadequate to bring about peaceful cooperation."[28]

He assessed the prevailing situation in the Little Entente countries, analyzed the Hungarian revisionist ambitions, and its last version under the slogan of "peaceful revision."

> In reality, revision of the frontiers is not the fundamental issue, since it cannot satisfy the three basic needs of the Danubian basin, which are the dissemination of education, the alleviation of the agrarian crisis, and the efficient defense of national minorities. The racial mixture in the Danube basin and the Balkans would make it impossible for any frontier arrangement to solve the problem of minorities. Yet the present protection of national minorities by the League is mere hypocrisy. Even if the present minorities treaties were taken seriously, they would not suffice. What the national minorities need is not tolerance and a certain minimum of rights, but a system of cultural autonomy from elementary school to university....the members of the various nationality groups must have a proportional share in the administration and judiciary of the state. This means that "nationality" and "citizenship" should be separated and the new states become nationally federated like Switzerland or Estonia. It is manifest that these things cannot be accomplished under the present Danubian system. Instead of autarchy, the peoples need growing areas of free trade; instead of armed national sovereignties, they need a federal union; instead of tariffs protecting the wealthy farmers, they need a new technique of agriculture based on an efficient credit and cooperative system.

His final exhortation concluded that if the Danube states did not implement the necessary, basic reforms, war and a successive revolutionary change would take place with kolkhozes instead of co-operatives, councils instead of national autonomies, and Asian-type dictatorships instead of free federations. His admonitions of 1935 were "The Economic Crisis in the Danubian States" published in *Social Research* and "Neglected Aspects of the Danubian Drama" published in the *Slavonic Review.* The latter discussed the petty rivalries and the silent warfare of the Danube nations and concluded that small streams might swell into large rivers within a few years.

In July of 1939 Jászi gave a talk, "The Future of the Danubian States," at the Institute of Public Affairs. At that time he was open to the possibility that within the framework of the German *Grossraumwirtschaft* a coordinated and unified Central Europe might come true, even without military intervention. Furthermore, he hoped that when Hitler and the Nazis destroyed the political and customs borders, they would have established a new system of traffic and transportation that would deliver Central European nations to a federation. And, he concluded, "a Central European federalism, a kind of an Oriental Switzerland on a far vaster scale, based on democracy and social justice, would mean the end of the old power policy."

The next paper, "The Future of Danubia," was written and published in the July 1941 issue of the *Journal of Central European Affairs*, and was dedicated entirely to the past problems and future perspectives of the Danubian Federation. Jászi found that the consequences of World War I "completely demolished the moral unity of Europe." Now, he added, "we stand again before a turning point." The moment was, however, most inopportune for a forecast, since it was just before the end of the German–Soviet Pact. But Jászi emphasized correctly that "the burning problems of the Danube and of the Balkans cannot be solved without the cooperation of an enlightened and friendly Germany." Though he saw both the necessity and the possibility of a German democratization, he repeated his old mistake of 1915–16 when he supported the Mitteleuropa plan and hoped for beneficial and progressive effects from a hated and terrible war.

The same journal published in April 1945, just before the end of the war, one of his most important essays, "Central Europe and Russia." The paper was originally delivered before the Modern History Section of the American Historical Association in Chicago, December 28, 1944. Again, he tried to define, on the eve of a new epoch, the perspectives of the democratization and federalization of this area. He envisaged several possibilities, for better of worse, but his presumption and forecast were rather optimistic on the whole. He was realistic, however, in his assumption, that "all plans for an international organization will depend on a sincere and efficient cooperation between Russia and the democracies."[29]

A special contribution of his to the problems of Central European reorganization was made in 1944 at the University of Oklahoma where a series of lectures was held on "Federation: The Coming Structure of World Government," with the participation of Wendell Willkie, Henry Wallace, and others. Jászi's lecture was dedicated to "Postwar Pacification in Europe." He could already foresee some dangerous traits and argued with Beneš who anticipated a "transfer of populations" on a large scale and a protection of minorities within the context of "the defense of human democratic rights." The whole history of the former Austro-Hungarian Monarchy has amply demonstrated that "individual human rights alone cannot solve the nationality problem."[30]

His worries proved to be true after the war. In 1945-46 he was disgusted by the Czechoslovak nationality policy and the collective condemnation and mass deportation of German and Hungarian minorities because he felt twofold responsible, as a former flagellator of old Hungarian nationalism and as an old friend of the Republic of Czechoslovakia, who "overestimated our Czechs" between the two world wars.[31] He wrote letters of protest to President Beneš, made statements in *The New York Times*, and asked Harold J. Laski, British Labour Party politician, to use his influence with the Czech leaders to stop the disastrous policy.[32]

However, he was very pleased to respond to a letter from a Hungarian group of students, the Danube Association of the high school societies of Eger, and he responded in his own resurrected journal, the new *Huszadik Század* (Twentieth Century) in the spring of 1947. "Your letter gave great pleasure to me because I felt that my ideas had not died and my struggles had not been in vain. In approaching the end of my life it is satisfying to know that a serious and independent group of young Hungarians is aware of the truth that after the horrible catastrophe one cannot fathom a real democracy and freedom along the Danube without Kossuth's plan of the Danube Confederation that I aspired to continue with. The horrible suffering of all the Danube nations was not in vain if a brotherly association would arise from it and which would assure their national independence and human rights....However, I should not conceal the fact that the difficulties in realizing the plan have increased as, contrary to our hopes, the two world wars intensified chauvinistic-nationalistic feelings and stiffened the obsolete doctrine of sovereignty, instead of giving way to confederation."[33]

In the fall of 1947 Jászi paid his last visit to his beloved Danubia: Austria, Czechoslovakia (Prague, Košice), and his native Hungary, which he had not seen since 1919. The trip was conceived as an ultimate fact-finding investigation of the local situation and prospects, and, at the same time, a farewell to the scene and witnesses of his youth. Afterwards he drew up a masterly report of his experiences, entitled *Danubia: Old and New*. Some of its chapters, as "Austria as the Last Bulwark of the West," "Prague in the Twilight," "The Plight of Slovakia," and "Towards a Dictatorship in Hungary" described the conditions found by the old Jászi. After many interviews, talks with both leading members of governments, opposition parties, and independent intellectuals, he arrived at the conclusion that the new regimes were also unable to solve the problems of freedom and national reconciliation in the region.[34]

His stubborn optimism, however, could not be suppressed, and in another essay in 1948, "Federalism in Danubia?," he foresaw some hope for the future:

> Looking over the picture again, one cannot see any real move to federalism in spite of the noisy manifestations of the dictators and the controlled press for union and cooperation. ...The hidden animosity between the states is so strong that crossing frontiers is still an almost superhuman task for ordinary mortals. However, this does not mean that the present state of the new "federalism" is unstable. On the contrary, the present Soviet domination seems to be stronger than the previous one of the Nazis....And one can even expect that the new system may in the long run develop a more favorable atmosphere for the future federalization of the small nations because of the influence of two factors: one is that tight cooperation in the Soviet orbit may enhance the intensity of individual relations, in both the economic and cultural field. People may become conscious as participants in a larger unity. The second factor is that all the small nations will resent more intensely the pressure of an alien power and civilization. Already this pressure begins to outweigh the romanti-

> cism of Slav solidarity. Should the rule of tyranny be shaken inside and outside of Russia, and should the union of the West become a reality, the revolutionary spirit of 1848 may reawaken. Individual liberty and democratic constitutionalism might be proclaimed again, and the road toward a free and independent federation of peasants and workers' democracies under the guidance of a really creative intelligentsia would be opened. A unified West and a democratized Russia would be equally eager to help these small nations into a genuine federation.[35]

Apparent in the above discussion is Jászi's stubborn "developmental optimism," often refuted by himself also, and his haunting foresight of 1956 Eastern Europe.

With the iron curtain the Western-Eastern connections were disrupted and any direct move, action or intellectual influence for the sake of the Danube confederacy was impossible for Jászi. Still, he did not retreat; on the contrary, he took a few steps forward and found an indirect way leading from the general, that is from the Atlantic and European Union to the Danube integration. In America he found soulmates who strived for the same or similar goals. First and foremost he cooperated with his immediate American colleagues, Stephen Borsody and Clarence Streit. In 1952, along with Czech, Romanian, Bulgarian and other social scientists, they organized a symposium in Washington, "Liberation and Union: The Future of Danubian Federation and the Atlantic Union." Streit dedicated his introductory words to the idea that the "Atlantic Union as an ever-expanding Federation of the Free can best help the people of Central Europe to liberate themselves."[36]

Presumably this approach and sequence still holds up and will fulfill Oszkár Jászi's old dream about a Danube Union and those of several other Central European democrats.

NOTES

1. Szocializmus és hazafiság [Socialism and Patriotism], (*Huszadik Század*, 1905, I), 1-11.

2. Letter to Bódog Somló on July 20, 1907, in *Jászi Oszkár válogatott levelei* [Oszkár Jászi's Selected Letters], ed. György Litván and János F. Varga (Budapest, 1991), 150.

3. *A nemzeti államok kialakulása és a nemzetiségi kérdés* [The Evolution of National States and the Nationality Question] (Budapest, 1912), XVI. 544.

4. Ady, Oszkár Jászi's Book, (*Nyugat,* 1912), in *Ady Endre összes prózai művei* [Endre Ady's Complete Prosaic Writings, X.] (Budapest, 1973), 191-194.

5. *A nemzeti államok kialakulása és a nemzetiségi kérdés* [The Evolution of National States and the Nationality Question], (Budapest, 1912), XVI. 524.

6. See *Jászi Oszkár Bibliográfia* [Oszkár Jászi's Bibliography], ed. János Gyurgyák and György Litván (Budapest, 1991), 31-32, and *Duna-völgyi barátságok és viták. Jászi Oszkár közép-európai dossziéja* [Danube Basin Friendships and Debates. The Central European Portfolio of Oszkár Jászi], ed. György Litván and László Szarka (Budapest, 1991), 30-41.

7. Cited by Géza Jeszenszky, The Correspondence of Oszkár Jászi and R. W. Seton-Watson before World War I. (*Acta Historica Acad. Sc. Hung.* 26. 1980), 446.

8. *Duna-völgyi barátságok és viták. Jászi Oszkár közép-európai dossziéja* [Danube Basin Friendships and Debates. The Central-European Portfolio of Oszkár Jászi] ed. György Litván and László Szarka (Budapest, 1991), 75-77.

9. See György Ránki, A hit, az illuzió és a politika [Faith, Illusion, and Politics] (*Valóság*, 1977/9), 62.

10. Jászi, *A Monarchia jövője és a Dunai Egyesült Államok* [The Future of the Monarchy and the United States of Danubia] (Budapest, 1918), 6.

11. Ibid.

12. Ibid., 5.

13. Ibid., 37-39.

14. Péter Hanák, *Jászi Oszkár dunai patriotizmusa* [Oszkár Jászi's Danubian Patriotism] (Budapest, 1985), 69.

15. Oszkár Jászi, *Magyar kálvária–magyar föltámadás* [Hungarian Calvary–Hungarian Resurrection] (Vienna, 1920), 62-63.

16. Jászi Oszkár nyilatkozata jugoszláviai és romániai útjáról [Oszkár Jászi's Statements about His Trip to Jugoslavia and Romania] (*Bécsi Magyar Újság*, 1920 December 12.)

17. Jászi Oszkár nyilatkozata jugoszláviai és romániai útjáról [Oszkár Jászi's Statements about His Trip to Jugoslavia and Romania] (*Bécsi Magyar Újság*, 1920 December 25.)

18. A nemzetiségi kérdés Közép-Európában [The Nationality Question in Central Europe] (*Revista Vremii*, March 12, 1922); Egy Dunai Szövetség haszna [The use of a Danube Union] (*Revista Vremii*, March 26, 1922); A dunai népek kultúrális ligája [The Cultural League of the Danube Peoples] (*Revista Vremii,* April 9, 1922).

19. Árpád Paál, Jászi Oszkár nálunk [Oszkár Jászi Visiting Us] (*Keleti Újság*, Kolozsvár-Cluj, May 17, 1923), in *Duna-völgyi barátságok és viták. Jászi Oszkár közép-európai dossziéja* [Danube Basin Friendships and Debates. The Central-European Portfolio of Oszkár Jászi] ed. György Litván and László Szarka (Budapest, 1991), 165-170. The evolution of the idea of Transylvanianism and the Transylvanian aspects of Jászi's policy are outlined and analyzed by Zsolt K. Lengyel, *Auf der Suche nach dem Kompromiss. Ursprünge und Gestalten des frühen Transsilvanismus 1918-1928* [In Search of Compromise: Origins and Forms of Early Transylvanianism, 1918-1928] (München, 1993).

20. Péter Hanák, *Jászi Oszkár dunai patriotizmusa* [Oszkár Jászi's Danube Patriotism] (Budapest, 1985), 95–103.

21. Oszkár Jászi, *The Dissolution of the Habsburg Monarchy* (Chicago 1929).

22. Oszkár Jászi, Dismembered Hungary and Peace in Central Europe (Foreign Affairs, Vol. 2, No. 2. 1923), 270–281.

23. E.g., Hungary's Descent to Bolshevism and Reaction (*The New York Times Book Review*, July 20, 1924); Europe's Hope, America's Reality (*The New Republic*, September 10, 1924), 41–42; Hungary and the Peace of Europe (*The New Republic*, April 18, 1925), 273–274.

24. *Jászi Oszkár válogatott levelei* [Oszkár Jászi's Selected Letters] ed. György Litván and János F. Varga (Budapest, 1991), 302.

25. Ibid., 308.

26. "I accept the theory of Renouvier, of the reversibility of the historical process, and regard the chief utility of all historical and sociological investigations to be to admonish us of the alternative possibilities of history." Dissolution, 380.

27. *Jászi Oszkár válogatott levelei* [Oszkár Jászi's Selected Letters], 311.

28. War Germs in the Danube Basin (*The Nation*, November 14, 21, December 12, 26. 1934). The first two parts, "The Nationality Problem" and "Can We Avert War" were also published in *Homage to Danubia. Selected writings of Oszkár Jászi* ed. György Litván (Lanham, MD, 1995), 77–86.

29. *Journal of Central European Affairs*, Vol.5. 1945/46. No.1.1–16. Published in *Homage to Danubia*, 102–114.

30. *Homage to Danubia*, 91–101.

31. Letter to Anna Lesznai, May 19, 1945. (Columbia University, Butler Library, Jászi Papers.)

32. Oszkár Jászi's and Rusztem Vámbéri's letter to Eduard Beneš, September 11, 1945. (Columbia University, Butler Library, Jászi Papers.) Hungarians in Slovakia. No Solution of Minority Problem Seen in Czechoslovakia's Plan. *The New York Times*, December 2, 1946; Letter to Laski, September 19, 1945. (Jászi Papers)

33. Message to Eger students about the Danubian confederation (*Huszadik Század*, 1947), 97–99.

34. Danubia: Old and New. *Proceedings of the American Philosophical Society*, 1949.

35. *Homage to Danubia*, 122–130.

36. Liberation and Union. Introduction by Clarence Streit and edited by Stephen Borsody, 1952.

TRANSYLVANISM: REVISION OR REGIONALISM?

PIROSKA BALOGH

Research into the intellectual movement called Transylvanism, which has been flourishing since the 1970's, defined Transylvanism as an aesthetic and literary self-identification program of writers, poets, publicists, and literary editors who belonged to the circle of *Erdélyi Helikon.* This definition mostly excluded any political intentions from Transylvanian ideology.[1] However, Zsolt K. Lengyel views Transylvanism as a political concept whose representatives "gave up the claim to belong to their political nation, that is, to be part of their fatherland.[2] They believed in an independent regional, linguistic-cultural, and religious development, which strove to achieve an institutionalized compromise between—in the spirit of the best federative tradition—an identity of integration and acceptance of current living conditions on the one hand and regional independence and diversity on the other."[3]

Whether Transylvanism possesses political intentions is not the real issue. What these intentions are and whether they are embedded in political concepts or are manifested in political actions are the real issues. Representatives of modern Transylvanism borrowed the term from Péter Apor in the early 18th century and name Imre Mikó and Zsigmond Kemény from the 19th century as their predecessors. Until the end of the 19th century only cultural Transylvanism existed; some politicians and writers proclaimed the uniqueness of Transylvanian cultural and political traditions. Transylvanism became politically charged after the 1867 union of Hungary and Transylvania. The movement used the cultural "ideology" to protest against the centralizing efforts of the Hungarian government by means of statements demanding greater economic, cultural, and administrative autonomy for Transylvania. Modern Transylvanism became heavily politicized among Transylvanian Hungarian intellectuals as a reaction to the Trianon Peace Treaty, which attached Transylvania to Romania. In their interpretation, Transylvanism meant an autonomous Transylvania. Autonomy might entail an independent political status (the concept of independent Transylvania), or might be a minority autonomy (linguistic-cultural, religious, economic, territorial-administrative) within Romania or Hungary. Minority autonomy within Hungary clearly shows revisionist intentions, while the concept of an independent Transylvania or a minority autonomy within Romania might be considered revisionist if it is the first step towards a complete revision. The present paper discusses the following issues: (1) What interpretation of Transylvanism has been dominant among Transylvanian intellectuals in different periods of time? (2) What ideas and significant political concepts and actions impacted the political rhetoric of Transylvanism? (3) Has this ideology, which may seem regional and provincial for a superficial observer, developed practical alternative programs?

TRANSYLVANISM AS A REGIONAL ALTERNATIVE

The period between the Alba Iulia Resolutions and the acceptance of the 1923 Romanian Constitution was characterized by lively political activity among Transylvanian Hungarians, Saxons, and Romanians. Articles II and III of the Alba Iulia Resolutions made tentative promises of establishing a "temporary" minority autonomy in Transylvania and the Banat.[4] Primarily these obscure promises initiated political movements within Transylvanian German, Romanian, and Hungarian circles. It is in this political context that the evolution of the Transylvanian ideology is to be found.

Speaking about Transylvanian Germans, R. Brandsch, a member of the *Deutsch-Sächsischer Volksrat*, declared in 1920 that "in the East, Germans will survive and fulfill their duties both towards their nation and the state that they will belong to if they unite and occupy an appropriate place in the new political state. This they can do by developing and nurturing connections among the different German groups."[5] In Brandsch's view this task could be realized by establishing a cultural (not territorial) German minority autonomy based on cultural institutions established within the Kingdom, the Banat, Bessarabia, Bukovina, and Transylvania. Hans Otto Roth, member of the *Verband der Deutschen in Rumänie* and President of the Romanian Deutsche Partei, advocated the same ideas and identified the tasks of these institutions as protecting against extreme centralization and defending self-governing institutions.

A significant number of Transylvanian Romanians joined the Partidul National Român led by Iuliu Maniu, thereby focussing on the autonomy of Transylvania and the Banat. In 1918–1919 Maniu led the Governing Council to establish just such a territorial-administrative autonomy around such centers as Kolozsvár (Cluj) and Nagyszeben (Sibiu). Unfortunately, these were subsequently destroyed by Averescu's People's Party. Yet the Romanian National Party did not fully renounce the alternative of territorial autonomy, even though its political propaganda focused on the establishment of cultural autonomy by emphasizing the cultural superiority of the Romanians. The People's Party in power until 1927, and the National Liberal Party denounced these ambitions as chauvinistic, irredentist, and secessionist, while Octavian Goga ran a publicized campaign against them in the name of "national self-defense."

In March of 1919 Hungarians in Romania agitated for an independent Transylvania; but their effort remained isolated.[6] The beginning of their political activities is usually associated with the publication of the pamphlet "Calling Voice," drawn up by Károly Kós, Árpád Paál, and István Zágoni.[7] The pamphlet set minority "national autonomy" as a goal in order to maintain national language and culture and social security, and to enhance the economic development of the minority. In return, it declared loyalty to the Romanian government. Similar to Saxon demands, institutional and not territorial autonomy was demanded for all Hungarians in Romania.

After 1921 Hungarians dominated Transylvanian institutions through aristocratic and intellectual representatives, mostly publiscists and writers. These gathered around two political institutions–the Hungarian Alliance and the Hungarian Peoples's Party.[8] This kind of institutional dualism existed only in 1921 but an underlying bifurcated interpretation of Transylvanism prevailed during the whole period. Both interpretations focused on Transylvania offering options for settling German and Romanian ethnic issues. Both views assumed territorial autonomy for Transylvania with independent administrative, cultural, and economic institutions. Romanian, Hungarian, and German ethnic issues would be federatively arranged and modelled after the Swiss example.[9] They based their arguments was founded on economic, geopolitical,[10] cultural,[11] and historical points,[12] supported by the history of ideas and the science of national characteristics, in order to support the idea of a specific "Transylvanian soul."[13] According to the Hungarian People's Party, Transylvania would remain within the political framework of Romania in a loose, federative dependence as a "minority nation." This perspective disassociated itself from Hungary and the idea of revisionism, while blaming the centralist policy of Dualism for the problem of Transylvanian Hungarians' "institutionlessness" condition in 1919.[14]

The Hungarian Alliance envisioned an independent Transylvania within the federation of a utopian "European United States,"[15] where Transylvania would embody Jászi's idea of a "Switzerland of the East."[16] This perspective did not separate itself from Hungary, although there was no statement made about a future unification with Hungary. These ideas would re-emerge in the United States in 1943 in one of the alternatives which proposed to settle the Hungarian–Romanian border issue by conferring independent status onto Transylvania within an Eastern-European or Danubian confederation.

Underlying the political activities of 1921–23 was what seemed to be an identity of interests among the nationalities of Transylvania and a need for a certain degree of national autonomy for Hungarians, Germans, and Romanians. However, the identity of interests was only realized in short-lived election alliances and in Hungarian efforts to expand Transylvanian ideology to demand territorial autonomy based on the co-operation of all three ethnicities.[17] However, beyond a few cultural gestures, there was no response from the Germans or the Romanians[18] and there was no regional co-operation on the political scene. Moreover, the 1923 centralist constitution squashed the "separatist" Romanian, Saxon, and Hungarian ambitions.

Between 1921 and 1923 Transylvanian ideology clearly distanced itself from Hungarian revisionism by rejecting the idea of an "independent Transylvania as a minimal program." As a result, Hungarian political circles showed no co-operative intentions beyond pure sympathy.[19]

A PRACTICAL TURN: THE GOALS OF CULTURAL AUTONOMY

Maniu and his party won the elections of 1927 and the Romanian National Party ceased to be a potential partner in representing autonomous ambitions, while those of German ethnicity started gravitating towards the mother-country from the late

1920's on. Advocates of Transylvanism had to face the fact that they did not have any more potential partners interested in a federation based on territorial autonomy and a common identity of interests. Therefore prominent representatives of Transylvanism came to advocate a minimal program of cultural and religious autonomy.

The myth of the significance of the "Transylvanian soul" became the myth of the significance of cultural, religious, and ethical renewal. "Minority means minority in politics and universality in literature and culture,"[20] ran the slogan. "Minorities can only be united by intellectual means and can adjust their relationship to majority nationalities by moral truths."[21] Yet beyond the mythical-literary developments, lively organizational activities were going on. In 1926 János Kemény convened a literary-cultural meeting in his Marosvécs castle with the democratic Károly Kós, the bourgeois-radical Ernő Ligeti, and the conservative Miklós Bánffy present. They continued to meet annually, developing into an informal organization called the *Erdélyi Helikon*, releasing a magazine under the same name, and starting literary publishing activities.[22]

This intensive cultural activity manifested itself indirectly in politics also. Cultural-political questions were sometimes discussed at international forums, where minority grievances and needs for cultural autonomy could gain international attention. This is how Elemér Gyárfás, one of the most active Transylvanian politicians, made it into the records of the League of Nations discussing a temporary settlement concluded with the Romanian government about compulsory Romanian language exams for ethnic Hungarian teachers.[23]

Under the guise of cultural interchange, Hungarian circles in Hungary proper also became involved transferring cultural and religious grievances, and propaganda disguised as statistical data abroad, especially to Anglo-Saxon countries. These materials did not contain direct revisionist demands. Rather, their goal was to prove that the Romanian government did not observe the minority provision of the Paris Area Treaties. Two Transylvania experts of the *Magyar Szemle*, Zsombor Szász and Benedek Jancsó, are typical examples of Hungarians who did this type of activity. (Jancsó himself was a Transylvanian and a professor at the University of Cluj.)

Zsombor Szász's *The Minorities in Roumania. Transylvania* was published in Great Britain in 1927.[24] With references to the Alba

Iulia resolutions and the minority provision of the Paris Peace Treaties, his book discussed the inadaquacies of the Romanian government's policies towards international minority rights. It extensively described the struggle for cultural and religious autonomy and the chapter "Transylvania against the Regat" described the history of the Transylvanian movement. This chapter especially emphasized Romanian separatism and quoted Professor Iorga, who declared in the *Ellenzék* (Opposition) "I do not believe a single Transylvanian when he says that he is Hungarian, Saxon, or Romanian; they are all Transylvanians. Centuries ago Hungarians, Saxons, and Romanians gathered among the Transylvanian mountains and developed a peculiar Transylvanian spirit. It should be protected." Underlying this effort was the desire–also manifested in István Bethlen's lecture in England–to justify the existence of local patriotism, even among Romanians, by describing Transylvanism as the ideology of an independent, ideal Transylvania. For tactical reasons, whether this would be the first step of revisionism or was its own objective was not clear from either the Transylvanian side or in the Hungarian propaganda materials.

In 1926–1927 the President of the *Székely* (Székler) Society, Benedek Jancsó, became involved in a lengthy correspondence with an American Unitarian minister, Louis L. Cornish.[25] Under the pretext of discussing religious problems Jancsó wished to publish propaganda materials in the United States through the Unitarian organization. The material was based on Transylvanian data and its aim was to refute H. Tichner's propaganda document which accused the Transylvanian Hungarian minority of seditious acts. There was so much significance attached to the correspondence that Jancsó even sought Pál Teleki's opinion concerning responses to Cornish. The only result of the correspondence was that Zsombor Szász's book was sent to the United States. One lesson from the correspondence experience was Cornish's warning about the indifference of American public opinion to foreign policy in the inter-war period.

> Permit me at once to answer your question concerning the proposed book by Mr. Zsombor. I have read with good interest the topics of his book which you list. I am sorry not to be able to encourage you or him to believe that there would be any large sales or any considerable notice of such a book in the United States...You will readily understand that at this dis-

tance, Transylvania is not a territory well known in our country, and the problems in Transylvania are of little interest outside of the groups affiliated in religion with the groups in Transylvania.[26]

Jancsó's manuscript proposed granting cultural autonomy to Transylvania's ethnic groups in order to resolve the problems they face and suggested that "a Hungarian, German, and Romanian department should be attached to each municipal authority, lawcourt, and existing other authority."[27] It summarized the strategy underlying those propaganda efforts which demanded cultural autonomy based of minority rights.

Both the government and the public opinion of Hungarians in Hungary are fully aware that there are two issues: territorial integrity and racial, that is cultural integrity. But they are also fully aware that if, under present circumstances, territorial integrity is set as an objective, then their own statehood and national independence will be at risk. Still Hungarians, cannot and will not renounce racial or cultural integrity under any circumstances....And they can do it without being suspected or accused of irredentism since the minority provision of the Paris Area Treaties entitle them to do so. The minority provision removed racial, national, and religious minority issues from among the domestic issues of individual countries and exposed them as international issues controlled by the League of Nations.[28]

Transylvanian ideology was disseminated beyond the borders of Transylvania by the revival of connections between Hungarian and Transylvanian cultural societies and institutions. The Society of Transylvanian Youth, an offshoot of the Transylvanian Helikon, advocated moral renewal, popular social programs, and the realization of Danube Valley co-operation as essence of Transylvanism. Its chief representative was Sándor Makkai.[29] Initially the social, political, and cultural profile of The Society of Transylvanian Youth closely resembled that of the Miklós Bartha Society[30] and The Art Collegium of the Szeged Youth with whom they communicated.

The Transylvanian freemason movement also helped to popularize Transylvanism beyond its regional bounds. Several prominent members of the Transylvanian Helikon (such as János Kemény, the host of Marosvécs meetings of Helikon, and Jenő Szentimrei, a radical pro-independence "Transylvanianist" of the 1920's) were members of Transylvanian freemasonic lodges.[31] The group, which founded the Transylvanian Endre Ady Society, presided over by Elemér Jancsó, broke off from the Transylvanian Helikon. They had intense connections with political, cultural, and freemasonic circles in Hungary.[32] Although quite a few Transylvanian freemasons were advocates of Transylvanism, freemasons as a group did not take a specific stance on the status of Transylvania. In his book on the history of the Cluj Unio Lodge, Miklós Jancsó alluded to views which might have approached thee idea of a Danubian Confederation.[33] It is possible that such views carried international significance in the 1920's since the Transylvanian Hungarian Lodges were the focus of attention by Swiss, American, and French masonic organizations.[34]

However, by the 1930's, Transylvanism, both as a regional alternative and a cultural movement and ideology, gradually lost ground in Transylvania. This was partially the result of weakened connections between the Germans and Romanians in Transylvania and by the plasticity of the ideology itself. Starting as a system of arguments demanding cultural autonomy, Transylvanism grew into a collage of ideas some parts of which were absorbed by the ideologies of diverse political and cultural groups which developed antagonisms for each other.[35] Even with this change, the demand for cultural autonomy for Transylvania remained an integral part of the propaganda Hungarian circles disseminated internationally. Arguments for cultural autonomy were convincingly supported with references to international minority rights, thereby increasing the justification for the idea of an independent Transylvania. These arguments ranged from the revisionism of Zsombor Szász's and Benedek Jancsó's minimal program to the utopian Danubian Confederation plan of many popular societies and some freemasons to the developed ideas of Oszkár Jászi and László Németh.[36]

POSTLUDE OF TRANSYLVANISM

While Transylvanism was losing ground in Transylvania proper, paradoxically it thrived in Hungary in the 1930's. The ideology was readily integrated into political concepts and statements about territorial revision.[37]

In November 1933 István Bethlen gave a talk to the British Royal Society of Foreign Affairs. He argued that Transylvanism would stabilize Romanian–Hungarian relations and, thus, indirectly, the Paris Area Treaties.[38] Enumerating geo-political, geographic, demographic, and historical arguments, Bethlen proposed four alternatives: 1) territorial division along linguistic borders, 2) territorial division and population exchange, 3) eradication of linguistic borders by guaranteeing minority rights, and 4) an independent Transylvania where "all the peoples receive national territorial autonomy and self-government through emancipation."[39] He presented counter-arguments against the first three options and argued for the fourth option. Bethlen saw Transylvania as a potential "Eastern Switzerland" due to its historical traditions. The "...prerequisites of success in both cases are full equality and the fact that, among the people living in the same area, geographic characteristics, a common past, and common struggles created familiar interests, sentiments, and mentality which distinguishes them from their co-nationalities beyond the area."[40] Bethlen substantiated the latter claim by pointing to the existence of an idiosyncratic local patriotism–an argument which proved to be the least convincing about the Romanians.[41] To sum up, while propaganda from Hungary of the late 1920's demanded cultural autonomy for Transylvania based on minority rights, Bethlen evoked concepts from 1921–23 Transylvanism to support a claim for an independent Transylvania.

As Hungarian foreign policy changed as chances for revision also changed, advocates of Transylvanism raised increasingly radical demands. At his lecture in England, István Bethlen made no allusions to rejoin an independent Transylvania to Hungary. However, László Ravasz's article in the October 1934 István Bethlen issue of the *Magyar Szemle,*[42] "István Bethlen's Transylvanism," was a classic example of Transylvanian ideology and welcomed Bethlen's "Transylvanian concept ...about the independent state of Transylvania comprising three nations."[43] Dezső Keresztury's "Transylvanism of the Youth" and Zsombor Szász's "István Bethlen and the Transylvanian Hungarians" repeated earlier minority right arguments.[44] Keresztury, while alluding to the viewpoints of The Transylvanian Youth, nevertheless stressed moral renewal and the importance of social programs, while Szász quoted contemporary Transylvanian Hungarian intellectuals about minority autonomy and rejection of irredentism. The issue of an independent Transylvania was not raised and even the final Benedek Jancsó quotation on cultural integrity seemed idealistic since it disregarded territorial revision. In contrast, most of the eight articles were politicized scientific studies of historical and cultural topics which indirectly emphasized the common connection between Hungary and Transylvania.[45] Two of the articles offered information on contemporary Transylvania from minority points of view, one article mentioned the independent Transylvania concept, and eight articles argued for the integrity of a united Transylvania and Hungary (using increasingly revisonist arguments).

Obviously arguments based on the Transylvanism ideology had become increasingly revisionist and decreasingly significant. This process ended with the Second Vienna Award when the arguments of Transylvanism became obsolete, although not for long. In 1943, after Germany's defeat at Stalingrad and Mussolini's downfall, there was a chance for Hungary to leave the German alliance with subsequent negotiations with the Allies. Simultaneously, Romanian refugees in the West initiated a campaign against Hungary on the issue of Transylvania. Seton-Watson also joined this campaign with his political pamphlet "Transylvania: a Key Problem."[46] To counter-balance this effort, the Hungarian Revision League[47] approached Endre Bajcsy-Zsilinszky to write a political pamphlet on Transylvania, which was published in English in Switzerland in 1943 by the representative of the League, Ferenc Honti.[48] Bajcsy-Zsilinszky had a wide circle of Transylvanian connections, such as Áron Tamási and Ernő Ligeti, who were familiar with Transylvanism and with whom he discussed different aspects of his writing.[49] In his book Bajcsy-Zsilinszky discussed a number of historical arguments, most of which were a combination of the historical basis of St. Stephen's political state and the autonomy-centered Transylvanian view of history. Bajcsy-Zsilinszky centered the history of Transylvania around four points: the history of the Transylvanian Voivodship (self-government on the level of the 1868 Croat Compromise); the Principality of Transylvania (sovereign state in close alliance with the motherland and in an ideological union with the Holy Crown), and for comparative purposes, the exemplary 1868 Croat autonomy; and the 1867 Austrian–Hungarian union. He claimed that "Transylvania should seek the terms of its free and independent existence along the lines of the degree of autonomy that Croatia enjoyed with the 1868 Hungarian–Croat Compromise (an obvious and satisfying solution). Otherwise, due to historical necessity, a Hungarian-Transylvanian Union should be accepted."[50] Internal relations would be based on the "Eastern Switzerland" concept—apart from the issue of independence—thus corresponding to the popular 1921-23 Transylvanian tradition, which had conceptualized territorial autonomy within the Romanian state. Bajcsy-Zsilinszky prepared a draft constitution concordant with the concepts of Transylvanism. Each ethnic group would be granted territorial autonomy within a system of banate modelled after the system of Swiss cantons. There were provisions for cultural autonomy and for central administrative, legislative, and jurisdictional organs to function via proportional ethnic representation.[51] Bajcsy-Zsilinszky's ideas integrated elements of the original idea of Transylvanism and discussed the subject fully, although in a different context—that is, territorial autonomy within Hungary.

How much did this proposal correspond to the views of the Great Powers? The idea of an autonomous Transylvania arose among Anglo-American preliminary peace plans. The Peace Advisory Committee in the United States considered the status of Transylvania in 1943 as well. A plan for an Eastern-European Confederation with an independent Transylvania arose also, but it was gradually forced into the background due to conflicts within the Advisory Committee, to the strategic situation, and to Soviet demands. The fact that this alternative emerged at all could be attributed both to Ottó Habsburg's and Eckhardt-Pelényi's drafts, and to Oszkár Jászi's and Rusztem Vámbéry's political connections.[52] During his Romanian tours of 1920 and 1923, Oszkár Jászi became aquainted with several intellectuals who advocated Transylvanism such that his views came to resemble several features of Transylvanism.[53] The idea of an independent Transylvania as an alternative buffer state with a Swiss type canton system appeared at the meetings of the Danube workshop of Toynbee's research group in England.[54] Their ideas resembled those raised by István Bethlen's lecture in England. However, Toynbee's draft and underlying confederative idea fared the same way as the American plan.

To sum up, the 1921 version of Transylvanism and its underlying political motivations underwent a unique metamorphosis by the time of World War II. At the beginning of the 1920's Transylvanism spread extensively among Transylvanian Hungarian intellectuals. However, beyond Transylvania it was considered to be a provincial self-identification ideology which offered a regional alternative to Transylvania's different ethnicities of an independent Transylvania or of an autonomous Transylvania within Romania. Its realization was politically impossible after 1923. From then on, Transylvanism focused on establishing cultural autonomy for Transylvanian Hungarians claiming minority rights. Its arguments and demands, especially minority grievances, became gradually integrated into propaganda materials, that were communicated from Hungary to the West.

By the 1930's both forms of Transylvanism had lost ground in Transylvania. However, their arguments and concepts appeared in the statements of Hungarian politicians, ranging from minority demands for cultural autonomies, to the concept of an independent Transylvania to demanding an autonomous Transylvania joined with Hungary. Despite apparent similarities between the ideas of Transylvanism and the Anglo-American plans concerning an independent Transylvania, they were eventually discarded. Still Hungarian propaganda which had incorporated the arguments of Transylvanism seems not to have been completely ineffectual on the Anglo-Americans who were inclined towards federative solutions anyway.

NOTES

1. Béla Pomogáts, *A transzilvánizmus. Az Erdélyi Helikon ideológiája* [Transylvanism: The Ideology of Erdélyi Helikon] (Budapest, 1983); Gusztáv Láng, Egy önmeghatározás tanulságai [Morals of Self-identification] (*Kortárs*, 1989, 8), 89-100; Gusztáv Láng, Jegyzetek a transzilvanizmusról [Notes on Transylvanism] (*Utunk*, 1973, 59), 3-4; Ernő Fábián, Azonosság és kultúra [Identity and Culture] in *A tudatosság fokozatai* [The Grades of Consciousness] ed. Fábián (Bucharest, 1982), 43-82; Sándor Sárréti, A transzilvanizmus fogalmáról [On the Theory of Transylvanism] (*Tiszatáj*, 1979, 8), 54-47; György Nagy, A kisebbségi helytállástól a közösségi desirabilitásig és vissza [From Minority Responsibility to an Appealing Community and Back] (*Korunk*, 1993, 1), 18-32; Attila Balogh Gajdos, A transzilvanizmus román nézőpontból [Transylvanism from a Romanian Viewpoint] (*Korunk*, 1991), 1275-1278; J. Wittsock, A transzilvanizmusról—német szempontból [Transylvanism from a German Viewpoint] (*Látó*, 1992, 1), 69-72; Ernő Gáll, A "kisebbségi humánum" ["Minority Humanity"], in *A humanizmus viszontagságai* [The Adventures of Humanism] ed. Ernő Gáll (Bukarest, 1972), 43-82; Éva Cs. Gyimesi, Gyöngy és homok. Egy jelkép ideologikuma [Pearl and Sand: The Ideology of a Symbol] (*Korunk*, 1991), 1201-1206.

2. Zsolt K. Lengyel, *Kulturális kapcsolatok, regionalizmus, szövetkezési kompromisszum* [Cultural Connections, Regionalism, Federative Compromise]

(*Erdélyi Múzeum*, 1992), 127–142; Lengyel, Transzilvanizmus és regionalizmus a huszas évek Erdélyében [Transylvanism and Regionalism in Transylvania of the 1920's] (*Korunk*, 1993, 6), 59–64; Lengyel, A meghiúsult kompromisszum [A Failed Compromise] (*Magyar Szemle*, 1993), 845–856.

3. Id., Cultural Connections, 140.

4. Gyulafehérvári határozatok, II. cikkely [Alba Iulia Resolutins, Article II], "Until the legislative assembly convenes, elected by universal suffrage, the National Assembly maintains temporary autonomy for the populations of these areas (Transylvania and the Banat)"; Article III, "Total national freedom for coexisting peoples. Each people has the right to education and government in its own tongue, with its own administration, and with its own elected individuals. Every people is proportionately entitled to participate in legislative bodies and in the government of the country."; Zsombor Szász, *Erdély Romániában* [Transylvania in Romania] (Budapest, 1927), 361.

5. Zsolt K. Lengyel, Kulturális kapcsolatok, regionalizmus, szövetkezési kompromisszum [Cultural Connections, Regionalism, Federative Compromises] (*Erdélyi Múzeum*, 1992), 130; For German minority aspirations for autonomy in Romania, see J. Wittsock, A transzilvanizmusról–német szempontból [Transylvanism from a German Perspective] (*Látó,* 1992,1), 69–72.

6. The 12 points, elaborating ideas about an independent Transylvania, were submitted to Minister E. Hategan in May 1919: (1) The three nations of Transylvania–Hungarian, Romanian, and Saxon–are forming a Union; (2) Independent Transylvania considers relationships with Hungary or Romanian as foreign policy issues and seeks solutions which will not violate its independence; (3) Territorial demands from both countries are foreign policy issues; (4) Establishment of a 24 member Government Council with ten Hungarian, ten Romanian, and four Saxon members; (5) The members of the Government Council will fulfill the twelve ministerial portfolios with five Romanian, five Hungarian, and two Saxon representatives; (6) Laws which date back before October 31, 1918, remain valid. Rights and authorities of the Hungarian government and the king are delegated to the Government Council; (7) Gyulafehérvár (Alba Iulia) is the seat of the Government Council; (8) Office holders keep their offices; (9) New officials will take the oath of office to the constitution of Transylvania; (10) The Government Council will convene Parliament within three months of its establishment and elections will take place according to the effective elective franchise; (11) The following bills will be tabled by the Parliament: (a) Establishment of an independent Transylvanian legislative system and establishment of national symbols, (b) Universal suffrage, (c) Agrarian Reform, (d) Changing Article XLIV:1868 on nationality rights and emancipation of all the nationalities, (e) Adjusting county and electoral district borders to language borders, (f) modification of criminal code: violating the sovereignty of Transylvania is high treason; and (12) The Legislature will naturalize citizens who were born in Transylvania before October 31, 1918, or held public offices. Az erdélyi három nemzet uniójának alapelvei [The Basic Principles of the Union of Transylvania's Three Nations] in Elemér Gyárfás, *Erdélyi problémák* [Transylvanian Problems] (Cluj–Kolozsvár, 1923), 149–153.

7. *Kiáltó szó Erdély, Bánság, Kőrös-vidék és Máramaros magyarságához* [Calling Voice to the Hungarians of Transylvania, Banat, Kőrös Area, and Máramaros] (Cluj–Kolozsvár, 1921).

8. The Hungarian Alliance was banned in 1921 and the Hungarian People's Party fused with the conservative Hungarian National Party to become the Hungarian Party in 1922.

9. There would be separate administrative, legal, economic, and cultural institutions for all the three parties and proportionately distributed mandates in the Kolozsvár (Cluj) Parliament.

10. For economic and geopolitical arguments see Elemér Jakabffy, *Erdély statisztikája* [The Statistics of Transylvania] (Lugos, 1923); István Sulyok and László Fritz, *Erdélyi magyar évkönyv 1918–1929* [Transylvanian Hungarian Almanac 1918-1929] (Kolozsvár, 1930); Károly Kós, *Erdély. Kultúrtörténeti vázlat* [Transylvania: a Cultural Historical Outline] (Kolozsvár, 1929); Elemér Gyárfás, *Erdélyi problémák* [Transylvanian Problems] (Kolozsvár, 1923).

11. Cultural arguments include the concept of cultural supremacy which attributes cultural achievements to certain ethnic groups and demands political-strategic priorities for them based on these achievements. See Károly Kós, *Erdély. Kultúrtörténeti vázlat* [Transylvania. A Cultural Historical Outline] (Kolozsvár, 1929); Lajos György, *Az erdélyi magyarság szellemi élete* [The Intellectual Life of Transylvanian Hungarians] (Budapest, 1926); Lajos Czézer, Modern transylvanizmus [Modern Transylvanism] (*Zord Idő*, 1920), 609-612.

12. Miklós Asztalos sums up the historical arguments and goals of minority historiography. "The Transylvanian past of Transylvanian Hungarians and Transylvanian Saxons serves the moral purpose for them to adjust efficiently to life in the Romanian state. The fate of the Hungarian minority in Romania depends on adjustment to historical lessons...Every layer of the Hungarian minority should be aware of its rights and obligations, based on historical development, within the Romanian state with respect to ethnic, political, and general issues." in *A magyar kisebbség és a történelem Erdélyben* [Hungarian Minority and History In Transylvania] (Kolozsvár, 1927). The debate in the *Napkelet* about writing the history of Transylvania is also illuminating. The conclusion was that a popularizing version of history emphasizing the cultural-historical achievements of Transylvanian Hungarians would suggest that Transylvania should be perceived as a mixing bowl of peoples and ethnicities and as a hotbed of both stifling and progressive ideas that is the whole global society on a small scale. In Jenő Szentimrei, Szempontok a megirandó "Erdély történeté"-hez [Points of View for a Future Book on History of Transylvania] (*Napkelet* V, 1925), 86. Transylvanian historiography emphasized the early independence of Transylvania–as early as the 16th century–applying Fichte's concept of "Kulturnationen" supported by analyses of the history of diplomacy and cultural history which stress the tolerance of the Transylvanian constitution and the successful cooperation of the three nations. See Miklós Gyárfás, *Bethlen Miklós kancellár* [Chancellor Miklós Bethlen] (Dicsőszentmárton, 1924); Károly Rass, *Erdélyi iskoláztatás és tudományosság a középkorban* [Transylvanian Schooling and Scholarship in the Middle Ages] (Kolozsvár, 1921); Vencel Biró, *Erdély követei a portán* [Transylvanian Envoys at the Porte] (Kolozsvár, 1921); Miklós Asztalos, Az erdélyi tudat kialakulása [The Evolution of Transylvanian Consciousness] in *Barta Miklós Társaság Évkönyve 1925* [The Almanac of the Miklós Barta Society, 1925], 31-58; etc.

13. Referring to the Swiss example Ferenc Albrecht claims that "in Transylvania we can state it as a fact that besides Hungarian, Romanian, and Saxon national consciousness, there exists a Transylvanian consciousness which endows a unique feature–as unique as Transylvania itself–to each nation's consciousness. Transylvanian consciousness is the same for each nation irrespective of ethnic differences. Thus their national characters have common features to this extent." In Ferenc Albrecht, Erdélyi öntudat [Transylvanian Consciousness] (*Pásztortűz*, 1922), 321-324. For the "Transylvanian soul" as national consciousness see László Ravasz, Erdélyi lélek [Transylvanian Soul] in *Nagyenyedi album* [Album of Nagyenyed], ed. Imre Lukinich (Budapest, 1926), 13-24; Sándor Makkai, Erdélyi szellem [Transylvanian Spirit] (1925) in S. Makkai, *Erdélyi szemmel* [From Transylvanian Perspective] (Kolozsvár, 1932), 123-132; György Bartók, Erdély lelke irodalmában [Transylvanian Spirit Reflected in its Literature] (*Pásztortűz*, 1925), 143-145; Sándor Imre, Töredékes gondolatok az erdélyi szellemről [Fragmented Thoughts on Transylvanian Spirit], in *Nagyenyedi album* [Album of Nagyenyed], ed. Imre Lukinich (Budapest, 1926), 25-38. Saxon intellectuals generally accepted the notion of a "Transylvanian spirit", while Romanians did not. See Béla Pomogáts, *A transzilvánizmus. Az Erdélyi Helikon ideológiája* [Transylvanism: The Ideology of "Erdélyi Helikon"] (Budapest, 1983), 126.

14. This train of thought appeared in political publication, although it was not outlined in a draft. For the pattern of reasoning see Elemér Gyárfás, *Erdélyi problémák* [Transylvanian Problems] (Kolozsvár, 1923).

15. "Transylvania is both a geographical, an economic, and a political unit. During long centuries its interconnections have not developed into a cohesive force either in the East or the West. Therefore, I cannot envision it as either part of Romania or Hungary. It should be a part of Central Europe and, in the distant future, of the European United States." Jenő Szentimrei, Szempontok a megirandó "Erdély történeté"-hez [Points of View for a Future Book on History of Transylvania] (*Napkelet* V, 1925), 84.

16. For the concept of "Transylvanian Switzerland" see Miklós Nagy, Erdély jövője [The Future of Transylvania] (*Budapesti Szemle*, 1926), 339-358.

17. Obviously the Germans and Romanians did not sabotage a functioning alternative. There was simply no response towards an offer of co-operation. When analyzing the Transylvanian concept, one has to keep in mind that the federative concept–whether a potential internal Transylvanian system or incorporating an independent Transylvania into a Danubian Federation–stands on very shaky theoretical grounds whether looking back from 1997 or 1946. "It is a very dangerous concept because in this region there has already been a supra-national federation–the Habsburg Empire. It fell apart and had driven the whole area into hopeless uncertainty because it was unable to develop internal separations among the nations within the Empire. ... Any potential federation will survive only if the minimal stability developed along the borders meets the psychological requirement for a federation. Nations usually unite in federations when they have enough to defend to require the security of a federation." István Bibó, A kelet-európai kisállamok nyomorúsága (The Misery of Eastern European Small Nations) in *Demokratikus Magyarország. Válogatás Bibó István tanulmányaiból* [Democratic Hungary. Selections from István Bibó's Essays] (Budapest, 1994), 198-199.

18. For German and Romanian reception of Transylvanism see Attila Balogh Gajdos, A transzilvanizmus–román nézőpontból [Transylvanism from the Romanian Aspect] (*Korunk,* 1991), 1275-1278; J. Wittsock, A transzilvánizmusról–német szempontból [About Transylvanism–From a German Point of View] (*Látó,* 1992, 1), 69-72; Béla Pomogáts, *A transzilvánizmus. Az Erdélyi Helikon ideológiája* [Transylvanism–Transylvanian Helikon's Ideology] (Budapest, 1983), 97-112.

19. This is in the background of the Transylvanian Debate provoked by Gyula Szekfű. Szekfű challenges the historical arguments of Transylvanism in order to prove that, throughout its history, Transylvania has always been an integral part of Hungary, while its periods of independence were initiated by foreign aggression. See Gyula Szekfű, Az erdélyi probléma [The Transylvanian Problem] (*Napkelet* V, 1925), 5-25, and *Magyar Kisebbség* [Hungarian Minority], 1925, 365-376, 407-417; Bálint Hóman and Gyula Szekfű, *Magyar történet III* [Hungarian History III] (Budapest, 1935), 602-603, 286.

20. Aladár Kuncz's motto quoted by Gusztáv Láng, Egy önmeghatározás tanulságai [The Moral of a Self-identification] (*Kortárs,* 1989, 8), 91.

21. See Gábor Tusa, Gróf Mikó Imre mint kisebbségi politikus [Count Imre Mikó as a Minority Politician] (*Erdélyi Helikon*, April 1945), 245-247; Sándor Makkai, Magunk revíziója [Our Own Revision], lecture series in Sándor Makkai, *Az élet kérdezett I* [Life Has Posed Questions] (Budapest, 1935), 207-256.

22. About the operation, aesthetic system, and debates of Erdélyi Helikon see Béla Pomogáts, *A transzilvánizmus. Az Erdélyi Helikon ideológiája* [Transylvanism–The Ideology of Erdélyi Helikon] (Budapest, 1983).

23. National Széchenyi Library, Archive of Manuscripts, marked as Fol. Hung. 2748 and titled Iratok az erdélyi magyarság történetéből 1921-1927 [Manuscripts from the History of Transylvanian Hungarians 1921-1927], which is a copy of the minutes, along with several documents containing data on Transylvanian educational and religious issues.

24. Zsombor Szász, *The Minorities in Roumania. Transylvania* (London, 1927)–in Hungarian, *Erdély Romániában. Népkisebbségi tanulmány* (Budapest, 1927). Six chapters discuss educational issues, one discusses administrative, and one economic problems (of the 23 chapters). The ratio, as well as the fact that it is based on minority rights, corresponds to contemporary arguments. Zsombor Szász continued to participate in propaganda activities abroad, probably within the Hungarian Revisionist League. See Die Entstehung Grossrumänien (Budapest, 1944) article from *Siebenbürgische Frage;* Hungarians–Rumanians (Budapest, 1941) article from *The Hungarian Quarterly*; Le oribkéme transylvain (Budapest, 1944) article from *Nouvelle Revue de Hongrie.*

25. The correspondence is available in the National Széchenyi Library, Archive of Manuscripts, marked as Fol.Hung.2748, titled Az erdélyi magyar kisebbség sérelmeivel kapcsolatos levélváltás Louis L. Cornish amerikai unitárius lelkésszel [Correspondence about the Grievances of Transylvanian Hungarian Minorities with Louis L. Cornish American Unitarian Minister]. The manuscript propaganda material is available also, *Tichner Henriette könyvének V. Az államellenes iskola és VI. Az egyházak az állam ellen című fejezetére adott válasz. Jancsó Benedek, 1927* [Response to Henriette Tichner's book, Chapter V: Anti-State School, and Chapter VI: Churches against the State, Benedek Jancsó, 1927].

26. Louis L. Cornish Jancsó Benedeknek [Louis L. Cornish to Benedek Jancsó] (Boston, 1926.03.04), (National Széchenyi Archive, Archive of Manuscripts, marked as Fol.Hung.2748.

27. *Tichner Henriette könyvének V. Az államellenes iskola és VI. Az egyházak az állam ellen című fejezetére adott válasz. Jancsó Benedek, 1927* [Response to Henriette Tichner's book, Chapter V: Anti-State School, and Chapter VI: Churches against the State, Benedek Jancsó, 1927] (National Széchenyi Archive, Archive of Manuscripts, marked as Fol.Hung.2748.)

28. Ibid.

29. About The Society of Transylvanian Youth see Dezső László, Erdélyi fiatalok [Transylvanian Youth] (*Korunk*, 1973), 923–929; Imre Mikó, Az erdélyi fiatalok egy emberöltő múlva [Transylvanian Youth After a Generation] in László, *Akik előttem jártak* [Those Who Came Before Me] (Bukarest, 1976), 14–34.

30. Among the founders of the Miklós Bartha Society was Miklós Asztalos who was an advocate of the Transylvanian historical concept. See Miklós Asztalos, Az erdélyi tudat kialakulása [The Evolution of Transylvanian Consciousness] in *Bartha Miklós Társaság Évkönyve 1925* [The Almanac of the Miklós Barta Society, 1925], 31–58;

31. László Teleki, Ernő Makkai, Jenő Szentimrei, László Ravasz, Zsigmond Remenyik, Elemér Jancsó, Imre Mikó, János Kemény, Géza Tabéry, Áron Tamási; Zsuzsa L. Nagy, *Szabadkőművesség a XX. században* [Freemasonry in the 20th Century] (Budapest, 1977); Zsuzsa L. Nagy, A magyarországi és erdélyi szabadkőművesség kapcsolatai a két világháború között [Connections between Hungarian and Transylvanian Freemasonry between the Two World Wars], in *Tanulmányok Erdély történetéből* [Essays on the History of Transylvania] ed. István Rácz (Debrecen, 1988), 151–159; Elemér Jancsó, *Az Unio szabadkőműves páholy ötven éve, 1886–1936* [Fifty Years of the Freemasonic Lodge Unio, 1886–1936] (Cluj, 1937). Relating to the 1943 Transylvanian Freemasonic trial, József Palatinus published lists which were not always based on lodge documents and several people were among the names due to political trials. József Palatinus, *Szabadkőművesek Magyarországon, I–II.* [Freemasonry in Hungary] (Budapest, 1944). Benedek Jancsó, President of the Székely Society and the Transylvanian expert of the *Magyar Szemle* [Hungarian Review] also mentioned in connection with the Cornish correspondence, was also a freemason and a member of the Cluj Unio Lodge. Oszkár Jászi and Rusztem Vámbéry (the latter was the leader of the Hungarian affiliation of the English Old Falles Lodge) were also freemasons. They participated in the Eckhardt, Pelényi, and Otto Plans and owing to them the alternative of establishing a Danube Confederation with an independent Transylvania was discussed during the peace preparatory talks in the United States in 1943.

32. Zsuzsa L. Nagy, A magyarországi és erdélyi szabadkőművesség kapcsolatai a két világháború között [Connections between Hungarian and Transylvanian Freemasonry between the Two World Wars], in *Tanulmányok Erdély történetéből* [Essays on History of Transylvania] ed. István Rácz (Debrecen, 1988), 155–156.

33. "Although the future does not look hopeful, we must start on the road that was set for the Hungarians and the Danubian people by the greatest freemason

and poet of all times, Endre Ady." He advocated cooperation above the ruins for a better and humane future. "Why isn't there a strong will evoked by a thousand lame desires–Hungarian, Romanian, Slavic sorrows eternally remain one grief," in Elemér Jancsó, *Az Unio szabadkőműves páholy ötven éve, 1886–1936* [Fifty Years of the Unio Freemasonic Lodge, 1886–1936], (Cluj, 1937), 29; see also note 31.

34. Relating to the issue of the Transylvanian Lodges Revechon, the Grand Master of the Swiss Alpina Grand Lodge, István Bethlen, and Miklós Bánffy, who incorporated the Transylvanian concept into his literary pieces as well, conferred in the summer of 1922. The discussions were followed by Ossian Lang's, the Grand Master of New York, trip to Hungary and Romania. See Zsuzsa L. Nagy, A magyarországi és erdélyi szabadkőművesség kapcsolatai a két világháború között [Connections between the Hungarian and Transylvanian Freemasonry between the Two World Wars] in *Tanulmányok Erdély történetéből* [Essays on the History of Transylvania] ed. István Rácz (Debrecen, 1988), 154–155; Zsuzsa L. Nagy, *Szabadkőművesség a XX. században* [Freemasonry in the 20th Century] (Budapest, 1977), 67.

35. Thus, the foundation of the Ady Endre Society, the Transylvanian Realists, Transylvanian Youth, etc., the polemics between the *Erdélyi Helikon* and *Korunk* (socialist, edited by Gábor Gaál), and the debate following Ferenc Szemlér's essay *Jelszó és mithosz* [Motto and Myth], all gave reason for which every significant Transylvanian intellectual stated his/her opinion about Transylvanism. Károly Kós, one of the most prominent Transylvan ideologists, had to admit that Transylvanism had lost its importance. For the debate see Béla Pomogáts, *A transzilvánizmus. Az Erdélyi Helikon ideológiája* [Transylvanism: the Ideology of Erdélyi Helikon] (Budapest, 1983), 200–204.

36. Mostly the concept of "Transylvania as an Eastern Switzerland" is presented in László Németh's works. He criticizes Gyula Szekfű's Transylvanian image because he moved from the original appropriate Transylvania-Hungary parallel towards a "labanc" (overzealously loyal to the Habsburg dynasty) concept which considers Transylvania as an artificial formation. See András Gergely, Németh László vitája Szekfű Gyulával [László Németh's Debate with Gyula Szekfű] (*Valóság,* 1984, 1), 47–62.

37. Mihály Babits, who contributed to every significant cultural-political concepts, expressed his views on Transylvanism in 1935. See Mihály Babits, Az én erdélyiségem [My Transylvanism] in Babits, *Könyvről könyvre* [From Book to Book], ed., György Belia (Budapest, 1973), 255–260.

38. *Bethlen István angliai előadásai* [István Bethlen's Lectures in England] (Budapest, 1933), 61–91.

39. Ibid., 84.

40. Ibid., 87.

41. "It was first in the Hungarian Parliament, of which I had been a member since 1901, that I heard the most beautiful lectures about Transylvania as an Eastern Switzerland, from Maniu and Vajda, who represent Transylvania in Romania today. ...Transylvania as an Eastern Switzerland was the program of the Romanian national party . ... I am convinced that the will still exists for this construction in a wide strata of the public. Local patriotism, that is, the so called Transylvanism, is still alive in the souls of Transylvanian Romanian people. The proof for this is the

deep antipathy which separates the Transylvanian Romanian from the Romanian in the Regat, in the old Romanian kingdom, in whom they recognize people who want to use them and destroy them out of selfishness–more so today than 15 years ago." Ibid., 90; Bethlen tactfully uses the arguments which made Transylvanism of the 1920's a regional alternative, but which were not valid in the 1930's any more. László Németh must have started out on his Romanian tour with a similar attitude. However, the situation was different from what he expected.

42. *Magyar Szemle* is a forum for public ideas which strongly follows government guidelines. About its significance and its views on revision and Transylvania see Domonkos Szőke, A Magyar Szemle és az Erdély-kérdés [The Magyar Szemle and the Transylvanian Issue], in *Tanulmányok Erdély történetéből* [Essays on the History of Transylvania] ed. István Rácz (Debrecen, 1988), 160–166.

43. László Ravasz, Bethlen István erdélyisége [István Bethlen's Transylvanism] (*Magyar Szemle*, 1934, XXII), 105–107. The quoted sentence is on p. 107.

44. Dezső Keresztury, Az ifjúság Erdélyszemlélete [The Transylvanism of the Youth] (*Magyar Szemle*, 1934, XXII), 265–272; Zsombor Szász, Bethlen István és az erdélyi magyarság [István Bethlen and the Transylvanian Hungarians], (*Magyar Szemle*, 1934, XXII), 136–150.

45. József Deér, A középkori Erdély [The Medieval Transylvania] (*Magyar Szemle,* 1934. XXII), 194–206; Ferenc Eckhart, Erdély alkotmánya [Transylvania's Constitution] (*Magyar Szemle*, 1934, XXII), 206–215. Following Szekfű's footsteps, they refute Transylvania's independent historical development and consider its separation from Hungary due to political interests. Also in *Magyar Szemle* 1934, XXII: Raymund Rapaics, Az erdélyi táj színelváltozása [Discoloration of the Transylvanian Landscape], 185–194; Gyula Farkas, Erdélyiség a magyar irodalomban [Transylvanism in Hungarian Literature], 215–225; Tibor Gerevich, Erdélyi művészet [Transylvanian Art], 225–242; István Genthon, Az orthodoxia művészete Erdélyben [The Art of Orthodoxy in Transylvania], 242–256; Károly Viski, Erdély népe [The People of Transylvania], 250–265; Lajos Tamás, Az oláh történetírás régi és új arca [The Old and New Face of Wallachian Historiography], 265–272.

46. R.W. Seton-Watson, *Transylvania: A Key-Problem* (Oxford, 1943) and reviewed by István Gál, Erdély: egy kulcskérdés [Transylvania: A Key Problem] (*Külügyi Szemle*, 1943, 9), 396–398.

47. On the work of the Hungarian Revisionist League and on publishing Endre Bajcsy-Zsilinszky's Transylvania book, see Miklós Zeidler, A Magyar Revíziós Liga. Trianontól Rothermere-ig [The Hungarian Revisionist League: From Trianon to Rothermere] (*Századok*, 1997, 2), 303–352.

48. Andrew, Bajcsy-Zsilinszky, *Transylvania: Past and Future* (Kundig-Geneva, 1944).

49. For Bajcsy-Zsilinszky's Transylvanian connections and about the circumstances of writing his *Transylvania,* see Endre Bajcsy-Zsilinszky, *Erdély múltja és jövője* [The Past and Future of Transylvania] (Budapest, 1990) with Károly Vigh's Postscript; Loránt Tilkovszky, Bajcsy-Zsilinszky Endre könyve Erdélyről [Endre Bajcsy-Zsilinszky's Book about Transylvania] (*Világosság*, 1990.10), 767–779.

50. Endre Bajcsy-Zsilinszky, *Erdély múltja és jövője* [The Past and Future of Transylvania] (Budapest, 1990), 110.

51. Az autonóm Erdély alkotmánytervezete [The Constitutional Draft of Autonomous Transylvania], in Endre Bajcsy-Zsilinszky, *Erdély múltja és jövője* [The Past and Future of Transylvania] (Budapest, 1990), 91–111.

52. See Ignác Romsics, A State Department és Magyarország, 1942–1947 [The State Department and Hungary, 1942–1947], in Romsics, *Helyünk és sorsunk a Duna-medencében* [Our Place and Fate in the Danube Basin] (Budapest, 1996), 234–301.

53. For Oszkár Jászi's Romanian trips, see György Litván, Jászi Oszkár romániai naplójegyzeteiből [From Oszkár Jászi's Romanian Journals] (*Századok,* 1985, 5-6), 1234–1271; for his concept and Transylvanism see Zsolt K. Lengyel, Kulturális kapcsolatok, regionalizmus, szövetkezési kompromisszum [Cultural Connections, Regionalism, Federative Compromises] (*Erdélyi Múzeum*, 1992), 132.

54. Ignác Romsics, A brit külpolitika és a "magyar kérdés," 1914–1946 [The British Foreign Policy and the Hungarian Question, 1914–1946] (Budapest, 1996), 34–131, in Romsics, *Helyünk és sorsunk a Duna-medencében* [Our Place and Fate in the Danube Basin] (Budapest, 1996), 34–131.

ISTVÁN BIBÓ ON THE CONDITIONS OF DANUBIAN RECONCILIATION

TIBOR ZS. LUKÁCS

István Bibó, well-known as a political theoretician and a writer of legal theory, political science, and history greatly influenced intellectual life in the 1980's.[1]

It is not my intention to examine István Bibó's entire political career,[2] but to analyze his writings which specifically bear upon the Trianon settlement and questions about Hungarian revisionist intentions. As he has not written separate reviews of these issues, his ideas must be gleaned from his analyses of European and Hungarian democratization, and from his papers examining democratic developments, particularly those addressing national border questions.[3]

Born in 1911, Bibó was brought up in Trianon Hungary. His background was urban upper middle-class, his father being the director of the Szeged University Library and very interested in cultural history. Bibó graduated from Szeged Law School in 1933 and pursued further studies in Vienna, Geneva and the Hague. Guglielmo Ferrero had the greatest influence on his view of history,[4] but biographers also allude to the influences of Max Weber, Emil Durkheim, Benedetto Croce, Johan Huizinga, István Hajnal, and István Szabó.[5]

CONCEPTS AND INTERPRETATION OF BIBÓ'S HISTORY

Most of the essays analyzed in this paper date from before and shortly after World War II. *On European Equilibrium and Peace*,[6] his first systematic work, reveals that Bibó's method of analysis has its own "world view, social representation, epistemiological reflection, style and organic composition" and it also outlines the concepts that Bibó applies later.[7]

After 1945, Bibó resigns from the role of professional scholar as his essays come to resemble much more analytical political pamphlets than scholarly monographs. In essence, his writings after 1945 are functional political essays.[8]

In *On European Equilibrium and Peace* Bibó predicts that after World War II, which will end with the defeat of the Axis Powers, a new European order will develop. The future of Eastern Europe lies in the hands of the negotiators at the peace conferences and is dependent on how much they comprehend regional peculiarities and are able to avoid the mistakes committed at Versailles and Trianon. His analysis offers a program both for the promoters of peace and for the political leaders of post-war Hungary and other Eastern-European countries. It is neither economic processes nor the ensuing power relationships and structures that determine Bibó's historical views. Instead, ideology determines "politics, and politics is not camarilla fights or political games. It is rather the relationship of the polis to the human being." After analyzing the motives which caused the War, he concludes that "conflicting interests of economic ideology and racial issues are secondary or extraneous compared with politics and its mass psychological effect."[9] Starting from this theory Bibó discusses the malfunctions which beset certain political communities as examples of social-psychological phenomena, and constrasts political or mass hysteria with the state of political equilibrium.[10]

POLITICAL EQUILIBRIUM AND PUBLIC HYSTERIA

Bibó's perspective was that healthy public and political attitudes are the result of "...proportionate existence of agility and stability, a situation when power relations and the guiding principles of a community make it possible for the public to place itself flexibly and with optimal stability between the extremes of rigidity and flexibility."[11] Political or public hysteria is a permanent threat, and the sensation is triggered by historical upheaval. In case of bona fide mass hysteria "all the typical symptoms show at once; a community departs from reality, it fails to solve the problems of life, it fosters insecure and exaggerated self-esteem, and it wallows in unreasonable reactions towards the world at large."[12]

Post-Trianon Hungarian society revealed symptoms of mass hysteria. Failure in war, revolutionary chaos, collapsed political prestige and lost territories induced anxiety in society at large producing an irrational reaction. And importantly, victorious neighbors feared a vengeful, "hysterical" Hungary, especially when they themselves were insecure in integrating newly gained territories. Angst spread like an epidemic to neighboring states.

Equilibrium may be thrown out of balance in inter-state relations whenever ideas become ossified. Extreme rigidity suggests that international balances can only be guaranteed by the presence of a super-state power, whereas extreme flexibility stipulates that inter-state relationships are dependent on momentary power. This is why no rule or principle will permanently prevail. "The Classic System of European Equilibrium" is the result of counterbalancing the two extremes. Its historically varying instances are founded on the *sine qua non* that equilibrium in inter-state relationships is necessary and possible. Territorial equilibrium has proved to be the most important condition of European equilibrium. "The state of equilibrium in each society is related to a certain material momentum." Domestically these momentums may be sacred places or traditional possessions whilst "state territory is the central material momentum of international equilibrium."[13]

DEMOCRATIC NATIONALISM AND SELF-DETERMINATION

In Bibó's system, political equilibrium cannot be achieved without democracy. Implementation of democracy is an indispensable condition of permanent arrangements because the development of nationalism is as much the result of democratization as the result of the propagation of the principle of self-determination.

Modern nationalism is treated as a positive historical phenomenon arising from the democratization of emotions relating to the nation. Up to 1789 the nobility were the conscious representation of a nation. The influx of professionals and the bourgeoisie, that is the third class of society, started at the end of the Middle Ages. However, in the French Revolution this influx took place in the form of instant and triumphant occupation of property leading to modern nationalism. The heat and tensile strength of modern nationalism are fed by two emotions: the third class takes possession of a country of kings and nobility, with all its prestige, appealing and challenging its values, and adorns it with all the positive emotions citizens have associated with their own immediate environment.[14]

In the case of Central and Eastern European nations, a national framework had to be created first. Usually the national and state frameworks did not coincide, which meant that state administration, political culture, and economic machinery did not conjoin. Establishing a modern national framework in these countries necessitated internal political movements, democratization, along with territorial rearrangement. Disrupting internal political equilibrium upset international equilibrium and as a result the democratic character of Central and Eastern European nationalism started to diminish. Only a limited democratic content remained to inculcate nationalism and so national solutions were pushed into the background.

In Bibó's theories, self-determination as the bedrock attribute of democracy is also important. During monarchical-feudal times wars were fought without support from the civilian population, and armies remained discrete from the multitude. However, modern war brings millions to arms making it a popular matter. Therefore, in addition to sovereignty, self-determination of the people was supposed to replace the old monarchical-feudal principles. A new democratic international commonwealth has to "replace the solidarity of kings and, in contrast with the kings, autonomous peoples cannot politely and gentlemanly relate to war. Instead, after concluding a treaty according to mutually accepted principles and methods, they have to create a system which does not resort to belligerence to resolve emerging conflicts.... This process would have required as much, or perhaps even more, mutual trust amongst peoples than that which existed amongst kings."[15]

Bibó's attitude toward self-determination as a democratic principle can be summarized in two axioms: (1) in the 20th century any legitimate power of the State should be founded on the two principles of popular sovereignty and national self-determination since the two together are the only valid principles of modern legitimacy; and (2) self-determination by its nature is a democratic and liberal principle, similar to popular sovereignty. However, while popular sovereignty refers to an existing state framework and its functions, self-determination somehow raises the issue of the state framework, and has territorial implications. Territorial disposition by the people is expressed in the principle of self-determination.[16]

Both stabilizing and destabilizing effects of self-determination as sources of legitimacy in modern times can be powerfully manifest. Self-determination does not take priority either in international law or in state charters over the issues of territorial stability and territorial sanctity. Therefore, self-determination and territorial stability are opposing viewpoints. Bibó recognizes this but claims that the contradiction is resolvable. He argues that conflict arises only when self-determination does not prevail, since it is not consistently observed.[17] He is convinced that "the principle of self-determination is the only possible and valid state-forming and country planning principle of the international commonwealth."[18] However, he emphasizes that the principle of self-determination is worth applying only when it has stabilizing effects and not when the intent is to destabilize existing state frameworks. The given point in history and circumstances should always be taken into consideration. Consequently, self-determination has its appropriate time and place. Bibó elaborates on this topic in connection with the Trianon borders.

A CRITIQUE OF THE NEW EUROPEAN SETTLEMENT ENDING WORLD WAR I

PERPETUAL DEFICIENCY OF POLITICAL EQUILIBRIUM

World War I brought forth important historical experiences for the whole of Europe. It offered possibilities for a general, global European democratic reorganization, since the War had driven away both German dynasties and Russian Czarism.

> It was an unparalleled situation when everything was present to bring the German matter to an issue and to reconstruct the confused territorial status of Central and Eastern Europe on a sound basis. The principle of self-determination was a suitable theoretical basis at the disposal of the 1918 peacemakers to arrange the various pending questions of Europe. They recognized relatively clearly that ethnographic borders should be drawn up on several controversial geographic points in Central and Eastern Europe.[19]

Bibó felt that, from the perspective of East Central Europe, the processes working towards uniting Germany were decisive. According to him, if the principle of self-determination was consistently observed, all of German–Austria could join Germany thus generously compensating the Germans for their territorial concessions to France and Poland. Bibó optimistically explained that "Germany would have gained territorially. However, it would have been less dangerous with the dissolution of the Habsburg Monarchy which had brought the Danube Basin into the German sphere of interest. A power bloc of the liberated Polish, Czechs, Hungarians, and Southern Slavs would have easily counter-balanced a possible German expansion towards the East, not imminent anyway, should German unity have been realized."[20] Such an arrangement would have been edifying for the Germans because it would have healed that political hysteria caused by the unity won through the assistance of the power and aggression of Prussian militarism. If German political ambitions were fulfilled despite a lost war, their paranoia would have ceased or at least been diminished, and they would have gained a definite, positive experience in democratic problem solving.

In reality, the Germans gained a completely different historical experience. To avoid this different negative experience "German democracy should have concluded a rational peace with Western democracies. However, for the first time in the history of democracy it happened that a peace agreement impacting the political structure and territorial status of the whole of Europe was concluded via exclusively democratic administration and methods. And at this first experiment, democracy failed."[21]

History has passed judgment on the Versailles Treaty as a dictated peace, one that did not even try to reach an agreement on its provisions. The Treaty branded the Germans as responsible for the War, although collective responsibility is justified only in a democratic country. The Victors humiliated the Germans with reparations, disarmament, and a prohibition against Anschluss with Austria. In Bibó's interpretation, the gravest mistake of the postwar transformation and power structure was that it did not raise, did not clarify, and did not respond to the question that had led to the war—the question of German unity, that is, the ultimate national and political goal of the Germans.

In Bibó's view European post—World War I political equilibrium depended upon three factors: (1) the power struggle among the coalitions or groups to be formed by large and small states, (2) the vitality of the League of Nations, and (3) the maturity of those principles to be used to resolve disputes. The 1919–1939 history of the League of Nations is a desperate struggle to supply legal and institutional guarantees to compensate for the imbalance of power within the European community. In the inter-war period there were several initiatives for peaceful dispute resolution and for the implementation of international jurisdiction. The latter, however, stumbled over the point that not a single country was willing to accept international jurisdiction over political problems since political disputes were synonymous with territorial disputes. Although a power balance was created, it remained fragile since the League of Nations proved to be unsuitable to deal with vital conflicts. Since the regulating mechanism of international law was based on contradictory principles, joint acceptance of self-determination and territorial sanctity—and since this did not correspond to power relations, the result was that it made its theoretical foundation impossible.

The permanent political imbalance in inter-war Europe called forth "a Europe that lived in persistent fear of territorial changes and in the belief that a possible onset of territorial changes might upset the whole European system."[22]

THE TRIANON TREATY AND CRITICISM OF HUNGARIAN REVISIONISM

Bibó said in 1936 that "Hungarians, as a European political unit, are known abroad by two things: (1) the Hungarian revisionist movement and (2) Hungarian political conservatism"[23] and considered both characterizations to be unfavorable. Bibó could not identify with the difficult burdens of political conservatism and revisionism that Hungary inherited from the Monarchy, as both were contradictory to his democratic mindset. Even in his later writings, he envisioned a Hungary that was able to break with feudal-conservative traditions and was able to move beyond militant revisionism.

To understand Bibó's views about the Trianon Treaty, his views on national sentiments are revealing. Bibó offers a historical overview of the evolution of Hungarian nationalism in two of his writings, *The Balance of Hungarian Democracy* and *The Misery of Small Eastern-European States.* In his interpretation, the dream of the Hungarian democratic movement was to establish a democratic state within historic Hungary. This process, both in Hungary and in Central-Eastern Europe, had evolved into a linguistic nationalism that assumed the existence of a unilingual country. As the ideal of an independent, historic Hungary encountered the reality of a Hungary that was not unilingual, the view evolved that the ancient historic frame ought to be made unilingual. The defeat of the 1848–49 Revolution and War of Independence added to the unfortunate incitement.

> However, the defeat did not fatally harm the development of Hungarian democracy; it was damaged by confronting a diverse language population when it firmly stood by the principle of independence and democratic freedom....The moral of 1848–49 was that Hungarian independence and democratic freedom could not rely on the help of Europe. What is more, the danger of dissolution and dismemberment of the historical Hungarian political state was brought forth by the process.[24]

The Compromise drew the lesson from it: "partial independence and partial democracy while maintaining the complete historic state."[25] This "untruthful political compromise" took place because of an illusionary hope that in this way the dismemberment of a thousand-year-old historic Hungary could be avoided.

The collapse of the Monarchy and the establishment of successor states traumatized the political elite, which had not faced reality. Although Mihály Károlyi headed a force that embarked on "the difficult mission of setting democracy in motion for the second time," the democratic experiment failed again. The second Hungarian democratic republic was unable to survive the shock of the demarcation lines drawn by the later Trianon borders since they gratuitously detached Hungarian national territories.[26]

According to Bibó's sharp criticism, the Horthy regime had been founded on a greater political untruthfulness than Dualism, since the regime had signed the Trianon Treaty, something which neither the People's Republic nor the Hungarian Soviet Republic had done before it. To justify and to compensate for this ignominious act, which was the proviso for international recognition of the regime, they tried to shift the responsibility upon the People's Republic and the Hungarian Soviet Republic. Lacking political equilibrium and feeling, vulnerable Hungarian nationalism was transformed into irredentism and revisionism. Soon the view became widespread that the dismemberment was an act of brutal force and hypocrisy by the victors who were "unable to distinguish between territories justly and unreasonably detached. Therefore the regime remained obsessed with the illusion of a historical Greater Hungary and moved towards the sentiment that Europe had become indebted to them due to a great injustice."[27] Bibó uses the model of disequilibrium to explain the prevalent political hysteria of the times.

Besides denouncing the hysterical attitude towards Trianon, Bibó frequently points out that the Treaty made a mockery of democratic principles and was a significant obstacle in the process of democratization. "We do not remember any more...that the collapse of Mihály Károlyi's democratic Hungarian republic was due to the disclosure of the peace conditions by the Entente. Károlyi's only hope was the strength of the proletariat to counter the absurdity of the peace conditions. The 1919 democratic Hungarian republic would have looked forward to a totally different future had it received better conditions than the Trianon ones."[28] Bibó considered the national secessionist ambitions natural and justified and was an advocate of reconciliaton with successor states.

Bibó insisted that it was of utmost importance to reach a permanent settlement.

> 1919 differed from 1815 in that the peacemakers publicized a theory in 1919 also but, unlike 1815, they did not have the strength to apply it. They did not allow for clearly demonstrated unification ambitions, did not liquidate all the historical units mature enough for liquidation; and when they did liquidate, they did not pay attention to historical sentiments attached to regions, while foolishly respecting geographical, strategic, transportation, and rounding-off aspects...[29]

The fate of the very democratically chosen Czech political elite exemplifies the result of inconsistency and unprincipledness, according to Bibó's criticism. Whilst Czechoslovakia successfully applied the principle of self-determination and attained independence for itself, it then denied these rights to the Hungarian and Sudeten-German population and also to the Slovaks, an ironic attitude since the Czechs "parted from" the territorial unity of historic Hungary on behalf of the Slovaks as well as themselves. A higher level of internal democracy does not exempt the Czechs from understanding their own responsibility for the reaction of the Bohemian Germans, Hungarians, and Slovaks alienated by their policy.[30] Democracy is but one insufficient condition of regional stabilization and of permanent border consolidation.

POSSIBILITIES AND CONDITIONS OF BORDER CONSOLIDATION IN THE REGION

From a distance of 30 years after both wars the settlement following the dissolution of the Monarchy, Bibó finds it inexpedient to refer to historical rights or the status quo when speaking about territorial and border disputes in Eastern and Central Europe. Such a perspective simply endorses theoretical demands which ignore reality. Hungarian "historical arguments" and the Czech "status quo standpoint" are both equally unfounded and arbitrary. The Hungarians refuse to face "the Central and Eastern European political status and the dissolution of the historical state-system. The Czech version is completely baseless since it wants to restore those elements of the 1918 peace treaty which had already led to collapse once before."[31]

In Bibó's system, ethnic self-determination should be the only primary organizing principle, if the goal is to stabilize political states. At the same time, in the case of existing stable state structures, the principle of self-determination ought not to be given priority, since this would simply destabilize things, therefore peacemakers are rightfully averse to it.

When the Monarchy collapsed, at the moment of historical boundary dissolution, people living in that area should have been able to choose their change in national status through self-determination. Peacemakers did not consistently abide by this principle. Beyond the well-known political impotence of the victors, the reason was that they did not understand the typical Central-Eastern European problem of transition from historical borders to linguistic boundaries.[32] For the victors, disputes did not belong to the realm of self-determination which rather entailed "secession or independence of whole nations such as the foundation of the United States or secession of Belgium from the Netherlands...On the same ground, they were pleased when those Eastern European nations which had lost their independent statehood, such as Poland, Czechoslovakia, Yugoslavia, gained them."[33] In short, peacemakers after World War I endorsed the idea of self-determination for the liberation of nations, but did not endorse plebiscitary decisions about cities and regions.

Applying Bibó's views on self-determination and the inescapable disintegration of historical boundaries, he would have considered the Danube Basin settlement following the collapse of the Monarchy fair and just if the peoples of the region could have decided upon their national status equally. Similar to Germany, the Monarchy had not been a democratic state, therefore it should not have been charged with collective responsibility or guilt. Consequently, the right of self-determination should have been equally applied throughout the Monarchy. Furthermore, if the population of each region could have decided on their national status in compliance with the principle of self-determination, border disputes would have been minimal with more stable and permanent borders. Bibó claimed this not to be a prophecy since it is proven by the successful Sopron area referendum which solved an Austro–Hungarian border dispute.

Peacemakers, however, missed the historical moment for self-determination. Settlements closing World War I, especially the Trianon Treaty, evaded the most obvious and effective way of political consolidation in the Danube Basin and laid stress upon circumstances which were obstacles rather than means towards permanent stability in the area. In the case of permanent border settlements, Bibó viewed economic, transport, and strategic considerations to be useless. Historically, he also did not believe in the "almightiness" of federal solutions either. "Borders are primarily means of stabilization, and if stabilization is not formed by rational factors, it is not of tragic consequence if a border proves to be economically or geographically absurd."[34]

Drawing a lesson from the inter-war period, Bibó presumes "that in Central and Eastern Europe every serious border dispute originates from two contrasting aspects, one of which is a kind of historical status, status quo, or an aspect of historical sentiment or need. The other aspect is the aspect of ethnic and language status...[35] Contrary to the inter-war opinions and arguments about the supremacy of the historical status quo, he maintains that borders should be linguistically determined since that is the only way of assuring permanent border consolidation. "If we want democratically legitimate borders, then we want to adjust to a separating principle which truly separates peoples. Well, that is the linguistic and ethnic aspect."[36] In 1946, before the peace treaties concluding World War II, Bibó was confident that the new borders would really be the means of stabilization.

Therefore a referendum ought to be held only in controversial cases where the linguistic border is not clearly defined.[37] Border consolidation is the main consideration, with strictly controlled population exchanges or resettlements as acceptable alternatives. If the lack of a linguistic border were to block reconciliation, then population exchange seems to be a reasonable alternative to achieve a higher degree of stability. Otherwise "the last footing in Europe to stabilize borders, the continuity of population, would disappear." Population exchange is justified if "in certain areas the ethnographic borders are impossible to follow, yet owing to unbearable antagonisms neither the historical status nor the status quo can be sustained. It should also be declared that population exchanges are to be mutual, in compliance with the resolution and the supervision of the community of nations. Once the exchange is completed, it cannot be reversed."[38]

PROSPECTS OF TRIANON BORDER CONSOLIDATION FOLLOWING WORLD WAR II

THE PARIS PEACE AND THE RE-ESTABLISHMENT OF TRIANON BORDERS

It is striking that Bibó attaches gratuitously little significance to the rivalries of great powers and their influence on the region up to the 1946 Paris peace talks, but rather blames internal problems of Hungarian development for missed historical opportunities. Partly his legal theoretical approach, and partly his theory of hysteria-equilibrium help explain why great powers' assertions of interest are not given greater emphasis in his summaries.

While he himself writes in early 1946 that

> although we have narrowed down our examinations of the problems of East Central Europe,...we believe that we have approached the central and most important question in the consolidation of the world....A war might break out in this area and even if the attack does not originate here, it might be directed towards this area. East Central Europe, that is the territory of small nations east of Germany, is not a large area, yet it remains a threat to world peace as long as it remains the area of the greatest anarchy, uncertainty, and dissatisfaction.[39]

Bibó was aware that settling the Danube Basin situation is the central question of world consolidation, yet he did not even attempt to analyze it with regard to power politics.

Disappointed and disillusioned by the Paris Peace talks, he finally raises the question of the role of the great powers in "The Peace Treaty and Hungarian Democracy," but he still considers the Horthy regime responsible for the postwar border arrangement which was "bad and unjust...and it is a world-renowned cliche."[40]

In Bibó's view the responsibility of the peacemakers lies in the fact that "the allied great powers and other states are presently divided into two rival power groups. Between the groups there is a crisis of confidence, and the ebbs and flows of the crisis randomly juggle every concrete question of the Peace Treaty." The struggle for spheres of influence "does not allow for the assertion of any theory in the course of peace talks and peace treaties."[41] His earlier writings testify that Bibó considered it a serious negligence towards peoples living in this area that peacemakers did not consistently observe basic principles and thus, the territorial settlement was devoid of any theoretical basis.

Bibó was a convinced democrat and could not forgive the damage done to Hungarian democratic development by the insistence on democracy in order to conceal unprincipledness. "It is obvious that peacemaking will be connected with democracy and that public sentiment will now blame democracy for the peace treaty, and will conclude from the injustice of the peace agreement that democracy is basically untruthful."[42] "The injustice of the Peace Treaty and the readiness for democratization still correlate....Each advantage obtained in bad faith, as for example the way that Czechoslovakia obtains advantages both territorially and in connection with resettlement, is a wicked obstacle on the hard road leading towards the democratization of Hungary."[43]

Bibó does not question compliance with the new Peace Treaty. In his view, in the long run peoples of the area will have to settle for this situation and will find prosperity within the Trianon borders.[44] However, knowing his views on Trianon and border consolidation, it is hard to imagine that he honestly believed that a repetition of the much criticized bad settlement and its extension would really bring stability to the area.

Although he claims that the restored Trianon borders should be accepted and the Peace Treaty should be observed, he also points out "on behalf of the nation" that Hungary "cannot renounce its political interest towards minorities."[45] The renewed Trianon settlement is acceptable only with an effective minority protection policy. Inter-war minority laws did not provide opportunities for the mother nation to intervene on behalf of its people living in different states and Bibó, being familiar with international law, understood that this perspective would hardly change in the future. "The lives of minorities can be made bearable only by political effort which, directly or indirectly, is the task of the mother country, that is, ours."[46]

He warns about the responsibility resting upon the peacemakers for resettling the population of whole areas unilaterally while claiming that in this way "an unreasonable border will become a good border." Unprincipledness and confused references to principles when passing resolutions–in the spirit of momentary political opportunism–dealing with questions of vital consequences that "may have lasting effects for decades or centuries, yet which could also be solved appropriately, will receive annihilating criticism from the whole world."[47]

THE RESPONSIBILITY OF HUNGARIAN POLITICS

Bibó is rather biased when he declares that "Horthy's, and his administration's, primary responsibility for the outcome of the peace treaty...can be pointed out with historical validity."[48] According to his arguments, "Hungary, with all the burdens of a satellite state and for the sake of a right standpoint, was in the position to seek and hope for encouragement in questions which at present make the Hungarian Peace Treaty so devastating." The right standpoint would have been for Horthy to firmly resist the March 1944 German invasion or, half a year later, for him to have had the strength to bring the October breakaway to success.[49] The Horthy regime is certainly responsible for the extraordinarily unfavorable international verdict Hungary received. However, it calls for strong bias to write that "we owe the Peace Treaty to Miklós Horthy and his government."[50] This obviously reflects the fresh and strong emotions of disappointment and disillusionment of the impending Peace Treaty. It is even more surprising to read a similar view in a paper from 1948 when Bibó circumstantially and carefully explains how inter-war Hungarian politics missed the opportunity to revise Trianon.[51]

> Horthy's government came into power with the proviso that they would sign the Trianon Treaty. The counter-revolutionary government counter-balanced this severe birth defect by nursing the ensuing irredentism.... Consequently, when the world political situation opened up the possibility of reannexation, its first reaction was to grasp this opportunity to make restitution on Hungary's earlier injustice, yet ignoring the fact that this very act also constituted a different injustice.[52]

Horthy's government disregarded principles, indiscriminately accepted any territory of historical Hungary to be reannexed, ignored the hatred the act created among the population, and conducted an even more unsuccessful nationality policy than the dualist government.

Again Bibó offers his theories of community hysteria and the loss of political equilibrium as explanations for the inter-war policy which had been foredoomed to failure.

> The new dead-end of the political, social, and national aspects of the counter-revolution fatally undermined the political intelligence and moral judgment of our leaders....Consequently, the untruthfulness of the whole counter-revolutionary construction recreated the very danger and fear for which it had been created. To safeguard the new territorial changes and to protect social immobility, the country maneuvered itself into a war which resulted in the restoration of the prewar status and the collapse of the centuries old social hierarchy.[53]

Bibó may be right in his belief that wars are caused by "the lack of political equilibrium" stemming from society's morale being saturated with fear and not necessarily from changes occurring in economics or power politics. However, if we consistently follow through Bibó's train of thoughts, the question comes up as to whether accelerated technological development and the ensuing intensive military competition do not evoke increasing fears in the political life of all participating nations equally. If this fear becomes permanent, we might infer that mass hysteria is a chronic symptom of the modern age.

NOTES

1. "I had conceived my career such that utilizing all the available opportunities, I would become a university professor and acquire relative independence for participation in public life and politics. After all, I have always wanted to be in politics, just like Ferenc Erdei." From Tibor Huszár's interview, Beszélgetés Bibó Istvánnal (A Discussion with István Bibó] (*Valóság*, 1980, 9), 27.

2. "He joined the March Front in 1937 but had no political role till the end of the War. In 1945 he joined the National Peasants' Party and for a while was member of the Provisionary National Government. In 1956 as a member of the Petőfi Party (former National Peasants' Party) he became the State Secretary of the Imre Nagy Government for a few days." Tibor Huszár, Bibó István—a gondolkodó, a politikus [István Bibó, the Theoretician and Politician] in *Bibó István—Válogatott tanulmányok*, III. [Selected Writings] ed. Tibor Huszár, (Budapest, 1986), 385–534.

3. István Bibó's writings on the Trianon Treaty and border revisions are the following in the four-volume *Válogatott tanulmányok* [Selected Writings]: A mai

külföld szemlélete a magyarságról (1936) [Hungarians through Foreign Eyes]; Az európai egyensúlyról és békéről (1943–44) [On European Equilibrium and Peace]; A magyar demokrácia mérlege (1946) [The Balance of Hungarian Democracy]; A kelet-európai kisállamok nyomorúsága (1946) [The Misery of Eastern-European Small States]; A békeszerződés és a magyar demokrácia (1946) [The Peace Treaty and Hungarian Democracy]; Eltorzult magyar alkat, zsákutcás történetelem (1948) [Distorted Hungarian Temper, Dead-end Hungarian History]; Az európai társadalomfejlődés értelme (1971–72) [The Significance of European Social Development]; A nemzetközi államközösség bénultsága és annak orvosságai. Önrendelkezés, nagyhatalmi egyetértés, politikai önbíráskodás (1965–74) [The Lameness of International Commonwealth and Its Remedies. Self-determination, Great Power Accord, Political Lynch-law].

4. László Ferenczi, *Guglielmo Ferrero*, in *A hatalom humanizálása. Tanulmányok Bibó István életművéről* [Humanization of Power: Essays on István Bibó's Life-Work] ed. Zoltán Iván Dénes (Pécs, 1993).

5. In Huszár, *Bibó*, III; László Lakatos, Hajnal István hatása [István Hajnal's Influence]; Ágnes Zsidai, Bibó István, a jogfilozófus [István Bibó, the Legal Philosopher], in ed. Dénes, *Humanization.*

6. Bibó, Az európai egyensúlyról és békéről, in *Selected Writings*, I. 295–604.

7. In Huszár, *Bibó*, I.

8. Bibó, A kelet-európai kisállamok nyomorúsága (1946) [The Misery of Eastern-European Small States]; A békeszerződés és a magyar demokrácia (1946) [The Peace Treaty and the Hungarian Democracy]; Eltorzult magyar alkat, zsákutcás történetelem (1948) [Distorted Hungarian Temper, Dead-End Hungarian History].

9. Huszár, *Bibó*, 402–404.

10. Huszár, *Bibó*, 403.

11. Bibó, On European Equilibrium and Peace, in *Selected Writings*, I. 300.

12. Ibid., 374.

13. Ibid., 302.

14. Ibid., 388.

15. Bibó, The Lameness of International Commonwealth, in *Selected Writings*, IV. 326–327.

16. I am relying on Péter Kende's analysis of the principle of self-determination: Péter Kende, Önrendelkezés Kelet-Európában tegnap és ma [Self-determination in Eastern Europe—Yesterday and Today], in ed. Dénes, *Humanization*, 166.

17. Bibó, The Lameness of International Commonwealth, 400.

18. Ibid., 415–416.

19. Bibó, On European Equilibrium and Peace, in *Selected Writings*, I. 432.

20. Ibid., 433.

21. Ibid., 433.

22. Ibid., 519–521.

23. Bibó, Hungarians through Foreign Eyes, in *Selected Writings*, I. 145.

24. Bibó, Balance, in *Selected Writings*, II. 124–125; Misery, in *Selected Writings*, II. 203.

25. Ibid., 125.

26. Ibid., 125, 126–127; Bibó, Distorted Hungarian Temper, Dead-end Hungarian History, in *Selected Writings*, II. 597–599.

27. Bibó, Misery, 204.
28. Ibid., 282.
29. Ibid., 259.
30. Ibid., 205–212.
31. Ibid., 234.
32. Ibid., 250–251.
33. Ibid., 251.
34. Ibid., 246.
35. Ibid., 242.
36. Ibid., 261.
37. Ibid., 253.
38. Ibid., 254–255.
39. Ibid., 265.
40. Bibó, The Peace Treaty and Hungarian Democracy, in *Selected Writings*, II. 269.
41. Ibid., 278.
42. Ibid., 270.
43. Ibid., 281–282.
44. Ibid., 295–296.
45. Ibid., 296.
46. Ibid., 293.
47. Ibid., 280.
48. Ibid., 273.
49. Since satellite Hungary could not count on support against Czechoslovakia and Yugoslavia, Bibó alludes to Transylvania's status which was undetermined for a long time. However, Transylvania did not finally end up under Romanian control because the Hungarian break-away experiment was unsuccessful. We cannot declare that the outcome of peace talks would have been different with respect to borders, if in March 1944 Hungarian politics had assumed the 'right' position and had 'asked and hoped' amid better international judgment.
50. Bibó, The Peace Treaty, 273.
51. Bibó, Distorted, 569–619.
52. Ibid., 599–600.
53. Ibid., 602–603.

NATIONAL INDEPENDENCE, NEUTRALITY, AND COOPERATION IN THE DANUBE REGION: IMRE NAGY'S FOREIGN POLICY IDEAS

JÁNOS M. RAINER

Although Imre Nagy's foreign policy ideas and his practical foreign policy activities hold great interest, they are the most debated parts of his political oeuvre. Most analysts acknowledge that his boldest and most significant accomplishment is his essay against the "Soviet bloc-policy," which discussed the independence of states within the Soviet system.[1] Yet even that historiography which deals with the Hungarian Revolution with objectivity and sympathy has shown an underlying concern about Imre Nagy's foreign policy during the Revolution. Was withdrawal from the Warsaw Pact and the Declaration of Neutrality prudent? Did it contribute to the second Soviet intervention and the defeat of the Revolution in a major way?

These significant historical decisions are grounds enough for a detailed analysis of the development of Nagy's foreign policy ideas in order to place them in the proper political context. Two further circumstances substantiate the necessity for such an analysis. One is that Imre Nagy is an important figure in the history of Hungarian foreign policy. After World War II, the scope of Hungary's political maneuver was minimal and Hungarian diplomacy was confined to fending off the extreme negative effects of the Paris Peace Treaty.[2] After the Peace Treaty, from the late 1940's on, independent Hungarian foreign policy ceased to exist and Hungary's foreign relations were subordinated to Soviet Imperial foreign policy. Independent foreign policy initiatives appeared only in the early 1970's, in the spirit of detente and in the interest of Hungarian minorities living across the border. Independence, unique concepts, foreign policy concepts, and/or concepts for furthering one's interests were still limited notions in that period. Imre Nagy was the only one during the two decades since the war who had both a definite foreign policy program and also the chance to implement it, due to the extraordinary circumstances of the 1956 Revolution.

The second circumstance is connected to the posthumous events concerning both Imre Nagy himself and his foreign policy concepts. Developing an independent foreign policy became one of the basic questions of the Hungarian democratic transformation after the 1989 collapse of the East Central European communist systems and the 1991 dissolution of the Soviet Union. The direction chosen was to join the large western political-military organizations (EU, NATO). There was only one relevant alternative, which surfaced for a short time: Imre Nagy's idea of neutrality, that is, existence outside of any power-bloc. In the first phase of the democratic transformation, the fight with the party state, this idea was deemed just as much unlawful and destructive to the existing state structure as the events of 1956 and Imre Nagy's rehabilitation. Although it was not explicitly stated as a foreign policy doctrine, neutrality still emerges in professional discussions and in public pronouncements.[3] It might occur that the lurking nostalgia for neutrality will intensify in the coming years, parallel with regionalism and "Euroskepticism," as a unique Hungarian version of these international trends and supported by arguments from Hungary's history.

The question is whether the idea of neutrality and life outside a power-bloc was something the nation as a whole wanted or was Imre Nagy's own creation. Generally any alternative to the Soviet occupation and the Warsaw Pact was popular with the public and drew massive support. On the one hand in October of 1956 Hungarian society openly declared the type of international relation the country should have–independence of the Soviet Bloc. On the other hand, of their own free will, society restrained itself in the spirit of "Realpolitik" and, instead of advocating joining the western alliance, accepted the situation of an Austrian–Swiss type of neutrality. Imre Nagy became the recognized leader of the Hungarian revolution although his earlier concepts of foreign policy, paradoxically, were not very well known despite the fact that they coincided with the social-national will. However, it could not have been accidental that a person in such a key position would have concluded from his own deep-seated conviction that the country, of necessity, should withdraw from the Warsaw Pact on November 1, 1956, and declare itself neutral. Thus knowing the extraordinary circumstances of the revolution it is of relevance to describe the evolutionary processes of Imre Nagy's foreign policy views.

A preliminary note: there was not such an evolution by itself. Despite his quarter-century long political career preceding 1956,

Imre Nagy rarely dealt with foreign policy issues. Two factors affected the development of his foreign policy views: (1) he was a first generation communist politician with a universalist, messianic attitude, an *eo ipso* internationalist who viewed the problems of the "movement" (within the movement, the party) in an international perspective. Ever since the Soviet Union was established, the existence, interests, empirical interests and traditions of the Soviet State determined international perspectives for Nagy. (2) The second factor stemmed from his theoretical inclinations. Unique national forms of transition from capitalism to socialism (communism) were at the center of his theoretical interests. As he was an agrarian expert, Nagy usually started investigations from an agricultural perspective. Yet due to his universalist approach, he came to general conclusions. His foreign policy interests and views comprised international diplomacy, the international communist movement, the dogmas of the Soviet Empire, international communist alternatives, and the dilemmas of national independence–directly or indirectly.[4]

It is interesting to note that Nagy's first writing, published in Soviet Russia in 1920 in a newspaper for Hungarian prisoners of war, discussed a foreign political issue–the attack Poland waged on Soviet Russia.[5] After that, for one and a half decades he examined the condition and the future of Hungarian agriculture and entered unchartered international waters through comparative agrarian-statistical applications.[6] In 1930 after a decade of activities in Hungary, Nagy became an exile in the Soviet Union and worked for fifteen years as an agrarian policy maker, researcher, professional, and general publicist.[7] As a member of the KOMINTERN's International Agricultural Institute he designed a large-scale project in the mid-1930's which would have examined social democratic agrarian views and would have included the Social Democratic Party's theory about Hungarian capitalist development.[8] It is striking that although he understood the importance of national independence and the nationality questions of 19th century Hungary, he underestimated their significance. Moreover he considered them to be factors which would have hindered the transformation of capitalism into socialism. In his notes Nagy often criticized social democrats, who stood on the platform of Hungarian national independence and territorial integrity, for signing a pact with Hungarian capitalists instead of concluding an alliance with the national minority peasant masses by recognizing their right to self-determination. In a 1936 essay, Nagy took a similar position in a debate with another significant theoretician of the Hungarian communist movement, József Révai, with regard to evaluating the 1848 Revolution and War of Independence. Nagy emphasized the anti-feudal character and "class content" of 1848, something obviously wrong, against Révai who quickly assumed the views of the anti-fascist Popular Front policy and then became very sensitive towards any national independent rhetoric and to the problems of national democratic allies.[9] There are very few traces of the later independent politician in Nagy's first essay on foreign policy, published in the Hungarian exiles' journal in Moscow in the summer of 1938, which was the eve of the Munich Agreement.[10]

The re-annexation of the mostly Hungarian-populated Southern Slovakia was the first opportunity for Hungary to revise the Trianon Treaty. This move had not followed an international agreement or bilateral talks. The Western Powers tried to avoid any confrontation and yielded ground to Hitler. Nagy's position on the situation reflected the interests of the communist movement and the Soviet Union since the Soviet Union was an ally of Czechoslovakia. Nagy stated that democratic Hungarians were obliged to protect the Czechoslovak democratic system against German fascism. He was right. However, for Hungary, Czechoslovakia was not only a bourgeois democratic system, it was the merciless utilizer of the Trianon Treaty to keep hundreds of thousands of Hungarians under its rule (which was not necessarily an unbearable rule). However, Nagy did not even allude to this national aspect. But he raised an idea which was not even part of the received directives and which became a recurring motive later as well, "None of the small nations along the Danube can cope with the threatening common danger by itself. The common danger and the common fate stipulate that threatened small nations should cope with one another."[11] Progressive thinkers of the area had dealt with the idea of cooperation among the Danube Basin (Carpathian Basin, East Central European) small nations since the 19th century. However, cooperation among small nations was not among the goals of communist movements which, on one hand, expected consolation with the global revolutionary internationalism for common grievances of small nations and, on the other hand, represented Soviet interests, which did not support any cooperation in the region unless it was initiated by the Soviet Union.

After 1944 Nagy became a member of the Hungarian government, first as Minister of Agriculture and later as Minister of Internal Affairs. On some occasions he had to confront the occupying Soviet authorities because of repeated plundering and requisitioning by the Soviet military. In contrast with the majority of communist politicians, Nagy was not servile, which necessarily led to conflicts within his own party.[12] In 1946 he lost importance, was dismissed from the government, and the idea came up that he would be appointed ambassador to Warsaw or Bucharest. His deputation to the Foreign Affairs Committee of the National Assembly in the spring of 1946 must have been in preparation for this. As a representative of the Hungarian Communist Party Nagy participated in the work of the Committee's peace preparatory sub-committee which reviewed and finalized the Hungarian peace plans (political and economic peace proposals) prepared by the Ministry of Foreign Affairs for submission to the Paris Peace Talks starting in the fall of 1946. During this process Nagy was quite passive and did not make any noteworthy statements.[13] Yet he must have gained important experiences during the discussions. Plans of massive forced resettlement of Hungarians from Czechoslovakia and the Soviet reaction to a very moderate Hungarian territorial demand toward Romania (sometimes unfavorable, sometimes ambiguous) Soviet foreign policy. He must have shared the schizophrenia of other communist leaders: on the one side it was essential to have a good relationship with the Soviets because of the political situation and the goals of the Party. But on the other side, the recurrence of Trianon, a national grievance with possibly graver conditions now, must have distressed him as a Hungarian politician. In the fall of 1946 his diplomatic "suspense" was removed by his being recalled from the Parliament's Foreign Policy Committee by the Hungarian Communist Party.[14]

In the second half of the 1940's Nagy functioned as the primary agrarian political expert of the Hungarian Communist Party. He concerned himself with the large transformational processes of Hungarian agriculture, with a land reform policy that terminated the system of large estates, and with the dilemmas of a newer agrarian integration that was to replace the smallholders' structure. One of his essays indicated a familiarity with the regional dimensions of the question. He concluded that the countries of the Danubian Basin–Czechoslovakia, Romania, Yugoslavia, and Hungary–were interdependent owing to a similar agrarian structure and state of development. Hence, their economies ought to be coordinated. This was a response to western and overseas competitive agricultural challenges and also a reaction to federative plans raised by the Yugoslavs. In response to the Yugoslav federative plans, mostly dealing with the Balkans with Belgrade as the center, Nagy evoked Lajos Kossuth's Danubian Confederative Plan, whose political consequences he reviewed again under different circumstances in the mid-1950's. "The idea is not new. In Kossuth's confederative plans the perspectives of a Danube Basin cooperation unfolded, corresponding to the respective situation. The plan, however, remained a plan because the prerequisites of the realization were missing. Today they are available."[15] Hungary would play a significant role in this plan based on traditions and also because its agriculture, in spite of the similarities, was more developed than those of other countries. Beyond being the Hungarian Communist Party's agrarian expert, Imre Nagy appended his own personal dream to the end of the study:

> The theoretical and practical expansion of a close agricultural cooperation among the Danube Basin countries would be the task of a Danube Basin Agrarian Research Institute. That is what I had in mind when I first started working on the plans of such an institute as the Minister of Agriculture in the summer of 1945. At that point it was not implemented for various reasons. Yet a scientific institute of this kind is essential. However, it will bring results only if the prerequisites of independent and really scientific work are realized....Let us take the first steps on this field...[16]

These plans are not of interest from the perspectives of implementation since they were never implemented, not even by the Danube Basin Agrarian Research Institute. They are of interest because they explore the possibilities of the situation–a quest which was done by many. However, Nagy was the most characteristic figure of this process in the Hungary of the 1940's.

Imre Nagy and the "explorers" wondered just how different a route from the Soviet model the Soviets would allow their occupied countries (Nagy's countries of the Danube Basin) to take to "reach socialism" and how long the process would take. For a while these issues were debated in the Soviet Union as well.[17] According to the "explorers," the new or people's democracies were transitions to a new, unique system–different from the Soviet one. They contained the characteristics of a revolution but might exclude or limit certain aggressive elements since they did not possess the abrupt and pervasive character of a revolution being instead a several decades-long process. The character of the East Central European area, which was different from the Soviet Union, served as a starting point. The Danube Basin was more similar to the west, at least in terms of its more developed economic and social systems. The "explorers" criticized Stalin's Soviet system, although not openly. They were convinced that the implementation of the Soviet model was not possible in Hungary (or Poland or Czechoslovakia), not in an unaltered form anyway. They did not question the post-war Soviet imperial power policy, although the theory about the existence of different national models indirectly did question that assumption as well. Imre Nagy's transition concept and the ensuing debate contained international references as well and, in today's language, it was about the socio-political establishment of contemporary, and future third-world, Soviet satellite states.

In the political debates of the late 1940's, Nagy was defeated; exploratory theories were pushed to the background and then disappeared. After Stalin's death, however, differences were, at least partly, acknowledged leading to a policy of corrections. As a result, in June of 1953 Imre Nagy became Prime Minister of Hungary.

The Presidium of the Soviet Party appointed Nagy to Prime Minister during the summit meeting with the Hungarian leadership on June 13–16, 1953.[18] The same Presidium decided his political downfall—not about his replacement—during a similar meeting on January 12, 1955.[19] Both acts violated Hungarian independence and sovereignty. However, in the first instance, when intervention was essential to assert his political predominance, Nagy overlooked it. He assumed that the crisis justified the exploration process of 1945–49. As a result, the Communist Party should return to the East Central European (Danube Basin) alternative transition; namely to the period of 1947–48 which was characterized by the predominance, but not by the hegemony of the communists. Nagy tried to navigate towards this situation during his first government. He wanted to reinstate smallholders' agriculture, a relatively freer public life and press, some limited autonomies, the post-1947 bogus-coalition, the not-quite-illusionary Parliament, and ease the state of war against society.[20] His first prime-ministership (1953–1955) was characterized by heated internal political fights and consequently he did not have enough energy left for foreign policy initiatives. He did have to focus on Soviet relations and the successor fights in Moscow since they would decide the fate of Hungarian corrections and reform. Still, Hungary's first modest opening towards the West, due to foreign trade considerations, is connected to his name. Normalizing relations with Yugoslavia, which had reached bottom at the end of the 1940's following the Stalin–Tito break, began in this period as well.[21] Nagy also initiated talks to solve the "uncleared questions" of Hungarian–Romanian relations, but their content is still unknown.[22] Negotiations did not take place because at the beginning of 1955 Mátyás Rákosi, with Soviet assistance, toppled Nagy, stripping him of his state and party functions.

Both of Imre Nagy's two political downfalls (1949 and 1955) originate from the same reason. He sought for an adequate realization of "true socialism," but disregarded the basic feature of the Soviet model: it was not a system of communism or socialism, rather it was an empire. When Hungary came within the Soviet imperial sphere of interest, the entire process of consolidation, acceptance, and legitimation of these "acquisitions" would logically stipulate a slower and more cautious transformation to communism, taking local characteristics into account. In that fortunate moment, the explorers' ambitions and Soviet imperial interests coincided. However, when the moment was gone, the "exploration" process became futile, superfluous, and dangerous. How the changing post-Stalin Soviet leadership wished and considered the ideas of imperial rationalization, newer external consolidation, and probable internal reconsideration of the transformation model cannot be stated unambiguously because of the lack of historical sources. The imperial aspect, however, remained of fundamental importance for the Soviets in every crucial moment of Hungarian history (the turn of 1954–55 and October, 1956).

This was where Imre Nagy, living in internal exile in 1955–56, started from when he tried to review the classic Soviet model in its totality. Actually, only foreign policy and international relations factors were added to his existing ideas on the transition to socialism developed in the late 1940's. This starting point limited him to thinking within the framework of the Socialist Bloc. It is evident from his writings of 1955–56 that his main concerns were the foreign political interactions within the bloc. Even if he possessed information about the main tendencies of world politics, they were not incorporated into his theoretical work.

Nagy's ideas were significantly motivated by his personal grievance. In his pamphlet about the March decision, written in the fall of 1955, Nagy mentioned "open Soviet intrusion into the affairs of the Hungarian Party and State" for the first time. Nagy wrote about the fact that Suslov, a member of the Soviet Party Presidium, participated in the summit meeting of the Hungarian Party leadership where he supported the Rákosi-type orthodox, Stalinist position against Nagy and his policies.[23] Nagy did not dwell on the personal and political offense, but tried to examine the phenomenon theoretically. The central recognition of his studies, written between the summer of 1955 and early 1956, was that his type of socialism could not be implemented without an "all national policy" based on national independence. Nagy took the Stalinist dogma, incessantly repeated by the Stalinists, that socialism would take place within the framework of national states seriously and elaborated on it extensively. Underlying his work was the conviction that the Soviet leadership could be convinced about the right connection between the national state and building socialism and about its practical consequences. This obviously naive conviction was typical of the first generation of reform communists and clearly separated them from the second generation of the 1970's and 1980's. The first generation, while it contrasted the socialist ideal with the practice of Stalinism, believed in the power of criticism to change practice. The second reform communist generation of the 1970's and 1980's followed the reverse strategy. Based on the experiences of 1956 and 1968, the second generation recognized the immutability of the imperial framework and of Soviet interests. This was their point of departure for their own cautious reform policy and its implementation.

Nagy discussed international issues for the first time in a treatise written in the summer of 1955 where he refuted the accusation of "nationalism" brought against him and his policy. He quoted from his earlier essays (1938 and 1947) on cooperation in the Danube Basin and claimed that "As a son of the Hungarian people and the member of the Hungarian nation, I am proud of being Hungarian and I will not deny my Hungarianness. I love my Hungarian homeland and people, with true patriotism which, together with my love for other peoples and nations, form the basis and essence of my proletarian internationalism."[24] It is remarkable that his love for the Soviet Union, itself a Stalinist principle, was left out of this quotation.

In September of 1955 in his essay "Some Timely Questions of Applying Marxism–Leninism," Nagy finally declared unambiguously that the Soviet model of establishing socialism was of limited validity. This model had become exclusive and was mechanically reproduced because, by "the Stalinist monopoly of Marxism–Leninism,...Lenin's teachings were pushed into the background and diminished."[25] The right starting point would be the level-headed examination of national characteristics and conditions. As a result of this, "in Central and South-Eastern European countries, we too, not in the least, have to find and apply forms and methods... while building socialism. And we have to establish a progress whose pace would make it acceptable and desirable for the capitalist countries. Our present social, economic, and cultural conditions, from where we start building socialism, are similar to those of western capitalist countries in many respects."[26] On this theoretical basis the transition "would have to be a steady, slow, less painful and burdensome advancement," while the Soviet route was a "historical mistake which will have its mark on the outcome of socialism."[27]

Instead of analyzing just one region of Europe, Nagy analyzed the whole European system when, in the same essay, he took a stand for the peaceful co-existence of the two politico-economic systems and for "peaceful competition between the two systems." It was only half a year later that the 20th congress of the Soviet Communist Party brought a resolution of criticism of Stalin's denial of the above statement. Nagy considered this question so essential that very soon he dedicated a whole essay to this issue. Khrushchev's doing penance in Belgrade in May 1955 made a great impression on Nagy since the Soviet leader recognized the theoretical possibility of national ways leading to socialism, while obviously still refusing to accept criticism of the Soviet model.[28]

Finalizing his foreign policy, Imre Nagy started from five basic principles regulating international relations, all laid down in the so-called *Bandung Declaration*: national independence, sovereignty, equal rights, territorial sanctity, and non-interference in internal affairs. In 1955 he was more and more convinced that international détente was coming and that it had been progressing ever since Stalin's death. He was equally convinced that de-Stalinization had been progressing, was successful in the Soviet Union, and might even win the day. Without this historical optimism, his ideas are hardly comprehensible.[29]

Hence, Nagy's ideas originated from these five principles and, by building upon one another, he developed them from general principles into unique ones concerning Hungarian foreign policy and, finally, with a newer and final generalization, to a vision of an East Central European regional policy. According to his first two principles, the five principles–which were first raised in connection with the newly liberated countries of the third world–were of universal value.

On one hand, the principle of national independence, which Nagy considered the most important of the five, was not restricted to a certain period of history. It was a powerful factor that existed in the present time, irrespective of social system.

> The historical events of the past decade more and more convincingly prove us that national independence, sovereignty, equal rights and the principle of self-determination, which became the ideas of the masses through bourgeois transformation and national liberation movements, do not only characterize bourgeois transformation but are important factors during the transition from capitalism to socialism....As long as nations and nation states exist, and a whole historical period is ahead of us on this respect, the ideas of the five principles will be moving forces in the development of the socialist social system.[30]

While elaborating his theories, Nagy heavily criticized the Soviet bloc counties where, in the name of Stalinist ideology, the significance of national independence was minimized and even denied.

On the other hand, the five principles were meant not only to regulate the co-existence of countries of different political systems. "National independence, sovereignty, equal rights and the principle of self-determination carry the same meaning in every country with respect to any other country, whether they are capitalist, socialist, transitional people's democracies, or anything else."[31] National independence has not lost its significance during socialism or in the period of "transition." Thus these countries, including the Soviet Union, should regulate their relationships accordingly. "...Good neighborly and friendly relationship between the Soviet Union and Hungary is a historical necessity. Developing their connections have great potentials. However, these connections should be based on the five principles and should be mutually observed."[32] And Nagy added that it had not happened in the past, nor was it happening in the present. In the relationship between the Soviet Union and its satellite countries, the sixth principle: the principle of non-intervention should be observed as well. This statement referred to the unquestionable Soviet "arbitrage" role played in the relationships between and within the various national Communist Parties.

According to Nagy's third principle, "there is a contradistinction between the policies of the power blocs and the five principles defining national independence, sovereignty, and the peaceful co-existence of peoples. Allotting states to power blocs will sooner or later lead to armed conflicts. Instead of creating power blocs, they should be dissolved since this is the only feasible way to peaceful development and to avoid wars." Although this principle was indisputably right, there were "serious considerations" regarding their political realization.[33] Hardly half a year after the establishment of the Warsaw Pact, this statement, despite attached reservations, indicated undue audacity and optimism.

However, Imre Nagy did not intend to stop at this question mark and in his fourth principle he tried to propose alternative responses. "A synchronized foreign policy of progressive democratic, socialist, or countries of similar type and their cooperation against power bloc policies,...seems to be the most efficient on the basis of neutrality or active co-existence....The Hungarian people, keeping their own particular interests and the general interests of socialist countries in mind, have to pursue the policy of active co-existence in the field of international politics."[34] Nagy's application of the term "active co-existence" alluded to the beginnings of a loose political organization which later evolved into the movement of non-aligned nations. First of all, he alluded to Yugoslavia which played the role of initiator and leader in this field. It was not the dubious, and from many respects confusing, movement that Nagy and its Hungarian supporters had in mind. It was much rather a Yugoslavia which was becoming independent of Stalin. Although remaining a socialist regime, its leaders seemingly had achieved independence when the Soviet leadership reluctantly came to accept their separation in 1955/56.

Nagy's final three foreign policy principles had been outlined in order to solve the theoretical and practical Hungarian dilemma–an outcome of his deduction. His fifth principle was very simple: there was a need for an independent Hungarian foreign policy since there had not been one thus far. As a result of "Stalinist theoretical and political autocracy," foreign political thinking was substituted with established "dogmas and clichés;" foreign relations were characterized by Soviet "subordination and dependence," and foreign policy was limited to "a minimal checking for the sake of uniformity within the socialist bloc."[35] The main Hungarian foreign political goal was clear: "It is the sovereign right of the Hungarian people to decide whatever form it envisions as the most favorable international relations to assure its national independence, sovereignty, equal rights, and peaceful development."[36]

Nagy's sixth principle initiated a manifold opening to Soviet bloc countries (primarily that of the East Central European area).

> Isolation of countries building socialism from the rest of the world and the general community of the nations is harmful and disadvantageous....It cannot be held up for an extended period of time, especially in those cases of economically and culturally more developed European countries, because it creates domestic tensions and tensions in the international situation of individual countries, thus leading to serious shocks sooner or later. Historically, traditional international relations of a country should not be ignored since it is not a Gordian knot which can be cut into two as a solution.[37]

In connection with this Nagy also raised the "unsettled relationship" of the Soviet communist movement to socialist and social-democratic parties which replaced "cooperation within international and national domains"–a problem which disappeared only when the communist movement perished.[38]

In his last principle Imre Nagy referred to Lajos Kossuth's Danubian Confederation Plan. "He did not envision joining a great power or power group to assure the the country's independent, sovereign, and self-reliant national existence. Kossuth envisioned a close cooperation with neighboring nations within an equal federation of free nations. We have to return to these ideas..."[39]

Imre Nagy's essay on foreign policy played a prominent role in the evolution of his ideas. His precepts created a consistent, logical system and his language consciously blended Marxist terminology with patriotic pathos. His proposals, however, assumed that the Soviet system and its allies would proceed along the road of de-Stalinization. In retrospect it is easy to call his ideological experiment naive. He himself was aware that if the circumstances and conditions developed differently, there would not be any chance to realize his ideas and he would not have any chance for foreign political or political activities. However, early in 1956 and especially after the 20th Congress of the Soviet Communist Party, it seemed that the Soviet Empire was moving along according to Nagy's ideas. This momentum slowed down by the summer of 1956 and finally came to a halt. But then the 1956 October Polish crisis, with Khrushchev's retreat by acknowledging a Nagy-type leader, Władysław Gomulka, again raised Nagy's hopes.[40] Everything that Imre Nagy envisioned as the evolutionary process of Hungarian foreign policy appeared on the agenda during the Hungarian Revolution, an extreme crisis situation and as an unexpected challenge. The revolution wanted to break with the Soviet Empire, as much as was possible. However, Hungary belonged to the Soviet sphere of influence and not even the most hot-headed revolutionary could contest that. The fact that a politician headed the country who had been considering the possibilities of a turn of direction in policy—which would have assured independence for the country and would have found a *modus vivendi* with the empire—was of major significance.

The above does not mean that Nagy's ideas were perfect given the circumstances and conditions of the times. On the contrary, they are open to criticism on at least two points. First of all, Imre Nagy did not discuss the practical implementation of his ideas, either in his writings or otherwise. Events that he listed in his essays, the Soviet-Yugoslav reconciliation, his activities during the days of the Revolution, and his retrospections all indicate that he envisioned personal negotiations with the "enlightened members" of the Soviet leadership leading to small steps of progress and also hoped for Yugoslav and Chinese support. However, Hungary's situation was essentially different from Yugoslavia's since no Soviet military was stationed in Yugoslavia. And after 1955, even the "more liberal" Soviet leaders were suspicious towards Imre Nagy. Finally, China strove for equality in their relationship with the Soviets but opposed open de-Stalinization and offered very limited support to the independent aspirations of the small East Central European countries.[41]

Secondly, Nagy envisioned the whole question as an internal affair of the Soviet bloc, by itself a realistic approach. However, even when the possibility arose, Nagy did not get involved in negotiations in a wider international forum. He thought that if this method had brought success for Tito and Gomulka, and as long as the Soviet leadership with Mikoian was willing to listen, he would be able to achieve results. His historical optimism returned. Trusting in the enlightened "within the family" settlement of the issue, Nagy did not even think about dealing with other factors of international life, such as the West. This one-sidedness clearly manifested in Nagy's personal diplomatic activities during the days of the threatening catastrophe following November 1, 1956. Except for the Austrian ambassador, he did not seek contact with any other western diplomat although the announcement of neutrality would have required the support of four great powers. It is a different issue how the diplomats would have received his initiatives. They had been very distrustful of Imre Nagy until the last days, according to the Budapest reports, and were aware of the realities of imperial and bloc politics. According to his own and others' statements in 1957, it was not the unresponsiveness of the UN towards Hungarian neutrality, but the demonstrative change in the Chinese attitude that made him recognize at the last moment the coming catastrophe.[42] However, even in the last moment before the intervention, Nagy trusted that he could stave off the inevitable danger with the help of the same negotiating tactics of earlier days. That is why he had long discussions into the wee hours of the night of November 3 with Deputy Foreign Secretary Malnasan's Romanian delegation. He tried to convince them of his position and asked Chief Secretary Gheorgiu-Dej to intervene for a personal summit for him with Khrushchev. Nagy asked Dej to mediate while ironically the day before Dej had offered Khrushchev the participation of Romanian troops in crushing the Hungarian Revolution.[43]

The outbreak of the Hungarian Revolution dispelled Imre Nagy's ideas about the evolutionary implementation of an independent foreign policy. There was hardly any chance for joint action with the possible East Central European partners during the state of emergency. In spite of that, Nagy still found the way to receive first hand information about the events of the Polish October from a Polish Party delegation that had arrived in Budapest.[44] For the moment, this reinforced his conviction that his tactics of negotiations might be successful. By utilizing the emergency caused by the Revolution, he would extort as many concessions as possible from the Soviets, who had landed in a very uncomfortable situation. By October 31 he wanted the Soviet troops stationed in Hungary to withdraw. At this time, issue of withdrawing from the Warsaw Pact came up. The latter could not have been a unilateral undertaking; it would have required bi- or multi-lateral negotiations. The issue of Soviet troop withdrawal came up between October 28 and 30, 1956, during heated discussions within the Soviet leadership about the Hungarian Revolution.[45] However, Soviet leaders did not even allude to the transformation of the Pact or discuss Hungarian withdrawal from it. On October 31, 1956, the Soviet leadership made the decision to go ahead with the armed suppression of the Hungarian Revolution. The alliance that Imre Nagy had counted on for "Danube Basin" cooperation against the Soviet bloc policy was not established either by peoples aspiring for freedom or by national politicians. Rather, it was concluded between November 1–3, 1956, by Khrushchev, the Stalinist leaders of the region, and the "independent" Mashal Tito according to the directions of the Moscow Party Presidium in order to suppress the Hungarian Revolution.[46] Following that, Nagy's foreign policy steps were meant to avert the threatening catastrophe. His decisions of November 1, 1956, to withdraw unilaterally from the Warsaw Pact and to declare neutrality were made as a result of the Soviet intervention. The decisions, however, were historical choices since the communist Imre Nagy identified with the interests of the nation against the interests and dogmas of the Party and against the interests of the international communist movement. Obviously he did not offer it as a symbolic, heroic gesture—although it became one. Even in a state of hopelessness, and within a narrow diplomatic scope, he tried to influence the situation hoping that the United Nations Organization would secure some kind of a "protective umbrella" for Hungary or that the UN would at least step up, forcing the Soviets to reconsider their actions.[47] None of these happened and he could not ward off the catastrophe of November 4.

After the defeat of the Revolution Nagy was interned in Snagov, Romania. There he summarized his views of the Hungarian Revolution in a series of notes. They would become very significant, albeit unfinished documents. Nagy's political testament has not yet been published.[48] The political analysis of the 1956 Hungarian Revolution is in the middle of this work.

Nagy's basic dilemma was the irreconcilable antagonism between his own reform ideas and revolution as an act. The reform plan included democratization of the political system and national independence. Yet the revolution raised the former in a radical way–demands for a multi-party system and free elections–and the latter as an immediate requirement. In his Snagov documents Nagy tried to face the issue of whether his foreign policy program of 1955–56 and his decisions during the emergency of the revolution were logical and reconcilable. For him, it was not only the consistency between the idea and the political action that was at stake, but also his own integrity as a politician, a thinker, and a human being in the shadow of a trial and possible death.

Early in the analysis, Nagy blamed the narrow-mindedness of the Hungarian and the Soviet Party leadership for the intensification of the situation. The problem was that they evaluated the mass movement as "counter-revolutionary" and wanted to suppress it by arms.

> Stemming from this situation...[came] the demands which characterized the general national resistance brought forth by the armed Soviet intervention: withdrawal of Soviet troops, termination of the Warsaw Pact, declaration of neutrality, and the establishment of internal democratization of the country by involving other democratic and socialist forces and parties besides the Hungarian Workers' Party.[49]

In reality, and he was also aware of it, the demands of the revolution were stated before the armed suppression and only a very one-sided analysis would attribute them to the intervention of the State Defense Office or that of the Soviets. At a later point in his writing and amid a more detailed elaboration, Nagy himself was inclined to take a different approach stating that "...the demands, which included the progressive content of the revolutionary uprising and the national war of independence, were tightly blended with the protection of socialist achievements and required the expansion of socialist democracy." They had been rooted in the wide population and in every layer of the nation for long years.[50]

In his notes, Nagy did not define the 1956 events in a way that he could have adhered to consistently. However, it is obvious that the essence of October for him was in trying to gain national independence. "National liberating revolution" is the most frequently used term. The lack of national independence stimulated democratic aspirations and demands because the use of the Soviet model characterized the introduction of an anti-democratic system into Hungary.

> Peoples and countries are inclined to accept socialism if it assures or grants national independence, sovereignty, and equal rights. The essence of the Hungarian tragedy is that the ideas of socialism and national independence came into conflict. The basic meaning of the Hungarian uprising was to search for and find a solution to this antagonism and to create the unity and complete harmony of the two.[51]

In the above statement the criticism of the regime and directions for the change became secondary. A different attempt to establish a definition illuminates the statement above, "...for the first time in history, the working class was in the forefront of the fight for national independence, sovereignty, and equal rights....A characteristic feature of this fight for independence was that the working class relied on the unity of the whole nation. This national unity embraced every class, layer, and political trend from communist through democratic to the extreme right reactionary."[52]

The last utterance, however, revealed a recognition that there was a divergence within the nation with respect to the goals of the revolution. The content of the "unity concept" would have been weakened by a discussion about political fragmentation. "The working class led the fight for national independence from the barricades of the people's democracy and socialist achievements. This was the second special feature of the events in Hungary." The third characteristic feature was the definition of the opposing party. Nagy stated that the revolution "was characterized by the fight between the Hungarian people, who rose up for their independence, and the armed forces of the Soviet Union. The Hungarian working class, as the main force of the fight for Hungarian independence, was confronted in an armed fight with the Soviet armed forces, definitely a tragic situation."[53]

Imre Nagy defined another important feature of the revolution using an older concept of his–the people's democratic transition to socialism. Both in 1947–49 and in 1953–54 it was clear that he considered this as a basically tactical idea, formulated for the post-fascist and post-war situation. He thought the idea held strategic value and, in every situation he considered favorable, he reverted to using it after periods when it was "in hiding" and only a latent concept. In 1957, however, he seemed to have gone beyond this stance.

> Undeniably, if the Hungarian Revolution had conquered,...if the revolution had achieved its social and national goals, a

> new form of transition from capitalism to socialism would have developed, that is a new type of democratic development towards socialism. It would have demonstrated essential differences from the similarly modeled people's democracies and the terms socialism, democracy, independence, sovereignty, etc.—the whole socialist terminology fully dehumanized by Stalinism, would have gained back their original, real Marxist content and essence.[54]

Even in Snagov the role of the Soviet Party leadership in the evolution of the crisis situation touched a neurotic nerve in Nagy. The Soviet leadership embodied both the leaders of an oppressive great power who did not care about Hungary and also a kind of supreme court of appeal, a just judge who can be moved by reasons, and who were the security and hope of the humanist renewal of the international communist movement, especially after the 20th Congress. November 4, 1956, however, completely shattered this antagonistic confidence. Only his outrage over the mistakes and sins of the Rákosi-Gerő group and the personal mistakes and sins of János Kádár surpassed his disappointment in the Soviets.

Nagy did not have the time to accomplish the historical analysis of the whole Soviet socialism and its introduction in East Central Europe. At several points in his notes Imre Nagy mentioned the Soviet interference in the Hungarian revolution and always unfavorably. After specifying the events leading to the interference, there was a noticeable change in the tone of notes. At the beginning of his notes, Nagy mentioned two motives: (1) the recurring and surviving Stalinist methods, despite the 20th Congress, and (2) Russian imperial ambitions (without ideological attributes).

> The way the Soviet party leadership analyzes and characterizes the Hungarian and Polish events...and the way they shrink back from admitting their mistakes...and if they set aside the imperial chauvinism—which appears under the pretext of socialism—so that they themselves would eliminate the ideological and political monopoly—to place the relationship among the socialist countries upon the five basic principles, not only on paper and belatedly, but in reality and immediately—so that they would not use the Hungarian events as a return back to the Stalinist methods; all show that the tragic events of Hungary do not signify the termination of a catastrophic period of socialism but introduce a series

> of similar or even graver national and international tragedies.[55]

He described the establishment of the Warsaw Pact a tool for implementing this policy. "...The Warsaw Pact is nothing else but a tool of Soviet imperial ambitions,...imposing the Soviet military dictatorship over the participating countries."[56]

The closing thought of the first quotation proved to be a prophecy of later events. The thought, however, was the expression of an urgent wish and was based on the conviction that coexistence between a great power and a small country was possible on the basis of Nagy's "five basic principles" in a de-Stalinized "nominal" socialism. However, Imre Nagy himself felt that if he pointed out the real moving force of Soviet politics, besides Stalinism, that is the interests of a war-winning power which had been pursuing an aggressive expansionist policy for centuries, this wish for coexistence would prove to be a superfluous magic formula. What kind of ideological change or "enlightenment" might alter aspirations of such deep historical roots? Just as at certain other points his train of thought was controversial, it happened here also and his approach to the problem was typical of him as well. Since this formulation would have endangered his own theoretical pillars, Nagy assigned imperial chauvinism to be one of the components of Stalinism, that is subordinated chauvinism to Stalinism, and at further points in the notes he only spoke about Stalinism. He did not leave any doubts about his own opinion; still he sustained the possibility that, theoretically due to some abstract recognition, the so often mentioned "proletarian internationalism" would prevail.

Nagy, while getting ready for his political trial, wanted to interpret his human, intellectual, and political careers as an organic union of messianic communist conviction and service to Hungarian independence aspirations. He was able to blend Hungarian patriotism and the historical optimism of a democratic-national communist. The events of the Hungarian revolution and his own personal fate, which he had probably envisioned, undermined this union. In his Snagov notes, Nagy mostly built on his theoretical explorations and firmly believed that he had proposed adequate solutions founded on a proper theoretical base. If he had founded his defense on the decisions of the 1956 Revolution, it would have been based on a short episode in his life. Yet in his notes he tried to reconstruct the 1956 revolution, his life's decisive event, so that it would verify or at least not contradict his earlier explorations and so that conflicting values would coincide in their final perspectives. Imre Nagy's historical role is marked out by his practical steps during the Revolution and his loyalty to them until his death, and not primarily by his theoretical explorations. To remain loyal, he could not have placed the events outside of the frame of life, not even if the reassuring union of values and decisions only lived in him.

Nagy's foreign political ideas were significant experiments meant to solve the questions of national independence and regional cooperation in a period when, apart from him, not many elaborated on these issues. His assumption that Soviet imperial policy was moving towards a democratic socialism, and thus might evolve into an integrative force or into a benevolent partner of independent small nations, proved to be faulty. Several elements of his concept–independence, regional cooperation, the perils of bloc policy–fit into centuries-old trends of Hungarian foreign political thinking. Its attractiveness is assured by the fact that Imre Nagy–in the history of Hungarian politics–represented his conviction with rare moral force and personal integrity literary until his final end.

NOTES

1. Imre Nagy, A nemzetközi kapcsolatok öt alapelve és külpolitikánk kérdése [Five Basic Principles of International Relations and the Question of our Foreign Policy], in *Vitairatok és beszédek 1955–1956* [Polemical Essays and Speeches, 1955-1956] (Magyar Füzetek, Paris, 1984), 208–224; In English, *Imre Nagy on Communism: In Defense of the New Course* (New York, Praeger, 1957).

2. Sándor Balogh, *Magyarország külpolitikája 1945–1950* [Hungary's Foreign Policy, 1945-1950] (Budapest, 1988); Mihály Fülöp, *A befejezetlen béke. A Külügyminiszterek Tanácsa és a magyar békeszerződés, 1947* [Unfinished Peace: The Council of Foreign Ministers and the Hungarian Peace Treaty] (Budapest, 1994); Stephen D. Kertész, *Between Russia and the West: Hungary and the Illusions of the Peacemaking, 1945–1947* (Notre Dame, Ind., 1984).

3. *Semlegesség. Illúziók és realitás. Tanulmányok* [Neutrality: Illusions and Reality. Essays] (Budapest, 1997).

4. For Nagy's pre-1956 political career see János M. Rainer, *Nagy Imre: Politikai életrajz I. 1896–1953* [Imre Nagy. Political Biography, 1896-1953] (Budapest, 1996).

5. Imre Nagy, Sötétség. Forradalom [Darkness. Revolution] (*Irkutszk*, June 12, 1920).

6. See *Nagy Imre a magyar parasztságról és a mezőgazdaságról 1928–1933. Dokumentumválogatás.* [Imre Nagy on Hungarian Peasantry and Agriculture, 1928–1933. Selected Documents], ed. and introduction József Sipos (Nyiregyháza, 1996).

7. János M. Rainer, *Nagy Imre,* 149–242.

8. See in Hungarian National Archive XX-5-h, Legfelsőbb Bíróság Népbírósági Tanácsa [People's Tribunal of the Supreme Court (Lb. Nb.) V-150,000, Nagy Imre és társai pere. Operatív iratok [Legal Proceedings of Imre Nagy and Accomplices] (Op.ir), vol. 24, 86–114.

9. Károly Urbán, Nagy Imre kontra Révai József, 1936. [Imre Nagy versus József Révai, 1936] (*Társadalmi Szemle*, 1991, 6), 83–94.

10. Imre Nagy, Dunavölgyi népek szabadságharca [The Freedom Fights of the Danube Valley Peoples] (*Új Hang*, Moscow, June 1938)

11. Ibid.

12. János M. Rainer, *Nagy Imre,* 285–288, 300–301.

13. See the records of the sub-committee. Tamás Stark, Út a békeszerződéshez [Road to the Peace Treaty] (*Századok*, 1993, 5–6), 781–851.

14. The Archive of the Political History Institute, 274.f.3/60. Jegyzőkönyv az MKP Politikai Bizottsága 1946. nov. 21-i üléséről [Minutes of the November 21, 1946, Session of the Political Committee of the Hungarian Communist Party].

15. Imre Nagy, Dunavölgyi agrárproblémák [Danube Basin Agrarian Problems] (*Közgazdaság*, March 30, 1947), in Imre Nagy, *Egy évtized: Válogatott beszédek és cikkek, 1945–1954* [One Decade: Selected Speeches and Articles, 1945–1954] (Budapest, 1954,1), 370.

16. Ibid., 371.

17. William O. McCagg, Jr, *Stalin Embattled, 1943–1948* (Detroit, 1978).

18. Minutes of Meetings Between Soviet and Hungarian Party and State Leaders, June 13–16, 1953. Published by György T. Varga (*Múltunk*, 1992, 2,3), 234–269.

19. Konzultációk. Dokumentumok a magyar és a szovjet pártvezetők két moszkvai találkozójáról 1954–1955-ben [Consultations: Documents about the Moscow Meetings of Hungarian and Soviet Party Leaders in 1954–1955], published by János M. Rainer and Károly Urbán (*Múltunk,* 1992,4), 141–148.

20. János M. Rainer, The Development of Imre Nagy as a Politician and a Thinker (*Contemporary European History*, 6, 3, 1997), 263–277.

21. *Magyar–Jugoszláv kapcsolatok 1956. Az állami- és pátkapcsolatok rendezése, az októberi felkelés és a Nagy Imre-csoport sorsa. Dokumentumok* [Hungarian–Yugoslav Connections, 1956: Settling State and Party Relations: the Fate of the October Uprising and that of Imre Nagy: Documents] ed. and introduction by József Kiss, Zoltán Ripp, István Vida (Budapest, 1996).

22. Hungarian National Archive XIX-A-2-v, Imre Nagy's Prime Ministerial Documents, box 71, III-240./1954: G. Gheorghiu-Dej's letter to Imre Nagy on October 6, 1954. (Dej's letter is in response to Nagy's initiative. Nagy's letter is so far unknown.)

23. Hungarian National Archive XX-5-h Lb. Nb. V-150.000. Nagy Imre és társai pere: Vizsgálati iratok [Legal Proceedings of Imre Nagy and His Comrades: Documents], vol. 7, 223; This page was omitted from the compilation that László

Kardos and Árpád Göncz smuggled to the West in 1957. It was published by the Strassbourg Hungarian Revolutionary Council in the same year, titled *A magyar nép védelmében* [In Defense of the Hungarian People].

24. Imre Nagy, *A magyar nép védelmében* [In Defense of the Hungarian People], 147. The quotation is from the essay, Nacionalizmus és proletárnemzetköziség [Nationalism and Proletarian Internationalism].

25. Ibid., 192, A marxizmus-leninizmus alkalmazásának néhány időszerű kérdése [Some Timely Questions of Applying Marxism-Leninism].

26. Ibid., 196.

27. Ibid., 197-198.

28. Ibid., 200-206. A két rendszer békés egymás mellett élése [Peaceful Coexistence of the Two Systems].

29. Imre Nagy, A nemzetközi kapcsolatok öt alapelve és külpolitikánk kérdése [Five Principles of International Relations and the Question of Our Foreign Policy] in *A magyar nép védelmében. Vitairatok és beszédek, 1955-1956* [In Defense of the Hungarian People: Treatises and Speeches, 1955-1956] (Magyar Füzetek, Paris, 1984), 208-224.

30. Ibid., 226-228.

31. Ibid., 231.

32. Ibid., 233.

33. Ibid., 235.

34. Ibid., 236-237.

35. Ibid., 239-240.

36. Ibid., 236.

37. Ibid., 238-239.

38. Ibid., 238.

39. Ibid., 237.

40. Tibor Hajdu, Szovjet diplomácia Magyarországon Sztálin halála előtt és után [Soviet Diplomacy in Hungary Before and After Stalin's Death] in *Magyarország és a nagyhatalmak a 20. században: Tanulmányok* [Hungary and the Great Powers in the 20th Century: Essays] ed. and introduction Ignác Romsics (Budapest, 1995), 195-201; Leo Gluchowski, Poland 1956. Khrushchev, Gomulka, and the 'Polish October.' (*Cold War International History Project Bulletin*, 5, Spring 1995,1), 38-49; SSSR i Polsa: oktyabr 1956-go. Postanovleniya i rabochie zapisi Prezidiuma CK KPSS. Publ. pdg. Ye. D. Orehova, V. T. Sereda. (Istoricheski Arkhiv, 1996, 5-6), 178-191.

41. For the attitude of Soviet politicians towards Nagy, Konzultációk. Dokumentumok a magyar és a szovjet pártvezetők két moszkvai találkozójáról 1954-1955-ben [Consultations: Documents about the Moscow Meetings of Hungarian and Soviet Party Leaders in 1954-1955], published by János M. Rainer and Károly Urbán (*Múltunk,* 1992, 4), 141-148; for Mikoian's July 1956 standpoint, *Hiányzó lapok 1956 történetéből: Dokumentumok a volt SZKP KB Levéltárából* [Missing Pages from the Archive of the Defunct Central Committee of the Soviet Communist Party], selected and introduction, Vjacheslav Sereda and Aleksandr Stikalin (Budapest, 1993), 21-82, 40-65; for China's role, Chen Jian, Peking és az 1956-os magyar válság [Beijing and the 1956 Hungarian Crisis] (*Rubicon,* 1996,8-9), 56-60.

42. After the New China Press declared solidarity with the aspirations of the Hungarian and Polish governments on November 1, 1956, Nagy was informed about the editorial, "Hail to the Grand Unity of the Socialist Countries" of the *Jenmin Jipao* late afternoon November 3. The article wrote about a "handful of Hungarian conspirators" who "try to reinstate capitalism" in Hungary and try "to break up the unity of socialist states." See Miklós Molnár, *Egy vereség diadala* [Triumph of a Defeat] (Paris-New Jersey, 1988), 181.

43. For Romania's role see István Vida, Miért Románia? A Nagy Imre csoport deportálása [Why Romania? The Deportation of the Imre Nagy Group] (*Rubicon,* 1993, 7), 26; Romanian documents related to the Hungarian Revolution, *1956. Explozia. Perceptii romane, iugoslave si sovietice aupre evenimentelor din Polonia si Ungaria.* ed., Corneliu Mihai Lungu, Mihai Retegan (Bucuresti, 1996).

44. Archive of the Supreme Court of the Hungarian Republic–Imre Nagy, *Gondolatok, emlékezések. Snagov, 1957.* [Thoughts and Memories: Snagov 1957], manuscript, 17-18; János Tischler, A lengyel pártvezetés és az 1956-os forradalom [The Polish Party Leadership and the 1956 Revolution] in *Évkönyv III, 1994* [Almanac, III, 1994] (Budapest, 1956-os Intézet [1956 Institute], 1994), 179-195.

45. Imre Nagy's October-November, 1956, foreign policy is analyzed in detail, Csaba Békés, Hungarian Neutrality in 1956, 111-131; Discusses it within a wider context, Csaba Békés, *Az 1956-os magyar forradalom a világpolitikában: Tanulmány és válogatott dokumentumok* [The 1956 Hungarian Revolution in World Politics: Essay and Selected Documents] (Budapest, 1996), 183.

46. *Döntés a Kremlben 1956. A szovjet pártelnökség vitái Magyarországról.* [Decision in the Kremlin, 1956: Debates of the Soviet Party Leadership about Hungary] ed. Sereda Vyacheslav and János M. Rainer (Budapest, 1996).

47. Csaba Békés, *Hungarian Neutrality in 1956*, 118-122.

48. His daughter and heiress denies permission for the publication of the document.

49. Imre Nagy, *Thoughts,* 1.

50. Ibid., 50-51.

51. Ibid., 54.

52. Ibid., 33.

53. Ibid.,

54. Imre Nagy, *Thoughts*, 53.

55. Imre Nagy, *Thoughts,* 17.

56. Imre Nagy, *Thoughts,* 19.

"WHY DID THE DANUBIAN FEDERATION PLANS FAIL?"

PÉTER HANÁK

Not long before his death Oszkár Jászi posed and responded to this question in his last essay.[1] The answer was that the "Danubian Federation" was too rational. At the beginning of the century it was an influential insightful theory, a late offshoot of the Enlightenment. The Danubian people should coexist peacefully within a federation rather than experience unending fights. This is an *a priori* consideration which should be so obvious that all people could understand it. Yet this rational utopia failed in 1918 because certain historical conditions militated against its success.

At the end of the war "the surrounding triumphant little states did not have a federation in mind; instead they wanted to extort any possible advantage." Contemporaneously, "extreme nationalism" survived in defeated areas while the idea of federation became alien to the public. The Monarchy had died an early death in the sentiments of its peoples even before it was dissolved politically. "The Empire including Hungary collapsed because every people's historical tradition viewed the experiences of other peoples with hostility and hatred."

Jászi's statements are still valid today. Yet from a certain distance and putting the federative plans into a wider historical perspective, research on the causes of the failure might be initiated on a different gauge. Why have these aspirations never been implemented even though they have existed in the political literature of all the peoples? There was rarely a concensus among participating parties concerning constitutional order of the federation. Only on rare occasions, such as in Yugoslavia, was concensus established. Most noteworthy are the periods just after World War I and, seemingly more extensively and firmly, after World War II. Yet the federation was never firmly established, leaving a major experiment to end in failure. The question arises whether establishing a multiethnic state or a permanent federation in this region is possible at all. Is a Danubian or Central European federation nothing more than an intellectual concept at odds with the reality of history?

Some distinction ought to be made between confederative plans, such as Czartoryski's Danubian Confederation draft from the summer of 1848, and federative plans, such as the Kremsier Constitution passed after lengthy negotiations by the Austrian *Reichstag*. Confederative plans include those aiming to establish a federation of states without prior existence, such as Kossuth's confederative plan of 1862. In contrast, federative plans wish to transform an existing formation into federation by reforming constitutional law. The question of historicity is not worth raising since both approaches were new orientations within the discipline of the history of ideas. However, investigating the reasons for the failures to achieve reforms in this century remains a pressing issue.

It is worth reflecting upon historical periods, situations, trends, and groups in trying to understand when and where federative plans emerged. They usually appeared amid political crises when the Monarchy was under great threat of dissolution or had already been dissolved. Hence, such plans became more prominent when the threat of a power vacuum was imminent and it had not yet been decided which great power would define the new Central European order–by the grace of God, on behalf of a higher civilization, or in the name of universal salvation. Federative plans were usually promulgated by the oppressed and the defeated after wars or freedom lost. Victors have never initiated fraternity because federative ideology was a compensation for defeat. Radical reformers also raised the idea of federation since it would serve as a new foundation for national and social reorganization. The weakness of these plans was that they depended on implementation either by a rational agreement among the various nationalities or by a monarch. Aurel Popovici's 1906 *Gross-Österreich* plan depended on Crown-Prince France Ferdinand, while Lammasch, Renner, and Jászi all placed high expectations on the rational workings of a representative constitutional body.

Federative plans were not born under lucky stars. Planning and execution, rationality and reality were not in harmony. Looking at the federative plans and experiments of the past one hundred years, the dissonance is evident. Why did not the history of our region encourage rationality? Why could not rational thinking and "ample holy will" realize peaceful co-existence?

At the end of the 20th century, in a time of regime changes and in a moment of historical review, the question is again raised: Why did not a confederation or loose alliance materialize in our region either in the last decades of, or during the dissolution of, the Monarchy, or after World War II, or after the bitter experiences of the Soviet occupation and dictatorship? It appears that the transformation of the Monarchy, which was supposed to be democratic and revolutionary, has been firmly conservative and anti-democratically intolerant towards small countries and nations of this area. Not only debatable theories or historical analyses, but also experiences might respond to the question raised—the terms of an institutionalized Central-European integration have not yet come to maturity.

First of all, economic conditions underpinning integration are absent. While at the end of the 20th century economic integration prevails even in our divided continent, in Central Europe the terms for integration are less pervasive than they used to be in the Monarchy. In the common market of the Monarchy of the turn of the century, an effective free exchange of capital, goods, technology, and manpower existed. The strict market, working by the principle of controlled comparative cost-benefit, prevailed and production took place where the cost of producing was lowest, an economic factor that spontaneously led to complementary industries. Although this kind of division of labor entailed the conservation of a traditional structure, national entrepreneurs were still able to develop specialties. For example, Hungary excelled in electrical and chemical industries.

Despite significant integrating advances, gradual grade differences remained all the way through the Monarchy. In an ethnically more homogeneous country it would have caused such pronounced economic antagonisms as the *Mezzogiorno* in Italy or the River Elbe demarcation line in Germany. However, in the multinational Monarchy, the regional antagonisms took the form of immediate nationalistic tensions and aggravated ethnic differences. It was evident that economic factors were not a firm base for political integration. The small statehood *Kleinstaaterei* concept dramatically weakened regional integration. An irrational autocratic economic policy prevailed. Years later Comecon (Council for Mutual Economic Assistance), the compulsory integration instituted by the Soviet Union, tore apart existing economic connections and it also rendered many traditional international economic policies dysfunctional.

Social conditions favoring federation were equally absent. A strong civil society with a middle class of autonomous individuals is the social base needed for permanent and peaceful coexistence. Unlike the West, in Central Europe there is a significant distinction between an aristocratic upper middle class and a populist lower middle class. A functioning civil society also means having a class-conscious working class trained in skills and solidarity. It appears that the social conditions for integration were more favorable at the turn of the century than at the present time.

The possibilities of a federation were also more reflectively considered than at the turn of the century. Both the Social-Democrats and the Bourgeois Radicals aimed to secure and operate the national autonomy while they also regulated the relationship between the central power and lesser political entities. Consolidation of new nation states was the central question of post-World War I reconstruction, with declaration of minority rights only a secondary consideration.

The social deficit was also heavy. Contradictions between the political system and the attitudes of the people proved to be major obstacles in the way of integration. Federative planmakers usually ignored international power relations and evaded any negative signs from the great powers. Nineteenth century confederative plans usually assumed the overthrow of the Habsburg Monarchy, as well as the Russian Empire, and counted upon either the support or benevolent neutrality of Western powers. At the end of World War I planmakers believed that because of its advantages, a new Danubian Federation would make the Poles give up their parts of the German Empire in order to join the Federation along with the South Slavs. Within the Danubian Federation, Illyria would unify Serbs, Croats, and Slovenes and "would solve the issue *sub specie aeternitatis* which had set Europe aflame." The Federation would then attract Romania, Bulgaria, and Greece because "one cannot fathom a more rational and unconstrained policy which would make them join than the Danubian Federation." Similar confidence prevailed at the end of World War II. It was believed that the confederation of Central and South Eastern European small states would be favored by the Allies.

The unsolved issue of minority autonomy was always an obstacle to regional integration. Within successor states there were millions within minority populations. In some sectors roles reversed when minorities became majorities. The direction of antagonisms shifted, but the fact that their relations were still antagonistic remained. The denial of minority autonomy and the curtailment of rights, notably among Hungarian and German irredentists, also obstructed political integration, especially in Romania and Yugoslavia where attitudes towards minorities were less progressive than elsewhere in the ex-Monarchy.

With the dissolution of the Monarchy the chances for a federation of sovereign small states of the region disappeared. Rivalry among successor states incited a paroxysm of nationalism and undermined federative ideas. Half a century of fascist and communist dictatorships reinforced prejudice, fixed enemy images, and nurtured xenophobia.

Recent research shows that in the 14th and 16th centuries amidst increasing Turkish threats the idea of interdependence prevailed among the leaders of the region. Christian solidarity existed among Czechs, Poles, Hungarians, Romanians, and the South Slavs. Under the first few centuries of Habsburg rule and the religious wars of counter-reformation this Central-European Christian solidarity declined. The ideological penetrations of the Age of Enlightenment and the institutional connections of freemasonry briefly awoke solidarity and interest in reform among the peoples of the Monarchy. But the idea of sharing a joint fate petered out under national romanticism and the mutual jealousy of nationalisms of the following period. The opinions and beliefs of Palacky, Rieger, László Teleki, Eötvös, and Kossuth and the later writings of Jászi, Hodža, and Popovici were forgotten or ignored by the majority of the leadership coming to power in 1918. Josef Helfert was the last to demand that a uniform patriotic history be taught all over the Monarchy. Crown Prince Rudolf's protegé Moritz Szeps was the last editor to publish a *schwarzgelb* paper with the comically pathetic Ten Commandments: "Thou shalt not have new beliefs but the belief in the old, the only, and undivided Austrian Empire...; Thou shalt not create new gods, new programs, new state conceptions and thou shalt be devoted to good old Austria." Regulation of the common army reflected the same spirit by designating unconditional loyalty towards the Emperor, a token of the unified diversity of the Monarchy. Helfert and Szeps can not be faulted for the nostalgic overtones of their writings. Their mistake was to juxtapose superannuated dynastic patriotism and pre-nationalistic loyalty to the Emperor next to the new, dynamic nationalisms. Neither pre-nationalistic loyalty nor post-nationalistic internationalism could supercede nationalistic feelings. Between outdated dynastic loyalty and premature internationalism, no regional community spirit evolved. Both the Austrian and Hungarian civic education were also responsible for intellectual and emotional partiality. The dynastic bias of Austrian public education did not counter-balance the resistance of other nationalities, while the nationalism of Hungarian education even provoked it. Both the deficient quality and assimilative content of civic education obstructed attempts at federative transformation. Ironically, in the inter-war period, the roles reversed with Romanian, Serbian, Czech, and Slovak public education obstructing and destroying Central-European integration.

Weakness in the aforementioned conditions, or even their absence answers the question raised in the introduction about why a confederation did not arise. Yet a second, very timely question remains. Lacking the economic, social, and political-ideological conditions necessary for integration, can there be anything meaningful or sensible done to advance a Central-European union and a united Europe, or does it remain only a dream? To answer this, let us contemplate whether our past and present advocates of Central European confederation understood what the political structure of Europe rested on during the past millenia. During this period, following major social and political change, the political system fell apart into its smallest constituents. It happened at the dissolution of the Roman and the German–Roman Empires and, partially, after the French Revolution. Disintegration to the smallest regional and/or ethnic units, however, stopped somewhere at the borders of Central-Europe, and remained incomplete both in 1918 and in 1945.

If freedom and equality prevail, fraternity may accompany them so that there is harmony among the three ideals postulated by the French Revolution, something neither that revolution nor the succeeding two centuries could achieve.

It has been a precarious existence in our region since 1918. And, the threatening instability created by the present power vacuum point to the following alternatives: insistence on an autotelic and discriminating political state in a multi-national area, leading to constant conflicts or even wars; or the opportunity to raise a very timely question, even though the situation was unfavorable and the conditions immature in 1989 for a confederation to arise when communist rule collapsed in Central Europe. It is still difficult to give an unambiguous and well-grounded response. Obviously, the economy of the region during the past fifty years has developed while society has become more homogeneous. But the economy is still far behind the West and its civil society is less unified. On the one hand a shared fate among generations who suffered and survived fascism, World Wars, and communism has generated a kind of democratic solidarity. On the other hand, it was clear that the ideology of "socialist patriotism" was only a cover for Soviet imperial nationalism. Still, it is evident that the legal/semilegal Polish Solidarity, Czech Charter 77, and the members of the Hungarian democratic opposition were all connected by intellectual affinities, and that these movements awakened the hope of post-transitional cooperation and regional alliance among intellectuals. Yet they can all be criticized for the belief that the power of rational thinking can conquer centuries old hostilities and prejudices.

After the profound changes of 1989 ancient nationalism, motivated by fear and suspicion, reemerged in the region swamping any recognition of the requirements needed by an up-to-date Europe. Hence the Visegrád initiative, a promising program of an Alps–Adriatic alliance, along with the plan for a customs union broke down among keen competition by several countries for support from the European Union.

In the meantime, the small states of Central Europe have suffered several fiascoes. Both the cautious West and the contentious squabbling Middle East have reversed their policies due to the fateful off-balance of East Central Europe.

ASSETS OF CENTRAL EUROPE

Although Central Europe has recently missed an opportunity for regional integration, it still has the possibility of joining a wider European integration and from there to proceed towards an intracontinental association. In retrospect the federative plans of the past proved to be only utopias with powerless leaders. In the first half of the 20th century in spite of pressing historical motivation and rational federative plans, an amalgamation proved unrealistic. The immature concept of multi-nationalism was to be applied to an existing nationalistic small nationhood which firmly resisted any rationality. Yet at the end of the century, amidst the turmoil of continental integration, the possibility of integration has increased. It seems to be contradicted by today's spectacular political dissolutions: an explosive dissolution of Yugoslavia, the bitter separation of the Czechs and Slovaks, and a diminishing Russian Empire. These all indicate that disintegration is the prevailing tendency in this region, threatening any possible Central European federation as well as the Eastern Empire. However, contrary to this perspective there exists a realistic counter-alternative by viewing the present disintegration as an integral part and phase of the millenial past.

On our continent centralization and disintegration have periodically alternated. Changes and experiences break old social and political systems at a climactic point. For example, the dissolution of the Roman Empire was followed by the rise of small Christian kingdoms. Then it took a few centuries for the Carolingian Empire to evolve into the German–Roman Empire. At the beginning of modern times another disintegration into nation states occurred. This process climaxed in the 19th century in Western Europe, but was delayed in the Eastern and South-Eastern regions of the continent. After World War I the Habsburg Monarchy and the Ottoman Empire dissolved into smaller multi-national units, while the czarist colossus was salvaged by the Soviet socialist revolution. Thereafter the monolithic Soviet empire impeded disintegration. However, the process in Central Europe now seems to be complete.

Key questions remain: How long will the euphoria of sovereignty hold in Slovakia, Croatia, and other places? Will nationalistic emotionalism provide economic and political rationality? Will disintegration into smaller entities prevail or will these entities merge into the European Union? Furthermore, in the event that European integration continues, will external and internal motivations for Central European cooperation persist?

Several open questions and an unsettling alternative remain to be explored. One route, the cult of small nation states, will lead to seclusion, isolation, intolerance, discrimination, permanent ethnic conflicts, and finally to destabilization of the middle region of Europe. Another route, which is an untrodden path, assumes that the region is experiencing a profound democratic turn with a developed bourgeois mentality leading to European integration, yet where ethnic and regional diversities are maintained and a looser form of regional federation might develop.

Central Europe is neither an indisputable reality nor a visionary utopia; it is a historical alternative. Jászi's question about why the

Danubian Federation Plans failed is no longer vital. Today the question is how to accomplish peaceful Central European coexistence and cooperation under changed historical circumstances.

NOTE

1. Látóhatár, 1955.

PRESENT AND THE FUTURE

THE PROTECTION OF NATIONAL AND ETHNIC MINORITIES' RIGHTS IN HUNGARY (1989–1997)

JUDIT BODA PÁLOK

October 23, 1989, constitutes a milestone in Hungarian history: This was the date when the Hungarian Republic was proclaimed. On the same day the Hungarian Parliament instituted the Constitutional Amendment which changed the nature of the political regime leading to the establishment of a constitutional state. The legal protection of national and linguistic minorities was recognized, and their nation-forming status was established. The Constitutional Amendment recognizes the right of national and linguistic minorities to self-identity, including the right to their own culture, their own language and the right to receive education in their mother tongue.[1] The purpose of minority protection derives from the concept that minorities constitute a special bridge between countries and nations. The protection of their rights is neither a favor granted by the majority, nor the privilege of the minority, but rather belongs inherently to minority groups.

Due to the multiple political and public administration tasks generated by the change in regime, the work of drafting a specific law for the regulation of national and ethnic minority rights did not speed up until the fall of 1990. As the final outcome of a drafting process that extended over three years, the Hungarian Parliament passed by a majority of 96.5% the "Act on the Rights of National and Ethnic Minorities" (the National Minorities Act) on July 7, 1993.[2] The underlying premise of the whole legislative process was that the treatment of the minority issue presupposes an environment of trust. There can be no significant legislative work on regulations pertaining to minorities without the participation of the minority groups involved. Influenced by this concept, the codification procedure was truly unprecedented. The text of the Act was a result of negotiations among legislators, the representatives of minority groups, the Hungarian National and Ethnic Minorities Round Table, and specialists in the field. Due consideration was given to all their ideas and feasible propositions.

INDIVIDUAL AND COLLECTIVE MINORITY RIGHTS

In Hungary, the protection of national and ethnic minority rights is prevalent in a variety of laws and regulations. Some of the most outstanding examples are the Constitution, the National Minorities Act, laws and regulations on local public administrative governments, laws dealing with the election of representatives to local government and city mayors, the Act on Public Education, the Act on Higher Education, the Act on Radio and Television, and the Criminal Code.

According to the Constitution, national and ethnic minorities are part of the popular sovereignty; they are nation-creating factors. They have a constitutional right to participate in public life, to maintain their culture, to use their mother tongue, to receive education in their language and to use their names as they appear in the vernacular. National and ethnic minorities are entitled to establish minorities governments on the local and national level.[3] The Constitution adjudicates these rights based on communities. However, it also honors both the collective rights of minorities, as well as the individual rights of minority members.

The National Minorities Act assures that long-term security for the intellectual enrichment and linguistic and cultural survival of national minorities is in place. It can open new horizons for their participation in public life and in exercising public powers.

The Act is in concord with international agreements and documents regulating human rights and the rights of minorities. International documents on minorities adopted in the past few years all urge special measures in this matter. The Hungarian National Minorities Act may be considered the specific embodiment of these general commitments; it is the implementation of the "special measures" urged. During the drafting process of the law, legislators tried to fulfil as best possible the obligations and proposals contained in international legal and political documents. The Act contains multiple instances of solutions that can serve as examples for international practices. In its "Preamble" the law enumerates all the documents that the legislators relied on most consistently in the codification process.[4]

This piece of legislation is well suited to the specific situations facing Hungarian national and ethnic minorities. The following two tables summarize the total number and ratio of minorities in Hungarian society:

Table 1
Breakdown of population by nationality (1941–1990)

Year	Total	Hungarian	Slovak	Romanian	Croat	Serb	Slovenian, Wendic	German	Roma Gypsy	Other
1941	9,316,074	8,919,868	16,677	7,565	4,177	3,629	2,058	302,198	27,033	33,869
1949	9,204,799	9,104,640	7,808	8,500	4,106	4,190	666	2,617	37,598	34,674
1960	9,961,044	9,837,275	14,340	12,326	14,710*	3,888	...	8,640	56,121	13,744
1980	10,709,463	10,638,974	9,101	8,874	13,895	2,805	1,731	11,310	6,404	16,369
1990	10,374,823	10,142,000	10,459	10,740	13,570	2,905	1,930	30,824	142,683	19,640

*Including Slovenians and Wendic
Source: Central Bureau of Statistics (KSH). "Living Conditions of the National Minorities," Budapest, KSH 1995.

Table 2
Breakdown of Population by Mother Tongue (1900–1990)

Year	Total	Hungarian	Slovak	Romanian	Croat	Serb	Slovenian, Wendic	German	Roma Gypsy	Other
1900	6,854,415	5,890,999	192,227	26,975	68,161	24,254	7,922	604,751	5,662	33,464
1910	7,612,114	6,730,299	165,317	28,491	62,018	26,248	6,915	553,179	9,799	29,848
1920	7,986,875	7,155,979	141,877	23,695	58,931	17,132	6,087	550,062	6,989	26,123
1930	8,685,109	8,000,335	104,786	16,221	47,332	7,031	5,464	477,153	7,841	18,946
1941	9,316,074	8,655,798	75,877	14,142	37,885	5,442	4,816	475,491	18,640	27,983
1949	9,204,799	9,076,041	25,988	14,713	20,423	5,158	4,473	22,455	21,387	14,161
1960	9,961,044	9,786,038	30,690	15,787	33,014*	4,583	...	50,765	25,633	14,534
1970	10,322,099	10,166,237	21,176	12,624	21,855	7,989	4,205	35,594	34,957	17,462
1980	10,709,463	10,579,898	16,054	10,141	20,484	3,426	3,142	31,231	27,915	17,172
1990	10,374,823	10,222,529	12,745	8,730	17,577	2,953	2,627	37,511	48,072	22,079

*Including Slovenians and Wendic
Source: Central Bureau of Statistics (KSH). "Living Conditions of the National Minorities," Budapest, KSH 1995.

These minorities are in most cases immigrant ethnic groups that have coexisted with Hungarians and other nationalities for several centuries. They arrived in Hungary during a period when nation-forming processes were still in progress in their lands of origin, and did not share a unified national language. The traditional minority communities of villages and small communities disappeared as a result of the forced "Hungarianization" prevalent at the end of the 19th century and the period between the two World Wars, the expatriation and exchange of population following the World War II, discrimination against Southern Slav ethnic groups in the 1950's, the waves of urbanization and industrialization of the past decades, and misfired policies of community and educational development. Minorities are now characterized by dispersed and ethnically mixed patterns of settlement. Mixed marriages abound. As a result of all of the above, we are witnessing the advanced assimilation of minorities, as best reflected in their language use.

One of the basic aims of the National Minorities Act, therefore, is the active protection of minorities, namely the establishment of conditions allowing for the halting or reversing of the assimilation process. The decision regarding assimilation is always individual and never dictated in Hungary. Active protection means that the state cannot be indifferent to, but rather must embrace a policy, and establish the legal institutions, that delays or hinders renouncement of an individual's current self-identity (assimilation decision).

In the National Minorities Act—contrary to the European codification efforts for the protection of minorities—Hungary has been able to give a definition of national and ethnic minorities.[5] Under the Act, every Hungarian citizen or community of citizens living in Hungary shall be termed a minority if he or it considers themselves as belonging to a national/ethnic minority. The elements that define a minority are: a community of people residing in the area of the Hungarian Republic for at least one hundred years and currently existing in numerical minority in Hungarian society. Its members are all Hungarian citizens, only differing from the rest of the population in language, culture, or traditions. Furthermore, they retain a sense of community, driven by the effort to preserve their culture and traditions, as well as the expression and protection of their historic community values.

Currently the following communities qualify as national minorities in Hungary: Bulgarians, Gypsy/Roma People, Greeks, Croats, Poles, Germans, Armenians, Romanians, Transcarpathian Ukrainians (Ruthens), Serbs, Slovaks, Slovenians and Ukrainians. The list can be added to, if there are at least 1000 qualifying citizens of voting age from the same minority group who sign a public plea to the effect and present it to the President of the Hungarian Parliament. The law does not apply to refugees, immigrants, expatriates, and displaced persons residing in Hungary.

One of the fundamental principles of the law is the recognition of the right to national and ethnic identity as a basic human right. It is the legal right of both individuals and communities of minorities. From the aspect of individual minority rights, it is the exclusive and inalienable right of a person to consider and proclaim himself as belonging to a national or ethnic minority. From the aspect of minority communities, on the other hand, it denotes the inalienable collective rights of individual minority citizens to protect, strengthen, and transmit the identity of their community. The right to free choice of identity as a human right is basically the legitimacy of people to choose and embrace their ethnicity based on personal determination alone.

The Preamble to the law states that individual minority rights and community rights of minorities are fundamental freedoms. The legal practice of individual and community rights enumerated by the National Minorities Act cannot be impeded by state administration entities, while the guarantees to implementation of these rights are mainly of legal nature.

It is one of the fundamental components of the law that the rights of minorities are to benefit individuals as well as communities. The prevalence of these rights is guaranteed by detailed regulations until community rights are recognized on the international level.

One of the specifics of the Hungarian legislation recognizes that respect of individual minority rights will not by itself accomplish the global legal protection of minority communities. Acceptance, preservation and cultivation of a national identity is not exclusively an individual right. Rather, it also belongs to the community since the practice of a national identity is a collective issue. If we recognize that minority life is to be protected by a number of special/additional rights on the individual level, the same cannot be disputed on the collective level. Therefore, the appropriateness of legal protection to these communities is not to be disputed.

Individual minority rights are:

–the right to national or ethnic identity;
–the right to secretly and anonymously register their national identity during the national census;
–the right to honor traditions, keep up family ties, and celebrate family holidays in the vernacular;
–the right to register one's name and surname as well as that of one's children as they would appear in the vernacular;

–the right to learn, preserve, enrich, and transmit the mother tongue, history, culture and traditions;
–the right to partake in instruction and education in the mother tongue;
–the right to protection of personal data relating to national identity;
–the right to establish and maintain relations freely with the state and community institutions of one's mother country and linguistic nation, or national minorities of other countries; and
–the right to participate in public life.

The prerequisite of the establishment and survival of a community–and even more so in the case of minorities–is freedom of assembly. The Hungarian law on public assembly, the law on political parties, and the National Minorities Act all state the following: "Participation in public life of persons belonging to minorities shall not be restricted. Under Constitutional ruling, minority individuals may establish associations, political parties, or other organizations for the expression and protection of their rights."

Community minority rights are:

–the right to maintain its minority identity;
–the right to preserve, enrich, and develop its mother tongue and historic traditions;
–the right to establish social organizations;
–the right to have public radio and television programs in the national and ethnic minority language;
–the right to propose preschool and grade school education partially or wholly in the vernacular language;
–the right to develop its own cultural, educational, and scientific institutional network;
–the right to celebrate holidays and social events;
–the right to preserve architectural, cultural, religious mementos, and to use its own emblems;
–the right to Parliamentary representation.

The right to the establishment of autonomous minority governments is one of the most noteworthy of community minority rights.

MINORITIES AND THE STATE ADMINISTRATION

The situation of national and ethnic minorities in Hungary fundamentally differs from that of other nationality groups commonly referred to in Europe. In most cases even the smaller, closely settled minority groups, such as the Slovenians or Romanians, live spread out over a vast area. For this reason–and because of the characteristic settlement patterns, the existence of mixed marriages, and the lack of linguistic homogeneity–it was not feasible to establish a regional autonomy system (an internationally recognized autonomy model) as the means for enforcing the rights of national and ethnic minorities in Hungary. This is why the National Minorities Act had to blend together local, individual, and functional autonomies with the local and national minority government systems in order to enforce collective minority rights. Thus, this Act creates a new form of minorities government unique in Europe.

Starting with the fact that national/ethnic minorities form part of society, the National Minorities Act integrates local autonomous minority governments into the already functioning local public administration system. A community is eligible to form a minority government if the majority of the resident population belongs to a group which in state wide sense is minority, or, even though they are not a majority, when their numbers are considerable. Finally, the Act also takes into account the "sporadic minorities," i.e., individuals in communities with a relatively small number of residents from a different nationality.

The life of a community is enriched by the coexistence of different cultures. Although a community could find foreign partners to help it, autonomous governments could also help in bringing local values to the surface. By the good offices of the autonomous governments, regional, bilateral, and multilateral relations could flourish. Also, they could share in implementing the agenda of the community. In addition, the system provides an administrative plenum where dialogue about minority issues and expressions of opposing or conflicting viewpoints can be aired. The autonomous government model is only a tool; it is the means by which minorities express, assert, and protect their rights. Ultimately it contributes to their survival as a minority and promotes the accomplishment of their social and political integration. The basic task of the minority governments is the representation and protection of minority rights. It is the exclusive right of local autonomous governments to define their organization and rules of procedure, their name and emblems, awards conferred and local holidays observed. The only thing the local government can determine in their resolutions is the budgeted support for the autonomies. For their turn, local authorities can decide how they want to make use of the allocated assets. They draw up their budget and divide the resources obtained from the local government.

Under the National Minorities Act, autonomous governments have a more effective access to public administration than other types of associations. They hold consenting rights in local legislative procedures, especially in issues pertaining to their culture and education. The Act grants the consenting right to the autonomous governments when the regulations being debated on the local level influence their lives directly, are connected to public education on the local level, or pertain to the media, preservation of traditions, cultural issues, or the collective usage of their language. They can also exercise this right when decisions are prepared concerning the appointment of principals of minorities' educational institutions or that involve the schooling of minority groups. The right of consent means that the local government can only finalize legislation in the issues mentioned above once the autonomous government has expressed its consent with the proposed decision. Minority governments have a variety of other legal tools to secure their rights and influence the decision-making process. They may file formal requisitions of information, issue proposals, present recommendations, and present objections. The agencies addressed by these legal measures have the obligation to consider in merit the issues discussed.

The establishment of the autonomous governments has been greatly facilitated by the 1994 Amendment to the Act on the Election of Local Representatives and City Majors. This law applied positive discrimination in the case of minority voters by requiring a considerably smaller number of votes for the nomination of a majority candidate. As for the operation of the autonomous governments, it was considerably simplified by the 1994 Revision to the Law on Local Governments.

During the municipal elections held on December 11, 1994, autonomous minority governments were also elected in Hungary for the first time. In the 1,850 communities of the country with substantial minority population, 679 autonomous governments were formed. In the capital city, eight national minorities chose to be represented by an autonomous government. There was a second round of elections held on November 19, 1995, for communities that had not held elections the previous December or whose government had been dissolved. As a result, the number of autonomous minority governments rose to 817 (see Table 3).

Table 3
Number of autonomous minority governments
Combined total of the December 11, 1994, and
November 19, 1995, elections

Name of minority group	Total minority governments	Name of minority group	Total minority governments
Bulgarian	4	Romanian	11
Gypsy/Roma	477	Transcarpathian	
Greek	6	Ukrainians (Ruthenians)	1
Croat	57	Serb	19
Polish	7	Slovak	51
German	162	Slovenian	6
Armenian	16	*Total:*	817

Source: "The Election of National and Ethnic Minorities Autonomous Governments in the Capital and on the National Level," 1995, Min. of Int. Affairs, "OVI Választási füzetek 27. sz." (Election booklets No. 27), and the "Report of the National Election Work-Group on the November 19, 1995 election," 1995, Min. of Int. Affairs.

It is known that the rights of national and ethnic minorities may be represented by regulating the decision-making process even without actual representation of minorities in the legislative body. The prerequisite for this is the constitutionally supported establishment of national personal autonomies and their mainstreaming into the legislative process. Eleven national minorities residing in Hungary (with the exception of Ruthenians and Ukrainians) elected their national autonomous government during the first quarter of 1995. By exercising their rights of decision, proposition, consent, and opinion, these autonomies provide for representation and protection of minority rights on the national and regional level, and are competent political partners for the executive branch of the country's government.

The national autonomous minority government has complete freedom of decision in its own internal issues. One of their more important scopes of authority is the participation in overseeing the instruction in the vernacular of the minorities that they represent. They have consenting right in the development of the curriculum for minorities–with the exception of higher education. They can express their opinion about proposed legislation concerning minorities, which constitutes an essential means to influence state decisions pertaining to minority groups.

It is clear from this brief presentation of the minority governments that by establishing them on the local and national levels, a new base has been generated for the enforcement of minority rights. Furthermore, by endowing these elected bodies with considerable legal powers, the system provides for the possibility of strong and legitimate representation of minority issues at the local and national levels.

The state has introduced a multi-channel financing system for covering the costs of enforcement of minority rights. The state budget allocates supplementary capitation fees to support minority preschools and the instruction of the vernacular language in schools. Within the framework of institutional financing, minority governments receive a once only allocation of assets and real estate property. Furthermore, budgetary regulations and parliamentary decisions prescribe the operating conditions for minority governments, and allocate financial support to their social institutions. In terms of operations financing, the Hungarian National and Ethnic Minorities Fund was established in the first half of 1995 with the aim of promoting the preservation of national identities, transmission of minority traditions, and safeguarding of minority languages. The Fund also supports all activities that help mitigate cultural and political disadvantages stemming from a community's existence as a minority. The majority of the Fund's legislative body–the Board of Trustees–is elected by the national minority governments or, in their absence, by organizations of the given minority.

The governmental agency responsible for minority affairs, the National and Ethnic Minority Bureau, has been performing state administrative duties related to minorities since its establishment in September 1990. These entail such governmental tasks as participation in the preparatory and executive procedures of the National Minorities Act and support for implementation of minority rights. One of its most important duties, however, is the maintenance of relations with minority governments and other minority institutions. The Government reports to Parliament biannually on the situation of minorities in the country. In June of 1995, Parliament elected the Parliamentary Commissioner of National and Ethnic Minority Rights, the Parliamentary Commissioner of Civic Rights, his General Deputy and the Commissioner of Data Security.[6]

The legal agency responsible for protection of civic rights is of Scandinavian origin and is embodied by the Parliamentary Commissioner of Civic Rights, internationally known as the Ombudsman. "The reason for the international popularity of the Ombudsman is that the flaws of representative democracy are the same in every country. Therefore the solutions to these flaws are similar too."[7]

It is characteristic of democratic countries that when it comes to litigation between an individual and the state, protection of the individual is stressed. This is implemented through judicial independence, separation of powers, constitutional jurisdiction, the concepts of the constitutional state, and the activation and operation of civic grassroots movements. At the same time, we have to be aware of the changing role of public administration, the extension of its scope of authority, and its increasing activity in setting standards. Its function is no longer only the implementation of legislative measures, and despite various contrary efforts, bureaucracy has also increased. Citizens encounter public administration in an increasing number of situations and they increasingly expect to receive legally correct but also kind and fair litigation. "The institution of the Ombudsman is one of the most important–although not exclusive–means for maintaining the ties between Parliament and real life, for controlling and influencing bureaucracy."[8]

The legal institution of the Ombudsman was introduced in Hungary by the 1989 Amendment to the Constitution of the Hungarian Republic–one of the amendments that was a vehicle for changing the regime.[9] The June 1990 Amendment to the Constitution referred to the institution of collective minority Ombudsman, and so mentions side by side with the Ombudsman of Civic Rights.[10] Within the framework of that regulation, jurisdiction of the collective minorities Ombudsman was to be exercised by a group of representatives nominated by national and ethnic minorities and elected by Parliament, with one person per national or ethnic minority represented. In June of 1993, Parliament passed the Law on the Parliamentary Commissioner of Civic Rights (the Ombudsman Law).[11] This piece of legislation describes the Ombudsman's legal status and their rules of procedures.

Under the December 1994 Amendment to the Constitution,[12] the never implemented collective institution of Ombudsman introduced in 1990 was replaced by the Parliamentary Commissioner of National and Ethnic Minority Rights. The 1994 regulation of Parliament was in conformity with the National Minorities Act, which regulates that there should be one person exercising rights as the Commissioner of Minority Rights. The Act departs from the concept–also shared by the author–that the Ombudsman is an institution of judicial protection and not representation. The collective body of Ombudsmen earlier projected would have overstressed the role of representation.

The President of the Republic proposes candidates for Ombudsmen of general and specific scope of authority and after hearing the report of competent Committees of the Parliament, the Parliamentary Representatives elect them by qualified majority votes (two thirds of votes). In the case of the Minority Ombudsman, the president of the Republic solicits the opinion of national minority governments or, in their absence, of national representatives of the national minorities, before proposing a candidate.

"The Ombudsman is a specific, independent institution of parliamentary control, directly responsible only to Parliament. The degree of independence of the Parliamentary Commissioner is a fundamental issue."[13] Under the regulations of the Ombudsman Law, the Ombudsman is independent in his procedures, and makes decisions influenced exclusively by the Constitution and the laws of the country. One safeguarding measure of the Ombudsman's independence is the six-year term of office, so that his operation is independent of the parliamentary electoral cycles. There are several other instances of the Ombudsman Law securing the independence of the person and action of the Commissioner from the executive power or political parties.[14] The activity of the Ombudsman curtails the bureaucratic powers of the state–especially that of public administration.

The Constitution defines the tasks of the Minority Ombudsman as the investigation of irregularities concerning the rights of national and ethnic minorities and the initiation of measures to redress infringement on these rights. The Ombudsman may proceed in issues under the ruling of the National Minorities Act. The Preamble to the Ombudsman Law defines irregularities as the infringement of, or direct risk of infringing on constitutional rights and states that further specification of the concept is possible once the law is being applied.

The activity of the Minorities Ombudsman has three main areas. The first is the investigation of irregularities and grievances, their redress, and controlling infringement of individual or collective national and ethnic minorities rights. The Minorities Ombudsman investigates all the individually filed complaints against a public authority and all procedures or decisions of a public institution (or the lack thereof) which have generated grievances or risks of grievances about infringement on the minority rights of Hungarian citizens. He also controls the community rights of national/ethnic minorities (their social organizations and local and national autonomous governments), and conducts investigations if their rights are violated or there is a risk that they will be. The Ombudsman uses the legal means at his disposal to redress all irregularities and grievances. Cases of grievance may occur with the violation of one of these rights: the right prohibiting discrimination, the right of free choice of identity, the right of free use of the mother tongue, the right of use of name in the vernacular form, the right of freely maintaining relations, or the right of freely participating in instruction in the mother tongue. The scope of authority of the Minorities Ombudsman also covers petitions regarding the minorities autonomous governments, their conditions of operation (both financial and structural), other minorities activities and licenses, as well as education and instruction.

Secondly, the Minorities Ombudsman also issues proposals for amending existing laws and regulations or drafting new ones. Once the Minorities Ombudsman finds that minority rights were infringed as a result of inadequate dispositions of laws or other legal tools of the state administration, or the lack of these, he may initiate the amendment of such rules and regulations at the competent legislative body, requesting their publication, cancellation, or correction, as applicable. He may also appeal to the Constitutional Court.[15] Drawing on the experience from all the complaints filed with his office, the Minority Ombudsman has knowledge of the regulations that are unclear or legally confusing in legislation pertaining to minorities. As all new system models lacking previous experience—which does not subtract from the merits of the system—this too has had to be corrected to conform to practical experience. The Ombudsman aims to use his experience in helping to generate more coherence in the laws and regulations pertaining to minorities.

Thirdly, the Minorities Ombudsman also acts as a mediator and has an advisory role. In a number of cases, e.g. in cooperation between local and minority governments, conflicts of interest were

Table 4
Statistical data of cases filed between
September 1, 1995, and December 31, 1996

	September 1, 1995	December 31, 1996	Total
Petitions	63	335	398
Investigation ex officio	1	9	10
Definition, interpretation, advising	9	13	22
Total	73	357	430
Minorities involved in the filed cases			
Gypsy/Roma	41	261	302
German	13	43	56
Serb	3	6	9
Croat	1	5	6
Slovak	1	6	7
Greek	1	3	4
Armenian	2	4	6
Bulgarian	1	2	3
Ruthenian	1	1	2
Romanian	1	7	8
Polish	-	3	3
Ukrainian	-	-	-
Slovenian	-	-	-
Petitioner outside the jurisd. of the National Minorities Act	-	19	19
Case concerning all minorities	8	11	19
*Total**	73	371	443

*One case may concern several minority groups.
Source: J/4048 "Report on the activity of the Parliamentary Commissioner of National and Ethnic Minority Rights, July 1, 1995, to December 31, 1996," p. 101.

redressed by negotiations with the Ombudsman or his assistants. This role of mediator in the case of conflicts is directly related to the advisory/informative activity of the Ombudsman, and the preparation of publications.

The majority of the 400 plus complaints received by the office of the Minority Ombudsman between July 1, 1995, and December 31, 1996, were cases filed by individual citizens. The Ombudsman may also initiate an investigation based on information obtained from the written or electronic media, or that has become common knowledge in any other way. Statistically processed data of the cases filed between September 1, 1995, and December 31, 1996, are given in Table 4.

Table 5

Public authority involved in complaints or ex-officio investigation

	September 1, 1995	December 31, 1996	Total
Local government	13	148	161
Police	9	42	51
Court of Justice	10	32	42
Local minority govt.	4	23	27
Public Prosecutor	1	10	11
Financial institution	3	13	16
Govt. departments	5	11	16
Law enforcement Agencies	–	4	4
Press	–	4	4
Electronic media	4	3	7
Office of Reparations	2	5	7
Social Security Agency	2	7	9
State Audit Office	–	1	1
Other	20	56	76
*Total**	73	359	432

*One case may concern several public authorities.
Source: J/4048 "Report on the activity of the Parliamentary Commissioner of National and Ethnic Minority Rights, July 1, 1995, to December 31, 1996," p. 103.

The prohibition of any detrimental discrimination against national or ethnic minorities is a Constitutional principle. The largest minority community in Hungary is that of the Gypsies/Romas, and they are the ones filing the highest number of complaints. Improvement of their situation is part of the mainstream of government and local programs, state and social organizations. It is an unfortunate fact that the majority of the Gypsy population is a loser in the economic transition process following the change of

Table 6

Category of minority law infringed, according to the claimants

	September 1, 1995	December 31, 1996	Total
Individual minority right	3	21	24
Collective minority right	18	102	120
Both individual and collective minority right	52	218	270

Provisions adopted on the basis of the investigations

	September 1, 1995	December 31, 1996	Total
Case transferred	10	16	26
Dismissed without investigation	18	20	38
Dismissed following investigation*	–	123	123
Investigation successfully completed	27	73	100
Pending	17	55	
Concluded	56	302	358
Total	73	357	430

* In these cases we have conducted the investigation, but infringement of minority rights was not substantiated.
Source: J/4048 "Report on the activity of the Parliamentary Commissioner of National and Ethnic Minority Rights, July 1, 1995, to December 31, 1996," p. 105.

regime. Along with the total emancipation that took place in terms of minority recognition, reforms of public administration and reforms towards market economy have brought not only a halt to

Table 7

Total recommendations or proposals

	September 1, 1995	December 31, 1996	Total
Accepted recommendations or proposals	1	26	27
Pending recommendations	–	7	7
Public authorities involved Treasury	–	1	1
Local government	1	16	17
Dept. of Education	–	4	4
Dept. of Internal Aff.	–	3	3
Government	–	1	1
Radio	–	1	1
Public Prosecutor	–	2	2
County Public Admin. Office	–	3	3
Secr. Overseeing Civic Secret Service	–	1	1
Parliament	–	1	1
Total	1	33	34

* In these cases the investigation was completed, but the deadline of acceptance/dismissal of the recommendations had not elapsed by the end of the period reported.
Source: J/4048 "Report on the activity of the Parliamentary Commissioner of National and Ethnic Minority Rights, July 1, 1995, to December 31, 1996," p. 104.

the integration of Gypsies into society, but a downright retrogression.[16] Their social standing, special cultural features, habits, and traditions must all be considered when trying to solve their problems, while at the same time society tries to consider employment,

ployment, educational, social, housing, health policies, etc. The management of the specific and complex problems of the Gypsy/Roma population cannot be accomplished within the general scope of minority policy, with only the possibilities offered by the National Minorities Act. Intervention against discrimination in employment or social issues is often hindered by difficulty in verifying the allegations. With the 1996 correction of the Criminal Code, the legislators aimed to provide minorities with more efficient protection under criminal law against discriminative actions by defining new forms of criminal acts in the law and by modifying criminal factors that constitute an offence. This change in the Criminal Code was in accord with the 1948 Genocide Agreement, the 1956 Anti-Discrimination Agreement, and the 1973 Anti-Apartheid Agreement.

It is a prerequisite of the Ombudsman's investigation that the petitioner has exhausted all other available possibilities for public administration redress, i.e. that he should have no further potential for legal redress. No petitions are accepted for cases predating October 23, 1989, and/or if the legally binding resolution in the case is more than 12 months old. The scope of investigative authority of the Ombudsman extends to any public authority described by the law.[17]

The Ombudsman may request information, explanation, opinion or additional evidence in the cases under scrutiny. He may conduct a hearing of the parties involved or request the head of the agency or its supervising authority to run an investigation. In case irregularities are disclosed, the Ombudsman may suggest legal redress or disclose responsibility to the competent authorities.

"The Ombudsman has a specific scope of legal action, is not a legislative authority, cannot alter existing regulations and is not competent in issuing directives. However, he may formulate recommendations to pertinent authorities in his report of the offense against constitutional rights."

"With the release of the recommendation the Ombudsman may address the agencies involved, their supervising authorities, or the pertinent Department, even the Government, as needed. The power of mandate is in any case only a last resort in the enforcement of human rights."[18] If the Ombudsman is in disagreement about the opinion or measures of the authority involved, he may bring the case to Parliament in his Annual Report, requesting investigation. The Ombudsman's Annual Report has a fundamental role as the forum informing the public on the legal protection of national/ethnic minorities and disclosing results of earlier recommendations made by the Ombudsman.[19] The special features of the Hungarian Ombudsman system are described in the definition that the International Barristers Association, the IBA, gives of the Ombudsman system.[20]

EDUCATION AND LANGUAGE USE OF THE MINORITIES

Under the National Minorities Act, anybody can freely use his or her mother tongue, in any place and at any time. The state has the obligation to provide minorities with the conditions supporting the free use of their mother tongue. There are regulations of procedural law in place to guarantee the use of mother language in the course of public administration and civil and criminal procedures.

There are considerable differences in the language use of Hungarian minorities, even between the regional dialects of a given language. Bilingual usage of the vernacular is characterized by the choice of a different language in a different situation. In the past decades the use of minority languages was relegated to the private sphere, losing its social prestige. As a result, there are signs of linguistic assimilation, with primarily the older population still using the mother tongue.

Communication with local government constitutes a prominent area of maternal language use. Data collected from 249 communities shows that 43% of the oral and 6% of written communication between officials and local population is in the local minority language. The crux of the matter here is whether there are administrative workers who speak the language of the local minority. Again, data from the 249 communities show that 29% of officials working in the local governments belong to a minority group.[21] The National Minorities Act devotes a full chapter to language use, while securing several language-use related rights in other places of the Act. For example, it regulates language use related to family traditions, holidays, religious ceremonies, and the right to use names and family names as they appear in the native language. The Act provides an itemized list of all languages used by minorities in Hungary, and describes the state subsidies available for conducting church services or publishing laws and important government notices in the minority language.

The National Minorities Act also regulates the rights of Parliamentary and local government representatives to the use of their native language; regulates the bilingual drafting of minutes and resolutions; regulates the mandatory translation of public administration or service institution signs, resolutions, forms and public notices, and street names; and finally regulates the employment of administrative staff fluent in the language of the local minorities. All these rights constitute a considerable advancement.

The 1995 ratification of the European Charter on Regional or Minority Languages signified a further step ahead in the language use of minorities in Hungary. The Charter contains provisions on the use of languages in education, the court system and public administration, in the media, and in economic, cultural and social fields.

We know that the mother language is the innermost essence of a linguistic-national community. Blocking the process of maternal language acquisition will hinder development of self-identity in a minority group. The other extreme–exclusion of certain ethnic groups and the incitement of mutual distrust–is just as harmful. The conditions of peaceful coexistence and the integration of minority groups have to start in the schools. Minority languages have to be present in schools either in classes in the native language, in bilingual instruction, or in schooling exclusively in the minority language.

Hungarian laws on public and higher education address the fundamental concept of minority education and its contextual requirements with special attention. These laws make mention of applicable regulations of the National Minorities Act, also listing the tasks and responsibilities of local governments. The 1996 Act on Public Education had a positive impact on minority education issues since it eliminated a series of legal insecurities and helped generate the harmony between the National Minorities Act and the precepts of the National Curriculum.

The National Curriculum states that in order to preserve the identity of minority groups, the education of minorities has to pursue multilateral goals:

–By development of oral and written understanding and usage of the given minority language, supporting the emergence of the given language on an educated vernacular level;

- –Preserving and disseminating folk literature, folk music, folk art, and customs and traditions;
- –Educating about historical traditions, cultural environments of the mother tongue, and knowledge of nation and ethnicity;
- –Educating about tolerance and acceptance of different cultures by emphasizing the inherent values of these minority cultures;
- –Educating about the cultural life and history of the mother country including assistance to Gypsy/Roma people in their social development and integration.

The introduction to the National Minorities Act states that the cultures of the minorities living in Hungary are part of the country's cultural legacy. Parliament considers the cultural autonomy established by minority governments as the fundamental condition for implementing the specific rights of minority groups. The Act devotes a full chapter to the autonomous management of minority education and schooling. The most important points and elements of the Minority and Public Education law are the following:

- –The language of the education at schools is Hungarian or the language of the national/ethnic minority. School age children of national/ethnic minority shall receive public education in their mother tongue, or in both their mother tongue and Hungarian in pre-schools and schools throughout the country (see Table 8);
- –Children and parents have the right to free choice of school. The teaching curriculum of public pre-schools and schools shall accommodate the preservation of the language and culture of national/ethnic minority children, as well as offer education in the mother tongue, history, geography, culture and folklore relating to the minorities;
- –Classes or full education in the minority language may be conducted at minority pre-schools or schools or in minority classes/groups within public schools, based on local conditions or demands. Even exams may be taken in the vernacular, while bilingual report cards are to be issued in Hungarian and the mother tongue.

Local or national autonomous minority governments can also maintain their own educational institutions. National minority governments may also exercise their right to consent and provide opinion in the course of legislative processes related to education. This is especially the case when the local government or educa-

Table 8

Statistical data of national minority elementary schools 1995–96 school year (full cases)

Year	No. of Students	No. of Classes
1st	10,736	511
2nd	10,582	560
3rd	10,531	538
4th	10,676	544
5th	10,704	535
6th	10,730	545
7th	10,154	528
8th	10,299	541
Total	84,412	4,342

Source: MKM (Department of Culture and Education), 1996.

tional institution operating the pre-schools, schools, or day-care centers catering partially or fully to the needs of minority children plans changes in operation. Such changes may include the establishment or closing of these institutions, modification of their scope of activity, establishing or changing the name of an institution, establishing or modifying its budget, evaluating the professional work carried out in an institution, accepting new rules of procedure, and validating educational programs or pedagogical programs, pedagogical-cultural programs at the school or institution. The autonomous minority government has to be consulted about and must agree with the nomination and termination of school principals in all minority schools.

The interests of national and ethnic minorities must be well represented in the school system. The Act on Public Education prescribes that all local, city, county, and district (in Budapest) governments shall provide public minority for pre-school education for children of national or ethnic background. It is the obligation of county seats and the capital city to provide high school and technical education in the proper language(s). Before establishing school districts, local governments must obtain the consent of the local minority government or, if the school/institution is of national interest, the consent of the National Autonomous Minority Government.

Local and minorities governments have the obligation to cooperate in assessing the need for minority education in their area and organizing its deployment. It is the task of the state to provide training for minority language teachers. The Hungarian government has signed a series of international agreements to insure that minorities will receive full or partial education in foreign institutions where the language of teaching is their mother tongue. In the same way the state supports the employment of foreign visiting professors as well as the recognition of foreign degrees under international agreements.

The Secretary of Culture and Public Education, the Council of Public Education Policy, and the National Minorities Committee also play an active role in the development of minority education. Representatives of the National Autonomous Minorities Governments participate in the latter forums as well. These agencies are forums for preparing decisions and recommendations.

Grassroots social organizations play an important role in enforcing the individual and collective rights of national and ethnic minorities. The activity of these civil organizations is mostly geared towards investigating and redressing the violation of individual and collective rights of minority communities, although they also strive to alleviate conflicts that surface naturally due to democratic changes and the development of new social structures.

It is my opinion that the minority issue may be best addressed from the standpoint of both the minorities and the majority in the country by supporting a minority-friendly environment. In such an environment both parties may recognize their interdependence, accept "otherness" and the rights of those that are different and, finally, recognize that we should not enforce our own rights to the detriment of others, but to the best of everyone, so that we may protect our values together.

NOTES

1. Paragraph 34 of Act XXXI of 1989 states: "The following resolutions shall replace Chapter XII of the Constitution: Paragraph 68 of Chapter XII Fundamental Rights and Obligations, Section (1): National and linguistic minorities living in the Republic of Hungary form part of popular sovereignty. They are nation-creating factors.

Section (2): The Republic of Hungary protects all national and ethnic minorities. It assures their collective participation in public life, the enrichment of their culture, use of their mother tongue, instruction in the mother tongue and the right to use their names as it appears in the minority language.

Paragraph 70/A, Section (1): The Republic of Hungary guarantees human and civic rights to all persons residing in the country, with no distinction as to race, color, gender, language, religion, political or other conviction, national or social origin, financial or birth status.

Section (2): The law shall severely penalize any discriminatory action described under Section (1).

Section (3): The Republic of Hungary promotes equality before the law by adopting resolutions aimed at eliminating discrimination."

2. Act LXXVII of 1993 on the Rights of National and Ethnic Minorities came into force on October 20, 1993, with two reservations. One pertains to the Parliamentary Commissioner of National and Ethnic Minority rights, in terms of stating that there is a separate law that regulates the coming into force of

provisions concerning his election and jurisdiction. The other reservation pertains to the election of minority self-governments. Under the National Minorities Act, Law LXIV of 1990 on the Election of Minority Self-government Representatives and Mayors was replaced by a new chapter mandated by the entry of the National Minorities Act entitled "Legal Protection of National and Ethnic Minorities" on the day when the date for the 1994 general municipal elections was set.

3. The Constitution of the Republic of Hungary contains comprehensive regulations protecting national and ethnic minority rights, entered into force June 25, 1990 (Law XL of 1990 on the Amendment of the Constitution of the Republic of Hungary):

"Paragraph 68, Section (1): National and linguistic minorities living in the Republic of Hungary form part of popular sovereignty. They are nation-creating factors.

Section (2): The Republic of Hungary protects all national and ethnic minorities. It assures their collective participation in public life, the enrichment of their culture, use of their mother tongue, instruction in the mother tongue, and the right to use their names as it appears in the minority language.

Section (3): The laws of the Republic of Hungary assure representation for the national and ethnic minorities residing in the country.

Section (4): National and ethnic minorities may elect their autonomous governments on the local and national levels."

"Paragraph 70/A, Section (1): The Republic of Hungary guarantees human and civic rights to all persons residing in the country, with no distinction as to race, color, gender, language, religion, political or other conviction, national or social origin, or financial or birth status.

Section (2): The law shall severely penalize any discriminatory action described under Section (1).

Section (3): The Republic of Hungary promotes equality before the law by adopting resolutions aimed at eliminating discrimination."

4. The UN Charter, Universal Declaration of Human Rights, International Agreement on Civic and Political Rights, European Agreement of Human Rights, Paris Charter for the New Europe.

5. The Hungarian National Minorities Act considered the concept of minority as defined by Professor Francesco Capotori in his study commissioned by the UN Subcommittee on Anti-Discrimination and the Protection of Minorities. The study written in 1971 and published in 1979, states: "A minority is a group of persons, smaller in number than the rest of the population of a country, but not in a dominant position, whose members share an ethnic, religious or linguistic characteristic, differentiating them from the characteristics of the rest of the population. They are joined by the feeling of solidarity to protect their culture, traditions, religion or language." *Study on the Rights of Persons Belonging to Ethnic, Religious and Linguistic Minorities* (United Nations, New York, 1991). For the definition of minority and an overview of the relationship between minorities and majorities see Péter Kovács, *Nemzetközi jog és kisebbségvédelem* [International Law and the Protection of Minorities] (Budapest, 1996), 36–60. Under

Section (2) of Paragraph 1, Act LXXVII of 1993 on the Rights of National and Ethnic Minorities, "National and ethnic minorities (hereafter: minorities) are defined by this law as a community of people residing in the area of the Hungarian Republic for at least one hundred years and that is in numerical minority in Hungarian society. Its members are all Hungarian citizens, differing from the rest of the population in their language, culture, or traditions. Furthermore, they retain a sense of community, driven by the effort to preserve their culture and traditions, as well as the expression and protection of their historic community values."

6. Parliamentary Resolution No.84/1995 (July 6), on the Election of Parliamentary Commissioners, "Under Section (4) of Paragraph 32/B of the Constitution, and Sections (1) and (2) of Paragraph 2 of the LIX Law of 1993, Section (1), Paragraph 23, of the 1992 LXIII Law on the Security of Personal Data and the Publicity of Data of Public Interest, and Section (2), Paragraph 20 of the 1993 LXXVII Law on the Rights of National and Ethnic Minorities, the Parliament hereby elects Dr. Katalin Gönczöl for Parliamentary Commissioner of Civic Rights, Dr. Péter Polt for General Sub-Commissioner of Civic Rights, dr. László Majtényi for Commissioner of Data Security, and Dr. Jenő Kaltenbach for Parliamentary Commissioner for National and Ethnic Minority Rights."

7. László Majtényi, *Ombudsman Állampolgári Jogok Biztosa* [Ombudsman, Commissioner of Civic Rights] (Budapest, 1992), 25.

8. Ibid., 26.

9. Paragraph 18 of the 1989 XXXI Law on the Amendment of the Constitution states: "Paragraph 32/A of the Constitution shall be amended with the following Chapter V: Chapter V. Parliamentary Commissioner of Civic Rights.

Section (1) of Paragraph 32/B: It is the task of the Minority Ombudsman to investigate the procedural irregularities concerning the rights of national and ethnic minorities and to propose general or individual measures to redress the infringement of these rights.

Section (2): Any person, as defined by law, may initiate the procedure of the Parliamentary Commissioner.

Section (3): Proposed by the President of the Republic, the candidate for Parliamentary Commissioner is elected by Parliament. The Parliament may opt to elect a separate Commissioner for the protection of specific constitutional rights.

Section (4): The Parliamentary Commissioner shall report annually to Parliament on the experiences of his activity throughout the year.

Section (5): Constitutional laws regulate detailed regulations on Parliamentary Commissioners."

The above law was passed at the October 18, 1989, session of Parliament, and enacted 23 October, 1989.

10. Paragraph 32/B established by Section (2), Paragraph 24 of the 1990 XL Law on the Amendment of the Constitution of the Republic of Hungary, enacted 25 June, 1990.

11. Law LIX of 1993 on the Parliamentary Commissioner of Civic Rights, enacted 22 June, 1993.

12. Section (2), Paragraph 1 of the 1994 LXXIII law mandating the correction of Law XX of 1949 on the Constitution of the Republic of Hungary, enacted 2 December, 1994.

13. Márta Dezső, Klára Fűrész, István Kukorelli, János Sári, Péter Schmidt, Imre Takács, *Alkotmánytan* [Principles of Constitutional Law], (Budapest, 1994); István Kukorelli, *Az állampolgári jogok országgyűlési biztosa* [Parliamentary Commissioner of Civic Rights] (Budapest, 1994), 238.

14. The assurances guaranteeing the legal independence of the Ombudsman are regulated in detail in Paragraphs 11–15 and 3–8 of Law LIX of 1993 on the Parliamentary Commissioner of Civic Rights. The provisions on the personal qualities that are prerequisite for the position are that the candidate must be a renowned lawyer with outstanding theoretical knowledge, or at least ten years of professional practice, with vast experience in procedures pertaining to constitutional law. The Ombudsman must comply with the rules and regulations of incompatibility. Thus in the four years predating his nomination the candidate cannot have been Parliamentary representative, President of the Republic, member of the Constitutional Court, or the Government, Under-Secretary of State, Assistant Under-Secretary of State, Representative of a local government, Notary-General of the local government, District Attorney, or full-time employee of the armed forces, the police, or security forces, or any political party. His nomination is also incompatible with any other state, local government, social, or political office or position. The provisions of the law also contain the preconditions for dismissal of the Ombudsman.

The Ombudsman is not subordinated to any authority, while his investigations are immune from external mandates. The Ombudsman may not be held accountable—except in cases of libel, defamation, or those pertaining to the Civil Code—for any fact or opinion expressed while exercising his mandate.

15. Paragraph 22, Act LIX of 1993 on the Parliamentary Commissioner of Civic Rights: "The Parliamentary Commissioner may propose to the Constitutional Court:

a. the subsequent investigation of unconstitutionality of laws, regulations, or other legal measures of the state administration;
b. investigation of the conflict of laws, regulations or other legal measures of the state administration with existing international agreements;
c. ruling in the case of complaints of violation of constitutional rights;
d. termination of unconstitutionality manifest in negligence or default; or
e. interpretation of provisions in the Constitution."

16. Csaba Tabajdi, *Látlelet a magyarországi cigányság helyzetéről* [Diagnosis of the Situation of the Hungarian Gypsy People] (Budapest, 1996), 29.

17. Paragraph 29, Act LIX of 1993 on the Parliamentary Commissioner of Civic Rights defines which organizations can be considered public authorities in terms of the investigations carried out by Ombudsmen of general and specific scope of authority. Under this law, all organizations of state power, state administration, other agencies with public administration mandate, armed forces, police, security forces, judicial agencies—with the exception of courts of justice—local gov-

ernments, and agencies ruling in out-of-court litigation are to be considered a public authority.

18. Katalin Gönczöl, Kétezer ügy: Az állampolgári jogok országgyűlési biztosának első féléves tapasztalatai [Two Thousand Cases: Semi-annual Report of the Parliamentary Commissioner of Civic Rights] (*Kritika,* 1996/6), 3.

19. The Parliament accepted the report on the activity of the Parliamentary Commissioner of National and Ethnic Minority Rights in its Resolution 54/1997 (V.21.) OGY. The Report covered the period between July 1, 1995 and December 31, 1996.

20. The definition of the Ombudsman system and the description of its terms of operation state the following: "The institution of the Ombudsman is an office established by the Constitution, legislature, or Parliament, and is directed by an independent government official of high standing, responsible only to the legislature or the Parliament. The Ombudsman receives the complaints from persons whose rights were violated by government or agencies, or the government, or public officials. The Ombudsman operates out of his own discretion, has the authority to conduct investigations, propose legal redress for complaints, and prepare reports."

The report of the IBA put forth a 12-point summary of the Ombudsman system. These are:

1. The Ombudsman has the authority to pass judgement on any government agencies and its employees, with the exception of courts of justice, legislative agencies and the supreme executive power, and its staff.
2. Officials of the government, except the legislature, to which it is responsible, cannot control the Ombudsman.
3. The legislative body, or the executive power based on a set majority of votes from the legislative body, nominates the Ombudsman. It is desirable that the nomination be based on more than the simple majority of votes, i.e. a two-thirds majority of votes should be obtained.
4. The independence of the Ombudsman shall be assured by a longer period of office, which shall last for more than 5 years. The Ombudsman is irrevocable, except if two thirds of the legislative power sees a substantial reason for recalling his person.
5. The Ombudsman is entitled to a salary conmesurate with those of the highest government officials in the country.
6. The Ombudsman has the right to freely select his own staff.
7. The Ombudsman has the right to investigate the decisions or the absence of decision of any government agency or its employee.
8. The Ombudsman shall have full access to any document he deems relevant in terms of his investigation.
9. The Ombudsman has the right to investigate the reasons, meaning, and effectiveness of decisions, or the absence of decisions, of any public office or its employees, and to receive competent answers to questions posed in this respect.

10. The Ombudsman has the discretionary right to decide which claims he is going to investigate, and what ruling he shall adopt in the given case, or what cases he deems to be made public.
11. Every Public office or public officer has the right to receive a preliminary copy of the Ombudsman's judgment referring to his case, and may publicly answer the criticism.
12. The Ombudsman and his staff may not be held responsible for investigations he has carried out properly.

G. Gaiden, *International Handbook of the Ombudsman, Evolution and Present Function* (Grenwood Press, 1983), 10, quoted in Tamás Földesi, Miért nincs, ha van? Gondolatok az ombudsmannrendszerről [Where is it, if it's here? Thoughts on the Ombudsman System] (*Társadalmi Szemle* 1992/11), 69-70.

21. Radó, Péter, *Kisebbségi nyelvhasználati jogok és gyakorlat Magyarországon* [Minority Language Use in Hungary, Rights and Practical Implementation] Data Base of Minority Communities established by the Minority Research Group of the National Foreign Language Library. (Budapest, 1994), 91-97.

BILATERAL TREATIES BETWEEN HUNGARY AND ITS NEIGHBORS AFTER 1989

GÁSPÁR BÍRÓ

Since 1989 Hungary has signed treaties of cooperation and good neighborly relations with Ukraine, Slovenia, Croatia, the Slovak Republic, and Romania. The common feature of these agreements, which attracted international attention, is the mutual recognition of borders accompanied in the case of Ukraine, the Slovak Republic, and Romania by the explicit renunciation by the contracting parties to any future claims regarding each other's territory. Some of the treaties contain extensive provisions on the protection of national minorities, while others only mention it because they are complemented by separate legal instruments on this issue. By signing the agreements Hungary has also implicitly renounced its claim as a protector of the Hungarian minorities living in the neighboring countries. By including in each treaty references to international instruments relating to the protection of national minorities, the signatory Hungarian governments[1] made it clear that in their view the problems of Hungarians abroad are internal matters of the states concerned. At the same time, this stance advances the view that the situation of Hungarian minority rights is a part of the international protection of human rights and thus a legitimate object of international attention. The clause on the inviolability of borders and the mutual renunciation of territorial claims is in some respect self-operating and carries a pronounced declarative and symbolic character because state frontiers in Europe are established under international law by several multilateral international instruments, guaranteed by the great powers.[2] In addition, Hungary and its neighbors, except the new Yugoslav federation, have undertaken in the 1990's unilateral obligations regarding the inviolability of borders and territorial integrity of states as part of the process aimed at the institutionalization of their relationship with the European Union (EU) and NATO. These unilateral undertakings are *de facto* guaranteed by the threat of the suspension or even termination of this entry into either organization should the respective governments not comply with their assumed obligations. Nevertheless, the political significance attached to these declarations, and their inclusion in bilateral international treaties signed by Hungary, has proved to be important. However, the provisions on minority protection contained in these documents has raised several and yet largely unresolved questions regarding their interpretation and implementation.

It is important to emphasize at this stage the fact that in order to include minority protection clauses in the treaties with its neighbors, both the Antall and Horn governments have made decisive compromises. In certain phases of the negotiation process they have put into brackets (their 1990 and 1994 program's) theses on Hungarian minorities living in neighboring countries and disregarded some of the minority protection endeavors on specific claims formulated by the political organizations and interest-defending associations of these minorities. Compromises consisting mainly of concessions were possible to some extent due to the fact that in Hungary no significant political force formulated irredentist policies. In addition. public opinion (according to repeated polls) became overwhelmingly uninterested in the situation of Hungarians abroad. More importantly, no Hungarian organization in Eastern and Central Europe tried to secede or to use violence or threatened the use of violence, including inflammatory language, in defending interests or policies of Hungarian minorities. However, concessions were heavily criticized by significant parts of the political spectrum in Hungary and abroad chiefly because it appeared that after 1995 dealing with the problems of the Hungarians abroad had dropped from among the country's foreign policy priorities. Since 1990 there has also been an unequivocally explicit consensus between government and the opposition that Hungarian governments, irrespective of their political orientation, should support the claims of the legitimate representatives of Hungarians abroad in accordance with international norms. The Hungarian Constitution, in Article 6 paragraph 3, states that the Hungarian state bears a sense of "responsibility" towards Hungarians abroad, and it promotes the development of their relations with Hungary.

At the level of political rhetoric, Hungary's foreign policy has been continuously characterized, both by the government and the opposition, as placing the same emphasis on the Euro-Atlantic integration of the country and on developing good relations with neighbors as on the constitutional responsibility regarding Hungarians abroad (the so-called "triple-priorities" policy). In reality, these expectations regarding future membership in the EU and NATO have constantly prevailed. The present chapter does not allow for a comprehensive and detailed analysis of the causes and developments of the process which has led all Hungarian governments after 1989 from a basically autonomy-centered minority policy towards national and ethnic minorities at home and support for a limited autonomy abroad, to the essential concessions made in order to cope with the opposite views and policies followed in the period under discussion for instance by the Slovak Republic and Romania. The remarks made in this regard should be understood in the context of the Hungarian general stand as described above, with a special emphasis on the absolute priority given by Hungary to the integration process with the West. The present chapter contains no comprehensive analysis of the situation of Hungarian minorities in Central and Eastern Europe, and it is limited to the minimum of descriptions necessary for the understanding of certain provisions of the treaties.

UKRAINE

A Declaration on the principles of cooperation on the question of national minorities[3] was signed in Budapest on 31 May 1991. A Treaty on Good Neighborly Relations and Cooperation signed in Kiev on 6 December 1991 reaffirmed the Declaration, following the 1 December 1991 referendum on the independence of Ukraine. Hungary was the first state after Poland to give international recognition to the newly independent Ukrainian state. Article 2 of the Treaty states that:

> The (Contracting) Parties respect each other's territorial integrity and state that they have no, nor will they have, territorial demands on each other.

A distinct paragraph of the first article emphasizes that the signatory parties will be guided by the principles of sovereign equality, territorial integrity, inviolability of borders and will refrain themselves from the use of or threatening with the use of force. One of the most important provisions on national minorities in the Declaration is contained in Article 6 which states that,

> The Parties consider that the right of national minorities to establish and operate, the Parties' territories and in accordance with their respective legislation, organizations and associations for the purpose of preserving their national identities is an element of a democratic state ruled by law. Such organizations or associations may establish or maintain relations with such organizations or associations of other countries with which they share a common ethnic or national origin, cultural heritage, or religion. Such organizations or associations may solicit voluntary financial or other assistance and apply for support from the state. Concrete questions of such support by the Parties shall be decided upon by a joint committee to be set up under article 16.

After seven decades of Soviet rule the importance of such a statement can hardly be overstated. The Treaty re-affirms and strengthens the principles laid down in the Declaration, according to which membership in a national minority is based on the free choice of identity and is protected against any adverse consequences. National minorities are regarded by the Parties as "organic parts" of their societies, "possessing appropriate rights, both individually and as a community." The Parties undertake not to adopt administrative, economic, or other measures designed to assimilate minorities or change the composition of populations in territories inhabited by national minorities. To guarantee the freedom to usc one's mother tongue, both orally and in writing, with no detriment to the obligation to learn the official language or languages recognized on the territories of the Parties. The use of names, family names, and forenames by persons belonging to national minorities, in accordance with the orthography of the mother language and its culture, is also guaranteed. Article 10 of the declaration states that:

> The Parties agree that they shall make it possible for the national minorities to learn their mother tongue and to study in their mother tongue at all levels of education.

Freedom of religion for people belonging to national minorities is also guaranteed, including worship and religious education. Several provisions deal with the cooperation of Parties in the field of culture, science, education, and generally, the exchange and dissemination of information. According to Article 5 of the Declaration:

> The Parties express their readiness to encourage efforts to attain for the national minorities a status that will guarantee their

rights to effective participation in public affairs, including aspects of protecting and developing their identities as well as adoption and implementation of decisions affecting their place of residence.

It is worth mentioning that during the 1 December 1991 referendum on the independence of Ukraine, in the Sub-Carpathian administrative area (in Western Ukraine, bordering the Slovak Republic, Romania and Hungary) complementary questions were asked regarding the status of local administrations. More than 86% of the local population voted for a special status of the Sub-Carpathian *oblast* (The percentage of the Hungarian population in the area at that time was 12.7). In the Beregszász district, the part of the *oblast* that is 78% Hungarian, only 81% voted for the district to obtain special status within the Sub-Carpathian administration. However, under neither the former legislation nor under the new constitution of 28 July 1996 was a special status enacted for the region or its component districts. Also, the participation of the Hungarian minority in public affairs, in those areas where it is living in compact blocks and usually constitutes a majority, is realized through democratic, multi-party elections. There is one Hungarian member in the Kiev parliament, elected in 1994.

With regard to monitoring and resolving disputes over the interpretation and implementation of the principles and provisions of the Treaty and the Declaration, Article 8 of the Treaty emphasizes that the parties shall "promote the development of constant and regular contacts" between various state organs and bodies, on the national level, and regional and local administration. Meetings and contracts on the highest level are regular, including periodical consultations of the Ministries of Foreign Affairs. The contracting parties, in exceptional cases, are ready to appeal to the existing UN and OSCE dispute resolution mechanisms. The joint committee mentioned by Article 16 of the Declaration consist of the delegations nominated by the parties. The Protocol attached to the Declaration provides for two meetings every year, alternately on the territory of each contracting party, in order "to consider and resolve such problems as may arise." The delegations, led by Deputy Foreign Ministers, meet mainly with the purpose of "making recommendations, on the basis of agreement between the Parties, for their governments, concerning the implementation of the principles set forth in the declaration." The Parties, however, "shall rely on their appropriate national institutions for implementing" the recommendations of the committee. Representatives of the Ukrainian minority in Hungary and the Hungarian minority in Ukraine, delegated by their own political or cultural organizations participate with a consultative status in the meetings.

International instruments on the rights of people belonging to national minorities and minority protection usually include a limiting clause on the general interpretation of the provisions contained in such acts. Following this practice, the Declaration in its Article 18 provides that

> No provision of the present Declaration shall be construed as permitting any activities or acts contrary to the purposes of the UN Charter or other obligations under international law or the provisions of the 1975 Helsinki Final Act, including the principle of territorial integrity of states.

On December 15, 1991, the Government of Croatia and on November 6, 1992, the Government of Slovenia expressed their support regarding the Declaration.

SLOVENIA

A Treaty on Friendship and Cooperation was signed on 1 December 1992 between Hungary and Slovenia, following the two countries' signatures on November 6, 1992, in Ljubljana of a Convention on Providing Special Rights for Slovenian and Hungarian Minorities.[4] According to Article 16, the Convention is a legally binding document "subject to ratification in conformity with the relevant legislation of each Contracting Party." It was the first of this type signed by Hungary after 1989. The *rationale* of the Convention as explained in the preamble is the perception by the parties "that the real equality of the Hungarian and Slovenian national minorities, and the preservation of their national identities, can be achieved through ensuring special individual and common rights for them."[5] It should be emphasized that, unlike the Declaration signed with Ukraine, the present text refers to the Hungarian and the Slovenian minorities living on the territories of the parties and not to national minorities in general. The document pays considerable attention to the institutions and associations created and maintained by the two national groups. Article 3 provides that:

> The Contracting Parties shall encourage the full satisfaction of the cultural needs of the national minorities. They shall promote the establishment and operation of their cultural institutions, associations, and foundations.

Article 9 (dealing with political participation) in its paragraph 3 takes up again the issue. "The Parties, in conformity with their national legislation shall ensure the conditions for the activity of the nation-wide organizations of the national minorities"[6] in order to protect their "interests." Far beyond usual forms of political participation, Article 11 states that:

> The Parties shall ensure the participation of the representatives of the national minorities in the conclusion of treaties directly concerning their situation and rights derived from this Convention.

The seventeen articles Convention includes detailed provisions on legal protection, preservation, and development of the cultural, linguistic, religious and "full Slovenian and Hungarian" identities of the respective minorities; on the right to use the minority language; on the individual rights regarding the use of names in accordance with the orthography of the Slovenian and Hungarian languages; on the right to education, in particular "the learning of and studying in the mother tongue" on all levels; on freedom of religion; on freedom of information; on access to mass media; and on free contacts at home and abroad among persons belonging to the Slovenian and Hungarian minorities. The Preamble makes reference to a series of United Nations, Council of Europe (CE), and Conference on Security and Cooperation in Europe (CSCE) conventions and declarations. The Treaty on Friendship and Cooperation in Article 16, paragraph 1, states that the Parties agree that they will regard the provisions and principles on the protection of national minorities laid down in the 1990 CSCE Copenhagen Declaration and other CSCE documents as legally binding on them.[7] It should be noted that before signing the Slovenian–Hungarian Convention in November 1992 only two legally binding international instruments, to which both states were signatory parties, have been in force with regard to the issue.[8] It is important to emphasize this circumstance because it underlines the fact that, once the political will to deal with the question of minorities exists, agreements can be reached and effectively implemented at the inter-government level despite the absence of a detailed framework of international instruments. On the contrary, as recent developments in East Central Europe demonstrate, a sophisticated international legal system and mechanism on the protection of national minorities by itself is not sufficient to counterbalance differences of approach and policies aimed at curtailing existing minority rights.

In the area of monitoring and dispute resolution, Article 15 of the Convention provides for the creation of a "special inter-governmental minority Commission," which will include persons "from the respective national minorities ... appointed upon the proposal of their organizations." The main tasks of the Commission are to evaluate the implementation of the Convention and to prepare and adopt recommendations for their governments concerning adjustment, and, in case of necessity, even the amendment of the Convention.

The question of territorial integrity of States is addressed by the signatory Parties in Article 2 of the Treaty on Friendship and Cooperation by reaffirming that each party:

> will refrain from force or threat by force directed against the territorial integrity or political independence of the other Contracting Party, and from actions incompatible for whatever reasons with the UN Charter or the purposes of and the principles laid down in the CSCE Helsinki Final Act.

CROATIA

On December 16, 1992 the Prime Ministers of the Hungarian and the Croat governments signed, in Budapest, a Treaty on friendly relations and cooperation between their two countries. The wording of Article 2, paragraph 3, of the Treaty regarding the principles of territorial integrity and political independence of States is identical to the above cited provision of the Slovenian–Hungarian Treaty. In paragraph 4 of the Article, the signatory Parties declare that they

> regard national minorities as a natural bridge between peoples and are convinced that they contribute in a valuable manner to the life of their societies.

As mentioned earlier Croatia had already expressed its support of the 31 May 1991 Declaration between Hungary and Ukraine. Still the two prime ministers agreed to continue negotiations on a separate

Convention on national minorities based on the precedent-setting model of the Slovenian–Hungarian Convention. However, developments in the successor states of the former Yugoslavia, in particular the war between Croatia and Serbia which had dramatic results on the situation of the Hungarian minority living in the eastern part of Croatia, have delayed the completion of the agreement. Due to the war, a significant part of the Hungarian community there was displaced or sought refuge in Hungary and other countries. In addition, the general situation in war-torn Croatia, made it difficult to conclude an agreement which necessarily had not only to take into account, but also to elaborate on certain basic principles of human rights and fundamental freedoms.

Despite all these difficulties, after the 1994 election the new Hungarian government decided to accelerate and complete the drafting of the Convention.[9] The document was signed on 5 April 1995 in Osijek (Eszék) Croatia. In the meticulous Preamble to the eighteen articles of the document the parties expressed their conviction that

> the integration of minorities (*the Hungarian minority in Croatia and the Croatian minority in Hungary*) is possible only through the preservation of their features as ethnic communities, and that an important element is their effective participation at various levels in the decisions concerning their identity.

Further, the Preamble confirmed that

> the Hungarian minority have the right to return to those presently occupied territories of the Republic of Croatia from which they were driven out in 1991. This is one of the prerequisites for the implementation of the protection of their minority rights ensured by this Convention.

Along the same lines, in Article 8

> the Contracting Parties undertake that, making plans on economic development, they shall take into account the special interests of the minorities including the reconstruction of the war-affected areas of the Republic of Croatia inhabited by Hungarians and shall ensure the economic and social development in areas inhabited by minorities in order to guarantee their economic and social equality.

They shall also support "such kind of economic development measures which eliminate the causes of the emigration and the alteration, in any forms, of the ethnic composition of the population" of minority areas. Further, in line with Article 10 the parties agree that they "shall endeavor, with the help of the international community, to enable the displaced persons and refugees, including those who belong to the Hungarian minority, to return freely and voluntarily to their homes in the presently occupied areas of the Republic of Croatia."

A new element in the Convention is the reference to minority self-governments and cultural autonomy. Article 9 is entirely dedicated to this issue and deserves to be reiterated here.

> The Contracting Parties, in compliance with their domestic legislation, shall ensure the appropriate participation of minorities in the local, regional and national decision-making process relevant to the rights and the status of minorities and shall ensure the material and other conditions required for the election and work of minority representatives in the Hungarian and Croatian representative bodies. The Contracting Parties undertake not to change the administrative and territorial organizations of the State and local governments as well as the electoral districts to the detriment of minorities. The Republic of Hungary shall confirm to ensure the material conditions for the establishment and effective operation of Croatian minority self-governments in Hungary within the framework of current regulations and the appointed date. The Republic of Croatia shall confirm to ensure, in accordance with its domestic legislation, the right of the Hungarian minority to cultural autonomy. And, in addition, shall promote the free union and association of the Hungarian minority intended to preserve their national and cultural identity.

Extensive provisions deal with the rights of the concerned minorities to freely express, preserve, and develop their ethnic, cultural, linguistic, or religious identity; to use their mother tongue in private and public; to register officially their original first names and surnames; to gain information and access to the media; and to enjoy freedom of religion. Article 2 provides that the parties shall be,

> consistent with the requirements of the minority organizations and based on the requests by the parents, support the operation

of educational institutions, which can take the following forms: a) full educational process in the language of the respective minority; b) bilingual educational process; or c) additionally arranged optional teaching of the language and culture of the respective minority.

Hungary and Croatia outlined several further undertakings in order to give effect to the provisions of the Convention. For instance, for the realization of the provisions regarding freedom of religion, in Article 6 the Parties agree that their competent "authorities will permit the mutual exchange of priests for the religious minority communities operating in their territories." Trans-frontier cooperation is supported also in other fields of activity. An inter-government joint committee for minorities was set up in order to monitor the implementation of the provisions of the Convention. Based on the proposal of the concerned minority organizations, the parties agreed to appoint to the joint committee members of minorities. As in the previous cases after evaluating the initial implementation of the Convention the committee has the task of preparing recommendations for the governments on its realization, and where necessary, its modification.

THE SLOVAK REPUBLIC

Slovakia reached independent statehood on January 1, 1993 following a peaceful separation from the Czechoslovak federation, and based on a political agreement between the Czech and the Slovak governments. No referendum was held on the question of separation. However, before the formal separation and just after the election of June 1992, the newly elected parliament, the Slovak National Council, proclaimed the sovereignty of the Slovak Republic. The Constitution of the new independent state was adopted by the Slovak parliament on 1 September 1992. Article 1 defined the new state as a "sovereign, democratic state" under the rule of law and without any religious or ideological aspect or connection. The preamble of the 1992 Constitution begins with the words "We, the Slovak nation" and makes explicit references to the spiritual legacy of Ss. Cyril and Method, the historical heritage of the Great Moravian Empire, and the "natural right of national self-determination" in order to buttress its historical and political legitimacy.

From the outset, there was ambiguity about the constituents of the new state. The Preamble states, "We, the Slovak nation...in common with members of national minorities and ethnic groups,...that is, we, the citizens of the Slovak Republic, through our elected representatives we have adopted the following Constitution." As representatives of two Hungarian parties and a political movement elected with an overwhelming majority of the votes of ethnic Hungarians in Slovakia, the Hungarian members of the Slovak National Council unanimously rejected the Constitution and left the room of the Council before the vote. The move was a protest against the fact that the parliamentary majority completely ignored the amendments to the text proposed by the Hungarian MPs during the preparatory works of the Constitution. They claimed also that the language of the Preamble on the constituents of the state, combined with Article 6 which declares the Slovak language as the official language of the state, reduced ethnic Hungarians in Slovakia to the status of second-class citizen. Against this background, negotiations on the bilateral treaty between Hungary and Slovakia were resumed in the Summer of 1994 after a long break.

Since February 1992 when Czechoslovakia signed a treaty with Germany containing fairly acceptable provisions on the rights and protection of national minorities, several political developments have taken place which has changed the political situation both internally and on the European level. The split of the Czech and the Slovak federation is one of them. It should be underlined that the ethnic Hungarian parties, represented in Prague, in the federal Parliament, and in Bratislava, were firmly opposed to the separation. As mentioned, a referendum was never held, although several polls indicated that the majority of the citizens in Slovakia were not in favor of the separation.

Although the question of a bilateral treaty between Hungary and Czechoslovakia (and after 1993 between Hungary and the Slovak Republic) was on the agenda, due to the political situation no progress has occurred. On 30 June 1993 the Slovak Republic, together with the Czech Republic joined the Council of Europe (CE). The Hungarian government, after hesitating partly due to the position of some of the Hungarian political parties in Slovakia, finally decided not to oppose the accession of the Slovak Republic to the CE. The diplomatic vacillation of Hungary, however, was an another step contributing to the ongoing decline in bilateral relations. Upon accession, the Slovak Republic made a series of unilateral commitments on the rights of national minorities. In Opinion 175 of 29 June 1993 supporting Slovakia's accession, the CE Parliamentary Assembly states that it

> ...takes note of the Slovak authorities' commitment to adopt legislation granting to every person belonging to a minority the right to use his/her surname and first names in his/her mother tongue and, in the regions in which substantial numbers of a minority are settled, the right of the persons belonging to this minority to display in their language local names, signs, inscriptions and other similar information, in accordance with the principles contained in Recommendation 1201/1993. It encourages the authorities of the Slovak Republic to continue the efforts they have begun to eliminate from its legislation all the laws or decrees adopted by previous governments which are likely to contain elements discriminating against a group of persons or an ethnic, national community living on its territory, particularly those containing 'collective guilt.' It also takes note, whatever administrative divisions may be introduced in the Slovak Republic, of the declaration made by the Slovak authorities that they will respect the rights of national minorities.

The Hungarian government and the organizations of Hungarians in Slovakia reasonably expected the government of the Slovak Republic to proceed with the implementation of these unilateral undertakings. However, nothing happened between July and October of 1993. Hungarian Prime Minister József Antall died in December 1993 after spending almost two months hospitalized. Soon after the new Prime Minister, Péter Boross, took office, the campaign of the May 1994 election began. This was one of the reasons why negotiations on the bilateral treaty were in practice suspended between June 1993 and August 1994.

The other reason for no progress until just before the opening ceremony of the Conference on the Pact on Stability in Europe (PSE), held in Paris between 20 and 21 March 1995, was apparently the Pact itself. Launched in the Spring of 1993 by French Prime Minister E. Balladur, the idea of an overarching stability agreement in Europe (known also as the Balladur Plan) was discussed for the first time at the inaugural Conference in Paris (26 and 27 May 1993) and formalized during the June 1993 Copenhagen Summit of the EU. The plan envisaged a series of (bi- and multilateral) regional inter-government agreements between a specific group of states in Eastern and Central Europe, and focusing on security issues, in the broad sense of interest for the whole of Europe.[10] At the top of the list was the question of national minorities and the prevention of possible border and territorial disputes. These were considered to be manageable by means of an intensive preventive diplomacy backed by agreements embodied in international conventions, all part of a comprehensive single European pact. Since most of the concerned countries were at the same time candidates for EU membership, it was hypothetically possible for the EU to suspend or even cancel negotiations on accession should any of the East Central European parties not comply with obligations assumed under the Pact. There were only two problems with this. First, from the beginning the initiative excluded really hot areas such as the territory of the former Yugoslavia. Second, it did not provide any mechanism for including in the process those parties most concerned, that is, national minority groups and communities from all over Eastern and Central Europe. In addition, Russia, one of the major players, was virtually not participating in the process either.

The PSE, signed finally in Paris in March 1995, consists of a declaration, together with a list of 96 good neighborliness and cooperation agreements and arrangements.[11] Apparently all the parties ignored that in January 1994 both Hungary and Slovakia (and Romania) had announced and subsequently signed the NATO Partnership for Peace initiative document, which *inter alia* provided that the signatory states will refrain from the threat or use of force against the territorial integrity or political independence of any state, will respect existing borders, and will settle disputes by peaceful means.[12] Again, non-compliance with these unilateral undertakings would presumably result in the undermining of future prospects for NATO membership of the countries concerned.

One of the effects of the proposal for the Pact, and the resulting diplomatic maneuvers taking place between June 1993 and March 1995, was that each of the parties to the Hungarian–Slovak negotiations on the bilateral treaty expected the other side to compromise on issues of interest. While the Slovak government expected its Hungarian counterpart to make a clear declaration that it will renounce forever any territorial claims, it was more than rigid on the question of the rights of national minorities. For example, the Slovak Ministry of Foreign Affairs in August 1994 sent to Budapest a draft proposal for the upcoming bargaining phase, in which its one-typed-page article on minorities mentioned the word "right" only once, but emphasized in detail the loyalty due to the State by persons belonging to minorities as well as the new related would-be obligations of the contracting parties.[13] In order to bypass the deadlock, in January 1995 Hungary proposed a draft of a separate agreement on the rights of national minorities to be signed after the signature of the main treaty. The new draft made no reference to collective rights or autonomy and was even more restrictive in some aspects than the related provisions of the conventions signed with Croatia and Slovenia. This initiative, as well as different versions of an extended article of the bi-lateral treaty on minorities, was rejected by the Slovak government's delegates to the negotiations. It should be born in mind that the Hungarian government has agreed from the outset of the negotiations with Slovakia to go far beyond the so-called "Helsinki territorial clause" (as included and cited supra in the treaties with Ukraine, Croatia, and Slovenia) and to make a solemn declaration that it does not have, nor will it ever have, any territorial claims against the Slovak Republic. Critics at home and abroad maintained that the Antall government's stubbornness in sticking with the language of the 1975 Helsinki Final Act and other international instruments ("to refrain from the threat or use of force against the territorial integrity and political independence of other States") was in fact poorly veiled irredentism. Despite the fact that this "problem" was eliminated by the May 1994 election of a new Hungarian government, until mid-March 1995 negotiations made little effective progress because of disagreement on the article on minorities. It must be also mentioned that negotiations with Romania on the same topic were taking place and were also facing the same obstacles at the same time. There were credible reports of collusion over tactics behind the scene between the Slovak and the Romanian governments. But as the date of the signature of the PSE approached, internal and international pressure increased both on Hungary and on Slovakia and Romania to come to an agreement. The government of the Slovak Republic finally broke the stalemate. Four days before the Paris Summit on the PSE, the article on minorities was agreed upon in a closed meeting between the Hungarian and the Slovak Prime Ministers and their experts on minorities. The Hungarian–Slovak Treaty was signed on 19 March 1995 in Paris, in the presence of French Prime Minister E. Balladur, just one day before the opening of the PSE Conference.[14]

Knowing the history of the document, it is astonishing that Article 15 of the Treaty (comprising 6 paragraphs in 97 lines) is the most elaborated text from a legal point of view of all similar documents signed by Hungary after 1989. Both the Parliamentary and extra-parliamentary opposition in Hungary and Hungarian organizations in Slovakia criticized the weakness of the guarantees offered by the contracting parties on the realization of provisions on minority rights. Despite these criticisms, it is evident that, if duly applied in practice, Article 15 constitutes an appropriate framework for the realization of the rights and legitimate interests of Hungarians in Slovakia and Slovaks living in Hungary.[15] For example, the wording of Article 15 paragraph 2 (c, e and f) is a theoretically acceptable definition of a possible architecture of political and cultural autonomy for national and ethnic minorities, although it does not make any references to such things. Article 15 states that

> c) Persons belonging to national minorities shall have the right, individually or in community with the other members of their group, to freely express, maintain, and develop their ethnic, cultural, linguistic, or religious identity and to maintain and develop their culture in all its aspects....e) Persons belonging to national minorities shall have the right to establish and operate, in conformity with their respective legislation and with the objective of maintaining, developing, and transferring their identity, their own associations, including political parties and educational, cultural, and religious organizations. Both Governments shall create legal conditions to this effect. f) Persons belonging to national minorities shall have the right to take part effectively at the national and, where appropriate, at the regional level in the decisions affecting minorities or the regions inhabited by minorities, in a manner which is not incompatible with domestic legislation.

The Parties state in paragraph 1 that the protection of national minorities and of the rights of persons belonging to these minorities are not "an exclusively domestic affair of the States concerned but constitute a legitimate concern of the international community." They then proceed to define in detail a series of these rights including the rights to identity and free choice of identity, to the free use of the mother tongue in private and public, to education of the mother tongue and education in the mother tongue, to access to the media, and to use one's name according to the orthography of the mother tongue.

The rosy picture resulting from the agreed upon text soon faded away. Just minutes before the signature ceremony (Paris, 19 March 1995), the Slovak delegates handed the Hungarian delegation an untitled statement with an accompanying note verbally dated Bratislava, 19 March 1997. The statement is not only a unilateral interpretation of Article 15 but an attempt to amend unilaterally the agreed upon text.

> It (*The Slovak Government*) insists that it has agreed to mention the Recommendation of the Parliamentary Assembly of the Council of Europe 1201/1993 exclusively with the inclusion of the restricting clause: '...respecting individual human and civil rights, including the rights of persons belonging to national minorities.[16]

Needless to say no such a wording appears anywhere in the text of the Treaty. Upon signature, however, the Slovak delegation insisted that this Statement should be attached to the Treaty. This stand was not accepted by the Hungarian government and consequently the statement is not regarded as part of the Treaty. The problem originates in paragraph 4 (b) of the Treaty which, following the model of the treaties with Germany declares "the norms and political commitments laid down" in certain international documents "as legal obligations." One of these documents is Recommendation 1201/1993 of the Parliamentary Assembly of the Council of Europe, which in Article 11 reads: "In the regions where they are in a majority, the persons belonging to a national minority shall have the right to have at their disposal appropriate local or autonomous authorities or to have a special status, matching the specific historical and territorial situation, and in accordance with the domestic legislation of the state."

On the one hand, this Recommendation has no legally binding character *per se*. On the other hand, it is difficult to imagine how Article 11 of this Recommendation could function as a legal norm in the internal legislation of a given state without subsequent norms and regulations providing concrete details on implementation. The fact is that, as mentioned above, Slovakia upon accession to the Council of Europe made a unilateral undertaking to observe certain principles of the Recommendation (Article 11 was not mentioned explicitly). Slovakia did this after being called upon by the pre-quoted Assembly Opinion 175/1993, paragraph 8,

> to base their policy regarding the protection of minorities on the principles laid down in Recommendation 1201/1993 on an additional protocol on the rights of national minorities to the European Convention on Human Rights.

Further, the contracting parties have declared these principles "as legal obligations." It was not a problem for Hungary to undertake such a commitment since both the 1990 Act on Local Self-Governments and the 1993 Act of the Rights of National and Ethnic Minorities in Hungary contained already detailed provisions on the question of self-governing bodies created by national and ethnic minorities. It was–and it is still–not the case in the Slovak Republic. As of March 1998, despite several consultations at the level of Foreign Ministries, the interpretation dispute is not yet settled and the full implementation of the Treaty in Slovakia is still delayed.[17]

> On the question of territorial integrity, Article 3 of the Hungarian-Slovak treaty states that (1) The Contracting Parties, in accordance with the principles and norms of international law, confirm that they shall respect the inviolability of their common state border and each other's territorial integrity. They confirm that they have no territorial claims on each other and will not raise any such claims in the future. (2) The Contracting Parties declare that, in their mutual relations, they shall refrain from the use of force or the threat of use of force against the territorial integrity or political independence of, or from other acts or support for any such actions against, the other Party that would be contrary to the Charter of the United Nations or to international law, and they shall not allow a third party to use their territory for conducting similar actions against the other Party. They shall settle any disputes arising between them exclusively by peaceful means.

Differences of approach persist not only regarding the interpretation of the Treaty. The question of monitoring was left also unresolved. Article 15 paragraph 6 provides that

> The Contracting Parties shall cooperate to assist one another in following the implementation of the content of this Article....To this end, they shall set up an intergovernmental joint commis-

> sion, entitled to make recommendations, and consisting of sections whose composition will be determined as they deem necessary.

Unlike in the agreements with Ukraine, Croatia, and Slovenia, the Treaty with Slovakia lacks any provision on the participation of persons belonging to the concerned minorities in the joint commission.[18] As of March 1998 the joint commission was not set up.

ROMANIA

Hungary and Romania failed to conclude the negotiations on the bilateral treaty before the signing of the PSE in March 1995. The internal and external political context show certain similarities with the case of Slovakia, but of course there are several differences. After the fall of the Ceausescu dictatorship in December 1989, the National Salvation Front (NSF), Romania's *interim* governing body, released several statements in regards to the situation of national minorities and made public gestures toward the Hungarian community living in Romania. For instance, in a declaration of 5 January 1990 the Front recognized the idea of minority collective rights. Surprisingly, after less than three weeks the dominant mood of the Romanian political elite towards Hungarians started to deteriorate, and this general trend continued until the November 1996 election.[19] The 1991 Romanian Constitution has defined the state as a "unitary, national state" based on the "unity of the Romanian people" (Articles 1 and 4 (1)). Romania, according to Article 4 (2),

> is the common and indivisible homeland of all its citizens, without any discrimination on account of race, nationality, ethnic origin, language, religion, sex, opinion, political adherence, property, or social origin.

In Article 6

> (1) The State recognizes and guarantees the right of persons belonging to national minorities, to the preservation, development and expression of their ethnic, cultural, linguistic, and religious identity.

Paragraph 2 of the same Article prohibits positive discrimination in fulfillment of the guarantees of the right to identity.

> The protecting measures taken by the Romanian State for the preservation, development, and expression of identity of the persons belonging to national minorities shall conform to the principles of equality and non-discrimination in relation to other Romanian citizens.

This language, together with the constitutional provision declaring Romanian as the official language of the state, was considered by the parliamentary representatives of Hungarians as discriminating against them.[20] Amendments and proposals made by several Hungarian MPs during the preparatory works were not taken into consideration. Therefore, the Hungarian parliamentary group voted *en bloc* against the Constitution. During the constitutional referendum of 8 December 1991, different figures and polls indicated that the overwhelming majority of Hungarians also voted "no." The question of whether "Romanian" in the context of the constitutionally proclaimed unity of the Romanian people means "ethnic Romanian" or simply designate people holding Romanian citizenship remained unclear.

Until mid-1996 the different Romanian governments have kept a rather low profile on the issue of the country's Euro-Atlantic integration, especially NATO-membership. In 1993 Romania became a member of the Council of Europe. It signed the Partnership for Peace initiative in 1994 and the PSE in March 1995. While the relationship with Hungary was tense because of the situation of Hungarians in Romania, cooperation between the two countries' Ministries of Defense and their militaries became quite close after 1991. Ironically enough, the most intensive channel of commuication between Budapest and Bucharest in the meantime was the parliamentary group of the Democratic Alliance of Hungarians in Romania (DAHR), the Hungarian umbrella organization created in December 1989. With a fixed constituency, the DAHR was the most stable political party in the Romanian parliament after 1990. With a group of around 40 representatives and senators, the DAHR was able to pursue its policy taking into account the situation in Romania and Hungary at the same time. After the 1996 election, the DAHR entered the new Christian Democrat-led coalition government. This move undoubtedly contributed to the general political stabilization of the country. Since 1990, the DAHR has been constantly charged by representatives of different Romanian political forces of pursuing a veiled irredentist agenda under the cover of claims for minority rights, including cultural and political autonomy, and of giving priority in its organizational matters to the idea of internal self-determination. The charges were never substantiated and have completely lost ground since the DAHR undertook government responsibilities after November 1996. At the same time, except for the sporadic and unsuccessful proposals and attempts to ban political parties on an ethnic basis, the DAHR phenomena in Romania, as an imperfectly functioning model of political and cultural autonomy, including internal self-determination (i.e. the existence of a formally structured community scheme, based on democratic representation) was left to its own devices. The evident gap between the *de facto* and *de jure* situation and the rigidity of the majority produced the so-called "struggle for minority rights" of the DAHR. This struggle resulted in a significant amount of writing about political programs and legislative proposals, all of them in accordance with the Romanian legal order, yet at the same time sharply criticizing its imperfections. Within legal bounds the DAHR also continuously asked for a democratic review of certain constitutional principles. Regardless of the arguments put forward by these programs and legislative initiatives, they were uniformly rejected by the parliamentary majority until November 1996. An important segment of the Romanian non-governmental organiations (namely the Center for Human Rights of APADOR, the Romanian branch of the Helsinki Committee movement, and the Tîrgu-Mureş [Marosvásárhely] based Liga Pro Europa) made a difference in this regard, and started a dialogue and public debate on DAHR statements and documents, preparing the ground for promising political perspectives.[21]

At the end of 1995 the ruling coalition government began to consider more seriously the prospects of Romania's NATO-membership. The failure of concluding the treaty with Hungary announced on 15 March 1995, after the Romanian Foreign Minister's visit to Budapest and just days before the PSE Paris Conference, had had a negative impact on Romania's international position. Since negotiations had begun years ago, and since the Hungarian government after 1994 had agreed—as in the Slovak case—to go far beyond the language of international instruments in questions regarding the territorial integrity and political independence of states, the failure was due "at least in part" to the fact that the Romanian government refused to include a reference in the article concerning minority rights to the famous

Recommendation 1201/1993.[22] After one year of sterile diplomatic exercises, and when virtually all hopes to establish the treaty were lost, suddenly a Hungarian delegation led by a state-secretary of the Ministry of Foreign Affairs visited Bucharest on August 13–14, 1996, and announced agreement with his Romanian counterpart on the Article on minorities. A few weeks before this event unofficial reports indicated that the Romanian government would agree on most of the Hungarian proposals regarding the article on minority rights as long as the two parts added to the text a common interpretation of Recommendation 1201/1993 declaring that the parties do not interpret its Article 11 as imposing an obligation on CE member-states to grant national minorities territorial autonomy on an ethnic basis. Such a declaration would not have been unacceptable in principle to the Hungarian side. The fact is that on 21 August a Romanian delegation arrived in Budapest and, together with the Hungarian Ministry of Foreign Affairs, added the final "stylistic adjustments" to the text. A few days later it was announced that the Treaty was going to be signed by the two Prime Ministers on 16 September 1996 in Timişoara (Temesvár), Romania. Observers agreed that the approaching Brussels NATO foreign minister's summit of December 1996, which many believed in the summer of 1996, would name the first Eastern and Central European states to be invited to join NATO, had a decisive role in accelerating the Hungarian–Romanian negotiations. Hungary was already high on the list of the most possible candidates, and the Romanian government, following President Iliescu's 1995 visit to Washington D.C., considered that it still had a chance to "join the expansion train."

Article 3 of the Treaty states that

> (1) The Contracting Parties confirm that they shall, in their mutual relations, refrain from the use of or the threat of use of force against the territorial integrity or political independence of the other Contracting Party, as well as from any actions which are inconsistent with the purposes of the United Nations and the Helsinki Final Act. They shall also refrain from supporting such actions and they shall not allow a third party to use their territory for conducting similar actions, against the other Contracting Party. (2) The Contracting Parties shall settle any dispute arising between them exclusively by peaceful means.

Article 3 added also that

> The Contracting Parties confirm that, in accordance with the principles and norms of international law and the principles of the Helsinki Final Act, they shall respect the inviolability of their common border and the territorial integrity of the other party. They further confirm that they have no territorial claims on each other and that they shall not raise any such claims in the future.

That prospects of NATO-membership played a role in negotiations seems to be confirmed by the novelty of the provision contained in the first paragraph of Article 7.

> The Contracting Parties will broaden their relations and cooperation in international organizations, including regional and sub-regional organizations. They shall mutually support each other's efforts aimed at integration to the European Union, NATO, and the Western Union.

Article 15 contains in 12 paragraphs (93 lines) the provisions relating to the situation of minorities. Similar to the treaty with Slovakia, the Romanian–Hungarian Treaty uses such language as the "rights of persons belonging to national minorities" and "persons belonging to the Hungarian minority in Romania and the Romanian minority in Hungary." The list of international documents is annexed to the treaty. According to Article 15, paragraph 2 (b): "with the aim of protecting and developing the ethnic, cultural, linguistic, and religious identity of the Hungarian minority in Romania and the Romanian minority in Hungary," the Parties shall "apply as legal obligations the provisions defining the rights of persons belonging to such minorities" from the listed international instruments. In a real innovative manner, the Parties in an endnote of the Annex, provide an interpretation of Recommendation 1201/1993 of the CE.

> The Contracting Parties agree that Recommendation 1201 does not refer to collective rights, nor does it impose upon them the obligation to grant to the concerned persons any right to a special status of territorial autonomy based on ethnic criteria.

Unlike the Treaty with Slovakia, which contains precise, professionally elaborated provisions when referring to minority rights, the language of Article 15 of the Treaty with Romania is more evasive and, as such, more difficult to interpret from a legal point of view.

For instance, paragraph 3 on the sensitive issue of education states that the measures undertaken by the parties regarding the education and training of persons belonging to national minorities will be designed "according to their needs." Who will determine these needs and based on which criteria? Paragraph 2 provides that persons belonging to the Hungarian minority in Romania and Romanian minority in Hungary "shall have the right to establish and maintain their own educational, cultural, and religious institutions, organizations and associations which are entitled to seek voluntary financial and other contributions, as well as public support in accordance with the domestic legislation." For Hungary more or less the same team of experts, under the direction of the head of the International Law Department of the Ministry of Foreign Affairs, participated in the negotiation process and prepared the drafts of all these treaties. The weaknesses of Article 15 of the Treaty with Romania are due mainly to time pressures in concluding the draft since the political decision to proceed was made in the first part of August 1996. In comparing the different texts of the drafts of Article 15, those from the first round of negotiations in Bucharest (August 13–14) and the final, "stylistic" changes in Budapest (August 21–22), published in the Hungarian daily press, it is clear that it was from the Hungarian side that very serious last minute concessions were made. However, concessions were made not just on the formulation of provisions on minority rights. The most substantial compromise made by Hungary, and sharply criticized by the opposition in Budapest and by the DAHR, was the dropping of the previously planned reference on appropriate measures taken by the Romanian government regarding the restitution of real estate and other goods of the Hungarian Churches in Romania arbitrarily confiscated or nationalized under the communist regime. From the beginning, this issue was one of the most important Hungarian requests, enjoying overall consensus in Hungary and among Hungarians abroad. However, this request was put aside by the Hungarian government in August 1996 in order that a deal could be reached.

With regard to the issue of monitoring, the Treaty mentions only the establishment of an "intergovernmental expert commission" without specifying, unlike the other treaties, any of the commission's competencies. Once again, however, Article 15 in a final paragraph makes an explicit reference to the principle of territorial integrity of states in emphasizing that neither of the obligations contained in the present Article shall be interpreted as implying any right to engage in any activity or perform any act contrary to the purposes and principles of the Charter of the UN, other obligations of international law or the Helsinki Final Act, and the Paris Charter of the Conference on Security and Cooperation in Europe, including the principle of the territorial integrity of states.

Following the November 1996 election, the DAHR, with its usual average of seven percent of the ballots cast entered the new coalition government contributing to the stabilization of the political situation in a period which required particularly severe austerity measures in economic and social policy. The rhetoric regarding Hungarians in Romania and Hungary itself has since then completely changed. The new Romanian government, firmly committed to the Euro-Atlantic integration of the country announced a new policy toward its neighbors, defined as "strategic partnership." Hungary, Poland and Ukraine were named as the main partners. A shift has taken place from defensiveness regarding minority rights to a broad political dialogue with concrete measures to satisfy the legitimate interests of the Hungarians and other minority communities and groups in Romania. A cabinet post (minister without portfolio) was created to deal with the problems of minorities. The Minister is an ethnic Hungarian, one of the leaders of DAHR, and a member of the Romanian Parliament from the first legislature after 1990. If the present tends continue, the provisions of Article 15 of the Treaty will be overtaken by the events, saving hopeless disputes about interpretation.

CONCLUSIONS

In addition to the general remarks made in the introduction, the following should be added. After 1989 every Hungarian government, as a matter of constant policy, has held regular consultations on a variety of issues of common interest with representatives of political and cultural organizations of Hungarians abroad. Article 6, paragraph 3, of the Hungarian Constitution underlines the "responsibility" of the Republic of Hungary toward Hungarians living abroad and the fostering of their relations with Hungary. Obviously, it cannot be interpreted as prescribing an obligation to include Hungarian organizations abroad in the negotiation of international treaties by Hungary. However, consultations did take place during the preparatory work of all the mentioned treaties, including the longest round of negotiations on the treaty with Romania. Nevertheless, negotiations were conducted and concluded in every case by the Hungarian government and the governments of its neighbors without the formal participation of the minorities concerned. In some cases the aims of Hungarians abroad were reflected in the treaties; in others, they were not. It can be generally stated that during the whole period, each of the parties, that is the Hungarian governments and every organization of the Hungarians living in the neighboring countries, has preserved its autonomy of action. Hungarian irredentism of the inter-war period, feared by many observers, has not come back. As mentioned, the role of the provisions on the territorial integrity and inviolability of borders is merely symbolic since European borders, including Hungary's state frontiers, were and are guaranteed by separate political and legal arrangements and international conventions.

It appears that negotiations went smoothly and treaties were concluded in short order with countries where the number of Hungarians is relatively small. According to official census data the cases are Croatia (1991: 22,355 or 5.9%), Slovenia (1991: 8,499 or 0.4%) and Ukraine (1989: 155,711 or 12.5% in Western Ukraine, where Hungarians live in compact blocks). Whereas in the Slovak Republic (1991: 567,296 or 10.76%) and Romania (1992: 1,620,199 or 7.1%) with a relatively large number of politically active Hungarians, the process was more complicated. Without going into detail over the political situation in each country, two objections should be made against the argument that in Hungary's particular case a small minority community does not pose problems in bilateral relations while large numbers of minorities do. First against the background of international politics with particular regard to regional stability, the problem of Hungarians living in Serbia was virtually neglected when the issue of bilateral treaties between Hungary and its neighbors was considered on various occasions. This is despite the fact that in Serbia there is community of 340,946 Hungarians or 16.9 % in Voivodina (1991) living in compact blocks in the frontier zone, with politically very active representatives, with a higher percentage of recruitment during the war as compared to the average in the country, with attempts by authorities to change the ethnic composition of their homelands, with a high rate of emigration to

Hungary, and with a number of other real problems and sources of tension. A treaty with the Yugoslav federation is not likely to be concluded soon. The second point is the dilemma posed by the emigration of Hungarians abroad to Hungary. Census data show that members of smaller communities, more exposed to assimilation, are more likely to emigrate to Hungary. The causes of emigration (war, hate-speech, or concrete, personal threats by some individuals belonging to the majority, not held accountable by the authorities), the ways emigrants reach Hungary (crossing the green border, being smuggled, etc.), or even the cases of people who come for a specific period of time to work illegally have all generated and may continue to generate in the future social tensions within Hungary. These tendencies are more pronounced in the case of Croatia where, by 1994, roughly one third of the Hungarians were displaced by the war, one third fled to Hungary and Western Europe, and only a few hundred are still in their native villages. They are also pronounced in Serbia and in Ukraine, where mainly because of the general economic and social situation of the country, the emigration of intellectuals and illegal work is most common. One may wonder whether bilateral treaties could play any role in resolving these type of problems in addition to any regional security policy considerations. The fact is that despite the treaties concluded with Ukraine and Croatia between 1990 and 1992, the long term problems have not yet been settled in a satisfactory manner, and perhaps the most sensitive situation of the second half of the 1990's—the Hungarians in Serbia is not even addressed at this level. If the present emigration trends increase, or even extend to other neighbors, this may cause much more serious social and political tensions in Hungary than it has thus far. For all these reasons the link between the number of Hungarians in a country and the way the treaty was concluded should be considered in context.

Respect for the rights of national minorities in a given state is primarily a matter of political will. The situation of Hungarian communities in minority in countries neighboring to Hungary is no exception to this rule. Where the political will of the concerned parties exists to deal effectively with the question in the spirit of the principles laid down in international and regional instruments, appropriate legal arrangements could be worked out at the bilateral, inter-governmental, and/or national levels. Of paramount importance, however, is an internal agreement between the majorities and the minorities concerned over the terms of coexistence, making explicit the legal and political status of different ethnic and national minority groups. The best hopes in this regard are raised by the situation in Romania where, after the November 1996 election, the Hungarian political organization (DAHR) became a party in the coalition government.[23]

NOTES

1. Prime Minister József Antall's Conservative coalition government of three parties took office after the March 1990 election. Prime Minister Antall signed the treaties with Ukraine, Slovenia and Croatia. After the 1994 election a two party coalition of the Hungarian Socialist Party (MSZP) and the main Liberal party, the Free-Democrats (SZDSZ), replaced the Conservative government. Prime Minister Gyula Horn was involved personally in the conclusion of the negotiation process of the treaty with Slovakia and supervised the final preparations of the treaty with Romania, signed in 1995 and 1996 respectively. In the following, when referring to subsequent Hungarian governments, sometimes the terms Antall government and Horn government will be employed. The Horn government signed the separate convention on minorities with Croatia, while under the former government similar documents were concluded and signed with Ukraine and Slovenia, as described below.

2. For Hungary the basic document is the Paris Peace Treaty of February 10, 1947, signed by Hungary and the Allied Powers, including the Soviet Union, Great Britain, USA, Australia, SSR of Belarus, Canada, Czechoslovakia, India, New Zealand, SSR of the Ukraine, the South African Union, and the FR of Yugoslavia. Hungary, together with its neighbors, has also signed the 1975 CSCE Helsinki Final Act.

3. *Declaration on the Principles of Cooperation between the Republic of Hungary and the Ukrainian Socialist Federal Republic in the Field of Safeguarding the Rights of National Minorities.* Budapest, 31 May 1991. With an attached *Protocol* on a joint committee to monitor the implementation of the principles laid down in the Declaration as well as the fulfillment of the commitments undertaken. There are no official English translations of the treaties and instruments on minorities signed by Hungary and its neighbors which are agreed upon with the other parties. The author used the working translations made by the Hungarian Ministry of Foreign Affairs and the Office of Hungarians Abroad, adding his comments where he felt that the English version needed such comments after comparison with the original text in Hungarian.

4. *Convention for providing special rights for the Slovenian minority living in the Republic of Hungary and for the Hungarian minority living in the Republic of Slovenia.* Press Release of the Ministry of Foreign Affairs of the Republic of Hungary. Budapest, 20 January 1993.

5. The term "common" refers to group or communal rights.

6. That is, minority organizations at the national level.

7. Conference on the Human Dimension. CSCE, Copenhagen, 29 June 1990. The

idea of proclaiming that such provisions will be regarded in the future as "general legal obligations," or which "shall be applied as law," or "as commitments of a legal character" has occurred in bilateral treaties signed between Germany and Hungary (6 February 1992), Germany and Romania (21 April 1992) and Germany and the former Czechoslovakia (27 February 1992). The precise meaning of such statements, leaving aside their solemn character, is yet to be clarified.

8. These documents are the *UNESCO Convention against Discrimination in Education* (1960) and the *International Covenant on Civil and Political Rights*—(ICCPR-1966). See *International Instruments Relating to Human Rights. Classification and Status of Ratifications as of 1 January 1993* by Jean-Bernard Marie. *Human Rights Law Journal.* Vol. 14. No. 1–2.) Article 5. c of the UNESCO Convention states: "It is essential to recognize the rights of members of national minorities to carry on their own educational activities, including the maintenance of schools and, depending on the educational policy of each State, the use or the teaching of their own language, provided however (i) that this right is not exercised in a manner which prevents the members of these minorities from understanding the culture and language of the community as a whole and from participating in its activities, or which prejudices national sovereignty; (ii) that the standard of education is not lower than the general standard laid down or approved by the competent authorities; and (iii) that attendance at such schools is optional." According to Article 27 of the ICCPR, "In those States in which ethnic, religious, or linguistic minorities exist, persons belonging to such minorities shall not be denied the right, in community with the other members of their group, to enjoy their own culture, to profess and practice their own religion, or to use their own language."

9. *Convention between the Republic of Hungary and the Republic of Croatia on the protection of the Hungarian minority in the Republic of Croatia and the Croatian minority in the Republic of Hungary.*

10. Two regional round-tables were set up, chaired by the EU. The first brought together Estonia, Latvia, Lithuania, and Poland and those invited by them. The second round-table on the regional basis included Bulgaria, Hungary, Poland, Romania, Slovakia and the Czech Republic, and those invited by them, including Slovenia.

11. The PSE expressed, in the view of its signatories, their "common, continuing effort to prevent and put an end to threats of tensions and crises and to create an area of lasting good-neighborliness and cooperation in Europe, in order to promote and render irreversible the achievements of democracy, respect for human rights, the rule of law, economic progress, social justice, and peace." *Introduction to the Declaration of the PSE,* Paris, 21 March 1995. The countries signing the attached agreements were: Bulgaria, the Czech Republic, Estonia, Hungary, Latvia, Lithuania, Poland, Romania, and Slovakia.

12. As of February 1995 the following states joined by signing the PFP initiative document: Albania, Armenia, Austria, Azarbaijan, Belarus, Bulgaria, Czech Republic, Estonia, Finland, Georgia, Hungary, Kazakhstan, Kyrgyzistan, Latvia, Lithuania, Moldova, Poland, Romania, Russia, Slovakia, Slovenia, Sweden, Turkmenistan, Ukraine, and Uzbekistan.

13. The draft presented astonishing similarities with the minority provisions contained in the 1993 Slovak–Romanian bilateral treaty.

14. *Treaty on Good-Neighborly Relations and Friendly Cooperation Between the Republic of Hungary and the Slovak Republic.* Paris, 19 March 1995. English translation by the International Law department of the Ministry of Foreign Affairs of the Republic of Hungary.

15. Article 68 (1) of the Hungarian Constitution, after defining national and ethnic minorities living in Hungary as "constituent factors in the state („államalkotó tényezők" in Hungarian), thus sharing "the power of the people"(„részesei a nép hatalmának"), provides that "(2) The Republic of Hungary grants protection to national and ethnic minorities; it ensures the possibilities for their collective participation in public life, and enables them to foster their own culture, the use of the mother tongue, to receive school instruction in the mother tongue, and to freely use their names as spelled and pronounced in their own language. (3) The laws of the Republic of Hungary ensure representation of the national and ethnic minorities living in the territory of the country. (4) National and ethnic minorities may set up their own local and national government organizations." („helyi és országos önkormányzatok"–that is, self-governing bodies at the local and the national level)." Official English translation of the Hungarian Constitution. (*Magyar Közlöny.* No. 84, 24 August 1990) The question of guaranteed parliamentary representation of national and ethnic minorities as of March 1998 was not yet resolved, for disagreement among parliamentary parties regarding the electoral *technique* to be codified. There is a consensus, however, that the question should be solved in a positive way. In 1993, the Hungarian parliament voted with 97% majority, and with the prior consent of all minority organizations in Hungary to approve the *Act On the Rights of National and Ethnic Minorities*, a comprehensive piece of legislation, called sometimes as the *Minority Code*.

16. The text of the verbal note, in a "courtesy translation" by the Ministry of Foreign Affairs of the Slovak Republic, indicated the following arguments: "The Government of the Slovak Republic considers the agreed upon text of the treaty mutually acceptable, not putting any Contracting Party at an advantage, guaranteeing the inviolability of common State borders, precluding raising any territorial claims towards each other, and creating an adequate legal framework for the implementation of the rights of persons belonging to national minorities in conformity with the domestic legislation of the two countries.

However, the Government of the Slovak Republic has noted with surprise that, even before the Treaty has been signed, misinterpretation of the text of the agreed Treaty occurs on the part of the official Hungarian representatives, namely as regards the article which regulates the status of persons belonging to national minorities. The Government of the Slovak Republic refuses, in particular, those interpretations of the Hungarian Contracting Party according to which the Slovak Contracting Party accepted the Recommendation of the Parliamentary Assembly of the Council of Europe No. 1201/1993 in the sense enabling the creation of autonomous minority self-governing bodies.

The Government of the Slovak Republic emphasizes that it has never accepted and has not enshrined in the Treaty any formulation that would be based on the recognition of the principle of collective rights for minorities and that would admit the creation of autonomous structures on ethnic principle... In conjunction with other relevant provisions of the document, the Treaty consistently respects the recognized European standards based exclusively on individual rights of persons belonging to national minorities. Consequently, no other interpretation comes into question.

This statement of the Government of the Slovak Republic shall be submitted to the Government of the Republic of Hungary through diplomatic channels. In Bratislava, 18 March 1995."

17. Article 21 of the Slovak–Hungarian treaty states that: "(1) The Contracting Parties, in the event of a difference of view in connection with the interpretation or application of the present Treaty, shall consult with each other pursuant to the provisions of Article 5 of this Treaty. (2) If such consultations fail to eliminate, within reasonable time, the difference of view, the Contracting Parties shall consider what other methods in accordance with the principles and norms of international law can be achieved."

18. The Slovak–Hungarian Treaty is not consequent on the use of the term "national minorities." Most of the provisions of Article 15 refer to persons belonging to national minorities in general. The provision which declares norms and political commitments of certain international documents "as legal obligation" refers explicitly to persons belonging to the Hungarian minority in the Slovak Republic and the Slovak minority in Hungary. That there is a distinction in treatment in this regard appears to be endorsed by the provision in Article 15, paragraph 4 (a), which states. "That as regards the regulation of the rights of persons belonging to national minorities living in their respective territories, they shall apply the Framework Convention on the Protection of National Minorities" of the Council of Europe (1994) "unless their respective domestic legal systems provide a broader protection of rights of persons belonging to national minorities than does the Framework Convention." This provision is followed by the section on "legal obligations" and the list of international documents considered as such.

19. Ion Iliescu, as acting chairman of the Front's executive committee, delivered on 25 January 1990 a televised statement accusing Hungarians in Transylvania of separatism. The charge was based on the fact that, in major towns of Transylvania, local Hungarian representatives, most of them in their capacity as local Front activists, not only argued for the restitution of Hungarian teaching schools closed down or transformed into bi-lingual or only Romanian teaching institutions by the Ceausescu regime, but in certain cases effectively have "taken back" the school. The lowest point in Hungarian–Romanian relations in Transylvania did not come until the March 1990 street clashes in Tîrgu-Mureş (Marosvásárhely) which, as it was proven later on, were instigated by certain elements of the secret services.

20. Some of the quoted sections are mentioned in a publication by the Government of Romania entitled *The Legislative and Institutional Framework for the National Minorities of Romania.* (Bucureşti, 1994), p. 9. Article 1 of the Constitution on the national character of the state is not mentioned. The provision on the official language is also absent. However, Article 148 on the limits of the revision of the Constitution is mentioned. "The provisions of this Constitution with regard to the national, independent, unitary, and indivisible character of the Romanian State, its Republican form of government, territorial integrity,

independence of the judiciary, political pluralism, and official language shall not be subject to revision."

21. See for instance Gabriel Andreescu, Renate Weber and Valentin Stan, *Study on the Conception of Democratic Alliance of Hungarians in Romania on the Rights of National Minorities. A Critical Analysis of the DAHR Documents.* (Bucureşti, 1994). The trimestrial review *Altera* published in Tîrgu-Mureş (Marosvásárhely) since 1995, under the editorship of Smaranda Enache and Elek Szokoly, regularly addressed issues related to minority rights and inter-ethnic relations.

22. Gabriel Andreescu, *Recomandarea 1201, drepturile minoritátilor nationale si dezbaterile publice din Romania* [Recommendation 1201, the rights of national minorities and the public debates in Romania]. Revista Romana de Drepturile Omului. APADOR-CH. (Bucureşti, Aprilie-Mai-Iunie, 1995), p.40.

23. On the conditions and the terms of such a deal see Gáspár Bíró, Minority Rights in Eastern and Central Europe and the Role of International Institutions in *Searching for Moorings. East Central Europe in the International System*, ed. Jeffrey Laurenti, (New York, 1994), 97-127.

BIOGRAPHIES OF KEY PERSONALITIES

Ady, Endre (1877-1919), Hungarian poet, publicist, leading figure of the literary movement and review journal *Nyugat* (hallmarked by his name), closely connected with the Galilei Circle, celebrated as a revolutionary poet during the 1918 Fall Revolution in Hungary.

Alexander I (1777-1825), Russian Czar (1801-1825).

Andrássy, Gyula (1823-1890), Hungarian Prime Minister (1867-1871), common Austro-Hungarian Foreign Secretary (1871-1879).

Andrian-Werburg, Viktor Franz von (1813-1858), Austrian politician, publicist, government employee (1834-1846), member of the Frankfurt German National Assembly (1848-1849), emissary of the Assembly to London (August 1848-March 1849).

Antall, József (1932-1993), Hungarian historian, politician, director of the Semmelweis Museum of Medical History (1964-1991), member (from 1988) and president (from 1989) of the Hungarian Democratic Forum, Prime Minister of the Hungarian Republic (1990-1993).

Apor, Péter (1676-1752), Transylvanian Székler (Székely) aristocrat, baron, memoir writer, poet.

Árpád (ca.850/55-ca.907), conquering Hungarian chieftain, exclusive Prince after the death of Kurszán (904).

Averescu, Alexandru (1859-1938), Romanian general, politician, served in the War of Romanian Independence (1877-1878), as Minister of War (1907) undertook reorganization of the Romanian army, commanded attack on Bulgaria (1913), as Prime Minister (1918) conducted peace negotiations with the Central Powers, Prime Minister of Romania (1920-21, 1926-27).

Babes, Emil (b. 1858), lawyer of Romanian nationality, publicist, prominent figure in the political and cultural life of Romanians in Hungary.

Bach, Alexander (1813-1893), baron, Austrian Minister of the Interior (1849-1859). Hungarian historiography calls his ministership the "Bach Era."

Bajcsy-Zsilinszky, Endre (1886-1944), Hungarian politician, Parliamentary Representative, journalist. Started as a right-wing politician, participated in extreme racist organizations, later joined the anti-German democratic opposition, became a leader of the antifascist resistance, executed by the Arrow-Cross in Sopronkőhida.

Bălcescu, Nicolae (1819–1852), Romanian politician, historian, a leader of the 1848 Wallachian Revolution. After the collapse of the Revolution mediated in Transylvania between the divided Hungarians and Romanians, hence had an important role in the creation of the 1849 Nationalities Act. Died in Palermo.

Balladur, Eduard (1929–), Secretary of State (1986–88), Parliamentary Representative (from 1988), French Prime Minister (1993–95), Republican presidential nominee in 1995.

Bánffy, Miklós (1873–1950), Transylvanian Hungarian count, writer, politician, Parliamentary Representative, participated in the establishment of the Budapest Székely National Council (1918), Hungarian Foreign Secretary (1921–22), Romanian citizen (from 1926), a leader of Transylvanian Hungarian intellectual life, on behalf of Miklós Kállay unsuccessfully negotiated with Iuliu Maniu about the return of Northern Transylvania to Hungary (1943).

Bartal, György (1820–1875), Hungarian Parliamentary Representative during the 1848/49 Revolution and War of Independence, Department Head of the Ministry of Finance.

Bartha, Miklós (1848–1905), Transylvanian Hungarian politician, publicist. The Miklós Bartha Society (1925–44) was named after him and was established to research the nationality question and the social problems of the countryside.

Bastide, Jules (1800–1879), French journalist, revolutionary, Foreign Secretary of France (May–December 1848).

Batthyány, Kázmér (1807–1854), count, Hungarian liberal politician, Foreign Secretary of the Szemere Government in 1849, exiled after the defeat of the War of Independence.

Batthyány, Lajos (1807–1849), count, Hungarian aristocratic liberal politician, Prime Minister of the first Hungarian Government in 1848, executed in Pest on October 6, 1849.

Bauer, Ottó (1881–1938), theoretician of the Austrian Social Democratic Party, statesman, Austrian Foreign Secretary after the end of World War I, signed a secret agreement on the Anschluss with Germany in the spring of 1919 which was later rejected by the Allies, resigned in the summer of 1919, was active as a member of the Austrian National Council (1929–1934), emigrated after the defeat of the Vienna Socialist Uprising in 1934.

Bem, Josef (1794–1850), Polish general during the 1830 Polish Uprising, honvéd Lieutenant General and the Commander-in-Chief of the Transylvanian Hungarian Army in 1848–49, exiled after the defeat of the War of Independence.

Beneš, Eduard (1884–1948), a leader of the Czechoslovak national movement, President of the State (1935–38), President of the Czechoslovak Provisional

Government in London (from July 1940), President of the Republic (1946-48).

Bethlen, István (1874-1946), Hungarian statesman, Prime Minister (1921-1931), retained his political significance even after his resignation as a leader of right-wing radical opposition, arrested by the Soviets and transported to Moscow (1945), died in the Soviet Union.

Bibó, István (1911-1979), Hungarian historian, political scientist, legal philosopher, Secretary of State of the Imre Nagy Government in 1956, imprisoned (1957-1963), rehabilitated in 1978, a paragon of the Hungarian democratic intellectuals.

Björnson, Björnstjerne Martinius (1832-1910), poet, playwright, novelist, journalist, editor, orator, theater director of Norwegian descent, emigrated to France due to political battles and literary debates, won the Nobel Prize in 1903.

Boross, Péter (1928-), Hungarian politician, member of the Hungarian Democratic Forum (from August 1992), Deputy President of the Forum (from February 1993), Minister without portfolio (July-December 1990), Minister of the Interior (December 1990-1993), Prime Minister (1993-1994).

Borsody, István (1911-), Hungarian journalist, historian, press attaché of the Hungarian Embassy in Washington D.C. (1946), settled in the United States (1947), friend and colleague of Oszkár Jászi.

Brandsch, Rudolf, Romanian politician of German descent who became a leader of the "Green Saxon" movement (1893), an important member of the German-Saxon People's Council.

Brăianu, Dumitru (1818-1892), Romanian politician of Wallachia, after 1849 representative of the Romanian exiles in the Central Democratic Committee in London. President of the National Liberal Party (1891-92).

Briand, Aristide (1862-1932), French politician, Socialist representative (from 1902), minister or prime minister in most of the governments (from 1906), advocate of rapprochement with Germany, initiator of the Kellog-Briand Pact (1928).

Brzezinski, Zbigniew (1928-), American political scientist, National Security Advisor to President Carter (1977-1981).

Carosini, Giuseppe, Italian merchant of Piemonte, political agent in Belgrade for Lajos Kossuth (January 1850), task included furthering Serb-Hungarian rapprochement.

Catherine II or Catherine the Great (1729-1796), Empress of Russia (1762-1796).

Charles IV (1887-1922), Hungarian king as Charles I, Austrian Emperor (1916-18).

Coudenhove-Kalergi, Richard Nikolaus (1894-1935), Austrian count, doctor of philosophy, founder and President of the Pan-European Union (1923).

Croce, Benedetto (1866-1952), Italian philosopher, historian, critic, Minister of Education (1920-21), had to resign as a professor in Naples after Mussolini came to power.

Csányi, László (1787-1849), Hungarian liberal politician, government commissioner (1848/49), Minister of Public Work and Transport in the Szemere Government, executed in Pest in 1849.

Cyril (827-869), Byzantine monk, missionary, brother of Methodius. Both are called the "Apostles of the Slavs" due to their influence on the religious-cultural development of the Danube Slavs.

Czartoryski, Adam (1770-1861), Polish politician, prince, Foreign Secretary for Alexander I at the beginning of the 19th century, leader of the 1830 Polish Revolution, head of the conservative wing of the Paris Polish exiles.

Czecz, János (1822-1904), Hungarian honvéd general and commander of an army corps in Transylvania during the 1848-49 War of Independence, emigrated in 1849.

Danilevski, Nikolai (1822-1865), Russian natural scientist and philosopher of history. In his view Russia and the Slavs ought to be neutral towards the West and strive to improve their cultural heritage, that is the system of political absolutism.

Deák, Ferenc (1803-1876), Hungarian statesman, a prominent figure of the Hungarian Reform Movement, Minister of Justice of the Batthyány Government (1848), isolated in 1849 moved to his country estates, after the defeat of the War of Independence pursued the policy of passive resistance, had a major role in negotiations leading to the Compromise and the establishment of the dualist Austro-Hungarian Monarchy in 1867.

Deák, Imre (1899-), Hungarian lawyer, member of the Populistic Literary Society, whose book *A száműzött Kossuth* [The Exiled Kossuth] (Budapest, 1939) relates to the Teleki-Kossuth debate.

Dembinski, Henryk (1791-1864), Polish count, general of the 1831 Polish Uprising, honvéd lieutenant general of the Hungarian War of Independence in 1848-49, commander-in-chief, commander of the army, chief of staff, emigrated after the defeat of the War of Independence.

Desprez, Hippolyte, 19th century French publicist, Balkans expert among the Polish exiles, traveled in Wallachia in 1847.

Dimitrov, Georgi (1882-1949), Bulgarian communist politician, first Prime Minister of Bulgaria after World War II. His speech for his defense denying Nazi accusations made him world famous in the Leipzig Trial after setting the Reichstag on fire (1933).

Dragoş, Ioan, Romanian politician in Hungary, Hungarian Parliamentary Representative during the 1848/49 War of Independence, delegated by Lajos Kossuth to start negotiations with the Romanian militiaman Avram Iancu, murdered in 1849.

Durkheim, Emile (1858–1917), French sociologist, developed efficient methodology which blended empirical research with sociological theory, considered to be the founder of the French school of sociology.

Eckhardt, Tibor (1888–1972), Hungarian politician, Parliamentary Representative, one of the founders and the leader of the extreme right wing Association of Awakening Hungarians, Deputy President of the Hungarian Revisionist League in 1930, joined the independent Small-holders' Party, became its president (1932–40), traveled to the USA as a government emissary to establish connections with the Anglo-Saxon powers to counter-balance German orientation, he did not return back to Hungary.

Eötvös, József (1813–1871), Hungarian novelist, essayist, statesman, dedicated his life and work to establish modern Hungarian literature and to the foundation of a new democratic Hungary, Minister of Religion and Education in the Batthyány Government in 1848, left the country before the War broke out, Minister of Religion and Public Education in the Gyula Andrássy Government (from 1867).

Fadeiev, Rostislav (1826–1884), Russian general, served in the Caucasus, Pan-Slav publicist.

Fényes, Elek (1807–1876), Hungarian statistician, geographic and economic writer, in 1848 he was commissioned by the Minister of the Interior Bertalan Szemere to establish the National Office of Statistics, after 1849 had to go into hiding terminating his scientific career.

Ferdinand V (1793–1875), Hungarian king, Austrian Emperor as Ferdinand I (from 1835 to December 2, 1848).

Ferrero, Guglielmo (1871–1943), Italian historian, professor in Geneva (from 1930), author of *Grandezza e decadenza di Roma* (1902–1907), *La ruine de la civilisation antigue* (1921), *Bonaparte en Italie* (1936).

Fichte, Johann Gottlieb (1762–1814), German philosopher, representative of transcendential idealism.

Franz I (1768–1835), Holy Roman Emperor (1792–1804), took the title of Austrian Emperor (1804), Hungarian king (1792–1835).

Franz Ferdinand (1863–1914), Austrian-Este Archduke and Hungarian Royal Prince, heir to the crown of Austria and Hungary, deputy commander-in-chief, morganatic marriage with Sophia Chotek (1900), killed by Serbian student Gavrilo Princip in Sarajevo (June 28, 1914).

Franz Joseph I (1830–1916), Austrian emperor and Hungarian king (1848–1916), established the dualist monarchy by dividing his Empire in 1867, entered into alliance with Germany (1879), launched World War I by giving an ultimatum to Serbia.

Gai, Liudevit (1809–1872), Croat politician, publicist, established Illyrism, developer of the Croatian literary language.

Gerő, Ernő (1898-1980), Hungarian politician, member of the Political Committee of the Hungarian Workers' Party (1945-1956), first secretary (July and October, 1956), Deputy Prime Minister (1949-1956), fled to the Soviet Union during the 1956 Revolution, lived in Budapest from 1960 onwards.

Gheorghiu-Dej, Gheorghe (1901-1965), Romanian communist politician, First Secretary of Romanian Communist Party (1945-1965), Prime Minister (1952-1955), statesman (1961-1965).

Ghica, Ion (1816-1897), man of letters, Prime Minister of Romania (1866, 1870-71), played a leading role in the revolutionary events of 1848, forced into exile, Prince of Samos (1854-1859), participated in overthrowing Alexandru Cuza, the first Prince of united Romania (1866).

Gladstone, William Ewart (1809-1898), English liberal politician, statesman, Prime Minister of Great Britain (1868-74, 1880-85, 1886, 1892-94).

Goga, Octavian (1881-1938), Romanian writer, politician, member of the Romanian delegation to the Peace Conference in Paris (1919), Minister of Religion (1920), Minister of the Interior (1926), Prime Minister (1937-38).

Golescu, Alexandru (1819-1881), Wallachian Romanian radical liberal politician, participated in the Wallachian Revolution of 1848, lived in exile, Prime Minister of Romania in 1870.

Gomulka, Władysłav (1905-1982), Polish communist politician, First Secretary of the Polish United Workers' Party (1944-1948 and 1956-1970), expelled from the Party (1949), imprisoned (1951-1954).

Gorove, István (1819-1881), Hungarian politician, economist, travel book writer, Parliamentary Representative during the Hungarian Revolution and the War of Independence, participated in writing the Declaration of Independence (April, 1849), lived in exile (1849-1857), Minister of Agriculture, Minister of Industry, Minister of Commerce (from 1867), Minister of Public Works and Transport (1870-71).

Gratz, Gusztáv (1875-1946), Hungarian publicist, legitimist politician, historiographer, from 1912 executive director of the National Alliance of Hungarian Industrialists, Minister of Finance (1917), Foreign Minister (1921), President of the Cultural Society of Germans of Hungary (1921-1938).

Grillparzer, Franz (1791-1872), Austrian poet, playwright, Director of Hofkammerarchiv (1832-1856).

Groza, Petru (1884-1958), Parliamentary Representative of the Romanian People's Party (1920-1927), ran on an anti-fascist program (1933), Prime Minister (1945-1952), President of the Presidium of the National Assembly (1952-1958).

Grünwald, Béla (1839-1891), Hungarian politician, publicist, historian, member of moderate opposition led by Albert Apponyi and Dezső Szilágyi (1880), concerned with administrative and nationality issues in his political writings, committed suicide in Paris.

Gyárfás, Elemér (1884-1945), Hungarian politician in Romania, economist, member of the Transylvanian National Party of Hungarians (1919), member of the Romanian Senate (1926), President of the Catholic People's Alliance.

Habsburg-Lotharingen, Otto von (1912-), son of Austrian Emperor and Hungarian king Charles IV, the head of the Habsburg-house (from 1922), member (from 1946) and president (from 1973) of the Pan-European Union, Bavarian Representative to the European Parliament (form 1979).

Habsburg-Lotharingen, Rudolph (1858-1889), Austrian archduke, heir to the Hungarian and Austrian thrones, only son of Franz Joseph I, committed suicide.

Hajnal, István (1892-1956), Hungarian historian, studied connections between culture, education, and social history.

Haller, Ferenc (1796-1875), Hungarian count, general, Croatian *Ban* (1841-1846), fought in Northern Italy with the imperial army (1848-49), A.D.C. for Military and Civic Governor of Hungary, Archduke Albrecht (1856).

Hantos, Elemér (1881-1942), Hungarian politician, legal and economic writer, economic expert of the League of Nations (1924), founder of the following institutes: National Union of Financial Institutes, Central European Institutes in Vienna, Brno, Budapest, Centre d'Études de l'Europe Centrale in Geneva, Mitteleuropäische Wirtschaftsagung.

Havliček, Karel (pseudonym **Havel Borovský** (1821-1856), Czech journalist, imprisoned and exiled because of his liberal articles (1851), considered a master prose stylist, influenced modern Czechs.

Helfert, Joseph Alexander (1820-1910), Austrian historiographer, Minister of Culture (1861-1863).

Herder, Johann Gottfried (1744-1803), German writer, poet, critic, literary translator, idealistic philosopher, an initiator of Sturm und Drang.

Hitler, Adolf (1889-1945), leader of the National Socialist German Workers' Party (NSDAP), chancellor (1933), "Führer" of the German people whose aggressive foreign policy led to World War II.

Hodoşiu, Josif (1830-1880), Transylvanian Romanian writer, politician, played important roles in the 1848-49 movements, became a leader of the intellectual life of Transylvanian Romanians.

Hodža, Milan (1878-1944), Czechoslovak politician, Member of Hungarian Parliament (1905-1918), Czechoslovakian Parliament (1918-1938), Prime Minister (1935-1938), went into exile following the Munich Agreement.

Hohenwart, Karl Siegmund (1824-1899), Austrian statesman, count, as Prime Minister of Austria (1871) wanted to restructure Austrian constitution on a federative basis.

Horn, Gyula (1932-), Hungarian politician, after the Revolution of 1956 participated in the aggressive stabilization of the Kádár-regime, Head of Foreign

Affairs Department of the Hungarian Socialist Workers' Party (1983–1985), Under-Secretary of Foreign Affairs (1985–1989), Foreign Secretary (1989–1990), Prime Minister (1994–1998).

Horthy, Miklós (1868–1957), naval officer, Regent of Hungary (1920–1944), by his own authority as Regent he led Hungary into the World War II with the subsequent consent of the Parliament, his unsuccessful attempt to jump out of the Axis Coalition on October 15, 1944 was followed by the Arrow-Cross take-over, after German and American captivity lived in Portugal until his death.

Horváth, Mihály (1809–1878), Hungarian historiographer, politician, Catholic prelate, Minister of Public Education of the Szemere Government (from May 12, 1849), after the defeat of the Revolution lived in exile in Belgium, France, Switzerland, his chief historical work was *Magyarország történelme, I–IV.* [History of Hungary, I–IV.], (Pest, 1860–1863).

Hugo, Victor (1802–1885), French poet, novelist, playwright, leading figure of romanticism.

Huizinga, Johann (1872–1945), Dutch cultural historian, representative of the counter-effects of the history of ideas of positivism, claimed that historians should detach from the objective historical process and should act as artists, in his view the task of historiography is to describe the life-style and the changes of emotional atmosphere characteristic of a period.

Irányi, Dániel (1822–1892), Hungarian publicist, politician, an important figure in the Pest events of 1848, government commissioner of Pest, lived in exile (1850–1868), Member of Parliament after returning to Hungary, rejected the 1867 constitutional law.

Irinyi, József (?1822–1859), Hungarian writer, journalist, literary translator, liberal politician, a leader of the "March Youth" in 1848, legation counselor in Paris (1849), sentenced to death after the defeat of the War of Independence, pardoned later.

Isac, Emil (b. 1855), Romanian writer, devotee of symbolism, reviewer of Hungarian literature for Romanians.

István I (ca. 971/75–1038), Prince of Hungary (from 997), first Hungarian king (from 1001), founder of the state.

Jancsó, Benedek (1854–1930), Transylvanian Hungarian publicist, historian, literary historian, from 1895 to 1899 co-worker of the Nationality Department of the Prime Minister's Office, worked in the Ministry of Culture (from 1907), most of his books discussed Romanian national aspirations.

Jancsó, Elemér (1905–1971), Transylvanian Hungarian literary historian, critic, member of Transylvanian Scientific Institute.

Jászi, Oszkár (1875–1957), Hungarian social scientist, publicist, politician, member of the National Council (1918), a leader of the 1918 Revolution, Minister of Nationality Affairs, emigrated in May 1919, President of the Democratic Alliance of American Hungarians during World War II.

Jelačić, Josip (1801-1859), baron, *Ban* of Croatia, Slavonia, and Dalmatia, imperial and royal lieutenant general, led an attack against Hungary during the fall of 1848 but the Hungarian Army blocked his way at Pákozd on September 28, 1848, then he left Hungary.

Kádár, János (1912-1989), Hungarian communist party functionary, Minister of the Interior (1948-1950), imprisoned on trumped-up charges (1950-1954), First Secretary of the Hungarian Workers' Party during the 1956 Revolution, Secretary of State in the Imre Nagy Government, later Head of Counter-Government in Szolnok, First Secretary of the Hungarian Socialist Workers' Party (1956-1988), President of the Party (1988-1989).

Kállay, Miklós (1887-1967), Hungarian politician, Minister of Agriculture (1932-1935), Prime Minister (1942-1944), pursued double-dealing policy between the Axis and the Western Powers, emigrated to the USA.

Kant, Immanuel (1724-1804), distinguished representative of classical German philosophy of idealism, dualism, and agnosticism.

Karacsay, Sándor (1813-1880), Hungarian liberal count, major of the National Guard in 1848-49, emigrated, major of the Hungarian Legion in Prussia (1866).

Károlyi, Mihály (1875-1955), Hungarian politician, memoir writer, count. As head of his party fought for ending the War from 1916 onwards, President of the National Council (established on October 25, 1918), Prime Minister of the Government of the successful Bourgeois Democratic Revolution, lived in exile in France and in England (from 1919) where he tried to establish connections for a Danube Confederation, returned to Hungary in 1946, ambassador in Paris until he turned against the Rákosi Regime (1949).

Kemény, Dénes (1803-1849), Transylvanian Hungarian liberal politician, baron, Parliamentary Representative (1848-49), Under-Secretary of the Ministry of the Interior (1848), later the leader of the Minister of the Interior.

Kemény, János (1903-1971), Transylvanian Hungarian writer, literary activist, theater director, baron, hosted the Erdélyi Helikon [Transylvanian Helikon] meeting in his Marosvécse castle (1921).

Kemény, Zsigmond (1814-1875), Hungarian writer, publicist, Parliamentary Representative (1848/49), member of the Peace Party, criticized Lajos Kossuth's policy in his political pamphlets (1850/51), as an editor of the *Pesti Napló* and as a publicist assisted in publicizing the Deák Party's program and in the preparation of the 1867 Austrian-Hungarian Compromise.

Keresztury, Dezső (1904-1998), Hungarian writer, literary historian, politician. Minister of Religion and Public Education as a member of the National Peasants' Party (1945-47).

Khrushchev, Nikita Sergeievich (1894–1971), Soviet politician, First Secretary of the Soviet Communist Party (1953–1964), Premier (1958–1964).

Klapka, György (1820–1892), general of the Hungarian (Honvéd) Army (1848–49), emigrated after the defeat of the War of Independence, a major figure in the Romanian-Hungarian reconciliation initiatives (1859–1864).

Klaus, Václav (1941–), Czech politician, economist, Minister of Finance and Deputy Prime Minister of Czechoslovakia (1989–1992), Prime Minister of the Czech Republic (1992–1998).

Klauzál, Gábor (1804–1866), eminent figure of Hungarian reform Diets/Parliaments, Minister of Agriculture, Industry, and Commerce of the Batthyány Government.

Kmet, Andrej (1841–1908), Slovak polymath, Roman Catholic priest.

Kollar, Jan (1793–1852), Slovak poet and linguist who wrote in Czech, prominent figure of Slovak national movement.

Kós, Károly (1883–1977), Transylvanian politician of Saxon descent, writer, based on the Wilsonian Principles organized the Republic of Kalotaszeg (spring of 1919), one of the authors of the pamphlet "Kiáltó Szó" [Crying Word] (1921), founder and secretary of the Hungarian People's Party and the Hungarian Alliance in Romania, participated in establishing the Erdélyi Helikon [Transylvanian Helikon] (1926), President of the Hungarian People's Alliance (1945).

Kossuth, Lajos (1802–1894), Hungarian reform politician, publicist, Finance Minister of the Batthyány Government (1848), President of the Hungarian Defense Committee, Governing President of Hungary (April 14, 1849), emigrated after the defeat of the War of Independence, rejected the Austrian-Hungarian Compromise until his death.

Kovács, Imre (1913–1980), writer, journalist, sociographer, rural sociologist, radical representative of peasant democracy, founding member of the March Front (1937). Member (1939), Secretary-General (1945), Vice President (1946) of the National Peasants' Party, Member of Parliament, emigrated to Switzerland (1947), later to the USA where he became a member of the Free Europe Committee.

Kvaternik, Slovko, Croatian colonel, violating the Belgrade Pact occupied Muraköz [Medimurje] with four thousand volunteers (December 1918).

Lammasch, Henrik (1853–1920), Austrian legal scientist, Prime Minister of Austria (1918).

Laski, Harold Joseph (1893–1950), British politician, philosopher, writer.

Laurian, August Treboniu (1810–1881), Transylvanian Romanian linguist, teacher, participated in Transylvanian Romanian movements (1848).

Leibniz, Gottfried Wilhelm (1646–1716), German philosopher, natural scientist, mathematician.

Ligeti, Ernő (1891–1945), Transylvanian Hungarian writer, poet, founding member of the *Erdélyi Helikon* [Transylvanian Helikon] (1926), moved to Hungary, murdered by the Arrow-Cross.

List, Friedrich (1789–1846), German economic theoretician, founder of the school advocating protective tariff system.

Ludendorff, Erich (1865–1937), German general, with Hindenburg major commanders of German military operations (from summer 1916), took part in the "beer-hall putsch" in Munich.

Lukács, Móric (1812–1881), Hungarian publicist, literary translator, forced into exile due to his involvement in 1848, after the 1867 Austro-Hungarian Compromise joined the Deák Party, concerned about the social contradictions of capitalism.

Madách, Imre (1823–1864), Hungarian playwright, poet, his sister and her officer husband were massacred by Romanian peasant revolutionaries, imprisoned and later under police supervision in Pest for sheltering Kossuth's secretary (1852–53), Parliamentary Representative (1861).

Maiorescu, Ioan (1811–1864), Transylvanian Romanian teacher, publicist, politician who later settled in Wallachia, emissary of the Wallachian Revolutionary Government in the German Assembly in Frankfurt (1848).

Makay, Miklós (1905–1977), Hungarian reformed minister, writer, first Hungarian representative of the ecumenical movement, organized the Danubian Ecumenical Youth Conference in Budapest.

Makkai, Sándor (1890–1951), Transylvanian Hungarian writer, fought for the cultural and political rights of Transylvanian Hungarians as a member of the Romanian Senate and as a Reformed bishop, settled in Hungary in 1936.

Malnasanu, Aurel, Romanian Deputy Foreign Secretary in 1956.

Maniu, Iuliu (1873–1951), founder and leader of the Romanian National Peasants' Party, Prime Minister (1928–30, 1932–33), imprisoned in 1947.

Marek, Antonin (1785–1877), Czech priest and writer.

Masaryk, Tomaš (1850–1937), Czech politician and philosopher, the first Prime Minister of Czechoslovakia (1918–1935).

Mazzini, Giuseppe (1805–1872), Italian revolutionary, leader of the republican side of Risorgimento, head of Roman Republic (March–July 1849).

Methodius (825–884), Byzantian monk, missionary, Cyril's brother. Both are called the "Apostles of the Slavs" due to their influence on the religious-cultural development of the Danube Slavs.

Metternich, M-W. Klemens Lothar von (1773–1859), prince, Austrian diplomat, statesman. Minister of Foreign Affairs (from 1809), Chancellor (from 1821), President of the Ministers' Council (1826), dominating figure of the Holy Alliance, emigrated due to the impact of the 1848 revolutions. Franz Joseph's advisor (1851–59).

Mikó, Imre (1911-1977), Transylvanian Hungarian writer of political law, literary translator, writer, representative in the Romanian Parliament (1937), Secretary General of the Bucharest Legal Consulting Office of the Hungarian People's Alliance (1939-40), after the Second Vienna Award Representative and Member of the Governing body of the Transylvanian Party in Budapest, returning home from Soviet captivity removed from his job.

Mikoian, Anastas Ivanovich (1895-1978), Soviet communist politician, member of the Presidium of the Central Committee of the Soviet Communist Party (1935-1966), Deputy Prime Minister (1937-1964).

Miletič Svetozar (1824-1901), Serbian writer, politician, participated in the Serbian movements of 1848-49. Representative in the Hungarian Parliament (from 1865), in spite of his immunity arrested (1876) and sentenced to five years imprisonment for high treason (January, 1878).

Mocsáry, Lajos (1826-1916), Hungarian politician, publicist, supporter of Deák's proposal at the 1861 Parliamentary session, opponent of the planned Austrian-Hungarian Compromise (1865), Parliamentary Representative with a left centrist program (until 1873), first President of the Independence Party (1874-1884), his Party delimited itself from his nationality policy (1887) and he was forced to resign, representative of mostly Romanian-inhabited Karánsebes (1888-1891), offered a nationality program with the most advantageous cultural and administrative opportunities for the nationalities of historical Hungary within a unified state.

Mussolini, Benito (1883-1945), Italian fascist politician, Prime Minister and dictator of Italy (1922-1943), leader of the "Salo Republic" (1943), executed by partisans.

Nagy, Imre (1896-1958), Hungarian communist politician, Minister of Agriculture in the Provisional National Government (1944-45), Minister of the Interior (November, 1945-March, 1946), Minister of Provision, Minister for Collecting Surplus, Produce, and Livestock (first half of 1950's), Vice President, later President of the Council of Ministers (1952-55), Prime Minister of Hungary during the 1956 Revolution, deported to Romania after the fall of the Revolution, sentenced to death and executed in Budapest.

Neumann, Friedrich (1860-1919), German clergyman, publicist, politician, early follower of Stoecker's Christian Social movement, a contributor to *Die Hilfe*, founder and first president (1896) of National Social Union, member of the Reichstag (1907-1912, 1913-1918), cofounder and leader (1918) of the German Democratic Party, wrote "Mitteleuropa" (1915).

Németh, László (1901-1975), Hungarian writer, essayist, literary translator, joined the group of peasant writers and the New Intellectual Front, condensed his nationality views in the so-called "foster-brother concept," was silenced in the 1950's.

Nicolaus I (1796-1855), Russian czar (1825-1855).

Nicolaus II (1868-1918), the last Russian czar (1894-1917).

Nyáry, Pál (1806-1871), Hungarian liberal politician, Parliamentary Representative during the 1848-49 War of Independence, Vice President of the National Military Committee, suffered castle imprisonment after the collapse of the War of Independence, Parliamentary Representative after the Austrian-Hungarian Compromise of 1867.

Paál, Árpád (1880?-1944?), President of the Székely National Council (1918-1919), one of the authors of the pamphlet "*Kiáltó Szó*" [Crying Word] (1921), Representative of Szatmár county in the Romanian Parliament (1926-1932), founding member of the Transylvanian Art Guild.

Palacky, František (1798-1876), Czech historiographer, politician, a leader of the Slav Congress of Prague in 1848, withdrew from political life (1849-1861), participated in the Moscow Pan-Slav Congress (1867).

Palacky, Jan (1830-1908), Czech scientist, professor of geographical botany at the University of Prague.

Palmerston, Viscount Henry John Temple (1784-1865), English liberal statesman, Minister of Foreign Affairs (1830-1841, 1846-1856), Prime Minister (1855-1858, 1859-1865).

Pelényi, János, ambassador to Washington D.C., resigned as ambassador when Hungary entered the War (1941), along with Tibor Eckhardt submitted to the Advisory Committee a common draft about the Danube Basin settlement (1942).

Peter I (1672-1725), Russian czar (1682-1725).

Pogodin, Mikhail Petrovich (1800-1875), Pan-Slav theoretician, connected Slavophilism with western thinking in order to unify all the Slavs politically.

Polit-Desančiš, Mihailo (1833-1920), Serbian publicist, Parliamentary Representative several times after the Compromise (1867) in Hungary.

Pop de Băseşti, Gheorghe [Illésfalvi Pap György], Romanian politician in Hungary, as a Deputy President of the Romanian National Party participated in the Memorandum movement which questioned the grounds for the Austrian-Hungarian Compromise, the Union, and the Nationalities Act, along with several companions was tried for the illegal publication of the Memorandum (1893), later became the President of the Romanian National Party.

Popovici, Aurel C. (1863-1917), Romanian teacher of Transylvanian descent, publicist, sentenced for the publication of the pamphlet *Replica* for subversive activity by the Kolozsvár [Cluj] Court (1893), emigrated to Romania, worked as a teacher in Bucharest, developed his federative Great-Austrian plan in Vienna.

Pulszky, Ferenc (1814-1897), Hungarian liberal politician, archeologist, art historian, Minister of Foreign Affairs during the 1848 Revolution, London emissary of the Hungarian Revolutionary Government (from early 1849), returned to Hungary in early 1866, Parliamentary Representative, well-known member of the Hungarian Freemasonry.

Rădulescu, Ioan Heliad (1802–1872), Romanian writer, founder and editor of the first Romanian periodical in Bucharest, the literary journal "*Albina Romaneasca*" (1829–1848), involved in revolutionary activities (1848), lived abroad but returned to his homeland (1859), author of plays, literary history and criticism, and a national epic poem.

Rákóczi, Ferenc, II. (1676–1735), Hungarian aristocrat, writer, statesman, general, leader of the 1703–1711 Hungarian anti-Habsburg War of Independence, exiled after the defeat of the War of Independence, his ashes were brought home to Kassa (Košice) in 1906.

Rákosi, Mátyás (1892–1971), Hungarian communist politician, his name hallmarks the establishment of the Soviet-style communist dictatorship in Hungary, Secretary-General of the Hungarian Communist Party and later of the Hungarian Workers' Party, Member of the National Chief Council (1945), Vice President of the Council of Ministers (1952–53), lived in the Soviet Union until his death (from 1956).

Ránki, György (1930–1988), Hungarian historian, his main area of research was the 19th and 20th century economic and political Hungarian and world history.

Rauch, Levin (1819–1890), *Ban* of Croatia, Slavonia, and Dalmatia (1867–1871).

Ravasz, László (1882–1975), Transylvanian Hungarian writer of philosophy and theology, Reformed bishop, was forced to resign in 1948.

Renner, Karl (1871–1950), Austrian social democratic politician, Austrian chancellor (1918–1920), formed the Austrian Provisional Government (April 1945), President of Austria (1945–1950).

Révai, József (1898–1959), Hungarian communist politician, member of the Political Committee of the Hungarian Workers' Party (1945–1953, 1956), Minister of Culture and Education (1949–1953).

Rieger, František Ladislav (1818–1903), Czech politician, leader with František Palacky of the conservative old-Czechs.

Romanul, Miron (1828–1898), Greek Orthodox metropolitan of Nagyszeben (Sibiu), a founder of the short-lived, moderate Romanian National Party which was pro-Compromise and pro-Union (1884).

Roth, Hans Otto, Romanian politician of German descent, lawyer of the German Alliance of Romania (1920's), President of the German Party in Romania.

Russo, Alecu (1819–1859), Moldavian Romanian prose writer, liberal politician.

Schlegel, August Wilhelm (1767–1845), German critic, one of the most significant theoreticians of early romanticism.

Schmerling, Anton von (1805-1893), Austrian statesman, knight, Austrian Minister of Justice (1849-1851, 1860-1865), his last period in power is called the "Schmerling provisional" by Hungarian historiography.

Schuselka, Franz (1812-1886), Austrian liberal publicist, politician, member of the Frankfurt German National Assembly (1848).

Seton-Watson, Robert William (1879-1951), English publicist, historian, from 1907 in English journals published essays describing nationality relations within the Austro-Hungarian Monarchy and expressed sympathy towards Slav national ambitions.

Šokčević, Josip (1811-1896), Austrian field marshal, Croatian and Slavonian *Ban* (1860-1867), Governor of Fiume.

Stalin (Djugasvilli) Iosif Vissarionovich (1879-1953), Soviet communist politician of Georgian descent, Party and Government Head, dictator, General Secretary of the Soviet Communist Party (1922-1953), Head of Government (1941-1953).

Steinacker, Edmund (b.1839), Saxon Representative of the Hungarian Parliament during Dualism.

Streith, Clarence K. (b.1896), American writer, journalist, published "*Union Now*" (1939) in which he argued that a federative government embracing democracies would enhance their power against dictatorships.

Strossmayer, Iosiph Iurai (1815-1905), Croatian politician from Hungary, Bishop of Diakóvár (from 1849), as politician fought for an independent Croatia.

Štúr, Ĺudovit (1815-1856), Slovak politician, writer, had significant role in the Slovak national movement, advocate of Austro-Slavism at the Slav Congress of Prague, organized irregular troops against the 1848/49 Hungarian Revolution and War of Independence.

Susaikov, Ivan Zakharovich (1903-1962), political officer, joined the Red Army (1924), and the Bolshevik Party (1925), graduated from the Mechanization Academy of the Red Army (1937), political officer in the tank forces of the Soviet Army before, during, and after World War II.

Suslov, Mikhail Andreievich (1902-1982), First Secretary of the Central Committee of the Soviet Communist Party (1947-1982).

Szabó, István (1898-1969), Hungarian historian, researcher of medieval and modern Hungarian agricultural history.

Szalay, László (1813-1864), Hungarian publicist, historian, critic, departmental head of the Ministry of Justice (1848), emissary to the Frankfurt German Legislative National Assembly (from May 1848), negotiated in London, Paris, and Brussels on behalf of the Government (fall of 1848), emigrated (May 1849), returned to Hungary (1855), Parliamentary Representative (1861), member of the Representation Party (Felirati Párt).

Szarvady, Frigyes (?1822–1882), Hungarian journalist, colleague of László Teleki in Paris (1848/49).

Szász, Zsombor (b. 1871), Transylvanian Hungarian lawyer, politician, legal writer, worked for the Peace Preparatory Committee and in the Office for Refugees (1919–1922), went to London on diplomatic mission, chief essay writer of the *Magyar Szemle.*

Széchenyi, István (1791–1860), Hungarian aristocratic liberal politician, political writer, theoretician, national educator. Minister of Transport and Public Works in the Batthyány Government (1848), was called by Lajos Kossuth "the greatest Hungarian," entered the mental asylum in Döbling (September 5, 1848) at the news that the Habsburgs revoked the April Laws, committed suicide (1860).

Szegedy-Maszák, Aladár (1903–1988), Hungarian diplomat, negotiated in Stockholm as the deputy head of the Political Department of the Ministry of Foreign Affairs, wrote memoirs in which he deemed the establishment of a Central European confederation hopeless (1943), ambassador to Washington D.C. (1945–47), nominated to be a member of the peace delegation to Paris (1946), resigned at the news of the force resignation of Prime Minister Ferenc Nagy (1947).

Szekfű, Gyula (1883–1955), Hungarian publicist, historian, ambassador to Moscow (1946–48), distinguished representative of the history of ideas, wrote historical works that greatly influenced public thinking in inter-war Hungary.

Szemere, Bertalan (1819–1869), Hungarian liberal oppositionist politician, Minister of the Interior of the Batthyány Government, member of the National Defense Committee, Prime Minister (from May 1849), emigrated after the defeat of the War of Independence.

Szentimrei, Jenő (1890–1959), Transylvanian Hungarian poet, writer, journalist, literary ombudsman, founding member of the Erdélyi Helikon.

Tamási, Áron (1897–1966), Transylvanian Hungarian writer, founding member of the *Erdélyi Helikon* (1926), developed an artistic approach that converged on that of the populistic writers (from 1935), urged withdrawal from the World War II as a member of the Transylvanian Hungarian Council (August 1944).

Tanárky, Gyula (1815–1886), Hungarian economic writer, manager of Ferenc Pulszky's estate, lived in Kossuth's environment in his London and Torino exile, became the chronicler of the exiles.

Tardieu, André-Rievre-Gabriel-Amédée (1876–1950), French politician, member of Chamber of Deputies (1914–1924, 1926–1936), delegated to the Paris Peace Conference and supporter of Clemenceau, Minister of the liberated regions (1919–1920), Minister of Public Works in the liberated regions (1926–28), Minister of the Interior (1828), Premier of France (1929–1930, 1932), Minister of Agriculture (1931–32).

Teleki, László (1811-1861), Transylvanian Hungarian aristocrat, writer, liberal politician, count, ambassador to Paris of the Hungarian Revolutionary Government (1848/49), member of the Hungarian National Administration (1859-1861), arrested in Dresden by the Austrian authorities (1861), after returning home became the leader of the newly organized opposition, committed suicide due to political pressure.

Teleki, Pál (1879-1941), Transylvanian landowner, count, scholar of geography, prominent statesman of the Horthy-era. President of the League for the Defense of Territory (1918-19), Minister of Culture and Foreign Affairs of the Counter-Revolutionary Government in Szeged, Foreign Affairs of the Simonyi-Semadam Government, Prime Minister (1920-21), founder of the Institute of Sociography (1926), the Institute of Political Science (1926), and the Revisionist League (1927), Minister of Religion and Public Education of the Imrédy Government (1938), Prime Minister (1939-1941), committed suicide on April 3, 1941 in protest to Hungary's drifting into the World War II.

Thun-Hohenstein, Leo von (1811-1888), descendant of a German Bohemian count, Minister of Religion and Public Education of the Austrian Empire (November 1848–October 1860).

Tisza, Kálmán (1830-1902), Hungarian statesman, a leader of the Resolution Party (Határozati Párt) of the Parliamentary Session of 1861, leader of the left center during the Parliamentary Session of 1865, Prime Minister and leader of the Liberal Party (Szabadelvű Párt) (1875-1890).

Tito (Broz), Josip (1892-1980), leader of Croatian descent of the Yugoslav Communist Party, commander of the Yugoslav communist partisan units (from 1941), President of the Provisional Government, Prime Minister (1945-1953), President of the Republic (1953-1980).

Tomič, Jasa, Serbian publicist in Hungary, leader of radical Serbians of the municipal board in Újvidék (Novi Sad), imprisoned for a short time for his views.

Toynbee, Arnold Joseph (1889-1975), English historiographer, developer of the kulturkreis (culture complex).

Török, János (1807-1874), Hungarian editor, publicist, specialist, Hungarian lieutenant-colonel in 1848-49, imprisoned, opposed the policy of passive resistance in his political publications (1850's).

Ubicini, Jean-Henry-Abdolonyme Honoré (1818-1884), pro-Romanian French journalist, historian, participated in the 1848 Bucharest revolution, supported Romanian national aspirations in his historical works.

Vajda, Imre (1900-1969), Hungarian economist, member of the Galilei Circle and the Austrian Social Democratic Party, leader of the left of the Hungarian Social Democratic Party (1938), Under-Secretary of Commerce and Cooperatives (1945-1947), President of the National Central Planning Bureau (1948-1950), imprisoned (1950-56), later rehabilitated.

Vámbéry, Rusztem (1872–1948), Hungarian legal scientist, publicist, lawyer, representative of bourgeois radicalism, member of the National Council (1918), emigrated to England and the United States (1938), Hungarian ambassador to Washington D.C. (1947–48), later resigned.

Vay, Miklós (1802–1894), Hungarian politician, Parliamentary Representative, royal commissioner (summer of 1848), sentenced to death after the defeat of the War of Independence despite loyalty, later received a reduced sentence of four years.

Visinski, Andrei Ianuarevich (1883–1954), Soviet lawyer of Polish descent, deputy chief public prosecutor of the Soviet Union (1933–35), chief public prosecutor (1935–39), Vice President of the Council of People's Commissaries (from 1939), Vice President of the Council of Ministers, Minister of Foreign Affairs of the Soviet Union (1949), UN Representative (1953–54).

Vukovics, Sebő (1811–1872), Hungarian liberal politician of Serbian origin, government commissioner (1848/49), Minister of Justice of the Szemere Government, emigrated after the defeat of the War of Independence, returned home in 1869, Parliamentary Representative with left centrist program.

Vulcan, Josif (1840–1907), Transylvanian Romanian writer, poet.

Wallace, Henry Agard (1888–1965), American Democratic Party politician, Secretary of Agriculture (1933–1940), Vice President (1941–45), Secretary of Commerce (1945–46).

Werbőczy, István (ca. 1458/65–ca.1541/42), Hungarian legal scientist, committed Hungarian customary law to writing in his *Hármaskönyv* [Tripartitum] which became an authoritative text in 1514, Palatine of Hungary (1525–26), chancellor of Hungarian king János Szapolyai, Chief justice in Buda Castle, died there during the Turkish occupation.

Wesselényi, Miklós (1796–1850), Transylvanian Hungarian aristocratic liberal politician, leader of the Hungarian opposition of the Pozsony Diet in the 1830's, prosecuted for disloyalty, sentenced to prison, went blind during his prison years, withdrew from political life after his release.

Willkie, Wendell Lewis (1892–1944), American politician, Republican Party presidential candidate (1940), opponent of Roosevelt's policy.

Zay, Károly (1797–1871), Hungarian count, member of the Upper House of the Diet, supporter of the reform movement, superintendent of the Hungarian Lutheran Church (from 1840).

BASIC BIBLIOGRAPHY

For the history of European ideas on integrating territories, Bernard Voyenne, *Histoire de l'idée européenne.* (Paris, 1964); Denis de Rougemont, *The Idea of Europe.* (New York, London, 1966); Derek Heater, *The Idea of European Unity*, (New York, 1992).

For federative restructuring of the Habsburg Monarchy, Robert A. Kann, *The Multinational Empire: Nationalism and National Reform in the Habsburg Monarchy 1848–1918.* 2 vols. (New York , 1950, 1964); Rudolf Wiere, *Der Föderalismus im Donauraum* (Federalism in the Danube Basin) (Graz, Köln, 1960).
For German Mitteleuropa concepts, Henry Cord Meyer, *Mitteleuropa in German Thought and Action 1815–1945* (The Hague, 1955); Jacques Droz, *L'Europe centrale. Évolution historique de l'idée de "Mitteleuropa"* [Central Europe: Historical Evolution of the Idea, "Mitteleuropa"] (Paris, 1960); *Mitteleuropa. History and Prospects,* ed., Peter Stirk, (Edinburgh University Press, 1994).

For Pan-Slavism and the history of Russian–Soviet expansionism, Louis Léger, *Le Panslavisme et L'Intérêt français* [Pan-Slavism and French Interest] (Paris, 1917); Alfred Fischel, *Der Panslawismus bis zum Weltkrieg*[Pan-Slavism until the World War] (Stuttgart, Berlin, 1919); Kálmán Rátz, *A pánszlávizmus története*[The History of Pan-Slavism] (Budapest, 1941); Hans Kohn, *Pan-Slavism. Its History and Ideology* (Notre Dame, Indiana, 1953); Géza Gecse, *Binzánctól Bizáncig. Epizódok az orosz pánszlávizmus történetéből* [From Byzantium to Byzantium. Episodes from the History of Russian Pan-Slavism] (Budapest, 1993); *Russian Diplomacy and Eastern Europe 1914–1917*, ed., Sarah Meiklejohn Terry, (New Haven, London, 1984); *Central and Eastern Europe: The Opening Curtain?* ed., William E. Griffith, (Boulder, 1989).

For confederative ideas, Joachim Kühl, *Föderationspläne im Donauraum und in Ostmitteleuropa* [Federative Plans in the Danube Basin and in East Central Europe], (Munich, 1958); Leften Stavros Stavrianos, *Balkan Federation. A History of the Movement Toward Balkan Unity in Modern Times*, (Hamden, Connecticut, 1964); Gyula Mérei, *Föderációs tervek Délkelet-Európában és a Habsburg Monarchiában 1840–1918* [Federative Plans in South-Eastern Europe and in the Habsburg Monarchy, 1840–1918], (Budapest, 1965); F. Stephen Larrabe, *East European Security After the Cold War,* (Santa Monica, 1994).

MAPS

AUSTRO-HUNGARIAN MONARCHY
Boundaries of the Monarchy (1878-1918)
Boundaries of Hungary (1867-1918)
Boundaries of Lands
Capital city of Lands
GERMAN EMPIRE
RUSSIAN EMPIRE
SWITZERLAND
Liechtenstein
ITALY
SAN MARINO
Corse (France)
Bohemia
Moravia
Silesia
Galicia
Bukovina
Upper-Austria
Lower-Austria
Salzburg
Tirol
Styria
Carniola
Crain
Coastal Dist.
Croatia
Slavonia
Dalmatia
Bosnia
HUNGARY
ROMANIA
SERBIA
MONTENEGRO
OTTOMAN EMPIRE
BULGARIA
Adriatic Sea
Prague
Pilsen
Budweis
Iglau
Olmütz
Brünn
Troppau
Bielitz
Krakau
Tarnów
Przemysl
Lemberg
Tarnopol
Kolomea
Kamenyec-Podolszkij
Czernowitz
Botosani
Regensburg
Ingolstadt
Munich
Linz
Salzburg
Vienna
Pozscny
Innsbruck
Bregenz
Bozen
Trient
Milánó
Verona
Mantova
Venice
Genova
Modena
Bologna
La Spezia
Livorno
Florenz
Ancona
Perugia
Roma
Graz
Klagenfurt
Marburg
Laibach
Zagreb
Trieszt
Rijeka
Pola
Zadar
Spalato
Mostar
Ragusa
Cetinje
Banja-Luka
Sarajevo
Zsolna
Besztercebánya
Nyitra
Komárom
Győr
Sopron
Szombathely
Székesfehérvár
Budapest
Pécs
Lőcse
Kassa
Miskolc
Ungvár
Szolnok
Kecskemét
Szeged
Szabadka
Osijek
Brod
Újvidék
Belgrad
Debrecen
Nagyvárad
Szatmárnémeti
Beszterce
Kolozsvár
Marosvásárhely
Gyulafehérvár
Arad
Temesvár
Déva
Nagyszeben
Brassó
Versec
Turnu-Severin
Craiova
Bukarest
Tutrakan
Vidin
Kragujevac
Niš
Novi Pazar
Priština
Plevna
Sofiao
Philippopolis
Jambol

"TRIANON" HUNGARY
CZECHOSLOVAKIA
POLAND
AUSTRIA
HUNGARY
ROMANIA
SERBIAN-CROATIAN-SLOVENIAN KINGDOM
To Poland:
589 km²
25.000 Inhabitants
To Czechoslovakia:
61.646 km²
3.517.000 Inhabitants
(1.072.000 Hungarian)
To Austria:
4.020 km²
292.000 Inhabitants
(26.000 Hungarian)
Hungary:
93.073 km²
7.615.000 Inhabitants
(6.718.000 Hungarian)
To Romania:
102.813 km²
5.237.000 Inhabitants
(1.664.000 Hungarian)
To Serbian-Croatian-Slovenian Kingdom:
20.829 km²
1.528.000 Inhabitants
(459.000 Hungarian)
To Italy:
21 km²
50.000 Inhabitants
(6.000 Hungarian)
Vienna
Pozsony
Besztercebánya
Léva
Kassa
Ungvár
Miskolc
Sopron
Győr
Budapest
Szombathely
Székesfehérvár
Debrecen
Szatmárnémeti
Nagyvárad
Beszterce
Kolozsvár
Marosvásárhely
Szeged
Szabadka
Arad
Pécs
Zagreb
Temesvár
Nagyszeben
Brassó
Eszék
Újvidék
Rijeka
Pancsova
Belgrad
Bukarest
Boundaries in 1914
Boundaries in 1920

HUNGARY IN 1941
Territorial increase of Hungary 1938-1941
① From Czechoslovakia (November 1938) 11925 km², 863.000 Inhabitants, 87% Hun.
② From Czechoslovakia (March 1939) 10700 km², 550.000 Inhabitants, 17% Hun.
③ From Romania (September 1940) 43591 km², 2.186.000 Inhabitants, 51% Hun.
④ From Yugoslavia, (April 1941) 11601 km², 1.145.000 Inhabitants, 32% Hun.
(Hun.: Hungarians)
Boundaries in 1938
Boundaries in 1941
Boundaries of Transylvania
POLAND
CZECHOSLOVAKIA
SLOVAKIA
AUSTRIA
HUNGARY
ROMANIA
YUGOSLAVIA
Vienna
Pozsony
Léva
Besztercebánya
Kassa
Ungvár
Miskolc
Sopron
Győr
Budapest
Szombathely
Székesfehérvár
Debrecen
Szatmárnémeti
Nagyvárad
Beszterce
Kolozsvár
Marosvásárhely
Szeged
Arad
Szabadka
Temesvár
Pécs
Zagreb
Osijek
Újvidék
Rijeka
Pancsova
Belgrad
Nagyszeben
Brassó
Bukarest

NAME INDEX

Page numbers in italics refer to "Biographies of key personalities"

GEOGRAPHICAL INDEX